New Selected Readings of ENGLISH LITERATURE

英国文学选读新编

（第二版）

主编 吕洪灵 汪 凯
编者 陈秋华 李钟涛
　　　秦 文 徐 晗

图书在版编目(CIP)数据

英国文学选读新编 / 吕洪灵, 汪凯主编. —2版. —北京：北京大学出版社, 2022.7
ISBN 978-7-301-33065-4

Ⅰ.①英… Ⅱ.①吕…②汪… Ⅲ.①英语－阅读教学－高等学校－教材②英国文学－文学欣赏 Ⅳ.①H319.37

中国版本图书馆CIP数据核字(2022)第096154号

书　　名	英国文学选读新编（第二版）
	YINGGUO WENXUE XUANDU XINBIAN (DI-ER BAN)
著作责任者	吕洪灵　汪　凯　主编
责任编辑	李　娜
标准书号	ISBN 978-7-301-33065-4
出版发行	北京大学出版社
地　　址	北京市海淀区成府路205号　100871
网　　址	http://www.pup.cn　新浪微博:@北京大学出版社
电子信箱	345014015@qq.com
电　　话	邮购部 010-62752015　发行部 010-62750672　编辑部 010-62754382
印刷者	河北文福旺印刷有限公司
经销者	新华书店
	787毫米×1092毫米　16开本　19.25印张　550千字
	2015年9月第1版
	2022年7月第2版　2022年7月第1次印刷
定　　价	78.00元

未经许可，不得以任何方式复制或抄袭本书之部分或全部内容。
版权所有，侵权必究
举报电话：010-62752024　电子信箱：fd@pup.pku.edu.cn
图书如有印装质量问题，请与出版部联系，电话：010-62756370

第二版序言

进入21世纪,在全球化浪潮的席卷之下,中国对外文化交流的深度与广度不断提升。在此过程中出现了大量介绍英、美、德、法等西方国家的文学作品和文学史的教材,虽称不上汗牛充栋,但也种类繁多,各有千秋。这本《英国文学选读新编》有别于诸多同类教材,不再以英国文学的发展历程以及文学流派为经纬编排作家作品,而是以文学主题为纲领、结合时代特点对英国文学中的经典作家作品进行梳理。整理归纳出的十个主题涵盖了人类社会的各个层面,重点关注人与自然、社会、自身之间的关系。这样的编排可以让学生更加充分理解文学跨时空、跨种族、跨国界、体现人类共通性的特点。在实际教学中,本教材第一版收获了良好的反响,同时,使用本教材的广大师生也向出版社和本书的编写组提出了一些有益的反馈意见。有鉴于此,在"'十三五'江苏省高等学校重点教材"项目的支持下,本书编写组经过充分准备后,着手对教材进行修订再版工作,以便与时俱进,更好地促进英国文学的教学与研究。

这次修订贯彻第一版以主题为统领、以时代为舞台、以作家作品为核心的原则,充实和完善各章的主题导读,加强主题与入选作家作品的契合性;修订对重点作家作品的引介与分析,删改相对陈旧的选篇并完善注释,增加引发学习者思考和探究的内容。同时,调整部分章节或选篇的顺序,使其在主题的范畴下更加贴合英国文学史的发展脉络,便于读者准确把握选读作品的创作背景与文化语境。修订后的《英国文学选读新编》与第一版相比,主要提高之处在于:

一、主题阐释内容更加深入丰富。文学主题在某种意义上展现了人类共同的集体意识,透过繁芜丛杂的多元文化表象,以文学创作作为媒介,直抵人类作为命运共同体所关注的一些基本问题和理念,因此文学主题性的梳理和研讨有助于引导读者从更加宏观的层面上理解文学创作作为一种永恒存在的精神追求,在人类发展的历史长河中发挥的重要作用,其内涵深植于某个国家、某种文化的历史与传统之中。在修订之后,相关主题的阐释重点更加突出鲜明,更加强调文学主题的共通性与文学形象的多样性。例如,重新撰写后的第一章主题"爱",更加凝练地阐释了爱作为最为经典和永恒的文学主题在不同时期以及不同文学作品中所呈现出的形象与意义,爱不仅仅是人类普遍经历的情感历程,也是个体向往幸福自由、反抗传统权威的精神追求。其他章节的主题陈述有相应的扩充或改动,更好地凸显了本教材以主题为纲的编写特色。

二、所选篇目在具备代表性的基础之上,更注重多样化,与主题的契合度也更加紧密。例如,再版增加了叶芝早期的另一首著名爱情诗歌《白鸟》,与原有选文《当你老了》相互映照,帮助读者更加深入了解叶芝的情感经历与精神世界,并体会其早期诗歌中浪漫主义、唯美主义和象征主义等多种文学元素相互碰撞、交织而形成的艺术风格。其他章节中的选篇也有一定程度的更新,体现了整本教材经典性与时代性并重的宗旨。

三、课后思考题更具有思辨性。对于文学作品的理解与分析必须带有问题意识,再版更改了若干选篇的课后思考问题,对某些选篇还增加了更具启发性和思辨性的问题,以期通过问题促使读者更准确地把握所学文本,增强文学批判意识和能力。

四、细节处理更加严谨与完善。由于涉及的作家作品众多,以及文学作品不同版本的版式差异,本教材第一版在作家介绍、作品选篇以及注释方面存在一定的问题。在修订过程中,编者注意更正所选版本,在作家介绍、选篇的勘误以及注释方面进行了一些实质性修改,确保选篇的权威性和准确性。

文学作为时代精神的体现与产物,亘古至今,一直处于不断探索、发展、提升的过程之中,随着一些开创性的批评理论和研究成果的涌现,传统意义上的经典文学正在经历被重新审视、重新建构、重新评述的变革过程,并被不断赋予新的历史意义和价值。英国文学同样不可避免要经受时代的洗礼。本教材编者力图与时俱进,但囿于自身的眼界与能力,必然无法充分展现英国文学的历史全貌与发展轨迹,入选的主题、选篇等只是英国文学宝库中的沧海一粟,导读、注释等也难免存在着不周或者谬误之处。恳请读者指正疏漏或不当之处,本教材编者必将虚心听取意见,本着严谨认真的态度,拓宽自身的视野,把握时代的脉搏,努力为英国文学的爱好者和学习者奉上一本好的教材。

最后,感谢"'十三五'江苏省高等学校重点教材"项目提供的支撑,感谢在编写过程中给予编写组支持的人们,并特别感谢北京大学出版社李娜编辑不辞辛劳使得该版顺利付梓面世。

编者

2022年5月

序　言

　　历经数年的筹备和编写，这本《英国文学选读新编》终于结稿完成。编写一本新的英国文学教材一直是英国文学教师的心愿，但是，如何在目前教材种类繁多的情况下寻找到新的方向，编写出有新意的文学教材，也一直是困扰编者的问题。为此，编者们集思广益，向具有多年英国文学教学经验的学者请教，经过反复论证而最终确定了教材编写的思路和纲目。

　　我们首先从《高等学校英语专业英语教学大纲》入手寻求理论的支持：英国文学属于专业知识课程，其目标之一在于培养学生的人文素质，增强学生对西方文学与文化的了解。换句话说，是要通过文学学习，促使学生了解英国文学的基本情况，培养对文化差异的领悟，提高进行跨文化交际的综合素质。这其中蕴涵着对学生情感智力和思维能力培养的要求。有鉴于此，在英语专业文学课程的教学改革中，如何把教材编写的重心由注重学生的认知智力的增强，转向不仅关注认知智力，而且更侧重学生情感智力和思维能力的培养，丰富深化英国文学教学的意义，成为我们编写教材的初衷之一。我们力图通过本教材的教学，促使学生更好地掌握所学习的语言，加深对文学内涵的领悟，培养起深切的人文关怀精神，提高他们的道德修养，以及思辨和批评的能力。

　　其次，英国文学教材的现状也促使我们去寻找编写的思路。目前，国内英国文学教材数目不少，各有特色，但大多按照文学史的编年顺序选择作家与作品，这样的做法有着它的优势，有助于教师和学生明晰作家作品的时代背景和英国文学的线性发展。然而，按照传统线性思路编写的英国文学教材虽然脉络清晰，整体性较强，但却多少忽视了学生对于文学作品共性认知的需求。由于文学作品体裁多样，具有明显的时代特色，学习者在阅读不同时期的文本时，如果能从横向进行比较学习，将会有更深刻的体会，也许更能够实现《大纲》的要求。本教材与传统英国文学选读教材相比一个重要特点就是，发掘不同时期文本蕴含的共性，并且按照主题将它们归类。这种以点带面的形式从教学上而言，有助于引领学生就某个文学主题展开认知与讨论，积极主动开展学习，更深层次地强化他们对英国文学与文化的认知。从研究角度而言，将不同时期的文学作品置于共同的语境之下，有助于开阔研究视角，丰富研究内容，启发学生对英国文学的研究兴趣。值得一提的是，本教材归纳的主题既具特色亦有普遍意义，通过英国文学对这些问题的展示，能够深化学生对人类共同问题的情感认同与理性辨析，从而在更高层次上加强对英国文学的认知与思辨。

　　总体上说，本教材打破传统的线性教材编写思路，选取英国文学作品的主要主题，将英国作家作品归类，既突出作家作品共通的主题意识，也强调作家作品个人所处的历史文化语境，点面结合地进行内容编排。在以主题统领篇章安排的前提下，本教材精选了经典作家代表作品的选段，为学生和老师都预留了充分施展思维能力、创新能力的空间，让文学课堂成为学习、研究、提高素质的场所。

　　本教材可作为各高校本科段英语专业高年级学生的外国文学教材及其他专业高年级学生辅修之用的教材，且各类高等院校专业教学均可使用。对于教师来说，利用本教材教学可操作性强，可灵活运用本教材的基本内容,根据课堂教学拓展书本知识,利于教师充分施展才华。对于学生来说,本教材内容所选材料均为经典作品,且形式多样,易于激发他们的学习兴趣,夯实他们的英国文学基础,开发思维能力与进行情智培养。

鉴于教材篇幅及教学实际需求,本教材选取英国文学作品中比较突出的十个主题,各主题下选择与之相关的三到五位经典英国作家及其作品。编者在每个主题前撰写了五百字左右的导读,对相关主题及选篇从宏观上进行了一定的阐释。每个篇目之后还附有若干针对作家、作品或相关创作思想和意图的思考性问题,教师可以结合实际情况,选用其中的一些作为课堂讨论或课后思考的材料。

本教材为集体承担项目,在学院的大力支持下得以顺利展开和完成。编写者均为高校英语系在职中青年骨干教师,长期从事英国文学的教学工作,教学经验丰富,具有较强的研究能力和丰富的实践阅历。傅俊教授从教材编写之初便对这项工作关注有加,从选题选篇到编写小组的组成以及编写过程中的疑难解答,她一直给予有益而有效的指导。在此还要感谢北京大学出版社的李娜编辑对于稿件的精心审读和悉心建议。

编写组各成员负责章节如下:陈秋华,Cultural Diversity, Utopia and Dystopia;李钟涛、徐晗,Love;吕洪灵,Faith and Skepticism, Female Individuality and Fulfillment;秦文,Human Race and Natural World;汪凯,Divinity and Secularity, Mythology and Reality, Civilization and Alienation;徐晗,Experience and Growth。各位编者在繁忙的教学工作中抽出时间,以严谨负责的态度完成了本书的编写。当然,由于编者水平有限,难免存在不足之处,故恳请使用本教材的专家、学者和读者批评指正,在此编者表示衷心的感谢。

编者
2015年7月

Contents

Chapter One Love 1
   William Shakespeare 2
   Robert Burns 4
   Oscar Wilde 6
   William Butler Yeats 13
   David Herbert Lawrence 16

Chapter Two Divinity and Secularity 29
   John Donne 30
   John Milton 34
   William Blake 37
   Bible 40

Chapter Three Experience and Growth 43
   Daniel Defoe 44
   Charles Dickens 54
   James Joyce 68

Chapter Four Human Race and Natural World 74
   William Wordsworth 76
   Percy Bysshe Shelley 79
   John Keats 84
   Robert Louis Stevenson 88
   Raymond Williams 93

Chapter Five Faith and Skepticism 101
   William Shakespeare 103
   William Makepeace Thackeray 105
   Matthew Arnold 116
   Thomas Hardy 119

Chapter Six Female Individuality and Fulfillment ... 123
   Geoffrey Chaucer 124
   Jane Austen 128

Charlotte Brontë ··· 138
　　Virginia Woolf ·· 149

Chapter Seven　Mythology and Reality ··· 155
　　Alfred Tennyson ·· 156
　　George Bernard Shaw ·· 160
　　Wystan Hugh Auden ··· 171

Chapter Eight　Civilization and Alienation ·································· 175
　　Joseph Conrad ··· 176
　　William Golding ·· 183
　　Thomas Stearns Eliot ··· 191
　　Harold Pinter ··· 196

Chapter Nine　Cultural Diversity ··· 203
　　Edward Morgan Forster ··· 205
　　Doris May Lessing ··· 218
　　Kazuo Ishiguro ··· 233

Chapter Ten　Utopia and Dystopia ··· 254
　　Thomas More ·· 256
　　Jonathan Swift ··· 264
　　Herbert George Wells ·· 277
　　George Orwell ··· 290

Chapter One Love

As a primeval sentiment that transcends time, races, cultures and territorial boundaries, it is natural that love has become one of the most prevalent motifs in all forms of artistic presentation throughout history. This is, of course, also true of literature, whether written or oral. The theme of love possesses a powerful and perpetual charm over writers, prominent or obscure, and finds its presence in almost all literary genres—highbrow or vulgar—probably from the very inception of literary creation. Love is generally manifested itself as an intense romantic and sexual attachment, but it would be too narrow-minded if love is simply understood as the palpitating sensation that stirs up young people's blood. Love is more of a spiritual affinity than a physical attraction. It is an all-embracing bond that connects and unites all people under the sun—among family members, friends, congregations and even strangers; and just like rays of sunshine in the harshest winters, love can bring warmth, hope and blessings to people who are leading a wretched existence in the four corners of the world, regardless of their race, belief, wealth and nationality.

Love is also as complicated as it is universal. From a literary perspective, the complexity of love is embodied by a broad spectrum of paradoxical depictions by writers out of different times. Love could be tender while violent, subtle while outspoken, healing while devastating, fleeting while everlasting. Love could become so disastrously entangled with death that to love literally means to destroy; but that, nevertheless, could not deter people from being drawn to this fatal attraction as moths to flames. Love sometimes could breed suffering and hate, and then miraculously out of hatred and torment, one comes to learn to love more intensely and forgive. Perhaps it is this very mystical quality of love that makes human nature so impenetrable and love a so captivating theme for writers.

The earliest narratives of love in western literature could be traced back to the times when they are preserved and passed on through oral tradition in forms like folktale, myth, saga and epic poem. And ever since, every age has nurtured quite a few prominent writers and great works on love that become that age's proud boast. For instance, love is a recurrent theme in Shakespeare's sonnets and comedies, and an indispensable element in his most famous tragedies as well. Robert Burns, though died young, is well remembered by the world for his lyric "A Red, Red Rose". William Yeats' early poems owed much of the inspiration to his somewhat fanatic love to Maud Gonne, a beautiful Irish nationalist. Oscar Wilde, probably "notorious" for his involvement in a relationship then strongly frowned on by the Victorian values, eulogizes that "love is a wonderful thing", and "it is more precious than emeralds, and dearer than fine opals". D. H. Lawrence, another controversial figure in his time, is a master in depicting the desire between men and women or love between parents and children. In a series of so-called "love novels", he puts the whole British society out of countenance by his "audacious" depictions of savage sensuality between men and women to counteract the dehumanizing effects imposed on by industrialization and social hierarchy. In a word, love makes one's existence rich and full. Like a precious stone—even in its crudest form, love can reflect the multiple facets of an individual's personality and human nature at large. And this is the very reason that elevates love to a timeless motif in the world of literature and the community of writers.

William Shakespeare
1564—1616

William Shakespeare, the giant of the English Renaissance, saw the light of day on 23 April, 1564; he was baptized three days later in Holy Trinity Church at Stratford-on-Avon. Written records on his life are scant but for some official documents and occasional references to him by his contemporary dramatists. He was born into a well-to-do family. His father was a merchant, and was appointed to High Bailiff in 1568, the highest position in the town. William Shakespeare is assumed to attend a grammar school free of charge and receive a good education in Latin, history, logic, and rhetoric. He married Anne Hathaway in 1582 and gave birth to one son and two daughters. He probably went to London in 1589. There he established himself as a narrative poet with *Venus and Adonis* (1593) and *The Rape of Lucrece* (1594), and

William Shakespeare

gradually prospered as an actor and more as a dramatist. He began his dramatic career in the late 1580s, and became a leading member of the Lord Chamberlain's Company in 1594. This company opened the Globe Theatre in 1598, where many of Shakespeare's plays were performed. Shakespeare may have retired to his hometown in 1610, and lived through the rest of his life till 23 April, 1616.

A writer of two narrative poems and 154 sonnets, William Shakespeare also established himself as the foremost playwright in the Elizabethan Age, a "golden age" of English literature. Between the late 1580 and 1613, he wrote thirty-seven plays, including comedies such as *A Midsummer Night's Dream, As You Like It, The Merchant of Venice*, history plays such as *Richard III, Henry IV* and *Henry V*, tragedies such as *Hamlet, Othello, King Lear, Macbeth, Antony and Cleopatra, Romeo and Juliet,* and romances such as *Pericles, Cymbeline, The Winter's Tale* and *The Tempest*.

Shakespeare's Epitaph

All his plays, except *Pericles*, were collected in *First Folio*, the earliest collection of his plays printed in 1623. Authoritative as it is, it presents many difficulties such as printing errors, confused passages and discrepancies between texts in this collection and some texts published earlier. However, such flaws can never obscure the brilliancy of Shakespeare and the profundity of his plays, for his literary creation is imbued with the spirit of humanism, thus provoking deep reflection about existence. Like his contemporary dramatists, Shakespeare often borrowed plots from older poems, plays, and stories, but he added to them his idiosyncratic poetry. Such way of recreating the old story is what to be valued. A master of the English language, William Shakespeare made his plays almost unsurpassable in English literature, just as his contemporary Ben Johnson wrote in the prefatory poem to the *First Folio*, "He was not of an age, but for all time!"

"Sonnet 18", often known as "Shall I compare thee to a summer's day?" is one of Shakespeare's most acclaimed sonnets. In the poem, the speaker, presumably the poet himself, compares his friend to the season of summer and expresses his wish that his friend will achieve immortality in his lines. The poem is written in the Shakespearean sonnet form composed of three quatrains and a rhymed couplet in iambic pentameter. It is generally believed by the critics that the poet intends to sublime artistic creation through the metaphor of eternal friendship.

Sonnet 18

Shall I compare thee[1] to a Summer's day?
Thou art[2] more lovely and more temperate[3]:
Rough winds do shake the darling buds of May,
And summer's lease hath all too short a date:
Sometime too hot the eye of heaven[4] shines,
And often is his gold complexion dimm'd;
And every fair from fair sometime declines[5],
By chance, or nature's changing course untrimm'd[6];
But thy eternal summer shall not fade,
Nor lose possession of that fair thou ow'st[7];
Nor shall Death brag thou wander'st[8] in his shade,
When in eternal lines to time thou grow'st[9]:
So long as men can breathe or eyes can see,
So long lives this[10], and this gives life to thee.

Shakespeare's Birthplace

Notes

1. thee: you
2. Thou art: You are
3. temperate: evenly-tempered; behaving in a calm and controlled way
4. the eye of heaven: the sun
5. And every fair from fair sometime declines: the beauty (fair) of everything beautiful (fair) at some uncertain times (sometime) will fade (declines), i.e., everything beautiful sometime will lose its beauty
6. untrimm'd: stripped (of its beauty)
7. that fair thou ow'st: that beauty you own/ possess. thou ow'st: thou ownest, i.e. you own.
8. thou wander'st: you wander

9. The poet is using a grafting metaphor in this line. Grafting is a technique used to join parts from two plants with cords so that they grow as one. Thus the beloved becomes immortal, grafted to time with the poet's cords (his "eternal lines"). eternal line: immortal lines such as the lines of this poem; to time thou grow'st: you become immortal.

10. this: this poem

Questions

1. What do you think is the theme of this sonnet?
2. What's the speaker's attitude to art?
3. What rhetoric devices are used by Shakespeare in the poem?

Robert Burns
1759—1796

Robert Burns

Robert Burns, a Scottish poet and lyricist, was born in South Ayrshire, Scotland. He was the eldest son of the seven children of a self-educated tenant farmer William, who taught his children a variety of subjects and also wrote for them *A Manual of Christian Belief*. Though Burns received little regular schooling, he had received education from John Murdoch (1747—1824), who opened an "adventure school" in Alloway in 1763 and taught Latin, French, and mathematics to both Robert and his brother Gilbert from 1765 to 1768. After a few years of home education, Burns was sent to Dalrymple Parish School during the summer of 1772 before returning at harvest time to full-time farm labouring until 1773, when he was sent to lodge with Murdoch for three weeks to study grammar, French, and Latin. In 1774, he exerted his first attempt at poetry, "O, Once I Lov'd a Bonnie Lass", which was inspired by Nelly Kilpatrick (1759—1820) who assisted him during the harvest of that year.

Burns is skilled in writing in the Scots language, though some of his works, such as "Love and Liberty" (also known as "The Jolly Beggars"), are written in both Scots and English for various effects. He also explores a variety of themes in his poems, including republicanism (he lived during the French Revolutionary period) and radicalism, Scottish patriotism, class inequalities, gender roles, Scottish cultural identity, poverty, sexuality, and the beneficial aspects of popular socialising (carousing, Scotch whisky, folk songs, and so forth).

Apart from making original compositions, Burns has also collected, revised or adapted many folk songs from across Scotland, which have also won him much fame. His poem (and song) "Auld Lang

Syne" is nowadays chanted around the globe and "Scots Wha Hae" serves for a long time as an unofficial national anthem of the country. Besides, such poems and songs as "A Red, Red Rose""A Man's A Man for A' That" "To a Louse" "To a Mouse" "Tam o' Shanter" and "Ae Fond Kiss" also remain well-known worldwide today.

Regarded as a pioneer of the Romantic Movement, Burns is also famous for his style marked by spontaneity, directness and sincerity. Besides, he is widely acclaimed as the national poet and a culture icon of Scotland, and has become a great source of inspiration to the founders of both liberalism and socialism.

"A Red, Red Rose", first published in 1794, is generally considered as one of the most famous songs of Robert Burns. Written in the form of a traditional ballad, the song has four stanzas of four lines each. It conveys its writer's feeling for love, which is straightforward in language and intent in emotion and therefore enchants the readers of all time.

A Red, Red Rose[1]

O, my Luve's[2] like a red, red rose,
That's newly sprung in June;
O, my Luve's like the melodie[3],
That's sweetly play'd in tune.

As fair art thou[4], my bonnie lass[5],
So deep in luve am I,
And I will luve thee still, my dear,
Till a' the seas gang dry![6]

Till a' the seas gang dry, my dear,
And the rocks melt wi'[7] the sun!
I will luve thee still, my dear,
While the sands o'[8] life shall run.[9]

And fare thee weel[10], my only Luve!
And fare thee weel, a while[11]!
And I will come again, my Luve,
Tho'[12] it were ten thousand mile!

Burns' Cottage

Notes

1. The metrical pattern of the poem is basically in a ballad form or quatrain, i.e. each stanza consists of four lines, with alternating lines of iambic tetrameter and iambic trimeter. While the first and third lines are iambic tetrameters, the second and fourth lines are iambic trimeters. The rhyme

scheme is ABCB.

2. Luve: love
3. melodie: melody
4. fair art thou: you are fair
5. bonnie lass: pretty girl
6. Till a' the seas gang dry: Till all the seas go dry
7. wi': with
8. o': of
9. While the sands o' life shall run: As long as I live. "sands" refers to the sand in the sand-glass, which was used for measuring time by the running of sand in ancient times, which is similar to an hour-glass.
10. weel: well
11. a while: a short time
12. Tho': Though

Robert Burns' Memorial

Questions

1. What's the connotation of the red rose? What rhetorical devices are used to help render the theme of this poem?
2. Find more English poems about love and make a comparison with this poem by Burns.

Oscar Wilde
1854—1900

Oscar Wilde

Oscar Wilde, celebrated Irish playwright and poet, was born in Dublin on October 16, 1854. His father, William Wilde, was an acclaimed doctor. His mother, Jane Francesca Elgee, was a poet and skilled linguist. From 1871 to 1874, Wilde attended Trinity College, Dublin, where he established himself as an outstanding student. Afterwards, he went to Magdalen College, Oxford before settling in London in 1878. Then, in 1884, he married Constance Lloyd, and later had a lecture tour of North America. Upon the conclusion of the American tour, Wilde returned home and commenced another lecture circuit of England and Ireland that lasted until the middle of 1884. Through his lectures, as well as his early poetry, Wilde established himself as a leading proponent of the aesthetic movement known as "art for art's sake".

Since the late 1880s, he witnessed the most creative period of his literary life. Two collections of children's stories, *The Happy Prince and Other Tales* (1888), and *A House of Pomegranates* (1891) got published. His first and only novel, *The Picture of Dorian Gray*, was published in 1891 in a book form, which caused a storm of criticism for its implied homoerotic theme that was considered very immoral by the Victorians. Oscar's first play, *Lady Windermere's Fan* (1892) brought him both great financial and critical success. Such subsequent plays as *A Woman of No Importance* (1892), *An Ideal Husband* (1895), and *The Importance of Being Earnest* (1895) further established him as one of the most successful playwrights of late Victorian London.

In the summer of 1891, Oscar met Lord Alfred Douglas and soon the two became lovers. However, in 1895, Oscar was sued by Douglas's father for libel, which finally led him to two years' imprisonment with hard labour. In 1897, he wrote *De Profundis* in prison and got it published in 1905. Upon his release he left immediately for France and never returned. In 1898, *The Ballad of Reading Gaol*, a response to the agony he experienced in prison, was published. On November 30, 1900, he died in Paris.

The Importance of Being Earnest, A Trivial Comedy for Serious People was first performed on 14 February 1895 at St. James's Theatre in London. In this farcical comedy, the wit of the author gets elaborated through his depiction of the protagonists who try to maintain fictitious personae and lead a double life so as to escape burdensome social obligations. Meanwhile, the Wildean wit also shows itself through the setting of the somewhat complicated but interesting love relationships among the major characters. Furthermore, Wilde also reveals such themes as the nature of marriage, morality and constraints, hypocrisy and inventiveness in the play, demonstrating his satire of the Victorian ways and conventions.

The Importance of Being Earnest

Oscar Wilde has firstly demonstrated his wit and talent through the implied pun of the title. Literally, "Earnest" means "seriousness and sincerity", a value emphasized among people; in the play, it is also wordplay with "Ernest"—the fake name of the protagonist Jack Worthing.

Jack Worthing is a pillar of the community in Hertfordshire. He is not only a guardian to Cecily Cardew, the pretty, eighteen-year-old granddaughter of the late Thomas Cardew, who found and adopted Jack when he was a baby; but also, as a major landowner and justice of the peace in Hertfordshire, he has to shoulder certain responsibilities and has a number of people all dependent on him. For years, whenever he goes to London, Jack goes by the name as Ernest. He has pretended Ernest as an irresponsible black-sheep brother who leads a scandalous life in pursuit of pleasure and is always getting into trouble of a sort that requires Jack to rush off to help him. As a matter of fact, Ernest is just an alibi for Jack, making an excuse for him to disappear for days at a time and do as he likes. He is the only person who knows the story behind all this.

Jack falls in love with Gwendolen Fairfax, the cousin of his best friend, Algernon Moncrieff. When the play opens, Algernon has begun to suspect something, having found an inscription inside Jack's cigarette case addressed to "Uncle Jack" from someone who refers to herself as "little Cecily".

Wilde's Memorial

Algernon suspects that Jack may be leading a double life, a practice he seems to regard as commonplace and indispensable to modern life. "Bunburyist" is the name he gives to such a kind of person with double life, which is in fact named after a nonexistent friend he pretends to have, a chronic invalid named Bunbury, to whose deathbed he is forever being summoned whenever he wants to get out of some tiresome social obligations.

At the beginning of Act I, Jack drops in on Algernon unexpectedly and announces his intention to propose to Gwendolen. Algernon confronts him with the cigarette case and forces him to tell the truth about the identity of "Jack" and "Cecily". Jack then confesses that Ernest is not his real name and that Cecily is his ward, a responsibility imposed on him by his adoptive father's will. Jack also tells Algernon about his fictional brother Ernest. Jack says he's been thinking of coming clean since Cecily has been showing too active an interest in him. Unexpectedly, Jack describes Cecily in terms that catch Algernon's attention and make him even more interested in her.

Gwendolen and her mother, Lady Bracknell, arrive, which gives Jack an opportunity to propose to Gwendolen. Jack is delighted to discover that Gwendolen returns his affections, but alarmed to find out that Gwendolen is fixated on the name Ernest as she makes clear that she would not consider marrying a man whose name was not Ernest, for it "inspires absolute confidence" in her mind.

Lady Bracknell interviews Jack to determine his eligibility as a possible son-in-law. During this interview, she asks about his family background. When Jack explains that he was an adoptive child without knowing who his parents were, Lady Bracknell is scandalized and forbids the match between Jack and her daughter.

ACT I

[...]

Jack: Charming day it has been, Miss Fairfax.

Gwendolen: Pray don't talk to me about the weather, Mr. Worthing. Whenever people talk to me about the weather, I always feel quite certain that they mean something else. And that makes me so nervous.

Jack: I do mean something else.

Gwendolen: I thought so. In fact, I am never wrong.

Jack: And I would like to be allowed to take advantage of Lady Bracknell's temporary absence ...

Gwendolen: I would certainly advise you to do so. Mamma has a way of coming back suddenly into a room that I have often had to speak to her about.

Jack: [Nervously.] Miss Fairfax, ever since I met you I have admired you more than any girl... I have ever met since ... I met you.

Chapter One　Love

Gwendolen: Yes, I am quite well aware of the fact. And I often wish that in public, at any rate, you had been more demonstrative. For me you have always had an irresistible fascination. Even before I met you I was far from indifferent to you. [Jack looks at her in amazement.] We live, as I hope you know, Mr. Worthing, in an age of ideals. The fact is constantly mentioned in the more expensive monthly magazines, and has reached the provincial pulpits, I am told; and my ideal has always been to love some one of the name of Ernest. There is something in that name that inspires absolute confidence. The moment Algernon first mentioned to me that he had a friend called Ernest, I knew I was destined to love you.

Jack: You really love me, Gwendolen?

Gwendolen: Passionately!

Jack: Darling! You don't know how happy you've made me.

Gwendolen: My own Ernest!

Jack: But you don't really mean to say that you couldn't love me if my name wasn't Ernest?

Gwendolen: But your name is Ernest.

Jack: Yes, I know it is. But supposing it was something else? Do you mean to say you couldn't love me then?

Gwendolen: [Glibly.] Ah! that is clearly a metaphysical speculation[1], and like most metaphysical speculations has very little reference at all to the actual facts of real life, as we know them.

Jack: Personally, darling, to speak quite candidly, I don't much care about the name of Ernest... I don't think the name suits me at all.

Gwendolen: It suits you perfectly. It is a divine name. It has a music of its own. It produces vibrations.

Jack: Well, really, Gwendolen, I must say that I think there are lots of other much nicer names. I think Jack, for instance, a charming name.

Gwendolen: Jack? ... No, there is very little music in the name Jack, if any at all, indeed. It does not thrill. It produces absolutely no vibrations... I have known several Jacks, and they all, without exception, were more than usually plain. Besides, Jack is a notorious domesticity for John! And I pity any woman who is married to a man called John. She would probably never be allowed to know the entrancing pleasure of a single moment's solitude. The only really safe name is Ernest.

Jack: Gwendolen, I must get christened at once—I mean we must get married at once. There is no time to be lost.

Gwendolen: Married, Mr. Worthing?

Jack: [Astounded.] Well ... surely. You know that I love you, and you led me to believe, Miss Fairfax, that you were not absolutely indifferent to me.

Gwendolen: I adore you. But you haven't proposed to me yet. Nothing has been said at all about marriage. The subject has not even been touched on.

Jack: Well... may I propose to you now?

Gwendolen: I think it would be an admirable opportunity. And to spare you any possible disappointment, Mr. Worthing, I think it only fair to tell you quite frankly beforehand that I am fully determined to accept you.

Jack: Gwendolen!

Gwendolen: Yes, Mr. Worthing, what have you got to say to me?

Jack: You know what I have got to say to you.

Gwendolen: Yes, but you don't say it.

Jack: Gwendolen, will you marry me? [Goes on his knees.]

Gwendolen: Of course I will, darling. How long you have been about it! I am afraid you have had very little experience in how to propose.

Jack: My own one[2], I have never loved any one in the world but you.

Gwendolen: Yes, but men often propose for practice. I know my brother Gerald does. All my girl-friends tell me so. What wonderfully blue eyes you have, Ernest! They are quite, quite, blue. I hope you will always look at me just like that, especially when there are other people present.

[Enter Lady Bracknell.]

Lady Bracknell: Mr. Worthing! Rise, sir, from this semi-recumbent posture. It is most indecorous.

Gwendolen: Mamma! [He tries to rise; she restrains him.] I must beg you to retire. This is no place for you. Besides, Mr. Worthing has not quite finished yet.

Lady Bracknell: Finished what, may I ask?

Gwendolen: I am engaged to Mr. Worthing, mamma. [They rise together.]

Lady Bracknell: Pardon me, you are not engaged to any one. When you do become engaged to some one, I, or your father, should his health permit him, will inform you of the fact. An engagement should come on a young girl as a surprise, pleasant or unpleasant, as the case may be. It is hardly a matter that she could be allowed to arrange for herself ... And now I have a few questions to put to you, Mr. Worthing. While I am making these inquiries, you, Gwendolen, will wait for me below in the carriage.

Gwendolen: [Reproachfully.] Mamma!

Lady Bracknell: In the carriage, Gwendolen!

[Gwendolen goes to the door. She and Jack blow kisses to each other behind Lady Bracknell's back. Lady Bracknell looks vaguely about as if she could not understand what the noise was. Finally turns round.] Gwendolen, the carriage!

Gwendolen: Yes, mamma. [Goes out, looking back at Jack.]

Lady Bracknell: [Sitting down.] You can take a seat, Mr. Worthing. [Looks in her pocket for note-book and pencil.]

Jack: Thank you, Lady Bracknell, I prefer standing.

Lady Bracknell: [Pencil and note-book in hand.] I feel bound to tell you that you are not down on my list of eligible young men, although I have the same list as the dear Duchess of Bolton has. We work together, in fact. However, I am quite ready to enter your name, should your answers be what a really affectionate mother requires. Do you smoke?

Jack: Well, yes, I must admit I smoke.

Lady Bracknell: I am glad to hear it. A man should always have an occupation of some kind. There are far too many idle men in London as it is. How old are you?

Jack: Twenty-nine.

Lady Bracknell: A very good age to be married at. I have always been of opinion that a man who desires to get married should know either everything or nothing. Which do you know?

Jack: [After some hesitation.] I know nothing, Lady Bracknell.

Lady Bracknell: I am pleased to hear it. I do not approve of anything that tampers with natural ignorance. Ignorance is like a delicate exotic fruit; touch it and the bloom is gone. The whole theory of modern education is radically unsound. Fortunately in England, at any rate, education produces no effect whatsoever. If it did, it would prove a serious danger to the upper classes, and probably lead to acts of violence in Grosvenor Square[3]. What is your income?

Jack: Between seven and eight thousand a year.

Lady Bracknell: [Makes a note in her book.] In land, or in investments?

Jack: In investments, chiefly.

Lady Bracknell: That is satisfactory. What between the duties expected of one during one's lifetime, and the duties exacted from one after one's death, land has ceased to be either a profit or a pleasure. It gives one position, and prevents one from keeping it up. That's all that can be said about land.

Jack: I have a country house with some land, of course, attached to it, about fifteen hundred acres, I believe; but I don't depend on that for my real income. In fact, as far as I can make out, the poachers are the only people who make anything out of it.

Lady Bracknell: A country house! How many bedrooms? Well, that point can be cleared up afterwards. You have a town house, I hope? A girl with a simple, unspoiled nature, like Gwendolen, could hardly be expected to reside in the country.

Jack: Well, I own a house in Belgrave Square, but it is let by the year to Lady Bloxham. Of course, I can get it back whenever I like, at six months' notice.

Lady Bracknell: Lady Bloxham? I don't know her.

Jack: Oh, she goes about very little. She is a lady considerably advanced in years.

Lady Bracknell: Ah, nowadays that is no guarantee of respectability of character. What number in Belgrave Square?

Jack: 149.

Lady Bracknell: [Shaking her head.] The unfashionable side.[4] I thought there was something. However, that could easily be altered.

Jack: Do you mean the fashion, or the side?

Lady Bracknell: [Sternly.] Both, if necessary, I presume. What are your politics?

Jack: Well, I am afraid I really have none. I am a Liberal Unionist[5].

Lady Bracknell: Oh, they count as Tories[6]. They dine with us. Or come in the evening, at any rate. Now to minor matters. Are your parents living?

Jack: I have lost both my parents.

Lady Bracknell: To lose one parent, Mr. Worthing, may be regarded as a misfortune; to lose both looks like carelessness. Who was your father? He was evidently a man of some wealth. Was he born in what the Radical papers call the purple of commerce[7], or did he rise from the ranks of the aristocracy?

Jack: I am afraid I really don't know. The fact is, Lady Bracknell, I said I had lost my parents. It would be nearer the truth to say that my parents seem to have lost me... I don't actually know who I am by birth. I was ... well, I was found.

Lady Bracknell: Found!

Jack: The late Mr. Thomas Cardew, an old gentleman of a very charitable and kindly disposition, found me, and gave me the name of Worthing, because he happened to have a first-class ticket for Worthing in his pocket at the time. Worthing is a place in Sussex. It is a seaside resort.

Lady Bracknell: Where did the charitable gentleman who had a first-class ticket for this seaside resort find you?

Jack: [Gravely.] In a hand-bag.

Lady Bracknell: A hand-bag?

Jack: [Very seriously.] Yes, Lady Bracknell. I was in a hand-bag—a somewhat large, black leather hand-bag, with handles to it—an ordinary hand-bag in fact.

Lady Bracknell: In what locality did this Mr. James, or Thomas, Cardew come across this ordinary hand-bag?

Jack: In the cloak-room at Victoria Station. It was given to him in mistake for his own.

Lady Bracknell: The cloak-room at Victoria Station?

Jack: Yes. The Brighton line.[8]

Lady Bracknell: The line is immaterial. Mr. Worthing, I confess I feel somewhat bewildered by what you have just told me. To be born, or at any rate bred, in a hand-bag, whether it had handles or not, seems to me to display a contempt for the ordinary decencies of family life that reminds one of the worst excesses[9] of the French Revolution. And I presume you know what that unfortunate movement[10] led to? As for the particular locality in which the hand-bag was found, a cloak-room at a railway station might serve to conceal a social indiscretion—has probably, indeed, been used for that purpose before now—but it could hardly be regarded as an assured basis for a recognized position in good society.

Jack: May I ask you then what you would advise me to do? I need hardly say I would do anything in the world to ensure Gwendolen's happiness.

Lady Bracknell: I would strongly advise you, Mr. Worthing, to try and acquire some relations as soon as possible, and to make a definite effort to produce at any rate one parent, of either sex, before the season[11] is quite over.

Jack: Well, I don't see how I could possibly manage to do that. I can produce the hand-bag at any moment. It is in my dressing-room at home. I really think that should satisfy you, Lady Bracknell.

Lady Bracknell: Me, sir! What has it to do with me? You can hardly imagine that I and Lord Bracknell would dream of allowing our only daughter — a girl brought up with the utmost care — to marry into a cloak-room, and form an alliance with a parcel? Good morning[12], Mr. Worthing!

[Lady Bracknell sweeps out in majestic indignation.]

Jack: Good morning! [Algernon, from the other room, strikes up the Wedding March. Jack looks perfectly furious, and goes to the door.] For goodness' sake don't play that ghastly tune, Algy[13]. How idiotic you are!

[The music stops and Algernon enters cheerily.]

Notes

1. metaphysical speculation: abstract philosophical inquiry
2. My own one: My darling
3. Grosvenor Square: a fashionable residential area in the fashionable West End of London
4. The unfashionable side: The "unfashionable" here suggests that those living in this side are not wealthy or have a high position.
5. Liberal Unionist: a British political party that was formed in 1886 by a faction that broke away from the Liberal Party and formed a political alliance with the Conservative Party in opposition to Irish Home Rule
6. Tories: members of the Conservative Party
7. born in ... the purple of commerce: "born in the purple" was traditionally a category of members of royal families born during the reign of their parents and was later expanded to include all children born of prominent or high ranking parents. "the purple of commerce", coined by Radical Papers, refers to the class of wealthy merchants. So, the sentence "Was he born in... commerce...?" means "Was he born in a wealthy merchant's family...?"
8. the Brighton line: the railway line which leads to Brighton, a seaside resort on the coast of the English Channel
9. excesses: the cruel acts in the French Revolution
10. that unfortunate movement: the French Revolution, which started in 1789 and ended in 1799
11. the season: referring to a period of time when great activities or events take place in the fashionable side
12. Good morning: Here it is used before parting, which means "Goodbye".
13. Algy: Algernon

Questions

1. Analyze the Wildean wit presented in the first act. Is there a difference between being "witty" and being "funny"?
2. Discuss the character of Lady Bracknell. What kind of person is she and what are the most striking traits in her character?

William Butler Yeats
1865—1939

William Butler Yeats, one of the foremost figures of 20th century literature, was born in Dublin, Ireland, in 1865. Born as the son of a well-known painter, John Butler Yeats, William spent his childhood in County Sligo and returned to Dublin at the age of fifteen to continue his education and

William Butler Yeats

study painting. But quickly, he discovered that he preferred poetry. In 1887, his first volume of verse appeared. Apart from being known as a great poet, William Butler Yeats is also remembered as a major playwright. Together with Lady Gregory, he founded the Irish Theatre which was to become the Abbey Theatre in 1904.

In 1923, Yeats was awarded the Nobel Prize in Literature. Being the first Irishman so honoured for the prize, he was described by the Nobel Committee as "inspired poetry, which in a highly artistic form gives expression to the spirit of a whole nation." However, Yeats is generally considered as one of the few writers who completed their greatest works after being awarded the Nobel Prize, which include *The Tower* (1928) and *The Winding Stair and Other Poems* (1933).

Besides, Yeats was also deeply involved in politics in Ireland and was active in societies and movement that sought to promote an Irish literary revival and fight against the cultural influences of English rule in Ireland during the Victorian period.

As a Symbolist poet, he uses allusive imagery and symbolic structures throughout his career. In the meantime, being a master of the traditional forms, Yeats distinguishes himself from other modernists who experiment with free verse. As for the themes under the pen of Yeats, such recurrent ones include the contrast of art and life, cyclical theories of life, and the ideal of beauty and ceremony contrasting with the hubbub of modern life.

"When You Are Old" and "The White Birds", written around the same time and dedicated to Maud Gonne, the inspiration of most of Yeats' love lyrics, were collected in his early anthology *The Rose* (1893)—a symbol generally related to love and beauty. Yeats met Maud in 1888 when he was 23. He then developed an obsessive infatuation with her beauty and outspoken manner. Yeats proposed marriage on several occasions, but was rejected each time. For Maud, a dedicated nationalist and political activist, the sole passion in her life was the pursuit of an independent Irish nation. Maud became his muse from the first moment they met. Yeats had celebrated her beauty in many of his early works, from the love lyrics (like the two below) to other poems and plays in which "he mythologized her as Helen, Cathleen Ni Houlihan, Pallas Athene, Dectora, and Deirdre".

When You Are Old

WHEN you are old and gray and full of sleep[1],
And nodding by the fire, take down this book,
And slowly read, and dream of the soft look
Your eyes had once, and of their shadows deep;

How many loved your moments of glad grace,
And loved your beauty with love false or true;
But one man loved the pilgrim[2] soul in you,
And loved the sorrows of your changing face.

And bending down beside the glowing bars[3],
Murmur[4], a little sadly, how Love fled
And paced upon the mountains overhead
And hid his face among a crowd of stars.

Notes

1. full of sleep: connotation of death
2. pilgrim: a person who journeys to sacred places as an act of devotion
3. glowing bars: Here referring to the sort of small electrical bar heater used in apartments to prevent the coldness of winter. The metaphor of death and age adds a further despondency to the image, and highlights the idea of solitude and loneliness.
4. Murmur suggests a whisper that shows she has no passion or zest left, reinforcing the imagery of age and weariness.

Questions

1. Why is "loved" repeated in the second stanza? And why does "Love" in the second line of the third stanza is capitalized?
2. What concrete images are used to present the broad notion of nearness to death and the subversive fears and sadness it connotes?
3. How do you interpret Yeats' intention of writing this poem? What strikes you most when you read it?

The White Birds[1]

I would that we were, my beloved, white birds on the foam[2] of the sea!
We tire of the flame of the meteor, before it can fade and flee;
And the flame of the blue star of twilight, hung low on the rim of the sky,
Has awaked in our hearts, my beloved, a sadness that may not die.
A weariness comes from those dreamers, dew-dabbled[3], the lily and rose;
Ah, dream not of them, my beloved, the flame of the meteor that goes,
Or the flame of the blue star that lingers[4] hung low in the fall of the dew:
For I would we were changed to white birds on the wandering foam:I and you!
I am haunted by numberless islands, and many a Danaan[5] shore,
Where Time would surely forget us, and Sorrow come near us no more;
Soon far from the rose and the lily and fret[6] of the flames would we be,
Were we only white birds, my beloved, buoyed[7] out on the foam of the sea!

Notes

1. This poem was delivered to Maud three days after she had rejected his first proposal. According to

Maud, when she and Yeats were taking a rest after a walk along the cliffs at Howth, she saw two white seagulls fly over their heads. Maud then said that if she were to become a bird, she would like to be a seagull above all. It was a commonplace remark, but "in three days he sent me the poem", with its gentle theme. And Yeats' note to the poem in the first printing—"I have read somewhere that the birds of faeryland are white as snow"—would also imply where he got the inspiration for the poem.

2. foam: a mass of small bubbles formed on the surface of water
3. dabble: to make wet by sprinkling, splashing, or dipping into water or other liquid
4. linger: to remain existent although waning in strength, importance, or influence
5. Danaan: also known as the Sidhe, is the fairy people of Irish folklore. Its full name is Tuatha de Danaan, meaning the folk of the goddess Danu. In his notes to the 1895 edition of *Poems*, Yeats says: "Tuatha De Danaan means the Race of the Gods of Dana. Dana was the mother of all the ancient gods of Ireland. They were the powers of light and life and warmth and did battle with the Fomoroh, or powers of night and death and cold. Robbed of offerings and honour, they [the Danaan] have gradually dwindled in the popular imagination until they have become the Faeries." Yeats also says that the Danaan can "take all shapes, and those that are in the waters often take the shapes of birds and are as white as snow."
6. fret: a state of anxiety or worry
7. buoy: to keep afloat or aloft

Questions

1. What is the rhyme scheme of this poem? And what kind of effect it might produce in recital?
2. According to the poem, what kind of quality is shared by the "flame of the meteor" and the "flame of the blue star"? Do you think they denote the same thing?
3. As a recurring image in Yeats' poetic creation, what does rose probably symbolize in this poem?
4. Apart from the love theme, do you feel there is a vein of escapism in this "white bird" image?

David Herbert Lawrence
1885—1930

David Herbert Lawrence, the famous English novelist, poet, playwright, essayist, and literary critic, was born on September 11, 1885 to a miner and his wife in the small village of Eastwood near Nottingham, England. Lawrence's father Arthur was a barely literate coal-miner, while his mother Lydia was originally lower middle-class and a former pupil-teacher. Owing to her family's financial difficulties, she had been forced into work in the lace industry. From the start, the couple had a troublesome marriage, and the tensions between them had its effect on young Lawrence and even provided the raw material for a number of Lawrence's early works. From 1891 to 1898, Lawrence received education in Beauvale Board School and then went into Nottingham High School. In 1908, he went on to become a full-time student and received a teaching certificate from the University College, Nottingham. During these years, he also worked on his first poems, some short stories, and a draft of a novel, *Laetitia*, which was eventually to become *The White Peacock*.

David Herbert Lawrence

In 1914, he married Frieda von Richthofen Weekley, who was six years his senior and was already married when they first met. During World War I, they resided in England in various towns and cities. After the war, they left for Italy in November 1919, and then the couple moved from place to place, including Australia, New Zealand, the South Seas, California, New Mexico, and Mexico. Lawrence died of tuberculosis in a sanatorium on March 2, 1930.

As one of the greatest English writers of the 20th century, Lawrence is perhaps best known for such novels as *The White Peacock* (1911), *Sons and Lovers* (1913), *The Rainbow* (1915), *Women in Love* (1920), and *Lady Chatterley's Lover* (1928). Many of his works were very controversial because of their sexually explicit material, and both *The Rainbow* and *Lady Chatterley's Lover* were banned during his lifetime. Besides novels, Lawrence also wrote many short stories as *The Captain's Doll, The Fox, The Ladybird, The Princess, The Rocking-Horse Winner* and almost 800 poems.

In his works, Lawrence shows an extended reflection upon the dehumanizing effects of modernity and industrialization to human relationship and power of love, and also makes profound exploration of psychological motivation in human behavior.

Sons and Lovers, the third published novel of D. H. Lawrence, is one of the author's most successful and popular works. Since many of the details in the plot of the novel parallel with Lawrence's own life, it is seen by some as semi-autobiographical. In this masterpiece, Lawrence portraits a working-class family in Nottinghamshire and mainly centers on Paul Morel, the second son in this family, and his relations with his mother and several other women. Similar to his other novels, Lawrence also depicts the influence of industrialization and rapid social change on the working families as they have to endure hardships and humiliation in order to survive, which thereby undermines their power of love and affects their relationships.

Sons and Lovers

Initially titled as *Paul Morel*, *Sons and Lovers* gets published in 1913. Divided into two parts, the first part explicates the background of the story and depicts the relationships among the members in the Morel family. Gertrude Coppard, a middle class girl raised in a strict family, marries Walter Morel, a coal miner, for love. They have four children, William, Annie, Paul and Arthur. However, facing with the reality of her limited social and economic status, Mrs. Morel becomes disillusioned and finds herself in an unhappy marriage. Thereafter, Mrs. Morel shifts her affections and hope for the future toward her four children, especially her sons. William, the eldest boy, is at first Mrs. Morel's favorite

 and also adores her mother a lot. Later, as William moves to London to seek a better future and gets involved with a flighty young woman named Gipsy, Mrs. Morel feels quite upset and tries to discourage the relationship. However, the sudden illness of William takes his life and makes his mother heartbroken.

Upon the death of William, Mrs. Morel rediscovers her love for her second son Paul as he catches pneumonia. Like his brother, Paul is drawn to his mother and bonded to her. In the second part of the novel, Paul falls into the relationship with two women—Miriam and Clara. Firstly, Paul meets Miriam, a girl in the nearby farm, and the two gradually falls in love with each other. As Mrs. Morel sees the power of Miriam taking Paul away from her, she disapproves the relationship and expresses her hatred towards the girl. Miriam is also aware of the influence Paul's mother casting over him and resents her interference. Caught in between, Paul constantly wavers in his feelings towards Miriam and he finally decides to break off with her. Paul meets Clara Dawes in the farm of Miriam's family. Clara is separated from her husband Baxter at then. Paul and Clara begin a passionate affair. Mrs. Morel doesn't discourage this relationship as she foresees that Clara doesn't have the emotional or intellectual depth to hold Paul. Gradually as Paul realizes there is something wrong with this relationship, he confesses to his mother that he realizes he doesn't really give himself to his women. Mrs. Morel is diagnosed with cancer. Paul and his sister give her a fatal dose of morphine for relief. After his mother's death, Paul sinks deep into depression and leaves for town for a new start.

The excerpt in the chapter below charts Paul's inner conflict towards the feeling over Miriam and his return to his mother's love. Paul decides to break off with Miriam and accuses her of having a negative attitude towards life and relationships. As Miriam understands that Paul cannot love her, she is angry with Paul constantly listening to his mother. Then in this chapter, Paul meets Clara in person for the first time, and as Paul taking his mother to Lincoln to see the cathedral, Mrs. Morel shows the first signs of illness. Paul falls into a fit of anguish. The chapter concludes with the end of the first phase of Paul's romance, though he still feels that he belongs to Miriam.

Chapter IX Defeat of Miriam (Excerpt)

PAUL WAS DISSATISFIED with himself and with everything. The deepest of his love belonged to his mother. When he felt he had hurt her, or wounded his love for her, he could not bear it. Now it was spring, and there was battle between him and Miriam. This year he had a good deal against her. She was vaguely aware of it. The old feeling that she was to be a sacrifice to this love, which she had had when she prayed, was mingled in all her emotions. She did not at the bottom believe she ever would have him. She did not believe in herself primarily: doubted whether she could ever be what he would demand of her. Certainly she never saw herself living happily through a lifetime with him. She saw tragedy, sorrow, and sacrifice ahead. And in sacrifice she was proud, in renunciation she was strong, for she did not trust herself to support everyday life. She was prepared for the big things and the deep things, like tragedy. It was the sufficiency of the small day-life she could not trust.

The Easter holidays began happily. Paul was his own frank self. Yet she felt it would go wrong. On the Sunday afternoon she stood at her bedroom window, looking across at the oak-trees of the wood, in whose branches a twilight was tangled, below the bright sky of the afternoon. Grey-green rosettes of honeysuckle leaves hung before the window, some already, she fancied, showing bud. It was spring, which she loved and dreaded.

Hearing the clack of the gate she stood in suspense. It was a bright grey day. Paul came into the yard with his bicycle, which glittered as he walked. Usually he rang his bell and laughed towards the house. To-day he walked with shut lips and cold, cruel bearing, that had something of a slouch and a sneer in it. She knew him well by now, and could tell from that keen-looking, aloof young body of his what was happening inside him. There was a cold correctness in the way he put his bicycle in its place, that made her heart sink.

She came downstairs nervously. She was wearing a new net blouse that she thought became her. It had a high collar with a tiny ruff, reminding her of Mary, Queen of Scots, and making her, she thought, look wonderfully a woman, and dignified. At twenty she was full-breasted and luxuriously formed. Her face was still like a soft rich mask, unchangeable. But her eyes, once lifted, were wonderful. She was afraid of him. He would notice her new blouse.

He, being in a hard, ironical mood, was entertaining the family to a description of a service given in the Primitive Methodist Chapel, conducted by one of the well-known preachers of the sect. He sat at the head of the table, his mobile face, with the eyes that could be so beautiful, shining with tenderness or dancing with laughter, now taking on one expression and then another, in imitation of various people he was mocking. His mockery always hurt her; it was too near the reality. He was too clever and cruel. She felt that when his eyes were like this, hard with mocking hate, he would spare neither himself nor anybody else. But Mrs. Leivers was wiping her eyes with laughter, and Mr. Leivers, just awake from his Sunday nap, was rubbing his head in amusement. The three brothers sat with ruffled, sleepy appearance in their shirt-sleeves, giving a guffaw from time to time. The whole family loved a "take-off" more than anything.

He took no notice of Miriam. Later, she saw him remark her new blouse, saw that the artist approved, but it won from him not a spark of warmth. She was nervous, could hardly reach the teacups from the shelves.

When the men went out to milk, she ventured to address him personally.

"You were late," she said.

"Was I?" he answered.

There was silence for a while.

"Was it rough riding?" she asked.

"I didn't notice it."

She continued quickly to lay the table. When she had finished—

"Tea won't be for a few minutes. Will you come and look at the daffodils?" she said.

He rose without answering. They went out into the back garden under the budding damson-trees. The hills and the sky were clean and cold. Everything looked washed, rather hard. Miriam glanced at Paul. He was pale and impassive. It seemed cruel to her that his eyes and brows, which she loved, could look so hurting.

"Has the wind made you tired?" she asked. She detected an underneath feeling of weariness about him.

"No, I think not," he answered.

"It must be rough on the road—the wood moans so."

"You can see by the clouds it's a south-west wind; that helps me here."

"You see, I don't cycle, so I don't understand," she murmured.

"Is there need to cycle to know that?" he said.

She thought his sarcasms were unnecessary. They went forward in silence. Round the wild, tussocky[1] lawn at the back of the house was a thorn hedge, under which daffodils were craning forward from among their sheaves of grey-green blades. The cheeks of the flowers were greenish with cold. But still some had burst, and their gold ruffled and glowed. Miriam went on her knees before one cluster, took a wild-looking daffodil between her hands, turned up its face of gold to her, and bowed down, caressing it with her mouth and cheeks and brow. He stood aside, with his hands in his pockets, watching her. One after another she turned up to him the faces of the yellow, bursten flowers appealingly, fondling them lavishly all the while.

"Aren't they magnificent?" she murmured.

"Magnificent! It's a bit thick—they're pretty!"

She bowed again to her flowers at his censure of her praise. He watched her crouching, sipping the flowers with fervid kisses.

"Why must you always be fondling things?" he said irritably.

"But I love to touch them," she replied, hurt.

"Can you never like things without clutching them as if you wanted to pull the heart out of them? Why don't you have a bit more restraint, or reserve, or something?"

She looked up at him full of pain, then continued slowly to stroke her lips against a ruffled flower. Their scent, as she smelled it, was so much kinder than he; it almost made her cry.

"You wheedle[2] the soul out of things," he said. "I would never wheedle—at any rate, I'd go straight."

He scarcely knew what he was saying. These things came from him mechanically. She looked at him. His body seemed one weapon, firm and hard against her.

"You're always begging things to love you," he said, "as if you were a beggar for love. Even the flowers, you have to fawn on them—"

Rhythmically, Miriam was swaying and stroking the flower with her mouth, inhaling the scent which ever after made her shudder as it came to her nostrils.

"You don't want to love—your eternal and abnormal craving is to be loved. You aren't positive, you're negative. You absorb, absorb, as if you must fill yourself up with love, because you've got a shortage somewhere."

She was stunned by his cruelty, and did not hear. He had not the faintest notion of what he was saying. It was as if his fretted, tortured soul, run hot by thwarted passion, jetted off these sayings like sparks from electricity. She did not grasp anything he said. She only sat crouched beneath his cruelty and his hatred of her. She never realised in a flash. Over everything she brooded and brooded.

After tea he stayed with Edgar and the brothers, taking no notice of Miriam. She, extremely unhappy on this looked for holiday, waited for him. And at last he yielded and came to her. She was determined to track this mood of his to its origin. She counted it not much more than a mood.

"Shall we go through the wood a little way?" she asked him, knowing he never refused a direct request.

They went down to the warren. On the middle path they passed a trap, a narrow horseshoe hedge of small fir-boughs, baited with the guts of a rabbit. Paul glanced at it frowning. She caught his eye.

"Isn't it dreadful?" she asked.

"I don't know! Is it worse than a weasel with its teeth in a rabbit's throat? One weasel or many rabbits? One or the other must go!"

He was taking the bitterness of life badly. She was rather sorry for him.

"We will go back to the house," he said. "I don't want to walk out."

They went past the lilac-tree, whose bronze leaf-buds were coming unfastened. Just a fragment remained of the haystack, a monument squared and brown, like a pillar of stone. There was a little bed of hay from the last cutting.

"Let us sit here a minute," said Miriam.

He sat down against his will, resting his back against the hard wall of hay. They faced the amphitheatre[3] of round hills that glowed with sunset, tiny white farms standing out, the meadows golden, the woods dark and yet luminous, tree-tops folded over tree-tops, distinct in the distance. The evening had cleared, and the east was tender with a magenta flush under which the land lay still and rich.

"Isn't it beautiful?" she pleaded.

But he only scowled. He would rather have had it ugly just then.

At that moment a big bull-terrier came rushing up, open-mouthed, pranced his two paws on the youth's shoulders, licking his face. Paul drew back, laughing. Bill was a great relief to him. He pushed the dog aside, but it came leaping back.

"Get out," said the lad, "or I'll dot thee one."

But the dog was not to be pushed away. So Paul had a little battle with the creature, pitching poor Bill away from him, who, however, only floundered tumultuously back again, wild with joy. The two fought together, the man laughing grudgingly, the dog grinning all over. Miriam watched them. There was something pathetic about the man. He wanted so badly to love, to be tender. The rough way he bowled the dog over was really loving. Bill got up, panting with happiness, his brown eyes rolling in his white face, and lumbered back again. He adored Paul. The lad frowned.

"Bill, I've had enough o' thee," he said.

But the dog only stood with two heavy paws, that quivered with love, upon his thigh, and flickered a red tongue at him. He drew back.

"No," he said—"no—I've had enough."

And in a minute the dog trotted off happily, to vary the fun.

He remained staring miserably across at the hills, whose still beauty he begrudged. He wanted to go and cycle with Edgar. Yet he had not the courage to leave Miriam.

"Why are you sad?" she asked humbly.

"I'm not sad; why should I be," he answered. "I'm only normal."

She wondered why he always claimed to be normal when he was disagreeable.

"But what is the matter?" she pleaded, coaxing him soothingly.

"Nothing!"

"Nay!" she murmured.

He picked up a stick and began to stab the earth with it.

"You'd far better not talk," he said.

"But I wish to know—" she replied.

He laughed resentfully.

"You always do," he said.

"It's not fair to me," she murmured.

He thrust, thrust, thrust at the ground with the pointed stick, digging up little clods of earth as if he were in a fever of irritation. She gently and firmly laid her hand on his wrist.

"Don't!" she said. "Put it away."

He flung the stick into the currant-bushes, and leaned back. Now he was bottled up.

"What is it?" she pleaded softly.

He lay perfectly still, only his eyes alive, and they full of torment.

"You know," he said at length, rather wearily—"you know—we'd better break off."

It was what she dreaded. Swiftly everything seemed to darken before her eyes.

"Why!" she murmured. "What has happened?"

"Nothing has happened. We only realise where we are. It's no good—"

She waited in silence, sadly, patiently. It was no good being impatient with him. At any rate, he would tell her now what ailed him.

"We agreed on friendship," he went on in a dull, monotonous voice. "How often HAVE we agreed for friendship! And yet—it neither stops there, nor gets anywhere else."

He was silent again. She brooded. What did he mean? He was so wearying. There was something he would not yield. Yet she must be patient with him.

"I can only give friendship—it's all I'm capable of—it's a flaw in my make-up. The thing overbalances to one side— I hate a toppling balance. Let us have done."

There was warmth of fury in his last phrases. He meant she loved him more than he her. Perhaps he could not love her. Perhaps she had not in herself that which he wanted. It was the deepest motive of her soul, this self-mistrust. It was so deep she dared neither realise nor acknowledge. Perhaps she was deficient. Like an infinitely subtle shame, it kept her always back. If it were so, she would do without him. She would never let herself want him. She would merely see.

"But what has happened?" she said.

"Nothing—it's all in myself—it only comes out just now. We're always like this towards Easter-time."

He grovelled so helplessly, she pitied him. At least she never floundered in such a pitiable way. After all, it was he who was chiefly humiliated.

"What do you want?" she asked him.

"Why—I mustn't come often—that's all. Why should I monopolise you when I'm not— You see, I'm deficient in something with regard to you—"

He was telling her he did not love her, and so ought to leave her a chance with another man. How foolish and blind and shamefully clumsy he was! What were other men to her! What were men to her at all! But he, ah! she loved his soul. Was he deficient in something? Perhaps he was.

"But I don't understand," she said huskily. "Yesterday—"

The night was turning jangled and hateful to him as the twilight faded. And she bowed under her suffering.

"I know," he cried, "you never will! You'll never believe that I can't—can't physically, any more than I can fly up like a skylark—"

"What?" she murmured. Now she dreaded.

"Love you."

He hated her bitterly at that moment because he made her suffer. Love her! She knew he loved her. He really belonged to her. This about not loving her, physically, bodily, was a mere perversity on his part, because he knew she loved him. He was stupid like a child. He belonged to her. His soul wanted her. She guessed somebody had been influencing him. She felt upon him the hardness, the foreignness of another influence.

"What have they been saying at home?" she asked.

"It's not that," he answered.

And then she knew it was. She despised them for their commonness, his people. They did not know what things were really worth.

He and she talked very little more that night. After all he left her to cycle with Edgar.

He had come back to his mother. Hers was the strongest tie in his life. When he thought round, Miriam shrank away. There was a vague, unreal feel about her. And nobody else mattered. There was one place in the world that stood solid and did not melt into unreality: the place where his mother was. Everybody else could grow shadowy, almost non-existent to him, but she could not. It was as if the pivot and pole of his life, from which he could not escape, was his mother.

And in the same way she waited for him. In him was established her life now. After all, the life beyond offered very little to Mrs. Morel. She saw that our chance for doing is here, and doing counted with her. Paul was going to prove that she had been right; he was going to make a man whom nothing should shift off his feet; he was going to alter the face of the earth in some way which mattered. Wherever he went she felt her soul went with him. Whatever he did she felt her soul stood by him, ready, as it were, to hand him his tools. She could not bear it when he was with Miriam. William was dead. She would fight to keep Paul.

And he came back to her. And in his soul was a feeling of the satisfaction of self-sacrifice because he was faithful to her. She loved him first; he loved her first. And yet it was not enough. His new young life, so strong and imperious, was urged towards something else. It made him mad with restlessness. She saw this, and wished bitterly that Miriam had been a woman who could take this new life of his, and leave her the roots. He fought against his mother almost as he fought against Miriam.

It was a week before he went again to Willey Farm. Miriam had suffered a great deal, and was afraid to see him again. Was she now to endure the ignominy[4] of his abandoning her? That would only be superficial and temporary. He would come back. She held the keys to his soul. But meanwhile, how he would torture her with his battle against her. She shrank from it.

However, the Sunday after Easter he came to tea. Mrs. Leivers was glad to see him. She gathered something was fretting him, that he found things hard. He seemed to drift to her for comfort. And she was good to him. She did him that great kindness of treating him almost with reverence.

He met her with the young children in the front garden.

"I'm glad you've come," said the mother, looking at him with her great appealing brown eyes. "It is such a sunny day. I was just going down the fields for the first time this year."

He felt she would like him to come. That soothed him. They went, talking simply, he gentle and humble. He could have wept with gratitude that she was deferential to him. He was feeling humiliated.

At the bottom of the Mow Close they found a thrush's nest.

"Shall I show you the eggs?" he said.

"Do!" replied Mrs. Leivers. "They seem such a sign of spring, and so hopeful."

He put aside the thorns, and took out the eggs, holding them in the palm of his hand.

"They are quite hot—I think we frightened her off them," he said.

"Ay, poor thing!" said Mrs. Leivers.

Miriam could not help touching the eggs, and his hand which, it seemed to her, cradled them so well.

"Isn't it a strange warmth!" she murmured, to get near him.

"Blood heat," he answered.

She watched him putting them back, his body pressed against the hedge, his arm reaching slowly through the thorns, his hand folded carefully over the eggs. He was concentrated on the act. Seeing him so, she loved him; he seemed so simple and sufficient to himself. And she could not get to him.

After tea she stood hesitating at the bookshelf. He took "Tartarin de Tarascon[5]". Again they sat on the bank of hay at the foot of the stack. He read a couple of pages, but without any heart for it. Again the dog came racing up to repeat the fun of the other day. He shoved his muzzle in the man's chest. Paul fingered his ear for a moment. Then he pushed him away.

"Go away, Bill," he said. "I don't want you."

Bill slunk off, and Miriam wondered and dreaded what was coming. There was a silence about the youth that made her still with apprehension. It was not his furies, but his quiet resolutions that she feared.

Turning his face a little to one side, so that she could not see him, he began, speaking slowly and painfully:

"Do you think—if I didn't come up so much—you might get to like somebody else—another man?"

So this was what he was still harping on.

"But I don't know any other men. Why do you ask?" she replied, in a low tone that should have been a reproach to him.

"Why," he blurted, "because they say I've no right to come up like this—without we mean to marry—"

Miriam was indignant at anybody's forcing the issues between them. She had been furious with her own father for suggesting to Paul, laughingly, that he knew why he came so much.

"Who says?" she asked, wondering if her people had anything to do with it. They had not.

"Mother—and the others. They say at this rate every-body will consider me engaged, and I ought to consider myself so, because it's not fair to you. And I've tried to find out—and I don't think I love you as a man ought to love his wife. What do you think about it?"

Miriam bowed her head moodily. She was angry at having this struggle. People should leave him and her alone.

"I don't know," she murmured.

"Do you think we love each other enough to marry?" he asked definitely. It made her tremble.

"No," she answered truthfully. "I don't think so—we're too young."

"I thought perhaps," he went on miserably, "that you, with your intensity in things, might have given me more— than I could ever make up to you. And even now—if you think it better—we'll be engaged."

Now Miriam wanted to cry. And she was angry, too. He was always such a child for people to do as they liked with.

"No, I don't think so," she said firmly.

He pondered a minute.

"You see," he said, "with me—I don't think one person would ever monopolize me—be everything to me—I think never."

This she did not consider.

"No," she murmured. Then, after a pause, she looked at him, and her dark eyes flashed.

"This is your mother," she said. "I know she never liked me."

"No, no, it isn't," he said hastily. "It was for your sake she spoke this time. She only said, if I was going on, I ought to consider myself engaged." There was a silence. "And if I ask you to come down any time, you won't stop away, will you?"

She did not answer. By this time she was very angry.

"Well, what shall we do?" she said shortly. "I suppose I'd better drop French. I was just beginning to get on with it. But I suppose I can go on alone."

"I don't see that we need," he said. "I can give you a French lesson, surely."

"Well—and there are Sunday nights. I shan't stop coming to chapel, because I enjoy it, and it's all the social life I get. But you've no need to come home with me. I can go alone."

"All right," he answered, rather taken aback. "But if I ask Edgar, he'll always come with us, and then they can say nothing."

There was silence. After all, then, she would not lose much. For all their talk down at his home there would not be much difference. She wished they would mind their own business.

"And you won't think about it, and let it trouble you, will you?" he asked.

"Oh no," replied Miriam, without looking at him.

He was silent. She thought him unstable. He had no fixity of purpose, no anchor of righteousness that held him.

"Because," he continued, "a man gets across his bicycle—and goes to work—and does all sorts of things. But a woman broods."

"No, I shan't bother," said Miriam. And she meant it.

It had gone rather chilly. They went indoors.

"How white Paul looks!" Mrs. Leivers exclaimed. "Miriam, you shouldn't have let him sit out of doors. Do you think you've taken cold, Paul?"

"Oh, no!" he laughed.

But he felt done up. It wore him out, the conflict in himself. Miriam pitied him now. But quite early, before nine o'clock, he rose to go.

"You're not going home, are you?" asked Mrs. Leivers anxiously.

"Yes," he replied. "I said I'd be early." He was very awkward.

"But this IS early," said Mrs. Leivers.

Miriam sat in the rocking-chair, and did not speak. He hesitated, expecting her to rise and go with him to the barn as usual for his bicycle. She remained as she was. He was at a loss.

"Well—good-night, all!" he faltered.

She spoke her good-night along with all the others. But as he went past the window he looked in. She saw him pale, his brows knit slightly in a way that had become constant with him, his eyes dark with pain.

She rose and went to the doorway to wave good-bye to him as he passed through the gate. He rode slowly under the pine-trees, feeling a cur and a miserable wretch. His bicycle went tilting down the hills at random. He thought it would be a relief to break one's neck.

Two days later he sent her up a book and a little note, urging her to read and be busy.

At this time he gave all his friendship to Edgar. He loved the family so much, he loved the farm so much; it was the dearest place on earth to him. His home was not so lovable. It was his mother. But then he would have been just as happy with his mother anywhere. Whereas Willey Farm he loved passionately. He loved the little pokey kitchen, where men's boots tramped, and the dog slept with one eye open for fear of being trodden on; where the lamp hung over the table at night, and everything was so silent. He loved Miriam's long, low parlour, with its atmosphere of romance, its flowers, its books, its high rose-wood piano. He loved the gardens and the buildings that stood with their scarlet roofs on the naked edges of the fields, crept towards the wood as if for cosiness, the wild country scooping down a valley and up the uncultured hills of the other side. Only to be there was an exhilaration and a joy to him. He loved Mrs. Leivers, with her unworldliness and her quaint cynicism; he loved Mr. Leivers, so warm and young and lovable; he loved Edgar, who lit up when he came, and the boys and the children and Bill—even the sow Circe and the Indian game-cock called Tippoo. All this besides Miriam. He could not give it up.

So he went as often, but he was usually with Edgar. Only all the family, including the father, joined in charades[6] and games at evening. And later, Miriam drew them together, and they read *Macbeth* out of penny books, taking parts. It was great excitement. Miriam was glad, and Mrs. Leivers was glad, and Mr. Leivers enjoyed it. Then they all learned songs together from tonic solfa, singing in a circle round the fire. But now Paul was very rarely alone with Miriam. She waited. When she and Edgar and he walked home together from chapel or from the literary society in Bestwood, she knew his

Chapter One Love

talk, so passionate and so unorthodox nowadays, was for her. She did envy Edgar, however, his cycling with Paul, his Friday nights, his days working in the fields. For her Friday nights and her French lessons were gone. She was nearly always alone, walking, pondering in the wood, reading, studying, dreaming, waiting. And he wrote to her frequently.

[…]

Paul could choose the lesser in place of the higher, she saw. He could be unfaithful to himself, unfaithful to the real, deep Paul Morel. There was a danger of his becoming frivolous, of his running after his satisfaction like any Arthur, or like his father. It made Miriam bitter to think that he should throw away his soul for this flippant traffic of triviality with Clara. She walked in bitterness and silence, while the other two rallied each other, and Paul sported.

And afterwards, he would not own it, but he was rather ashamed of himself, and prostrated himself before Miriam. Then again he rebelled.

"It's not religious to be religious," he said. "I reckon a crow is religious when it sails across the sky. But it only does it because it feels itself carried to where it's going, not because it thinks it is being eternal."

But Miriam knew that one should be religious in everything, have God, whatever God might be, present in everything.

"I don't believe God knows such a lot about Himself," he cried. "God doesn't KNOW things, He IS things. And I'm sure He's not soulful."

And then it seemed to her that Paul was arguing God on to his own side, because he wanted his own way and his own pleasure. There was a long battle between him and her. He was utterly unfaithful to her even in her own presence; then he was ashamed, then repentant; then he hated her, and went off again. Those were the ever-recurring conditions.

She fretted him to the bottom of his soul. There she remained—sad, pensive, a worshipper. And he caused her sorrow. Half the time he grieved for her, half the time he hated her. She was his conscience; and he felt, somehow, he had got a conscience that was too much for him. He could not leave her, because in one way she did hold the best of him. He could not stay with her because she did not take the rest of him, which was three-quarters. So he chafed himself into rawness over her.

When she was twenty-one he wrote her a letter which could only have been written to her.

"May I speak of our old, worn love, this last time. It, too, is changing, is it not? Say, has not the body of that love died, and left you its invulnerable soul? You see, I can give you a spirit love, I have given it you this long, long time; but not embodied passion. See, you are a nun. I have given you what I would give a holy nun—as a mystic monk to a mystic nun. Surely you esteem it best. Yet you regret—no, have regretted—the other. In all our relations no body enters. I do not talk to you through the senses—rather through the spirit. That is why we cannot love in the common sense. Ours is not an everyday affection. As yet we are mortal, and to live side by side with one another would be dreadful, for somehow with you I cannot long be trivial, and, you know, to be always beyond this mortal state would be to lose it. If people marry, they must live together as affectionate humans, who may be commonplace with each other without feeling awkward—not as two souls. So I feel it.

"Ought I to send this letter?—I doubt it. But there—it is best to understand. Au revoir."

Miriam read this letter twice, after which she sealed it up. A year later she broke the seal to show her mother the letter.

"You are a nun—you are a nun." The words went into her heart again and again. Nothing he ever had said had gone into her so deeply, fixedly, like a mortal wound.

She answered him two days after the party.

"'Our intimacy would have been all-beautiful but for one little mistake,'" she quoted. "Was the mistake mine?"

Almost immediately he replied to her from Nottingham, sending her at the same time a little "Omar Khayyam."

"I am glad you answered; you are so calm and natural you put me to shame. What a ranter I am! We are often out of sympathy. But in fundamentals we may always be together I think.

"I must thank you for your sympathy with my painting and drawing. Many a sketch is dedicated to you. I do look forward to your criticisms, which, to my shame and glory, are always grand appreciations. It is a lovely joke, that. Au revoir."

This was the end of the first phase of Paul's love affair. He was now about twenty-three years old, and, though still virgin, the sex instinct that Miriam had over-refined for so long now grew particularly strong. Often, as he talked to Clara Dawes, came that thickening and quickening of his blood, that peculiar concentration in the breast, as if something were alive there, a new self or a new centre of consciousness, warning him that sooner or later he would have to ask one woman or another. But he belonged to Miriam. Of that she was so fixedly sure that he allowed her right.

Notes

1. tussocky: adjective form of tussock, a small area of grass that is longer and thicker than the grass around it
2. wheedle: (disapproving) to persuade one to give you what you want or do something by saying nice things that you do not mean
3. amphitheatre: an open space that is surrounded by high land in a circular slope
4. ignominy: (*formal*) shame and public disgrace
5. Tartarin de Tarascon: (*French*) an 1872 novel written by the French author Alphonse Daudet
6. charades: a game for teams of players in which one team acts a word or phrase, syllable by syllable, until other players guess the whole word or phrase

Questions

1. Why does Paul change his mind so often? Trace his constantly changing feelings for Miriam throughout the novel.
2. Explain the meaning of the title in this chapter. Then, read each chapter title of the whole novel and think about the role they are playing in revealing the information about the story.
3. Read the whole novel and try to figure out the origin of Miriam's notion of self-sacrifice.

Chapter Two Divinity and Secularity

Religion is a popular subject because no one seems to be in agreement. Throughout the history of the West, some of the most memorable and acclaimed literary works have been rooted in one religious context or another, baiting readers to sink deep into the mysticism and possibilities they create. But the Reformation led by Martin Luther struck the very foundations of the institutionalism of the Roman Catholic Church. Faith (based on the word of the *Bible*) was alone thought competent to save, and salvation itself was regarded as a direct transaction with God in individual soul, without the necessity of intermediation by Church, priest, or sacrament. Protestantism, sometimes called "Renaissance individualism" soon developed its own type of institutionalism in the theocracy proposed by John Calvin and his Puritan followers. Although England officially broke with the Catholic church during the reign of Henry VIII, the new state religious establishment (the Anglican church) headed by the monarch retained many of the characteristics of the old church. The result was a political and theological compromise that remained the subject of heated debate for centuries, especially in literary works.

Theological works are one of the dominant forms of literature typically found in libraries in English literature. In Middle Ages, Catholic clerics were the intellectual center of society, and it is their literature that was produced in the greatest quantity. Countless hymns survived from this period. Religious scholars often attempted to reconcile the teachings of the Greek and Roman pagan authors with the doctrines of the Church. Under the strong influence of religion, many writers turned to the *Bible* for literary creation afterwards. They used religious allusions in their creative works. Whereas, with the incoming of Renaissance, their works were not just to eulogize the glory of Christianity, or the benevolence of God; what they wanted to express was their understanding of the worldly life, including fighting spirit, attitude toward life and love. Some even tried to condemn the cruelty and hypocrisy of religious institute. Therefore, it can be said that their works are the combination of religion and secularity. Take John Donne's poetry for example, they represent a sharp break with those written by his predecessors and most of his contemporaries. These poems give a more inherently theatrical impression by exhibiting a seemingly unfocused diversity of experiences and attitudes, and the faith in religion is often expressed with conflict or doubt. Other writers such as John Milton began literary creation following the tradition of Christian humanism, the most representative of which is *Paradise Lost*. This epic intends to expose the way of Satan and justify the ways of God to men. Satan is no longer an incarnation of monster, but a character with unconquerable will. Thus, the combination of Reformation and Renaissance is perfectly shown in the work. And in the poems of William Blake, the relation between an economic circumstance, which is the exploitation of child labor, and an ideological one, which is religion's role in making people compliant, is profoundly revealed. No matter what the form, the subject matter, or the theme is, these writers and the like are engaged in deep exploration between divinity and secularity.

John Donne
1572—1631

John Donne

John Donne, the author of multiple works like sonnets, epigrams, elegies, songs, satires, sermons, and Latin translations, was born into a Roman Catholic family in 1572 when practice of that religion was illegal in England. His father, also named John Donne, was of Welsh descent and a respected Roman Catholic. His mother was a great-niece of the Roman Catholic martyr Thomas More.

In his early teen years, Donne studied at both Oxford and Cambridge Universities without taking a degree at either school for, given his Catholic origin, he could not take the Oath of Supremacy required of graduates. At age twenty he studied law at Lincoln's Inn. In 1598, after returning from a two-year naval expedition against Spain, Donne was appointed private secretary to Sir Thomas Egerton. During the next four years, he fell in love with Egerton's niece Anne More. They were married just before Christmas in 1601. This wedding ruined Donne's career. He was imprisoned and dismissed from his post. After his release, he scraped a meager living as a lawyer, depending on his wife's cousin to house him, his wife, and the children. Pressed by hard life, despite much doubt and reluctance, he converted to Anglicanism, and became dean of Saint Paul's Cathedral in 1621. In his later years, Donne's writing reflected his fear of his inevitable death.

Donne shows in his secular love poems a quest for the union of spiritual and physical love; in his divine poems, he deconstructs while expressing his sense of guilt in the pursuit of true religion. Moreover, secular and religious images are used in the two types of poetry reciprocally. His thinking represents a kind of humane morality, and peculiar reasoning about religion, desire and art, which developed as well as deviated from his times. Out of his meticulous thinking, he was daring enough to challenge Death, and wrote poems like "Death Be Not Proud", from which come the famous lines "Death, be not proud, though some have called thee / Mighty and dreadful, for thou art not so."

Donne is known as the founder of the Metaphysical School, a term coined by the eighteenth-century English intellect Samuel Johnson. Donne's secular poems and divine poems are particularly famous for their metaphysical conceits. The conceit is an extended metaphor that combines vastly different ideas into a single idea, often using imagery, reliant on intellectual wit, learned imagery, and subtle argument. Donne used conceits in the two poems below to discuss religion and love. In "The Canonization", he equates lovers with saints, and in "The Flea", he requests love through the blood-sucking flea and even plays with the idea of trinity.

The Canonization

For God's sake hold your tongue, and let me love;
    Or chide my palsy, or my gout,
My five gray hairs, or ruined fortune, flout,
      With wealth your state, your mind with arts improve,
        Take you a course, get you a place,[1]
        Observe His Honor, or His Grace,
Or the king's real, or his stamped face[2]
    Contemplate; what you will, approve,
    So you will let me love.

Alas, alas, who's injured by my love?
    What merchant's ships have my sighs drowned?
Who says my tears have overflowed his ground?
    When did my colds a forward spring remove?
      When did the heats which my veins fill
      Add one more to the plaguy bill[3]?
Soldiers find wars, and lawyers find out still
    Litigious men, which quarrels move,
    Though she and I do love.

Call us what you will, we are made such by love;
    Call her one, me another fly,
We're tapers too, and at our own cost die,
And we in us find the eagle and the dove[4].
    The phoenix riddle hath more wit
    By us: we two being one, are it.
So, to one neutral thing both sexes fit.
    We die and rise the same, and prove
    Mysterious by this love.

We can die by it, if not live by love,
    And if unfit for tomb or hearse
Our legend be, it will be fit for verse;
    And if no piece of chronicle we prove,
      We'll build in sonnets pretty rooms;
      As well a well-wrought urn becomes[5]
The greatest ashes, as half-acre tombs,
    And by these hymns[6], all shall approve

Us canonized for love[7]:

And thus invoke us: You whom reverend love
    Made one another's hermitage;
You, to whom love was peace, that now is rage;
    Who did the whole world's soul contract, and drove
        Into the glasses of your eyes
        (So made such mirrors, and such spies,
That they did all to you epitomize)
    Countries, towns, courts[8]: Beg from above[9]
    A pattern of your love!

Notes

1. Take you a course, get you a place: Settle yourself in life. A place is an appointment at court or elsewhere
2. stamped face: on coins
3. plaguy bill: the deaths from the plague were recorded by parish in weekly bills
4. the eagle and the dove: the eagle signifies strength and vision; the dove, weakness and mercy
5. becomes: befits
6. hymns: the lover's own poems, which becomes hymns for a new love religion
7. all shall approve/Us canonized for love: posterity shall confirm us as lover's saints
8. Countries, towns, courts: "Countries, towns, courts" are the objects of the verb "drove".
9. above: heaven

Questions

1. What is the theme of the poem?
2. What do the images of eagle, dove, and phoenix symbolize respectively?

Death, Be Not Proud[1]

Death, be not proud, though some have called thee
Mighty and dreadful, for thou art not so;
For those whom thou think'st thou dost overthrow
Die not, poor Death, nor yet canst thou kill me.
From rest and sleep, which but thy pictures be,
Much pleasure; then from thee much more must flow,
And soonest our best men with thee do go,[2]
Rest of their bones, and soul's delivery.[3]

Thou art slave to fate, chance, kings, and desperate men,
And dost with poison, war, and sickness dwell,
And poppy[4] or charms can make us sleep as well
And better[5] than thy stroke; why swell'st thou then?[6]
One short sleep past, we wake eternally[7]
And Death shall be no more; Death, thou shalt die.

Notes

1. The sonnet is written in the Petrarchan pattern, with 14 lines of iambic pentameter rhyming abba abba cddc ee.
2. And soonest our best men with thee do go: Whom the Gods love die young.
3. Rest of their bones, and soul's delivery: To find rest for their bones and freedom for their souls.
4. poppy: opium
5. better: easier
6. why swell'st thou then?: why should you be proud?
7. One short sleep past, we wake eternally: Shortly after we die, we'll wake up and live eternally.

Questions

1. Analyse the form of the sonnet.
2. What does death mean to Donne? How does he develop his ideas in a logic and poetic way?

The Flea

Mark[1] but this flea, and mark in this,
How little that which thou deniest me is;
Me it sucked first, and now sucks thee,
And in this flea our two bloods mingled be;
Thou know'st that this cannot be said
A sin, or shame, or loss of maidenhead,
　　Yet this enjoys before it woo,
　　And pampered swells with one blood made of two,
　　And this, alas, is more than we would do.[2]

Oh stay, three lives in one flea spare,
Where we almost, nay more than married are.
This flea is you and I, and this
Our marriage bed and marriage temple is;
Though parents grudge, and you, we are met,

  And cloistered in these living walls of jet.
   Though use³ make you apt to kill me
   Let not to that, self-murder added be,
   And sacrilege, three sins in killing three.

  Cruel and sudden, hast thou since
  Purpled thy nail in blood of innocence⁴?
  Wherein could this flea guilty be,
  Except in that drop which it sucked from thee?
  Yet thou triumph'st, and say'st that thou
  Find'st not thy self nor me the weaker now;
   'Tis true; then learn how false fears be:
   Just so much honor, when thou yield'st to me,
   Will waste, as this flea's death took life from thee.

Notes

1. Mark: Look
2. And this, alas, is more than we would do: We don't dare hope for this consummation of our love, which the flea freely accepts. The idea of swelling suggests pregnancy.
3. use: habit
4. Purpled thy nail in blood of innocence: Donne's mistress has slaughtered the innocents and is now clothed in imperial purple.

Questions

1. What does flea symbolize?
2. What's Donne's feeling toward his mistress?

John Milton
1608—1674

  John Milton, English poet and polemicist, was born on December 9, 1608, in London. His father was both a scrivener and a composer of church music. He was first educated at St. Paul's School and then Christ's College, Cambridge. Milton was a hardworking and argumentative student in the college. After graduation in 1632, he retired to the home for years of private study and literary composition.

  In 1638, Milton set out for a tour through France, Switzerland, and Italy. But the tour of Europe was cut short with rumors of impending civil war in England. He returned to London and began writing pamphlets on political and religious matters. In 1649, Milton was appointed Latin Secretary to Cromwell's Council of State. He used his pen to serve his country, even when his eyesight was threatened with strains and went blind in 1652. In 1660 King Charles II was restored to the throne. Milton was arrested and thrown in prison for a short time and then retired to private life. In 1674 he died peacefully and was buried in the church of St. Giles. A monument to Milton rests in Poets' Corner at Westminster Abbey.

John Milton

Chronologically, Milton's literary works can be distinctively divided into three categories. In his early period, Milton created such works as *L'Allegro and Il Penseroso* (1632), *Lycidas* (1637), and *Comus* (1634), a masque. His middle period achievements include powerful pamphlets and tracts, among which *Doctrine and Discipline of Divorce* (1643), and *Areopagitica* (1644) are perhaps the best. The third period witnesses his three major poetic works: *Paradise Lost* (1667), *Paradise Regained* (1671), and *Samson Agonistes* (1671). Among the three, the first is the greatest and also the perfect example of the verse drama in English.

Milton's stories are mostly borrowed from the *Bible* but with profound significance. A real revolutionary, a master poet and a great prose writer, he fought for freedom in all respects as a Christian humanist. His poetry and prose reflect deep personal convictions, a passion for freedom and self-determination, and the urgent issues and political turbulence of his day. Writing in English, Latin, and Italian, he achieved international renown within his lifetime. What's more, Milton's use of blank verse, in addition to his stylistic innovations influenced many later poets.

Paradise Lost

Paradise Lost is an epic poem in blank verse by John Milton. It was originally published in 1667 in ten books, and then changed into twelve books in 1674.

The story is taken from the Old Testament. It concerns the Biblical story of the Fall of Man: the temptation of Adam and Eve by the fallen angel Satan and their expulsion from the Garden of Eden. In Heaven, Satan led a rebellion against the God, but failed. He and his rebel angels were cast into Hell. Refusing to accept his failure, Satan vowed that "all was not lost" and he would seek revenge. He tempted Adam and Eve to eat the forbidden fruit from the tree of knowledge. Then, Adam and Eve were driven out of Paradise for their disobedience. At the end of the poem, they walked away from Paradise and the gates of Eden were closed behind them.

Paradise Lost is widely considered one of the greatest literary works in the English language. Milton's purpose, stated in Book I, is to "justify the ways of God to men". However, Milton expresses his concern with freedom and choice; the freedom to submit to God's prohibition and the choice made for love. The following excerpt is from Book I.

Book I (Excerpt)

[...]
All is not lost; the unconquerable Will,
And study[1] of revenge, immortal hate,
And courage never to submit or yield:
And what is else not to be overcome?
That Glory[2] never shall his wrath or might
Extort from me[3]. To bow and sue for grace
With suppliant knee, and deifie his power[4]
Who from the terrour[5] of this Arm so late
Doubted his Empire[6], that were low indeed,
That were an ignominy and shame beneath
This downfall[7]; since by Fate the strength of Gods
And this Empyreal substance[8] cannot fail,
Since through experience of this great event[9]
In Arms not worse, in foresight much advanc't,
We may with more successful hope resolve
To wage by force or guile eternal Warr[10]
Irreconcilable, to our grand Foe[11],
Who now triumphs, and in th' excess of joy
Sole reigning holds the Tyranny of Heav'n.

Notes

1. study: pursuit, the earnest intention
2. That Glory: The glory of hearing Satan confess himself overcome
3. never shall his wrath or might/ Extort from me: his wrath or might shall never extort that glory from me
4. deifie his power: deify the power of him; deifie: deify
5. terrour: terror
6. Doubted his Empire: Feared for his sovereignty
7. That were an ignominy and shame beneath/ This downfall: That were an ignominy and shame beneath this downfall
8. Empyreal substance: heavenly, sublime power
9. this great event: the failure of Satan
10. eternal Warr: continuous war
11. grand Foe: the God

> Chapter Two Divinity and Secularity

> **Questions**

1. What does Satan try to express in the monologue?
2. How does Milton portray the image of Satan in this excerpt?

William Blake
1757—1827

William Blake

William Blake, an English poet, painter, and printmaker, was born on 28th November 1757 in London. His father was an Irish hosier. At the early age of ten, Blake attended a drawing school for four years. He started writing poetry at the age of twelve, and with the help of a friend he had his first collection of verses entitled *Poetical Sketches* printed many years later. Despite his obvious talents as a poet, his official profession was as an engraver because he could not afford to do a painter's apprenticeship and therefore began his apprenticeship with an engraver in 1772. After completing his apprenticeship six years later, he joined the Royal Academy of Art. In 1782, he married Catherine Boucher. The marriage proved to be a lifelong happiness though there were difficulties for a time. Blake taught Catherine to write, and she helped him colour his printed poems. Through all his life, Blake had been both a poet and an engraver. He also printed a few books of his own. He passed away at the age of sixty-nine in 1827 and was buried five days after his death—on the eve of his 45th wedding anniversary.

Blake was a pre-romantic poet. His representative works are *Songs of Innocence* and *Songs of Experience*. The former is a lovely volume of poems, presenting a happy and innocent world, though not without its evils and sufferings. The *Songs of Experience* paints a different world, a world of misery, poverty, disease, war, and repression with a melancholy tone. In poem "London", the misery of the English capital is reflected. The two books hold similar subject-matter, but the tone, emphasis and conclusion differ. Take "The Chimney Sweeper" for example: the poem in *Songs of Innocence* reveals the hypocrisy of religion and power in an innocent tone, while the one in the *Songs of Experience* exposes the hypocrisy explicitly from a more critical and sophisticated view. Blake's other important works include *Marriage of Heaven and Hell* (1790), *The French Revolution* (1791), *America a Prophecy* (1794), *Milton a Poem* (1804—1810).

Blake lived during revolutionary times and witnessed the downfall of London during Britain's war with republican France. His disgust with society grew as he matured. As well as having radical religious ideas for the time, he also had radical political ideas due to the day-to-day poverty he was forced to witness. Blake's preoccupation with good and evil as well as his strong philosophical and religious beliefs remained throughout his life and he never stopped depicting them in his poetry and engravings.

The Chimney Sweeper (from *Songs of Innocence*)

When my mother died I was very young,
And my father sold me while yet my tongue
Could scarcely cry " 'weep[1]! 'weep! 'weep! 'weep!"
So your chimneys I sweep & in soot I sleep.

There's little Tom Dacre, who cried when his head,
That curl'd like a lamb's back, was shav'd, so I said,
"Hush, Tom! never mind it, for when your head's bare,
You know that the soot cannot spoil your white hair."

And so he was quiet, and that very night,
As Tom was a-sleeping he had such a sight!
That thousands of sweepers, Dick, Joe, Ned, and Jack.
Were all of them lock'd up in coffins of black;

And by came an Angel who had a bright key,
And he open'd the coffins & set them all free;
Then down a green plain leaping, laughing, they run
And wash in a river, and shine in the sun.

Then naked & white, all their bags left behind,
They rise upon clouds, and sport in the wind,
And the Angel told Tom, if he'd be a good boy,
He'd have God for his father, and never want[2] joy.

And so Tom awoke; and we rose in the dark
And got with our bags & our brushes to work.
Tho'[3] the morning was cold, Tom was happy & warm;
So if all do their duty, they need not fear harm.

Songs of Innocence and of Experience

Notes

1. 'weep: sweep, which is the child's lisping attempt at the chimney sweeper's cry.

2. want: lack of
3. Tho': Though

Questions

1. What picture does the short poem present?
2. Is the world in the poem a harmonious one? Why or why not?

The Chimney Sweeper (from *Songs of Experience*)

A little black thing among the snow
Crying "'weep, 'weep!" in notes of woe!
Where are thy father & mother? say?
They are both gone up to the church to pray.

Because I was happy upon the heath[1],
And smil'd among the winters snow;
They clothed me in the clothes of death[2],
And taught me to sing the notes of woe.

And because I am happy & dance & sing,
They think they have done me no injury,
And are gone to praise God & his Priest & King,
Who make up a heaven of our misery.

Notes

1. heath: uncultivated land covered with shrubs
2. clothes of death: clothes in dark color

Questions

1. What are the differences between this poem and its counterpart in *Songs of Innocence*?
2. What is the role of religion in this poem?

Bible

A Christian Bible, consisting of the Old and New Testaments, is a set of books that a Christian denomination regards as divinely inspired and thus constituting scripture. It is a collection of 66 books written by about 40 authors, in three different languages, on three different continents, over approximately 1600 years. Basically, *Bible* describes the origin of man in the Garden of Eden along with his fall into sin and out of fellowship with God. The English Christian Bible has various versions, the significant of which includes the Douay-Rheims Bible, the Revised Standard Version, the Authorized King James Version, the American Standard Version, the English Standard Version, the New King James Version, and the New International Version. Groups within Christianity include different books as part of their sacred writings.

The Old Testament is a collection of selected writings composed and edited by members of the Hebrew-Jewish community between the twelfth century B.C. and the beginning of the Christian era. It includes such diverse materials as prophetic oracles, teachings of wise men, instructions of priests and ancient records of the royal courts. Some material is historical, some is legendary; some is legalistic, some is didactic.

The New Testament opens about 400 years later with the birth of Jesus Christ in Bethlehem. Jesus was the descendant to fulfill God's plan to redeem mankind and restore creation. Jesus faithfully completed His work—He died for sin and rose from the dead. The death of Christ is the basis for a new covenant (testament) with the world. All who have faith in Jesus will be saved from sin and live eternally.

Bible is not just a religious classic, but a book exerting profound significance in the western world. It contains many different styles of writing such as poetry, narration, fiction, history, law, and prophecy, which provide writers of different period with ample resources for literary creation.

The Story of Babel

"The Story of Babel" is a story from *The Old Testament*. After the Flood, man had again begun to multiply and fill the earth. They all spoke one language and understood one another well. The generations of people before the Flood had been interested only in themselves; they thought of themselves as supermen and lived each one for himself alone; they used violence and force against their weaker neighbors, paying no attention to laws and rules. However, the new generation of mankind after the Flood was different. They stressed the opposite code of living. The individual did not count for himself; he counted only as part of the community, and he had to subject his own interests to those of the group. Had they confined themselves to this kind of social life, all might have been well. But they overdid it. The tremendous strength that grew out of their organization and goodwill made them proud, and their pride made them turn against God.

They decided to build a tower which was to reach to heaven, to make them equal to God, and at the same time, to make it possible for them to stay together. This symbol of their divine strength, as they thought, was to be built in the valley of the Land of Shinar.

God decided to destroy their arrogance by destroying their ability to understand one another. He, therefore, confused the people by splitting them up into seventy different nations and tribes, each with a language of its own, (hence the name Babel, meaning "confusion").

When this happened, the project of the Tower had to be given up. The various groups migrated in different directions and settled in all parts of the world. The Tower itself was partly burned and partly swallowed by the earth.

The following excerpt is taken from the Genesis of *The Old Testament*.

{11:1} And the whole earth was of one language, and of one speech. {11:2} And it came to pass, as they journeyed from the east, that they found a plain in the land of Shinar[1]; and they dwelt there. {11:3} And they said one to another, Go to, let us make brick, and burn them throughly[2]. And they had brick for stone, and slime[3] had they for morter[4]. {11:4} And they said, Go to, let us build us a city and a tower, whose top [may reach] unto heaven; and let us make us a name, lest we be scattered abroad upon the face of the whole earth. {11:5} And the LORD came down to see the city and the tower, which the children of men builded. {11:6} And the LORD said, Behold, the people [is] one, and they have all one language; and this they begin to do: and now nothing will be restrained from them, which they have imagined to do. {11:7} Go to, let us go down, and there confound[5] their language, that they may not understand one another's speech. {11:8} So the LORD scattered them abroad from thence upon the face of all the earth: and they left off to build the city. {11:9} Therefore is the name of it called Babel[6]; because the LORD did there confound the language of all the earth: and from thence did the LORD scatter them abroad upon the face of all the earth.

Notes

1. the land of Shinar: a place located in Southern Mesopotamia, extending almost to the Persian Gulf
2. throughly: thoroughly
3. slime: a moist, soft, and slippery substance

4. morter: mortar, a mixture of lime with cement, sand, and water, used in building to bond bricks or stones
5. confound: cause confusion in someone
6. Babel: a scene of noisy confusion

Questions

1. Why did God sabotage people's effort? Was he jealous of his Creation's success? Why?
2. What lesson can we draw from this story?

Chapter Three Experience and Growth

Among various literary writings, Bildungsroman best presents a person's experience and growth. Bildungsroman, a German word brought into English, means "the novel of formation or education". It centers on the growth and coming-of-age of the protagonist through revealing the relationship between experience, education and identity formation. Moreover, according to J.H. Buckley, the principle elements of the Bildungsroman can be concluded as follows—childhood, the conflict of generations, provinciality, the larger society, self-education, alienation, ordeal by love, the search for a vocation and a working philosophy. Therefore, it is evident that experience and growth, as two related literary themes, are commonly connoted in the writings of Bildungsroman.

Since the publication of Goethe's *Wilhelm Meister's Apprenticeship*, novels of experience and growth have flourished, with such writers as James Joyce and Charles Dickens as the representatives. For instance, *A Portrait of the Artist as a Young Man* by James Joyce is generally regarded as a typical novel of Bildungsroman, or rather, *Künstlerroman* which traces the growth to maturity of a writer or an artist. *Araby*, a renowned work of Joyce, also presents a boy's growth from naivety to maturity. Such themes as coming of age, the loss of innocence and the danger of idealization are included in the story through the protagonist's journey to a bazaar. Charles Dickens also contributes to developing this artistic form in Britain. *David Copperfield* and *Great Expectations* are generally seen as novels of Bildungsroman. Widely recognized as an autobiographical novel, *David Copperfield* is the first novel that Dickens ever wrote in the first point of view with the narrator as the protagonist. Besides, numerous parallels can be drawn between David's life story from childhood to maturity with that of Dickens' since he has put his own real experiences into the novel. Thus, these unique features of the novel help distinguish it from other novels of Dickens and make it a shadow of the author himself. In *Robinson Crusoe*, Daniel Defoe traces the protagonist's growth from a naïve youth who was passionate about voyage to a tough and hardened man tempered by series of adventures and unexpected trials, especially by the experiences of those castaway years spent alone on a remote tropical island after a shipwreck.

To put it in a nutshell, the works mentioned above present the protagonists' evolving growth in their formative years and have the true world unveiled during their journey. For the young boy in *Araby*, he completes his initiation into the adult world at the end of his journey; for David Copperfield, he struggles with the psychical and moral growth in the world, experiencing the conflicts with the larger society and finally getting assimilated into the society; for Robinson Crusoe, he grows up into maturity in the process of struggling with the hostile nature and experiencing many vicissitudes of life.

Almost everyone has to witness his/her growth from youth through adolescence to old age, and those unforeseeable changes and experiences have endowed our life with surprises and made us constantly engaged in the process of learning. Therefore, writers of different times are easily charmed to elucidate the theme of experience and growth in their literary writings.

Daniel Defoe
1660—1731

Daniel Defoe

Daniel Defoe, a prolific and versatile writer, was born into a family of Presbyterian dissenters in London in 1660. Since young, the boy was sent to special schools for Dissenters. He studied first at the Reverend James Fisher's school at Dorking, Surrey, and later was educated for the Presbyterian Ministry at the famous Charles Morton's Academy in Newington Green, Middlesex. As the son of a successful tradesman and merchant, Defoe was greatly influenced by the commercial rather than the religious aspect of his father's life. By 1683, he had also established himself as a merchant in Cornhill, London. In 1684, he married Mary Tuffley, the daughter of another successful Dissenting merchant. Then, off and on for the rest of his life, Defoe worked as a businessman in England and Scotland. Though he was at times successful, he was often unfortunate, for his business dealings had forced him to suffer several lawsuits, two terms in prison, and two bankruptcies by 1703. Even so, Defoe had never abandoned his religious convictions, which pulled him into the social and political arena.

In 1685, James II who had converted to Catholicism succeeded his older brother as king. Consequently, many in England, especially among the Dissenters, were expected to lose religious privileges, which led to a substantial opposition to the crown. Defoe was among the oppositional side. In June of 1685, he joined a rebellion led by the illegitimate son of Charles II, the Protestant Duke of Monmouth. Though the rebellion failed, James II was deposed by William of Orange in the Glorious Revolution three years later. Due to his participation in this revolution, Defoe got a number of positions in the service of William and Queen Mary between 1689 and 1702. Then, his public service continued during the reign of Queen Anne, the successor of William and Mary. From 1703 to 1714, he served as an agent for Robert Harley, a leading Tory Member of Parliament and a cabinet member. After the Tories fell from power with the death of Anne, Defoe continued doing intelligence work for the Whig government.

The development of Defoe's writing career is inseparable from his commercial, political, and religious experience. His first notable publication *An Essay upon Projects* was published in 1697, which was a series of proposals for social and economic improvement. By 1702 when Anne had assumed the throne, Defoe had written several political pieces and published more than ten lengthy pamphlets and satiric poems. In 1702 he wrote a mocking pamphlet attacking the suppression of the dissenting Puritans by the Tory Government, and consequently was sentenced to stand three days in the pillory and imprisoned until 1704. In the same year, Defoe created the journal, *A Review of the Affairs of France, with Observations on Transactions at Home*, which became a forum for Defoe to express views on contemporary politics, economics, religion, morality, and journalism until June of 1713. Thanks to Defoe, the seeds for modern journalism were sowed during that period.

Throughout his lifetime, though Defoe had assumed such variety of roles as businessman, social activist, and journalist, he did not assume his most famous one as a novelist until the publication of *The Life and Strange Surprising Adventures of Robinson Crusoe of York, Mariner* in 1719, which is commonly known as *Robinson Crusoe*. Then he produced a number of other novels, including *Captain Singleton* (1720), *A Journal of the Plague Year* (1722), *Colonel Jack* (1722), *Moll Flanders* (1722), and *Roxana* (1724). In the final years of life, he also wrote several conduct manuals and published some works on the supernatural, foreign travel and trade, or on criticizing the breakdown of the social order.

Robinson Crusoe, the story of a man stuck on a deserted island, depicts the castaway's years of life and struggle on the remote island. Both his internal and external activities during his years of solitary existence are minutely explored by the author in the novel. And, those adventures and experiences of the fictional protagonist contribute to his growth and formation of character. Moreover, apart from its bildungsroman features and simplistic narrative style, *Robinson Crusoe* is wildly acclaimed as marking the beginning of realistic fiction as a literary genre.

Robinson Crusoe

Robinson Crusoe is an English sailor strongly appealed by the sea. After many adventures and perils, he boards a ship which is en route to Brazil, where Crusoe settles down and procures a plantation. Years later, the call of the sea is still too strong for him that he joins an expedition to bring slaves from Africa. However, in a storm, he is shipwrecked about forty miles out to sea on an island (which he calls the Island of Despair) on September 30, 1659. He manages to swim ashore, but the rest members of the crew are all drowned. As a result, only he and three animals, the captain's dog and two cats, survive the shipwreck. Overcoming his despair, he fetches arms, tools, and other supplies from the ship before it breaks apart and sinks. He builds a fenced-in habitat near a cave which he excavates. By making marks in a wooden cross, he creates a calendar. By using tools got from the ship and made by himself, he hunts, grows barley and rice, dries grapes to make raisins, learns to make pottery, and raises goats. He also adopts a small parrot. He reads the *Bible* and becomes religious, thanking God for his fate in which nothing is missing but human society. More years pass, Crusoe saves a savage from the native cannibals and makes him a servant thereafter. He names the servant "Friday" and teaches him English, Christian religion and civilised ways of life. For twenty-eight years, Crusoe manages to live on the island, first alone, then as the master of a small group of men. An English ship then appears one day; mutineers have commandeered the

vessel and intend to maroon their captain on the island. Crusoe and the ship's captain strike a deal in which Crusoe helps the captain retake the ship and the latter helps Crusoe leave the island. Crusoe finally leaves the island with Friday and arrives in England in 1687. Years later, Crusoe revisits his island, finding that it has become a prosperous colony.

The sections below show in minute detail how Crusoe builds up a new life on the so-called "Island of Despair" with his will power and hard labour. Also, he begins a journal in which he records the good and evil aspects of his experience until he runs out of ink. In the journal, he narrates such events as his discovery of the ship's remains, his salvaging of provisions, the storm that destroys the ship entirely, the construction of his house, etc.

FIRST DAYS

After I had been there about ten or twelve days, it came into my thoughts that I should lose my reckoning of time for want[1] of books[2] and pen and ink and should even forget the Sabbath[3] days from the working days; but to prevent this I cut with my knife upon a large post, in capital letters—and making it into a great cross, I set it up on the shore where I first landed, viz., "I came on shore here on the 30th September 1659." Upon the sides of this square post I cut every day a notch with my knife, and every seventh notch was as long again as the rest, and every first day of the month as long again as that long one; and thus I kept my calendar, or weekly, monthly, and yearly reckoning of time.

In the next place we are to observe that among the many things which I brought out of the ship in the several voyages which, as above mentioned, I made to it, I got several things of less value, but not at all less useful to me, which I omitted setting down before; as in particular, pens, ink, and paper, several parcels in the captain's, mate's, gunner's and carpenter's keeping, three or four compasses, some mathematical instruments, dials, perspectives[4], charts, and books of navigation, all which I huddled together, whether I might want them or no; also, I found three very good Bibles, which came to me in my cargo from England, and which I had packed up among my things; some Portuguese books also, and among them two or three Popish prayer-books[5], and several other books, all which I carefully secured. And I must not forget that we had in the ship a dog and two cats, of whose eminent history I may have occasion to say something in its place; for I carried both the cats with me, and as for the dog, he jumped out of the ship of himself and swam on shore to me the day after I went on shore with my first cargo and was a trusty servant to me many years; I wanted nothing that he could fetch me, nor any company that he could make up to me; I only wanted to have him talk to me, but that would not do. As I observed before, I found pens, ink, and paper, and I husbanded[6] them to the utmost; and I shall show that while my ink lasted, I kept things very exact, but after that was gone, I could not, for I could not make any ink by any means that I could devise.

And this put me in mind that I wanted many things, notwithstanding all that I had amassed together, and of these, this of ink was one, as also a spade, pickaxe, and shovel, to dig or remove the earth, needles, pins, and thread; as for linen, I soon learned to want that[7] without much difficulty.

This want of tools made every work I did go on heavily, and it was near a whole year before I had entirely finished my little pale, or surrounded my habitation. The piles, or stakes, which were as heavy as I could well lift, were a long time in cutting and preparing in the woods, and more by far in bringing home, so that I spent sometimes two days in cutting and bringing home one of those posts and a third day in driving it into the ground; for which purpose I got a heavy piece of wood at first, but at last bethought myself of one of the iron crows, which, however, though I found it, yet it made driving those posts or piles very laborious and tedious work.

But what need I ha' been concerned at the tediousness of anything I had to do, seeing I had time enough to do it in? Nor had I any other employment, if that had been over, at least that I could foresee, except the ranging the island to seek for food, which I did more or less every day.

I now began to consider seriously my condition, and the circumstance I was reduced to, and I drew up the state of my affairs in writing, not so much to leave them to any that were to come after me, for I was like to have but few heirs, as to deliver my thoughts from daily poring over them, and afflicting my mind; and as my reason began now to master my despondency, I began to comfort myself as well as I could and to set the good against the evil, that I might have something to distinguish my case from worse, and I stated very impartially, like debtor and creditor, the comforts I enjoyed, against the miseries I suffered, thus:

Evil: I am cast upon a horrible desolate island, void of all hope of recovery.

Good: But I am alive, and not drowned, as all my ship's company were.

Evil: I am singled out and separated, as it were, from all the world to be miserable.

Good: But I am singled out, too, from all the ship's crew to be spared from death; and He that miraculously saved me from death can deliver me from this condition.

Evil: I am divided from mankind, a solitaire, one banished from human society.

Good: But I am not starved and perishing on a barren place, affording no sustenance.

Evil: I have no clothes to cover me.

Good: But I am in a hot climate, where if I had clothes I could hardly wear them.

Evil: I am without any defense or means to resist any violence of man or beast.

Good: But I am cast on an island, where I see no wild beasts to hurt me, as I saw on the coast of Africa. And what if I had been shipwrecked there?

Evil: I have no soul to speak to, or relieve me.

Good: But God wonderfully sent the ship in near enough to the shore that I have got out as many necessary things as will either supply my wants, or enable me to supply myself even as long as I live.

Upon the whole, here was an undoubted testimony that there was scarce any condition in the world so miserable but there was something negative or something positive to be thankful for in it; and let this stand as a direction from the experience of the most miserable of all conditions in this world, that we may always find in it something to comfort ourselves from and to set in the description of good and evil on the credit side of the account.

Having now brought my mind a little to relish my condition, and given over looking out to sea to see if I could spy a ship; I say, giving over these things, I begun to apply myself to accommodate my way of living and to make things as easy to me as I could.

I have already described my habitation, which was a tent under the side of a rock, surrounded with a strong pale of posts and cables, but I might now rather call it a wall, for I raised a kind of wall up against it of turfs, about two foot thick on the outside, and after some time, I think it was a year and a half, I raised rafters from it leaning to the rock and thatched or covered it with boughs of trees and such things as I could get to keep out the rain, which I found at some times of the year very violent.

I have already observed how I brought all my goods into this pale, and into the cave which I had made behind me. But I must observe, too, that at first this was a confused heap of goods, which, as they lay in no order, so they took up all my place; I had no room to turn myself; so I set myself to enlarge my cave and works farther into the earth, for it was a loose sandy rock, which yielded easily to the labor I bestowed on it; and so, when I found I was pretty safe as to beasts of prey, I worked sideways to the right hand into the rock, and then turning to the right again, worked quite out, and made me a door to come out on the outside of my pale or fortification.

This gave me not only egress and regress, as it was a back way to my tent and to my storehouse, but gave me room to stow my goods.

THE JOURNAL: FOOD AND SHELTER

And now I began to apply myself to make such necessary things as I found I most wanted, as particularly a chair and a table, for without these I was not able to enjoy the few comforts I had in the world; I could not write, or eat, or do several things, with so much pleasure without a table.

So I went to work; and here I must needs observe, that as reason is the substance and origin of the mathematics, so by stating and squaring everything by reason and by making the most rational judgment of things, every man may be in time master of every mechanic art. I had never handled a tool in my life, and yet in time, by labor, application, and contrivance, I found at last that I wanted nothing but I could have made it, especially if I had had tools; however, I made abundance of things, even without tools, and some with no more tools than an adze and a hatchet, which perhaps were never made that way before, and that with infinite labor. For example, if I wanted a board, I had no other way but to cut down a tree, set it on an edge before me, and hew it flat on either side with my axe, till I brought it to be thin as a plank, and then dub it smooth with my adze. It is true, by this method I could make but one board out of a whole tree, but this I had no remedy for but patience, any more than I had for the prodigious deal of time and labor which it took me up to make a plank or board. But my time or labor was little worth, and so it was as well employed one way as another.

However, I made me a table and a chair, as I observed above, in the first place, and this I did out of the short pieces of boards that I brought on my raft from the ship. But when I had wrought out some boards, as above, I made large shelves of the breadth of a foot and a half one over another, all along one side of my cave, to lay all my tools, nails, and ironwork, and, in a word, to separate everything at large into their places, that I might come easily at them; I knocked pieces into the wall of the rock to hang my guns and all things that would hang up.

So that had my cave been to be seen, it looked like a general magazine of all necessary things, and

Chapter Three Experience and Growth

I had everything so ready at my hand, that it was a great pleasure to me to see all my goods in such order and especially to find my stock of all necessaries so great.

And now it was when I began to keep a journal of every day's employment; for, indeed, at first, I was in too much hurry, and not only hurry as to labor, but in too much discomposure of mind; and my journal would have been full of many dull things. For example, I must have said thus:

September the 30th. After I had got to shore and escaped drowning, instead of being thankful to God for my deliverance, having first vomited with the great quantity of salt water which had got into my stomach and recovering myself a little, I ran about the shore, wringing my hands and beating my head and face, exclaiming at my misery and crying out I was undone, undone[8], till, tired and faint, I was forced to lie down on the ground to repose, but durst not sleep, for fear of being devoured.

Some days after this, and after I had been on board the ship, and got all that I could out of her, yet I could not forbear getting up to the top of a little mountain and looking out to sea in hopes of seeing a ship; then fancy at a vast distance I spied a sail, please myself with the hopes of it and then, after looking steadily till I was almost blind, lose it quite and sit down and weep like a child, and thus increase my misery by my folly.

But having gotten over these things in some measure and having settled my household staff and habitation, made me a table and a chair, and all as handsome about me as I could, I began to keep my journal, of which I shall

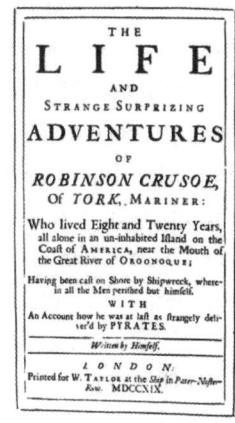

here give you the copy (though in it will be told all these particulars over again) as long as it lasted, for having no more ink, I was forced to leave it off.

THE JOURNAL

September 30, 1659. I, poor miserable Robinson Crusoe, being shipwrecked during a dreadful storm in the offing[9], came on shore on this dismal unfortunate island, which I called "the Island of Despair", all the rest of the ship's company being drowned and myself almost dead.

All the rest of the day I spent in afflicting myself at the dismal circumstances I was brought to, viz., I had neither food, house, clothes, weapon, or place to fly to, and in despair of any relief, saw nothing but death before me, either that I should be devoured by wild beasts, murdered by savages, or starved to death for want of food. At the approach of night, I slept in a tree for fear of wild creatures, but slept soundly, though it rained all night.

October 1. In the morning I saw to my great surprise the ship had floated with the high tide and was driven on shore again much nearer the island, which, as it was some comfort on one hand, for seeing her set upright and not broken to pieces, I hoped, if the wind abated, I might get on board, and get some food and necessaries out of her for my relief; so on the other hand, it renewed my grief at the loss of my comrades, who, I imagined, if we had all stayed on board, might have saved the ship, or at least that they would not have been all drowned as they were; and that had the men been saved, we might perhaps have built us a boat out of the ruins of the ship, to have carried us to some other part of the world. I spent great part of this day in perplexing myself on these things; but at length seeing the ship almost dry, I went upon the sand as near as I could, and then swam on board; this day also it continued raining, though with no wind at all.

FROM the *1st of October to the 24th*. All these days entirely spent in many several voyages to get all I could out of the ship, which I brought on shore, every tide of flood, upon rafts. Much rain also in the days, though with some intervals of fair weather. But, it seems, this was the rainy season.

October 20. I overset my raft, and all the goods I had got upon it, but being in shoal water, and the things being chiefly heavy, I recovered many of them when the tide was out.

October 25. It rained all night and all day, with some gusts of wind, during which time the ship broke in pieces, the wind blowing a little harder than before, and was no more to be seen, except the wreck of her, and that only at low water. I spent this day in covering and securing the goods which I had saved, that the rain might not spoil them.

October 26. I walked about the shore almost all day to find out a place to fix my habitation, greatly concerned to secure myself from any attack in the night, either from wild beasts or men. Towards night I fixed upon a proper place under a rock, and marked out a semicircle for my encampment, which I resolved to strengthen with a work, wall, or fortification made of double piles, lined within with cables, and without with turf.

From the 26th to the 30th I worked very hard in carrying all my goods to my new habitation, though some part of the time it rained exceedingly hard.

The 31st in the morning, I went out into the island with my gun to seek for some food, and discover the country, when I killed a she-goat, and her kid followed me home, which I afterwards killed also, because it would not feed.

November 1. I set up my tent under a rock, and lay there for the first night, making it as large as I could with stakes driven in to swing my hammock upon.

November 2. I set up all my chests and boards, and the pieces of timber which made my rafts, and with them formed a fence round me, a little within the place I had marked out for my fortification.

November 3. I went out with my gun and killed two fowls like ducks, which were very good food. In the afternoon went to work to make me a table.

November 4. This morning I began to order my times of work, of going out with my gun, time of sleep, and time of diversion, viz., every morning I walked out with my gun for two or three hours if it did not rain, then employed myself to work till about eleven o'clock; then eat what I had to live on and from twelve to two I lay down to sleep, the weather being excessively hot, and then in the evening to work again. The working part of this day and of the next were wholly employed in making my table, for I was yet but a very sorry workman, though time and necessity made me a complete natural mechanic soon after, as I believe it would do any one else.

November 5. This day went abroad with my gun and my dog, and killed a wild cat; her skin pretty soft, but her flesh good for nothing. Every creature I killed, I took off the skins and preserved them. Coming back by the seashore, I saw many sorts of sea fowls, which I did not understand, but was surprised and almost frightened with two or three seals, which, while I was gazing at, not well knowing what they were, got into the sea and escaped me for that time.

November 6. After my morning walk I went to work with my table again, and finished it, though not to my liking; nor was it long before I learned to mend it.

November 7. Now it began to be settled fair weather. The 7th, 8th, 9th, 10th, and part of the 12th (for the 11th was Sunday) I took wholly up to make me a chair and with much ado brought it to a tolerable shape, but never to please me, and even in the making I pulled it in pieces several times. Note: I soon neglected my keeping Sundays, for, omitting my mark for them on my post, I forgot which was which.

November 13. This day it rained, which refreshed me exceedingly and cooled the earth, but it was accompanied with terrible thunder and lightning, which frightened me dreadfully, for fear of my powder; as soon as it was over, I resolved to separate my stock of powder into as many little parcels as possible, that it might not be in danger.

November 14, 15, 16. These three days I spent in making little square chests or boxes, which might hold about a pound or two pounds, at most, of powder; and so, putting the powder in, I stowed it in places as secure and remote from one another as possible. On one of these three days I killed a large bird that was good to eat, but I knew not what to call it.

November 17. This day I began to dig behind my tent into the rock to make room for my further conveniency. *Note:* Three things I wanted exceedingly for this work, viz., a pickaxe, a shovel, and a wheelbarrow or basket, so I desisted from my work and began to consider how to supply that want and make me some tools. As for the pickaxe, I made use of the iron crows, which were proper enough, though heavy; but the next thing was a shovel or spade. This was so absolutely necessary, that indeed I could do nothing effectually without it, but what kind of one to make I knew not.

November 18. The next day in searching the woods I found a tree of that wood, or like it, which in the Brazils they call the iron tree, for its exceeding hardness; of this, with great labor, and almost spoiling my axe, I cut a piece and brought it home, too, with difficulty enough, for it was exceeding heavy.

The excessive hardness of the wood, and having no other way, made me a long while upon this machine, for I worked it effectually by little and little into the form of a shovel or spade, the handle exactly shaped like ours in England, only that the board part having no iron shod upon it at bottom, it would not last me so long; however, it served well enough for the uses which I had occasion to put it to; but never was a shovel, I believe, made after that fashion, or so long a-making.

I was still deficient, for I wanted a basket or a wheelbarrow; a basket I could not make by any means, having no such things as twigs that would bend to make wickerware, at least none yet found out; and as to a wheelbarrow, I fancied I could make all but the wheel, but that I had no notion of, neither did I know how to go about it; besides, I had no possible way to make the iron gudgeons for the spindle or axis of the wheel to run in, so I gave it over; and so for carrying away the earth which I dug out of the cave, I made me a thing like a hod which the laborers carry mortar in when they serve the bricklayers.

This was not so difficult to me as the making the shovel; and yet this and the shovel and the attempt which I made in vain to make a wheelbarrow took me up no less than four days, I mean always excepting my morning walk with my gun, which I seldom failed, and very seldom failed also bringing home something fit to eat.

November 23. My other work having now stood still because of my making these tools, when they were finished I went on, and working every day, as my strength and time allowed, I spent eighteen days entirely in widening and deepening my cave, that it might hold my goods commodiously. NOTE: During all this time, I worked to make this room or cave spacious enough to accommodate me as a warehouse or magazine, a kitchen, a dining-room, and a cellar; as for my lodging, I kept to the tent, except that sometimes in the wet season of the year it rained so hard that I could not keep myself dry, which caused me afterwards to cover all my place within my pale with long poles, in the form of rafters, leaning against the rock, and load them with flags and large leaves of trees, like a thatch.

December 10. I began now to think my cave or vault finished, when on a sudden (it seems I had made it too large) a great quantity of earth fell down from the top on one side, so much, that, in short, it frightened me, and not without reason too; for if I had been under it I had never wanted a gravedigger. Upon this disaster I had now a great deal of work to do over again; for I had the loose earth to carry out; and which was of more importance, I had the ceiling to prop up, so that I might be sure no more would come down.

December 11. This day I went to work with it accordingly and got two shores or posts pitched upright to the top, with two pieces of boards across over each post. This I finished the next day; and setting more posts up with boards, in about a week more I had the roof secured; and the posts, standing in rows, served me for partitions to part of my house.

December 17. From this day to the 20th I placed shelves and knocked up nails on the posts to hang everything up that could be hung up, and now I began to be in some order within doors.

December 20. Now I carried everything into the cave, and began to furnish my house, and set up some pieces of boards, like a dresser, to order my victuals upon, but boards began to be very scarce with me; also I made me another table.

December 24. Much rain all night and all day; no stirring out.

December 25. Rain all day.

December 26. No rain, and the earth much cooler than before, and pleasanter.

December 27. Killed a young goat, and lamed another, so that I caught it and led it home in a string; when I had it at home, I bound and splintered up its leg, which was broke. N.B. I took such care of it that it lived, and the leg grew well, and as strong as ever; but by my nursing it so long, it grew tame and fed upon the little green at my door and would not go away. This was the first time that I entertained a thought of breeding up some tame creatures, that I might have food when my powder and shot was all spent.

December 28,29,30. Great heats, and no breeze; so that there was no stirring abroad, except in the evening for food; this time I spent in putting all my things in order within doors.

January 1. Very hot still, but I went abroad early and late with my gun, and lay still in the middle of the day; this evening going farther into the valleys which lay towards the centre of the island, I found there were plenty of goats, though exceedingly shy and hard to come at; however, I resolved to try if I could not bring my dog to hunt them down.

January 2. Accordingly, the next day, I went out with my dog, and set him upon the goats, but I was mistaken, for they all faced about upon the dog, and he knew his danger too well, for he would not come near them.

January 3. I began my fence or wall; which, being still jealous of my being attacked by somebody, I resolved to make very thick and strong.

N.B. This wall being described before, I purposely omit what was said in the journal; it is sufficient to observe, that I was no less time than from the 3rd of January to the 14th of April working, finishing, and perfecting this wall, though it was no more than about twenty-four yards in length, being a half circle from one place in the rock to another place about eight yards from it, the door of the cave being in the centre behind it.

All this time I worked very hard, the rains hindering me many days, nay, sometimes weeks together; but I thought I should never be perfectly secure till this wall was finished; and it is scarce credible what inexpressible labor everything was done with, especially the bringing piles out of the woods, and driving them into the ground, for I made them much bigger than I needed to have done.

When this wall was finished, and the outside double-fenced with a turf wall raised up close to it, I perceived myself that if any people were to come on shore there, they would not perceive anything like a habitation; and it was very well I did so, as may be observed hereafter upon a very remarkable occasion.

Notes

FRIST DAYS

1. want: lack
2. book: notebook
3. the Sabbath: (in Judaism and Christianity) the holy day of the week that is used for resting and worshipping God. For Jews this day is Saturday and for Christians it is Sunday.
4. perspective: telescope
5. Popish prayer-book: prayer book from Roman Catholics
6. husband: use them very carefully and make sure that they are not wasted
7. want that: go without that

THE JOURNAL: FOOD AND SHELTER

8. undone: (*old use*) (of a person) defeated and without any hope for the future

THE JOURNAL

9. offing: part of the sea that is visible but away from the shore

Questions

1. What is the theme of *Robinson Crusoe*? How is the character of Robinson Crusoe revealed in the excerpts?
2. The author has his narrator practice two different types of writing in the novel. One type is the journal that Crusoe keeps for a few chapters until his ink runs out. The other is the bulk of the story told by Crusoe as an omniscient narrator. Both are in the first-person voice, but they produce different effects. What is the intention of Defoe to write in this way?
3. How essential is the setting to the story? Could the story have taken place anytime or anywhere else?

Charles Dickens
1812—1870

Charles Dickens

Charles Dickens, the great Victorian novelist, was born on February 7, 1812 in Portsmouth, Hampshire, England. His father, John Dickens, was a clerk in the Navy Pay Office. Though being a kind and likable man, John was incompetent with money and led to tremendous debts throughout his life. At the age of nine, his family moved to London, where his father was arrested and taken to debtors' prison two years later. his mother moved into prison together with his seven brothers and sisters, but she arranged for the young Charles to live alone outside the prison and work with other children in a blacking warehouse. Dickens returned to school after his father was released from prison. At fifteen he left school for working as a clerk in a lawyer's office. During his spare time he studied shorthand and visited the British Museum library, where he did much reading. At the age of nineteen, he became a Parliamentary reporter.

In 1833, his first story *A Dinner at Poplar Walk* was published in the *Monthly Magazine*. He also had some sketches published in the *Morning Chronicle* for which he began reporting in 1834 and adopted the pen name "Boz". His first book, a collection of stories titled *Sketches by Boz,* was published in 1836. In the same year, he married Catherine Hogarth, daughter of the editor of the *Evening Chronicle*. Also in 1836, Dickens became editor for *Bentley's Miscellany* in which *Pickwick Papers* (1836—1837) was first serialized.

Thereafter, Dickens began to witness a prolific and commercially successful period during his life. Most of his novels were first serialized in monthly magazines as it was a common practice of the time. *Oliver Twist* between 1837 and 1839 was followed by *Nicholas Nickleby* (1838—1839), *The Old Curiosity Shop* (1840—1841), and *Barnaby Rudge* (1841). Successively published were Dickens' series of five Christmas Books: *A Christmas Carol* (1843), *The Chimes* (1844), *The Cricket on the*

Hearth (1845), *The Battle of Life* (1846), and *The Haunted Man* (1848). Those works had won Dickens a readership eagerly anticipating his next installments.

In 1842 his journey to the United States and Canada contributed to *American Notes* (1842). *Martin Chuzzlewit* was then serialized in 1843. His trip to Italy and settlement in Genoa for the next two years led to *Pictures from Italy* (1846). The next two published novels were *Dombey and Son* (1846) and *David Copperfield* (1849). From 1850 on, he started his own weekly journal *Household Words* which circulated for the next nine years. More novels were written including *Bleak House* (1852—1853), *Hard Times* (1854), and *Little Dorrit* (1855—1857). In 1859, his second weekly journal *All the Year Round* was founded and *A Tale of Two Cities* (1859) was first serialized. Novels to follow were *Great Expectations* (1860—1861) and *Our Mutual Friend* (1864—1865). In 1870, Charles Dickens died from a cerebral hemorrhage and was buried in Poet's Corner of Westminster Abbey.

The Personal History, Adventures, Experience and Observation of David Copperfield the Younger of Blunderstone Rookery (Which He Never Meant to Publish on Any Account), which is simply known as *David Copperfield* today, originally appeared in serial form in 1849. In the novel, Dickens records the growth of David from youth to maturity, and many events the protagonist has experienced parallel his own, thus making the novel the most autobiographical one among his literary writings. Meanwhile, Dickens continues to make direct attacks on the capitalist world in the novel and shows his belief that happiness can be achieved for a hard-working and honest man in that society.

David Copperfield

The novel traces the life of David Copperfield from childhood to maturity. David spends his childhood with his mother and their housekeeper Peggotty since his father died six months before his birth. At the age of seven, his mother marries the overbearing Edward Murdstone. David is sent away by Murdstone to a boarding school, where he meets a ruthless headmaster, Mr. Creakle, and befriends James Steerforth and Tommy Traddles. His mother dies not long after giving birth to a boy. Then, Murdstone forces little David to work in a factory in London, where he meets his landlord Wilkins Micawber, a man of elastic quality. When Micawber has to move to Plymouth after his stay in the debtor's prison, David decides to run away from the factory.

He manages to find his only relative, his unmarried and eccentric aunt Betsey Trotwood in Dover. Betsey takes the responsibility to raise him. Under the help of Betsey, David manages to continue his education. He attends a school run by a man named Doctor Strong. Then, he moves in with Mr. Wickfield and befriends his daughter Agnes. He studies law and later becomes an apprentice in the law office of Spenlow and Jorkins. There, he falls in love with the daughter of his boss, the beautiful but naïve Dora Spenlow. Following the advice of Tommy Traddles, David learns shorthand and gets a job reporting government debates for the newspapers in his spare time. Gradually, David succeeds as a skilled journalist and marries Dora, but a few years later, Dora dies after failing to recover from a miscarriage. David then realizes Agnes's long affection for him and gets married with her. As for Uriah Heep, the cunning and fraudulent clerk of Mr. Wickfield, he is discovered to be guilty of multiple acts of fraud, and is later imprisoned for an attempted fraud on the Bank of England.

Furthermore, various characters enter, leave, and re-enter David's life as he grows up, taking his nurse Peggotty, her family and her orphaned niece "Little Em'ly" for example. As a young boy, Peggotty once takes him to visit her family in Yarmouth where he meets Peggotty's brother, Mr. Peggotty, and his two adopted children, Ham and Little Em'ly. After David graduates from Doctor Strong's school, he goes to Yarmouth to revisit Peggotty with James Steerforth. There, Steerforth befriends the Peggottys. Later on, Little Em'ly gets seduced by Steerforth and runs off with him. As self-serving as Steerforth is, he leaves Em'ly. David and Mr. Peggotty finally find Little Em'ly. Then, Mr. Peggotty and Little Em'ly decide to move to Australia, as do the Micawbers.

The section below offers a vivid description of little David as a child laborer. David is sent to work at Murdstone and Grinby's warehouse, where he suffers from a sense of unmerited degradation apart from the hard work. He gets befriended with his landlord, the Micawbers, who are constantly facing financial difficulties with an amazingly elastic quality. Mr. Micawber is thereafter sent to debtors' prison, followed by his family. Recalling his childhood experience, the adult narrator David shows a rather sympathetic stance.

Chapter 11

I BEGIN LIFE ON MY OWN ACCOUNT, AND DON'T LIKE IT

I know enough of the world, now, to have almost lost the capacity of being much surprised by anything, but it is matter of some surprise to me, even now, that I can have been so easily thrown away at such an age. A child of excellent abilities, and with strong powers of observation, quick, eager, delicate, and soon hurt bodily or mentally, it seems wonderful to me that nobody should have made any sign in my behalf. But none was made, and I became, at ten years old, a little labouring hind in the service of Murdstone and Grinby.

Murdstone and Grinby's warehouse was at the waterside. It was down in Blackfriars[1]. Modern improvements have altered the place, but it was the last house at the bottom of a narrow street, curving down hill to the river, with some stairs at the end, where people took boat. It was a crazy old house with a wharf of its own, abutting on the water when the tide was in, and on the mud when the tide was out, and literally overrun with rats. Its panelled rooms, discoloured with the dirt and smoke of a hundred years, I dare say, its decaying floors and staircase, the squeaking and scuffling of the old grey rats down in the cellars, and the dirt and rottenness of the place, are things, not of many years ago, in my mind, but of the present instant. They are all before me, just as they were in the evil hour when I went among them for the first time, with my trembling hand in Mr. Quinion's.

Murdstone and Grinby's trade was among a good many kinds of people, but an important branch of it was the supply of wines and spirits to certain packet-ships[2]. I forget now where they chiefly went, but I think there were some among them that made voyages both to the East and West Indies. I know that a great many empty bottles were one of the consequences of this traffic, and that certain men and boys were employed to examine them against the light, and reject those that were flawed, and to rinse and wash them. When the empty bottles ran short, there were labels to be pasted on full ones, or corks to be fitted to them, or seals to be put upon the corks, or finished bottles to be packed in casks. All this work was my work, and of the boys employed upon it. I was one.

Chapter Three Experience and Growth

There were three or four of us, counting me. My working place was established in a corner of the warehouse, where Mr. Quinion could see me, when he chose to stand up on the bottom rail of his stool in the counting-house, and look at me through a window above the desk. Hither, on the first morning of my so auspiciously beginning life on my own account, the oldest of the regular boys was summoned to show me my business. His name was Mick Walker, and he wore a ragged apron and a paper cap. He informed me that his father was a bargeman, and walked, in a black velvet head-dress, in the Lord Mayor's Show[3]. He also informed me that our principal associate would be another boy whom he introduced by the—to me—extraordinary name of Mealy Potatoes. I discovered, however, that this youth had not been christened by that name, but that it had been bestowed upon him in the warehouse, on account of his complexion, which was pale or mealy. Mealy's father was a waterman, who had the additional distinction of being a fireman, and was engaged as such at one of the large theatres; where some young relation of Mealy's—I think his little sister—did Imps in the Pantomimes[4].

No words can express the secret agony of my soul as I sunk into this companionship, compared these henceforth everyday associates with those of my happier childhood—not to say with Steerforth, Traddles, and the rest of those boys, and felt my hopes of growing up to be a learned and distinguished man crushed in my bosom. The deep remembrance of the sense I had of being utterly without hope now, of the shame I felt in my position; of the misery it was to my young heart to believe that day-by-day what I had learned and thought, and delighted in, and raised my fancy and my emulation up by, would pass away from me, little-by-little, never to be brought back any more, cannot be written. As often as Mick Walker went away in the course of that forenoon, I mingled my tears with the water in which I was washing the bottles, and sobbed as if there were a flaw in my own breast, and it were in danger of bursting.

The counting-house clock was at half past twelve, and there was general preparation for going to dinner, when Mr. Quinion tapped at the counting-house window, and beckoned to me to go in. I went in, and found there a stoutish, middle-aged person, in a brown surtout and black tights and shoes, with no more hair upon his head (which was a large one, and very shining) than there is upon an egg, and with a very extensive face, which he turned full upon me. His clothes were shabby, but he had an imposing shirt-collar on. He carried a jaunty sort of a stick, with a large pair of rusty tassels to it, and a quizzing-glass[5] hung outside his coat, for ornament, I afterwards found, as he very seldom looked through it, and couldn't see anything when he did.

"This," said Mr. Quinion, in allusion to myself, "is he."

"This," said the stranger, with a certain condescending roll in his voice, and a certain indescribable air of doing something genteel, which impressed me very much, "is Master Copperfield. I hope I see you well, sir?"

I said I was very well, and hoped he was. I was sufficiently ill at ease, Heaven knows, but it was not in my nature to complain much at that time of my life, so I said I was very well, and hoped he was.

"I am," said the stranger, "thank Heaven, quite well. I have received a letter from Mr. Murdstone, in which he mentions that he would desire me to receive into an apartment in the rear of my house, which is at present unoccupied—and is, in short, to be let as a—in short," said the stranger, with a smile and in a burst of confidence, "as a bedroom—the young beginner whom I have now the pleasure to—" and the stranger waved his hand, and settled his chin in his shirt-collar.

"This is Mr. Micawber," said Mr. Quinion to me.

"Ahem!" said the stranger, "that is my name."

"Mr. Micawber," said Mr. Quinion, "is known to Mr. Murdstone. He takes orders for us on commission, when he can get any. He has been written to by Mr. Murdstone, on the subject of your lodgings, and he will receive you as a lodger."

"My address," said Mr. Micawber, "is Windsor Terrace, City Road. I—in short," said Mr. Micawber, with the same genteel air, and in another burst of confidence—"I live there."

I made him a bow.

"Under the impression," said Mr. Micawber, "that your peregrinations[6] in this metropolis have not as yet been extensive, and that you might have some difficulty in penetrating the arcana of the Modern Babylon[7] in the direction of the City Road,—in short," said Mr. Micawber, in another burst of confidence, "that you might lose yourself—I shall be happy to call this evening, and instal you in the knowledge of the nearest way."

I thanked him with all my heart, for it was friendly in him to offer to take that trouble.

"At what hour," said Mr. Micawber, "shall I—"

"At about eight," said Mr. Quinion.

"At about eight," said Mr. Micawber. "I beg to wish you good day, Mr. Quinion. I will intrude no longer."

So he put on his hat, and went out with his cane under his arm, very upright, and humming a tune when he was clear of the counting-house.

Mr. Quinion then formally engaged me to be as useful as I could in the warehouse of Murdstone and Grinby, at a salary, I think, of six shillings a week. I am not clear whether it was six or seven. I am inclined to believe, from my uncertainty on this head, that it was six at first and seven afterwards. He paid me a week down (from his own pocket, I believe), and I gave Mealy sixpence out of it to get my trunk carried to Windsor Terrace at night, it being too heavy for my strength, small as it was. I paid sixpence more for my dinner, which was a meat pie and a turn at a neighbouring pump, and passed the hour which was allowed for that meal in walking about the streets.

At the appointed time in the evening, Mr. Micawber reappeared. I washed my hands and face, to do the greater honour to his gentility, and we walked to our house, as I suppose I must now call it, together, Mr. Micawber impressing the names of streets, and the shapes of corner houses upon me, as we went along, that I might find my way back, easily, in the morning.

Arrived at this house in Windsor Terrace (which I noticed was shabby like himself, but also, like himself, made all the show it could), he presented me to Mrs. Micawber, a thin and faded lady, not at all young, who was sitting in the parlour (the first floor was altogether unfurnished, and the blinds were kept down to delude the neighbours), with a baby at her breast. This baby was one of twins, and I may remark here that I hardly ever, in all my experience of the family, saw both the twins detached from Mrs. Micawber at the same time. One of them was always taking refreshment.

There were two other children; Master Micawber, aged about four, and Miss Micawber, aged about three. These, and a dark-complexioned young woman, with a habit of snorting, who was servant to the family, and informed me, before half an hour had expired, that she was "a Orfling[8]", and came

Chapter Three Experience and Growth

from St. Luke's workhouse, in the neighbourhood, completed the establishment. My room was at the top of the house, at the back, a close chamber, stencilled all over with an ornament which my young imagination represented as a blue muffin, and very scantily furnished.

"I never thought," said Mrs. Micawber, when she came up, twin and all, to show me the apartment, and sat down to take breath, "before I was married, when I lived with Papa and Mama, that I should ever find it necessary to take a lodger. But Mr. Micawber being in difficulties, all considerations of private feeling must give way."

I said: "Yes, ma'am."

"Mr. Micawber's difficulties are almost overwhelming just at present," said Mrs. Micawber; "and whether it is possible to bring him through them, I don't know. When I lived at home with Papa and Mama, I really should have hardly understood what the word meant, in the sense in which I now employ it, but experientia[9] does it,—as papa used to say."

I cannot satisfy myself whether she told me that Mr. Micawber had been an officer in the Marines, or whether I have imagined it. I only know that I believe to this hour that he WAS in the Marines once upon a time, without knowing why. He was a sort of town traveller for a number of miscellaneous houses, now, but made little or nothing of it, I am afraid.

"If Mr. Micawber's creditors will not give him time," said Mrs. Micawber, "they must take the consequences, and the sooner they bring it to an issue the better. Blood cannot be obtained from a stone, neither can anything on account be obtained at present (not to mention law expenses) from Mr. Micawber."

I never can quite understand whether my precocious self-dependence confused Mrs. Micawber in reference to my age, or whether she was so full of the subject that she would have talked about it to the very twins if there had been nobody else to communicate with, but this was the strain in which she began, and she went on accordingly all the time I knew her.

Poor Mrs. Micawber! She said she had tried to exert herself, and so, I have no doubt, she had. The centre of the street door was perfectly covered with a great brass-plate, on which was engraved "Mrs. Micawber's Boarding Establishment for Young Ladies", but I never found that any young lady had ever been to school there, or that any young lady ever came, or proposed to come, or that the least preparation was ever made to receive any young lady. The only visitors I ever saw or heard of were creditors. THEY used to come at all hours, and some of them were quite ferocious. One dirty-faced man, I think he was a boot-maker, used to edge himself into the passage as early as seven o'clock in the morning, and call up the stairs to Mr. Micawber: "Come! You ain't out yet, you know. Pay us, will you? Don't hide, you know; that's mean. I wouldn't be mean if I was you. Pay us, will you? You just pay us, d'ye hear? Come!" Receiving no answer to these taunts, he would mount in his wrath to the words "swindlers" and "robbers", and these being ineffectual too, would sometimes go to the extremity of crossing the street, and roaring up at the windows of the second floor, where he knew Mr. Micawber was. At these times, Mr. Micawber would be transported with grief and mortification, even to the length (as I was once made aware by a scream from his wife) of making motions at himself with a razor, but within half-an-hour afterwards, he would polish up his shoes with extraordinary pains, and go out, humming a tune with a greater air of gentility than ever. Mrs. Micawber was quite as elastic. I have known her to be thrown into fainting fits by the king's taxes[10] at three o'clock, and to eat lamp-chops breaded, and drink warm ale (paid for with two tea-spoons that had gone to the pawnbroker's) at four. On one occasion, when an execution had just been put in, coming home through some chance as early as six o'clock, I saw her lying (of course with a twin) under the grate in a swoon, with her hair all torn about her face, but I never knew her more cheerful than she was, that very same night, over a veal-cutlet before the kitchen fire, telling me stories about her papa and mama, and the company they used to keep.

In this house, and with this family, I passed my leisure time. My own exclusive breakfast of a penny loaf and a pennyworth of milk I provided myself. I kept another small loaf, and a modicum of cheese, on a particular shelf of a particular cupboard, to make my supper on when I came back at night. This made a hole in the six or seven shillings, I know well, and I was out at the warehouse all day, and had to support myself on that money all the week. From Monday morning until Saturday night, I had no advice, no counsel, no encouragement, no consolation, no assistance, no support, of any kind, from anyone, that I can call to mind, as I hope to go to Heaven!

I was so young and childish, and so little qualified—how could I be otherwise?—to undertake the whole charge of my own existence, that often, in going to Murdstone and Grinby's, of a morning, I could not resist the stale pastry put out for sale at half-price at the pastry-cooks' doors, and spent in that the money I should have kept for my dinner. Then, I went without my dinner, or bought a roll or a slice of pudding. I remember two pudding-shops, between which I was divided, according to my finances. One was in a court close to St. Martin's Church—at the back of the church—which is now removed altogether. The pudding at that shop was made of currants, and was rather a special pudding, but was dear, two pennyworth not being larger than a pennyworth of more ordinary pudding. A good shop for the latter was in the Strand, somewhere in that part which has been rebuilt since. It was a stout pale pudding, heavy and flabby, and with great flat raisins in it, stuck in whole at wide distances apart. It came up hot at about my time every day, and many a day did I dine off it. When I dined regularly and handsomely, I had a saveloy and a penny-loaf, or a four-penny plate of red beef from a cook's shop, or a plate of bread and cheese and a glass of beer, from a miserable old public-house opposite our place of business, called the Lion, or the Lion and something else that I have forgotten. Once, I remember carrying my own bread (which I had brought from home in the morning) under my arm, wrapped in a piece of paper, like a book, and going to a famous alamode beef-house near Drury Lane, and ordering a "small plate" of that delicacy to eat with it. What the waiter thought of such a strange little apparition coming in all alone, I don't know, but I can see him now, staring at me as I ate my dinner, and bringing up the other waiter to look. I gave him a half-penny to himself, and I wish he hadn't taken it.

We had half-an-hour, I think, for tea. When I had money enough, I used to get half-a-pint of ready-made coffee and a slice of bread and butter. When I had none, I used to look at a vension-shop in Fleet Street, or I have strolled, at such a time, as far as Covent Garden Market, and stared at the pineapples. I was fond of wandering about the Adelphi, because it was a mysterious place, with those dark arches. I see myself emerging one evening from some of these arches, on a little public-house close to the river, with an open space before it, where some coal-heavers were dancing, to look at whom I sat down upon a bench. I wonder what they thought of me!

Chapter Three   Experience and Growth

I was such a child, and so little, that frequently when I went into the bar of a strange public-house for a glass of ale or porter, to moisten what I had had for dinner, they were afraid to give it me. I remember one hot evening I went into the bar of a public-house, and said to the landlord: "What is your best—your very best—ale a glass?" For it was a special occasion. I don't know what. It may have been my birthday.

"Twopence-halfpenny," says the landlord, "is the price of the Genuine Stunning ale."

"Then," says I, producing the money, "just draw me a glass of the Genuine Stunning, if you please, with a good head to it."

The landlord looked at me in return over the bar, from head to foot, with a strange smile on his face, and instead of drawing the beer, looked round the screen and said something to his wife. She came out from behind it, with her work in her hand, and joined him in surveying me. Here we stand, all three, before me now. The landlord in his shirt-sleeves, leaning against the bar window-frame; his wife looking over the little half-door, and I, in some confusion, looking up at them from outside the partition. They asked me a good many questions, as, what my name was, how old I was, where I lived, how I was employed, and how I came there. To all of which, that I might commit nobody, I invented, I am afraid, appropriate answers. They served me with the ale, though I suspect it was not the Genuine Stunning, and the landlord's wife, opening the little half-door of the bar, and bending down, gave me my money back, and gave me a kiss that was half admiring, and half compassionate, but all womanly and good, I am sure.

I know I do not exaggerate, unconsciously and unintentionally, the scantiness of my resources or the difficulties of my life. I know that if a shilling were given me by Mr. Quinion at any time, I spent it in a dinner or a tea. I know that I worked from morning until night, with common men and boys, a shabby child. I know that I lounged about the streets, insufficiently and unsatisfactorily fed. I know that, but for the mercy of God, I might easily have been, for any care that was taken of me, a little robber or a little vagabond.

Yet I held some station at Murdstone and Grinby's too. Besides that, Mr. Quinion did what a careless man so occupied, and dealing with a thing so anomalous, could, to treat me as one upon a different footing from the rest. I never said, to man or boy, how it was that I came to be there, or gave the least indication of being sorry that I was there. That I suffered in secret, and that I suffered exquisitely, no one ever knew but I. How much I suffered, it is, as I have said already, utterly beyond my power to tell. But I kept my own counsel, and I did my work. I knew from the first that, if I could not do my work as well as any of the rest, I could not hold myself above slight and contempt. I soon became at least as expeditious and as skilful as either of the other boys. Though perfectly familiar with them, my conduct and manner were different enough from theirs to place a space between us. They and the men generally spoke of me as "the little gent", or "the young Suffolker." A certain man named Gregory, who was foreman of the packers, and another named Tipp, who was the carman, and wore a red jacket, used to address me sometimes as "David", but I think it was mostly when we were very confidential, and when I had made some efforts to entertain them, over our work, with some results of the old readings, which were fast perishing out of my remembrance. Mealy Potatoes uprose once, and rebelled against my being so distinguished, but Mick Walker settled him in no time.

My rescue from this kind of existence I considered quite hopeless, and abandoned, as such, altogether. I am solemnly convinced that I never for one hour was reconciled to it, or was otherwise than miserably unhappy, but I bore it, and even to Peggotty, partly for the love of her and partly for shame, never in any letter (though many passed between us) revealed the truth.

Mr. Micawber's difficulties were in addition to the distressed state of my mind. In my forlorn state I became quite attached to the family, and used to walk about, busy with Mrs. Micawber's calculations of ways and means, and heavy with the weight of Mr. Micawber's debts. On a Saturday night, which was my grand treat—partly because it was a great thing to walk home with six or seven shillings in my pocket, looking into the shops and thinking what such a sum would buy, and partly because I went home early—Mrs. Micawber would make the most heart-rending confidences to me—also on a Sunday morning, when I mixed the portion of tea or coffee I had bought overnight in a little shaving-pot, and sat late at my breakfast. It was nothing at all unusual for Mr. Micawber to sob violently at the beginning of one of these Saturday night conversations, and sing about Jack's delight being his lovely Nan[11] towards the end of it. I have known him come home to supper with a flood of tears, and a declaration that nothing was now left but a jail, and go to bed making a calculation of the expense of putting bow-windows to the house, "in case anything turned up", which was his favourite expression. And Mrs. Micawber was just the same.

A curious equality of friendship, originating, I suppose, in our respective circumstances, sprang up between me and these people, notwithstanding the ludicrous disparity in our years. But I never allowed myself to be prevailed upon to accept any invitation to eat and drink with them out of their stock (knowing that they got on badly with the butcher and baker, and had often not too much for themselves), until Mrs. Micawber took me into her entire confidence. This she did one evening as follows:

"Master Copperfield," said Mrs. Micawber, "I make no stranger of you, and therefore do not hesitate to say that Mr. Micawber's difficulties are coming to a crisis."

It made me very miserable to hear it, and I looked at Mrs. Micawber's red eyes with the utmost sympathy.

"With the exception of the heel of a Dutch cheese—which is not adapted to the wants of a young family"—said Mrs. Micawber, "there is really not a scrap of anything in the larder[12]. I was accustomed to speak of the larder when I lived with Papa and Mama, and I use the word almost unconsciously. What I mean to express is, that there is nothing to eat in the house."

"Dear me!" I said, in great concern.

I had two or three shillings of my week's money in my pocket—from which I presume that it must have been on a Wednesday night when we held this conversation—and I hastily produced them, and with heartfelt emotion begged Mrs. Micawber to accept of them as a loan. But that lady, kissing me, and making me put them back in my pocket, replied that she couldn't think of it.

"No, my dear Master Copperfield," said she, "far be it from my thoughts! But you have a discretion beyond your years, and can render me another kind of service, if you will, and a service I will thankfully accept of."

I begged Mrs. Micawber to name it.

Chapter Three Experience and Growth

"I have parted with the plate myself," said Mrs. Micawber. "Six tea, two salt, and a pair of sugars[13], I have at different times borrowed money on, in secret, with my own hands. But the twins are a great tie, and to me, with my recollections of Papa and Mama, these transactions are very painful. There are still a few trifles that we could part with. Mr. Micawber's feelings would never allow him to dispose of them; and Clickett"—this was the girl from the workhouse—"being of a vulgar mind, would take painful liberties if so much confidence was reposed in her. Master Copperfield, if I might ask you—"

I understood Mrs. Micawber now, and begged her to make use of me to any extent. I began to dispose of the more portable articles of property that very evening, and went out on a similar expedition almost every morning, before I went to Murdstone and Grinby's.

Mr. Micawber had a few books on a little chiffonier, which he called the library, and those went first. I carried them, one after another, to a bookstall in the City Road—one part of which, near our house, was almost all bookstalls and bird shops then—and sold them for whatever they would bring. The keeper of this bookstall, who lived in a little house behind it, used to get tipsy every night, and to be violently scolded by his wife every morning. More than once, when I went there early, I had audience of him in a turn-up bedstead, with a cut in his forehead or a black eye, bearing witness to his excesses over-night (I am afraid he was quarrelsome in his drink), and he, with a shaking hand, endeavouring to find the needful shillings in one or other of the pockets of his clothes, which lay upon the floor, while his wife, with a baby in her arms and her shoes down at heel, never left off rating him. Sometimes he had lost his money, and then he would ask me to call again, but his wife had always got some—had taken his, I dare say, while he was drunk—and secretly completed the bargain on the stairs, as we went down together.

At the pawnbroker's shop, too, I began to be very well-known. The principal gentleman who officiated behind the counter took a good deal of notice of me, and often got me, I recollect, to decline a Latin noun or adjective, or to conjugate a Latin verb, in his ear, while he transacted my business. After all these occasions Mrs. Micawber made a little treat, which was generally a supper, and there was a peculiar relish in these meals which I well remember.

At last Mr. Micawber's difficulties came to a crisis, and he was arrested early one morning, and carried over to the King's Bench[14] Prison in the Borough. He told me, as he went out of the house, that the God of day had now gone down upon him—and I really thought his heart was broken, and mine too. But I heard, afterwards, that he was seen to play a lively game at skittles[15] before noon.

On the first Sunday after he was taken there, I was to go and see him, and have dinner with him. I was to ask my way to such a place, and just short of that place I should see such another place, and just short of that I should see a yard, which I was to cross, and keep straight on until I saw a turnkey. All this I did, and when at last I did see a turnkey (poor little fellow that I was!), and thought how, when Roderick Random[16] was in a debtors' prison, there was a man there with nothing on him but an old rug, the turnkey swam before my dimmed eyes and my beating heart.

Mr. Micawber was waiting for me within the gate, and we went up to his room (top story but one), and cried very much. He solemnly conjured me, I remember, to take warning by his fate, and to observe that if a man had twenty pounds a year for his income, and spent nineteen pounds nineteen shillings and sixpence, he would be happy, but that if he spent twenty pounds one he would be miserable. After which he borrowed a shilling of me for porter, gave me a written order on Mrs. Micawber for the amount, and put away his pocket-handkerchief, and cheered up.

We sat before a little fire, with two bricks put within the rusted grate, one on each side, to prevent its burning too many coals, until another debtor, who shared the room with Mr. Micawber, came in from the bake-house with the loin of mutton which was our joint-stock repast. Then I was sent up to "Captain Hopkins" in the room overhead, with Mr. Micawber's compliments, and I was his young friend, and would Captain Hopkins lend me a knife and fork.

Captain Hopkins lent me the knife and fork, with his compliments to Mr. Micawber. There was a very dirty lady in his little room, and two wan girls, his daughters, with shock heads of hair. I thought it was better to borrow Captain Hopkins's knife and fork, than Captain Hopkins's comb. The Captain himself was in the last extremity of shabbiness, with large whiskers, and an old, old brown greatcoat with no other coat below it. I saw his bed rolled up in a corner, and what plates and dishes and pots he had on a shelf; and I divined (God knows how) that though the two girls with the shock heads of hair were Captain Hopkins's children, the dirty lady was not married to Captain Hopkins. My timid station on his threshold was not occupied more than a couple of minutes at most, but I came down again with all this in my knowledge, as surely as the knife and fork were in my hand.

There was something gipsy-like and agreeable in the dinner, after all. I took back Captain Hopkins's knife and fork early in the afternoon, and went home to comfort Mrs. Micawber with an account of my visit. She fainted when she saw me return, and made a little jug of egg-hot afterwards to console us while we talked it over.

I don't know how the household furniture came to be sold for the family benefit, or who sold it, except that I did not. Sold it was, however, and carried away in a van, except the bed, a few chairs, and the kitchen-table. With these possessions we encamped, as it were, in the two parlours of the emptied house in Windsor Terrace—Mrs. Micawber, the children, the Orfling, and myself; and lived in those rooms—night and day. I have no idea for how long, though it seems to me for a long time. At last Mrs. Micawber resolved to move into the prison, where Mr. Micawber had now secured a room to himself. So I took the key of the house to the landlord, who was very glad to get it, and the beds were sent over to the King's Bench, except mine, for which a little room was hired outside the walls in the neighbourhood of that Institution, very much to my satisfaction, since the Micawbers and I had become too used to one another, in our troubles, to part. The Orfling was likewise accommodated with an inexpensive lodging in the same neighbourhood. Mine was a quiet back-garret with a sloping roof, commanding a pleasant prospect of a timber-yard, and when I took possession of it, with the reflection that Mr. Micawber's troubles had come to a crisis at last, I thought it quite a paradise.

All this time I was working at Murdstone and Grinby's in the same common way, and with the same common companions, and with the same sense of unmerited degradation as at first. But I never, happily for me no doubt, made a single acquaintance, or spoke to any of the many boys whom I saw daily in going to the warehouse, in coming from it, and in prowling about the streets at meal-times. I led the same secretly unhappy life, but I led it in the same lonely, self-reliant manner. The only changes I am conscious of are, firstly, that I had grown more shabby, and secondly, that I was now relieved of much of the weight of Mr. and Mrs. Micawber's cares, for some relatives or friends had engaged to help them at their present pass, and they lived more comfortably in the prison than they had lived for a long while out of it. I used to breakfast with them now, in virtue of some arrangement, of which I have forgotten the details. I forget, too, at what hour the gates were opened in the morning, admitting of my going in, but I know that I was often up at six o'clock, and that my favourite lounging-place in the interval was old London Bridge, where I was wont[17] to sit in one of the stone recesses, watching the people going by, or to look over the balustrades[18] at the sun shining in the water, and lighting up the golden flame on the top of the Monument[19]. The Orfling met me here sometimes, to be told some astonishing fictions respecting the wharves and the Tower[20], of which I can say no more than that I hope I believed them myself. In the evening I used to go back to the prison, and walk up and down the parade with Mr. Micawber, or play casino with Mrs. Micawber, and hear reminiscences of her papa and mama. Whether Mr. Murdstone knew where I was, I am unable to say. I never told them at Murdstone and Grinby's.

Mr. Micawber's affairs, although past their crisis, were very much involved by reason of a certain "Deed", of which I used to hear a great deal, and which I suppose, now, to have been some former composition[21] with his creditors, though I was so far from being clear about it then, that I am conscious of having confounded it with those demoniacal parchments which are held to have, once upon a time, obtained to a great extent in Germany. At last this document appeared to be got out of the way, somehow; at all events, it ceased to be the rock ahead it had been, and Mrs. Micawber informed me that "her family" had decided that Mr. Micawber should apply for his release under the Insolvent Debtors Act[22], which would set him free, she expected, in about six weeks.

"And then," said Mr. Micawber, who was present, "I have no doubt I shall, please Heaven, begin to be beforehand with the world[23], and to live in a perfectly new manner, if—in short, if anything turns up."

By way of going in for anything that might be on the cards, I call to mind that Mr. Micawber, about this time, composed a petition to the House of Commons[24], praying for an alteration in the law of imprisonment for debt. I set down this remembrance here, because it is an instance to myself of the manner in which I fitted my old books to my altered life, and made stories for myself, out of the streets, and out of men and women, and how some main points in the character I shall unconsciously develop, I suppose, in writing my life, were gradually forming all this while.

There was a club in the prison, in which Mr. Micawber, as a gentleman, was a great authority. Mr. Micawber had stated his idea of this petition to the club, and the club had strongly approved of the same. Wherefore Mr. Micawber (who was a thoroughly good-natured man, and as active a creature about everything but his own affairs as ever existed, and never so happy as when he was busy about something that could never be of any profit to him) set to work at the petition, invented it, engrossed it on an immense sheet of paper, spread it out on a table, and appointed a time for all the club, and all within the walls if they chose, to come up to his room and sign it.

When I heard of this approaching ceremony, I was so anxious to see them all come in, one after another, though I knew the greater part of them already, and they me, that I got an hour's leave of absence from Murdstone and Grinby's, and established myself in a corner for that purpose. As many of the principal members of the club as could be got into the small room without filling it supported Mr.

Micawber in front of the petition, while my old friend Captain Hopkins (who had washed himself, to do honour to so solemn an occasion) stationed himself close to it, to read it to all who were unacquainted with its contents. The door was then thrown open, and the general population began to come in, in a long file, several waiting outside, while one entered, affixed his signature, and went out. To everybody in succession, Captain Hopkins said: "Have you read it?"—"No." "Would you like to hear it read?" If he weakly showed the least disposition to hear it, Captain Hopkins, in a loud sonorous voice, gave him every word of it. The Captain would have read it twenty thousand times, if twenty thousand people would have heard him, one by one. I remember a certain luscious roll he gave to such phrases as "The people's representatives in Parliament assembled," "Your petitioners therefore humbly approach your honourable house," "His gracious Majesty's unfortunate subjects," as if the words were something real in his mouth, and delicious to taste, Mr. Micawber, meanwhile, listening with a little of an author's vanity, and contemplating (not severely) the spikes on the opposite wall.

As I walked to and fro daily between Southwark and Blackfriars, and lounged about at meal-times in obscure streets, the stones of which may, for anything I know, be worn at this moment by my childish feet, I wonder how many of these people were wanting in the crowd that used to come filing before me in review again, to the echo of Captain Hopkins's voice! When my thoughts go back now, to that slow agony of my youth, I wonder how much of the histories I invented for such people hangs like a mist of fancy over well-remembered facts! When I tread the old ground, I do not wonder that I seem to see and pity, going on before me, an innocent romantic boy, making his imaginative world out of such strange experiences and sordid things!

Notes

1. Blackfriars: a district in London
2. packet-ship: also called packet boat, packet ship, a small vessel that carries mails, passengers, and goods regularly on a fixed route, especially on rivers or along coasts.
3. Lord Mayor's Show: one of the longest established and best known annual events in London which dates back to before 1535. The event is a procession through the City of London to celebrate the inauguration of a new Lord Mayor.
4. Imps: Imp is a small creature like a little man, that has magic powers and behaves badly in stories; Pantomimes: a play or entertainment in which the performers express themselves mutely by gestures, often to the accompaniment of music.
5. quizzing-glass: a monocle, a type of corrective lens used to correct or enhance the vision in only one eye. It consists of a circular lens.
6. peregrination: (*literary or humorous*) a journey, especially a long slow one
7. Babylon: the capital of the ancient empire of Babylonia in southwestern Asia
8. a Orfling: an orphan
9. experientia: (*Latin*) experience
10. the king's taxes: taxes levied by the state
11. Jack's delight being his lovely Nan: referring to a popular song at that time
12. larder: a room or place where food is kept; pantry

13. Six tea, two salt, and a pair of sugars: Six tea-spoons, two salt-spoons, and a pair of sugar-tongs
14. the King's Bench: a division of the British superior court system that hears criminal and civil cases. Used when the sovereign is a man.
15. skittles: (*plural; functioning as singular*) also called (esp. US) ninepins, a bowling game in which players knock over as many skittles as possible by rolling a wooden ball at them.
16. Roderick Random: the hero and narrator of *The Adventures of Roderick Random* by Tobias Smollett published in 1748.
17. wont: (*usually passive*) to become or cause to become accustomed
18. balustrade: an ornamental rail or coping with its supporting set of balusters
19. the Monument: referring to the Monument to the Great Fire of London, a stone Roman Doric column in the City of London, near the north eastern end of London Bridge, which commemorates the Great Fire of London in 1666.
20. the Tower: referring to the Tower of London, a historic castle on the north bank of the River Thames in central London, founded towards the end of 1066 as part of the Norman Conquest of England. The White Tower, which gives the entire castle its name, was built by William the Conqueror in 1078. The castle was used as a prison since at least 1100.
21. composition: a settlement by mutual consent, esp. a legal agreement whereby the creditors agree to accept partial payment of a debt in full settlement
22. Insolvent Debtors Act: an Act of Parliament passed by the United Kingdom Parliament in 1813, which was enacted in response to the demands on the prison system imposed by the numbers of those being incarcerated for debt, and some concern for their plight. Those imprisoned for debt could apply to the court to be released—unless they were in trade or guilty of fraudulent or other dishonest behavior—by reaching an agreement with their creditors that ensured a fair distribution of their present and future assets.
23. to be beforehand with the world: to pay, or ready to pay, every thing before it is due so as not to run into debt
24. House of Commons: the lower house of the Parliament of the United Kingdom. The Commons is a democratically elected body consisting of 650 members known as Members of Parliament (MPs).

Questions

1. Although the story is narrated by David as an adult, his memories, as he says, are similar to those of a child. Why does Dickens choose to narrate the story in the perspective as an adult, and how does it affect the way the readers understand the different characters in the novel?
2. What can you learn about the character of Mr. Micawber through Chapter 11? How does Dickens portray this character?

James Joyce
1882—1941

James Joyce

James Joyce, an Irish novelist and poet, was born to John Joyce and Mary Murray in Dublin on 2 February, 1882. In 1888, he was sent to the prestigious Clongowes Wood College, a boarding school run by the Jesuit order. From 1893 on, he went to another Jesuit school called Belvedere College in Dublin. In 1898, he entered University College. Upon graduation in 1902, Joyce enrolled as a medical student in Paris. Two years later, on one of his visits back in Dublin, Joyce met and fell in love with Nora Barnacle, a Galway country girl working in Dublin as a chambermaid. Then they left Ireland in 1904 to spend the rest of their life in exile in Trieste, Zürich and Paris and did not get married until 1931. Facing financial difficulties, Joyce had to support his family by writing, but always had to rely heavily on some forms of patronage. Having suffered from a deteriorating health, James had several operations on his eyes and died in Zürich from a perforated stomach ulcer on 13 January, 1941.

As one of the most influential writers in the modernist avant-garde of the early 20th century, Joyce is best-known for several works, which mainly include the short-story collection *Dubliners* (1914), the novels *A Portrait of the Artist as a Young Man* (1916), *Ulysses* (1922), and *Finnegans Wake* (1939). In addition, Joyce also wrote and published numerous pieces of non-fiction. In 1918, Joyce published his only play *Exiles*. Besides, a number of poetry collections were published, taking *Chamber Music* (1907) and *Collected Poems* (1936) for example. Among Joyce's literary works, *Ulysses* is probably the most famous one for its revolutionized structure and form as well as its development of stream of consciousness technique. *Finnegans Wake*, as Joyce's last work, has been known for being incomprehensible and unreadable. It is generally acclaimed as one of the most difficult works of fiction in the English language owing to its expansive linguistic experiments, stream of consciousness technique, literary allusions, and the abandonment of the conventional plot and character construction.

"Araby" is a short story in *Dubliners* which is intended to depict the life of middle class in and around Dublin in the early years of the 20th century. "Araby" tells the story of a boy trying to buy a worthy gift from the Araby bazaar for a girl whom he falls in love with, but eventually he fails in this quest. The whole story can be seen as the boy going on a journey, and it ends with a fruitless result as the boy goes back buying nothing. And this particular nature of the journey endows the story with some characteristics of Bildungsroman, such as coming of age and the loss of innocence.

Araby

North Richmond Street, being blind, was a quiet street except at the hour when the Christian Brothers' School set the boys free. An uninhabited house of two storeys stood at the blind end, detached from its neighbours in a square ground. The other houses of the street, conscious of decent lives within them, gazed at one another with brown imperturbable[1] faces.

The former tenant of our house, a priest, had died in the back drawing-room. Air, musty from having been long enclosed, hung in all the rooms, and the waste room behind the kitchen was littered with old useless papers. Among these I found a few paper-covered books, the pages of which were curled and damp: *The Abbot*[2], by Walter Scott[3], *The Devout Communicant*[4], and *The Memoirs of Vidocq*[5]. I liked the last best because its leaves were yellow. The wild garden behind the house contained a central apple-tree and a few straggling bushes, under one of which I found the late tenant's rusty bicycle-pump. He had been a very charitable priest; in his will he had left all his money to institutions and the furniture of his house to his sister.

When the short days of winter came, dusk fell before we had well eaten our dinners. When we met in the street the houses had grown sombre. The space of sky above us was the colour of ever-changing violet and towards it the lamps of the street lifted their feeble lanterns. The cold air stung us and we played till our bodies glowed. Our shouts echoed in the silent street. The career of our play brought us through the dark muddy lanes behind the houses where we ran the gauntlet[6] of the rough tribes from the cottages, to the back doors of the dark dripping gardens where odours arose from the ashpits, to the dark odorous stables where a coachman smoothed and combed the horse or shook music from the buckled harness. When we returned to the street, light from the kitchen windows had filled the areas. If my uncle was seen turning the corner, we hid in the shadow until we had seen him safely housed. Or if Mangan's sister came out on the doorstep to call her brother in to his tea, we watched her from our shadow peer up and down the street. We waited to see whether she would remain or go in and, if she remained, we left our shadow and walked up to Mangan's steps resignedly. She was waiting for us, her figure defined by the light from the half-opened door. Her brother always teased her before he obeyed, and I stood by the railings looking at her. Her dress swung as she moved her body, and the soft rope of her hair tossed from side to side.

Every morning I lay on the floor in the front parlour watching her door. The blind was pulled down to within an inch of the sash so that I could not be seen. When she came out on the doorstep my heart leaped. I ran to the hall, seized my books and followed her. I kept her brown figure always in my eye and, when we came near the point at which our ways diverged, I quickened my pace and passed her. This happened morning after morning. I had never spoken to her, except for a few casual words, and yet her name was like a

summons to all my foolish blood.

Her image accompanied me even in places the most hostile to romance. On Saturday evenings when my aunt went marketing I had to go to carry some of the parcels. We walked through the flaring streets, jostled by drunken men and bargaining women, amid the curses of labourers, the shrill litanies[7] of shop-boys who stood on guard by the barrels of pigs' cheeks, the nasal chanting of street-singers, who sang a *come-all-you* about O'Donovan Rossa[8], or a ballad about the troubles in our native land. These noises converged in a single sensation of life for me: I imagined that I bore my chalice[9] safely through a throng of foes. Her name sprang to my lips at moments in strange prayers and praises which I myself did not understand. My eyes were often full of tears (I could not tell why) and at times a flood from my heart seemed to pour itself out into my bosom. I thought little of the future. I did not know whether I would ever speak to her or not or, if I spoke to her, how I could tell her of my confused adoration. But my body was like a harp and her words and gestures were like fingers running upon the wires.

One evening I went into the back drawing-room in which the priest had died. It was a dark rainy evening and there was no sound in the house. Through one of the broken panes I heard the rain impinge upon the earth, the fine incessant needles of water playing in the sodden beds. Some distant lamp or lighted window gleamed below me. I was thankful that I could see so little. All my senses seemed to desire to veil themselves and, feeling that I was about to slip from them, I pressed the palms of my hands together until they trembled, murmuring: "*O love! O love!*" many times.

At last she spoke to me. When she addressed the first words to me I was so confused that I did not know what to answer. She asked me was I going to *Araby*. I forgot whether I answered yes or no. It would be a splendid bazaar; she said she would love to go.

"And why can't you?" I asked.

While she spoke she turned a silver bracelet round and round her wrist. She could not go, she said, because there would be a retreat that week in her convent[10]. Her brother and two other boys were fighting for their caps and I was alone at the railings. She held one of the spikes, bowing her head towards me. The light from the lamp opposite our door caught the white curve of her neck, lit up her hair that rested there and, falling, lit up the hand upon the railing. It fell over one side of her dress and caught the white border of a petticoat just visible as she stood at ease.

"It's well for you," she said.

"If I go," I said, "I will bring you something."

What innumerable follies laid waste my waking and sleeping thoughts after that evening! I wished to annihilate the tedious intervening days. I chafed against the work of school. At night in my bedroom and by day in the classroom her image came between me and the page I strove to read. The syllables of the word *Araby* were called to me through the silence in which my soul luxuriated and cast an Eastern enchantment over me. I asked for leave to go to the bazaar on Saturday night. My aunt was surprised and hoped it was not some Freemason[11] affair. I answered few questions in class. I watched my master's face pass from amiability to sternness; he hoped I was not beginning to idle. I could not call my wandering thoughts together. I had hardly any patience with the serious work of life which, now that it stood between me and my desire, seemed to me child's play, ugly monotonous child's play.

Chapter Three Experience and Growth

On Saturday morning I reminded my uncle that I wished to go to the bazaar in the evening. He was fussing at the hallstand, looking for the hat-brush, and answered me curtly:

"Yes, boy, I know."

As he was in the hall I could not go into the front parlour and lie at the window. I left the house in bad humour and walked slowly towards the school. The air was pitilessly raw and already my heart misgave me.

When I came home to dinner my uncle had not yet been home. Still it was early. I sat staring at the clock for some time and, when its ticking began to irritate me, I left the room. I mounted the staircase and gained the upper part of the house. The high cold empty gloomy rooms liberated me and I went from room to room singing. From the front window I saw my companions playing below in the street. Their cries reached me weakened and indistinct and, leaning my forehead, against the cool glass, I looked over at the dark house where she lived. I may have stood there for an hour, seeing nothing but the brown-clad figure cast by my imagination, touched discreetly by the lamplight at the curved neck, at the hand upon the railings and at the border below the dress.

When I came downstairs again I found Mrs. Mercer sitting at the fire. She was an old, garrulous woman, a pawnbroker's widow, who collected used stamps for some pious purpose. I had to endure the gossip of the tea-table. The meal was prolonged beyond an hour and still my uncle did not come. Mrs. Mercer stood up to go: she was sorry she couldn't wait any longer, but it was after eight o'clock and she did not like to be out late, as the night air was bad for her. When she had gone I began to walk up and down the room, clenching my fists. My aunt said:

"I'm afraid you may put off your bazaar for this night of our Lord[12]."

At nine o'clock I heard my uncle's latchkey in the hall door. I heard him talking to himself and heard the hallstand rocking when it had received the weight of his overcoat. I could interpret these signs. When he was midway through his dinner I asked him to give me the money to go to the bazaar. He had forgotten.

"The people are in bed and after their first sleep now," he said.

I did not smile. My aunt said to him energetically:

"Can't you give him the money and let him go? You've kept him late enough as it is."

My uncle said he was very sorry he had forgotten. He said he believed in the old saying: "All work and no play makes Jack a dull boy." He asked me where I was going and, when I had told him a second time he asked me did I know *The Arab's Farewell to His Steed*[13]. When I left the kitchen he was about to recite the opening lines of the piece to my aunt.

I held a florin[14] tightly in my hand as I strode down Buckingham Street towards the station. The sight of the streets thronged with buyers and glaring with gas recalled to me the purpose of my journey. I took my seat in a third-class carriage of a deserted train. After an intolerable delay the train moved out of the station slowly. It crept onward among ruinous houses and over the twinkling river. At Westland Row Station a crowd of people pressed to the carriage doors; but the porters moved them back, saying that it was a special train for the bazaar. I remained alone in the bare carriage. In a few minutes the train drew up beside an improvised wooden platform. I passed out on to the road and saw by the lighted dial of a clock that it was ten minutes to ten. In front of me was a large building which displayed the magical name.

I could not find any sixpenny entrance and, fearing that the bazaar would be closed, I passed in quickly through a turnstile, handing a shilling to a weary-looking man. I found myself in a big hall girdled at half its height by a gallery. Nearly all the stalls were closed and the greater part of the hall was in darkness. I recognised a silence like that which pervades a church after a service. I walked into the centre of the bazaar timidly. A few people were gathered about the stalls which were still open. Before a curtain, over which the words *Café Chantant* were written in coloured lamps, two men were counting money on a salver. I listened to the fall of the coins.

Remembering with difficulty why I had come I went over to one of the stalls and examined porcelain vases and flowered tea-sets. At the door of the stall a young lady was talking and laughing with two young gentlemen. I remarked their English accents and listened vaguely to their conversation.

"O, I never said such a thing!"

"O, but you did!"

"O, but I didn't!"

"Didn't she say that?"

"Yes. I heard her."

"O, there's a... fib[15]!"

Observing me, the young lady came over and asked me did I wish to buy anything. The tone of her voice was not encouraging; she seemed to have spoken to me out of a sense of duty. I looked humbly at the great jars that stood like eastern guards at either side of the dark entrance to the stall and murmured:

"No, thank you."

The young lady changed the position of one of the vases and went back to the two young men. They began to talk of the same subject. Once or twice the young lady glanced at me over her shoulder.

I lingered before her stall, though I knew my stay was useless, to make my interest in her wares seem the more real. Then I turned away slowly and walked down the middle of the bazaar. I allowed the two pennies to fall against the sixpence in my pocket. I heard a voice call from one end of the gallery that the light was out. The upper part of the hall was now completely dark.

Gazing up into the darkness I saw myself as a creature driven and derided by vanity; and my eyes burned with anguish and anger.

Notes

1. imperturbable: (*formal*) calm; not easily upset or worried by a difficult situation
2. *The Abbot* (1820) is a historical novel by Sir Walter Scott. A sequel to *The Monastery*, it is one of Scott's *Tales from Benedictine Sources* and is set in the time of Mary, Queen of Scots. The story follows the fortunes of certain characters Scott introduced in *The Monastery*, but it also introduces new characters such as Roland Graeme.
3. Walter Scott: Sir Walter Scott, 1st Baronet (1771—1832), a Scottish historical novelist, playwright, and poet, whose death marked the end of Romanticism.
4. *The Devout Communicant*: an 18th century Franciscan book by Pacificus Baker, a noted Catholic spiritual writer of the 18th century
5. *The Memoirs of Vidocq*: memoirs of Francois Eugene Vidocq (1775—1857), a French criminal and

criminalist and also known as an inspiration to great writers such as Honore de Balzac, Victor Hugo and Edgar Allen Poe.

6. gauntlet: a former punishment, chiefly military, in which the offender was made to run between two rows of men who struck at him with switches or weapons as he passed. "Run the gaunlet" refers to suffer severe criticism or tribulation.
7. litanies: a series of prayers to God for use in church services, spoken by a priest, etc., with set responses by the people. Here it refers to the repeated monotonous cries of the shop-boys.
8. The street singers earned their living by singing timely songs that usually began, "Come all your gallant Irishmen/ And listen to my song." Their subject is O'Donovan Ross whose full name is Jeremiah O'Donovan Rossa (1831—1915), a popular hero jailed by the British for advocating violent rebellion.
9. chalice: a large gold or silver cup, used especially to hold wine in the Christian religious services of Holy Communion
10. a retreat... in her convent: a week devoted to religious observances more intense than usual, at the convent school Miss Mangan attends.
11. Freemason: a man belonging to a large secret society whose members promise to help each other and use a system of secret signs in order to recognize each other
12. this night of our Lord: this Saturday evening
13. *The Arab's Farewell to His Steed*: a poem by Caroline Norton (1808—1877) which shows the love of man for his faithful horse. Here, the uncle mentioned this poem is due to the reason that he had misheard Araby for Arab.
14. florin: an old British coin that was worth two shillings
15. fib: (*informal*) a small, unimportant lie

Questions

1. From what point of view is the story told? What is the relation between the narrator and the boy? Are they exactly the same person? Is the chosen point of view an effective one?
2. What is the nature of the boy's sudden realization? How does Joyce prepare the readers for this moment of illumination?
3. How is the theme of "innocence and experience" conveyed in the story?
4. How are the opening description of the street and the description of the bazaar in the end related to the narrator?

Chapter Four   Human Race and Natural World

The development of human history has witnessed the inseparable relationship between human race and the natural world. Though there are some distinctions between man and nature, human instincts and natural laws are interrelated. Human behaviours can change the natural world, and the natural world can exert its power over human race.

The exploration of the relationship between man and nature runs through British literature. In medieval British literature, the relationship between man and nature shown in literary works was in a contradictory state. On the one hand, human race was curious about the magic nature; on the other hand, human race represented by the warriors in *Beowulf*, the national epic of English people, had to struggle against the evil forces of the natural world, which remained mysterious and unknown to them and was a great threat to the development of human civilization.

As time moved to Renaissance, nature became the embodiment of humanism, the ideal of Renaissance. Writers like William Shakespeare and Edmund Spencer began to use natural images in their sonnets and plays to praise the human beauty and human achievements, and advocated the harmony between human race and the natural world.

With the rapid development of capitalism after the Industrial Revolution in the eighteenth and nineteenth century, social conflicts became more and more serious. During this period, romanticism appeared in England as a new trend in literature. And the discussion between human race and the natural world came to a climax in literature. The romantic poets, such as William Wordsworth, Samuel Taylor Coleridge, George Gordon Byron, Percy Bysshe Shelley, and John Keats, had a deep veneration of nature, and drew their poetic inspiration from the natural world, especially the sublime aspect of a natural scene, as Wordswoth once said in the *Preface* to the *Lyrical Ballads* that the poet should describe in his poems "the primary law of our nature". The romantic poets read in nature some mysterious power. In their poems, such as Wordsworth's *The Solitary Reaper* and *The Daffodils*, Shelley's *Ode to the West Wind* and Keats's *To Autumn* and *On the Grasshopper and Crickets*, they regarded nature as the embodiment of Divine Spirit, used nature as the outlet of their dissatisfaction towards social injustice, turned nature into the revolutionary passion to fight against the corrupted government, and took nature as the fairyland of hope and dream. Under the strong influence of romantic poetry, there also appeared a group of romantic novelists, represented by Sir Walter Scott and Robert Louis Stevenson, who took nature as a medium to express their concern on human race.

Under the influence of two World Wars, more and more modern British writers turned their attention to rethink the relationship between human race and the natural world in their literary works. Some works examined the rapid urbanization and the degradation of the living environment, such as *The Country and the City* by Raymond Williams; some reflected the sordid aspects of modern city life or the decay of human culture after the war through natural symbols or images, such as The *Waste Land* by T. S. Eliot; and some satirized and criticized the corrupted and brutal material civilization through the description of the twisted relationship between man and nature, such as *The Lord of Flies* by William Golding.

And in today's world, the scientific development and productivity improvement accelerate the development of human civilization, but at the same time they bring severer problems like environmental pollution and ecological disruption. Thus, the discussion between man and nature becomes a hot subject of contemporary British literature and will be an eternal theme of world literature.

William Wordsworth
1770—1850

William Wordsworth

William Wordsworth, a great Romantic poet in English literature, was born in Cockermouth, West Cumberland, and grew up in the picturesque Lake District. The beautiful landscape of the Lake District not only stirred his poetic imagination, but also gave him a strong love for nature. Wordsworth lost his mother when he was only eight years old, and five years later, his lawyer father died. After that his beloved sister Dorothy became his lifelong companion.

With the help of his relatives, Wordsworth entered a school at Hawkshead and later continued his study at Cambridge from 1787 to 1791. Influenced by the Great French Revolution, and greatly impressed by its slogans of "liberty, equality, and fraternity", Wordsworth took a walking tour through revolutionary France during the summer vocation in 1790. In 1791, he went to France again, and stayed there a year to experience the revolutionary upsurge. But under the pressure of his relatives across the channel to call him back to England and with the establishment of the Jacobin dictatorship, his revolutionary enthusiasm died down and gave place to political conservatism.

In 1795, Wordsworth received a legacy and decided to settle down in his native Lake District with his sister Dorothy, where he met Samuel Taylor Coleridge (1772—1834), who became his best friend thereupon. In 1798, Wordsworth and Coleridge published their *Lyrical Ballads*, which marks the break with the conventional poetical tradition of the eighteenth century classicism and the beginning of the Romantic revival in English poetry. In the *Preface* to *Lyrical Ballads*, Wordsworth set forth his principles of poetry. He said, "All good poetry is the spontaneous overflow of powerful feelings." And the language used in poetry should be "near to the language of men". *The Preface* is regarded as the declaration of English Romanticism.

As a "worshipper of nature", Wordsworth is celebrated for his poems of nature. To him, nature is the embodiment of the Divine Spirit, a source of consolation and joy, and a great moral teacher. His deep love for nature runs through many of his lyrical poems as "Lines Written in Early Spring", "The Daffodils", "Lines Composed a Few Miles above Tintern Abbey", "To the Cuckoos" and "To a Skylark". In these poems he sings of the natural beauty of lakes, mountains, animals and the pastoral tranquility, and eulogizes the harmony between things in nature and the harmony between man and nature. Besides nature, Wordsworth also wrote many poems as "The Solitary Reaper", "We Are Seven", "The Ruined Cottage" and "Lucy" to draw pathetic pictures of the poor labouring people and reveal the harmony between humanity and natural world. In 1843, after the death of Robert Southey (1774—1843), another famous Romantic poet, Wordsworth was made Poet Laureate.

The Solitary Reaper[1]

Behold her, single in the field,
Yon[2] solitary Highland[3] Lass[4]!
Reaping and singing by herself;
Stop here, or gently pass!
Alone she cuts and binds the grain,
And sings a melancholy strain;
O listen! for the vale profound
Is overflowing with the sound.

No nightingale did ever chaunt[5]
More welcome notes to weary bands
Of travellers in some shady haunt,
Among Arabian sands[6]:
A voice so thrilling ne'er was heard
In spring-time from the cuckoo-bird,
Breaking the silence of the seas
Among the farthest Hebrides[7].

Will no one tell me what she sings?
Perhaps the plaintive numbers[8] flow
For old, unhappy, far-off things,
And battles long ago;
Or is it some more humble lay[9],
Familiar matter of to-day?
Some natural sorrow, loss, or pain,
That has been, and may be again?

Whate'er[10] the theme, the Maiden sang
As if her song could have no ending;
I saw her singing at work,
And o'er[11] the sickle bending;—
I listened, motionless and still;
And, as I mounted up the hill,
The music in my heart I bore,
Long after it was heard no more.

Notes

1. The poem is one of Wordsworth's most famous lyrics. It comprises four eight-lined stanzas in

iambic tetrameter and the rhyme scheme of each stanza is ababccdd.
2. Yon: Yonder, over there
3. Highland: Here referring to the mountainous area of Scotland.
4. Lass: (Scottish) a young girl
5. chaunt: old form of "chant"
6. Arabian sands: Arabian desert
7. Hebrides: an archipelago off the western coast of Scotland
8. plaintive numbers: a mournful song
9. lay: a short narrative poem meant to sung
10. Whate'er: Whatever
11. o'er: over

Questions

1. Who is talking in the poem? What does he see and hear?
2. In the second stanza, why does the speaker compare the song of the reaper with that of the cuckoo bird and nightingale?
3. In the first and third stanzas, the poet uses the present tense to describe the Highland Lass' singing, but in the last stanza he changes it into the past tense. Why?
4. What is the theme of the poem?

The Daffodils[1]

I wander'd lonely as a cloud
That floats on high o'er vales and hills,
When all at once I saw a crowd,
A host, of[2] golden daffodils;
Beside the lake, beneath the trees,
Fluttering and dancing in the breeze.

Continuous as the stars that shine
And twinkle on the Milky way,
They stretch'd in never-ending line
Along the margin of a bay:
Ten thousand saw I at a glance[3],
Tossing their heads in sprightly[4] dance.

The waves beside them danced, but they
Out-did the sparkling waves in glee[5]:
A poet could not but be gay
In such a jocund[6] company!

I gaze—and gazed—but little thought
What wealth[7] the show to me had brought:

For oft[8], when on my couch I lie
In vacant[9] or in pensive[10] mood,
They flash upon that inward eye[11]
Which is the bliss of solitude;
And then my heart with pleasure fills,
And dances with the daffodils.

Notes

1. The poem "Daffodils", also known by the title "I Wandered Lonely as a Cloud", is one of the most popular poems of the Romantic Age. According to a poll taken in 1995 by BBC Radio 4 Bookworm program, this poem ranked fifth in the nation's favorite poems.
2. a crowd/A host, of: a great number of
3. Ten thousand saw I at a glance: I saw ten thousand at a glance. The poet uses inversion here.
4. sprightly: lovely
5. but they / Out-did the sparkling waves in glee: the joyful dancing of daffodils is superior to the beautiful dancing of waves. "They" here refers to the daffodils.
6. jocund: cheerful
7. wealth: spiritual wealth
8. oft: often
9. vacant: empty, void of thought
10. pensive: contemplative, thoughtful
11. inward eye: the mind's eye

Questions

1. What major rhetorical devices are used by the poet? How does the poet use these rhetorical devices to achieve the unity of man and nature?
2. Recast the poem into prose.

Percy Bysshe Shelley
1792—1822

Percy Bysshe Shelley was born in Field Place, near Horsham, Sussex on 4 August, 1792. His ancestors had been Sussex aristocrats since early in the 17th century. His father, Sir Timothy was a

Percy Bysshe Shelley

conservative and narrow-minded country squire. Though Shelley was gentle and kind by nature, he had a brave and rebellious heart, and was an alien in his own family. Active, mischievous, and highly imaginative as a child, he was conventionally educated at Syon House Academy, Eton, and University College, Oxford. In his school-days, his rebellious spirit became stronger. At Eton, he was known as "Mad Shelley" for his opposition to the brutal fagging system at school, by which the younger students were required to serve for the students in high classes. And during the time in Oxford, he wrote and published a pamphlet called *The Necessity of Atheism* (1811), in which he said that religion was just an instrument of oppression. Because of his rebellious character, he was expelled from Oxford and disowned by his father.

Four months after being expelled, the 19-year-old Shelley eloped with 16-year-old Harriet Westbrook, his sister's friend, and got married with her. Later, they moved to Lake District of England to study and write. However, the marriage proved to be a failure and they got divorced. In 1814, he met William Godwin, a novelist and an atheist. Shelley was deeply attracted by his radical philosophy, and he also fell in love with his gifted daughter Mary Godwin, but their love affair was opposed by Godwin, and these two social rebels eloped to Europe. Later they returned to England and got married. They lived a happy life after marriage, but it was broken by the suicide of Harriet. Shelley's political enemies took the chance to attack him, and he was socially ostracized and suffered from poverty. Then in 1818, Shelley left England with Mary and spent the rest of his life in Italy with his friend George Gordon Byron (1788—1824). On 8 July, 1822, Shelley was drowned while sailing in a small boat along the coast of Italy. Byron buried his body and his ashes were buried in Rome.

Shelley is considered by many critics to be among the greatest of English Romantic poets. His poems are filled with his hatred toward injustice, cruelty, authority, religion, tyranny, war and exploitation, at the same time run over with his love for freedom and optimistic idealism. His social and political ideas are mainly reflected in his poems as *Queen Mab* (1813), his first long serious poem, *The Revolt of Islam* (1818), *England in 1819* (1819), *The Masque of Anarchy* (1819), *Song to the Men of England* (1819) and his verse dramas as *Prometheus Unbound* (1820) and *Cenci* (1819). Shelley is also called the "most wonderful lyric poet England has ever produced". His lyrics are full of passion, imagination, and symbolic meaning. To him, human spirit is interlinked with the natural world, and nature exists as an unseen Life of Universe, so in his lyrics, nature is endowed with life, and he merges himself with it to express his attitudes toward life and society. The famous *Ode to the West Wind* (1819) is a typical example.

Ode to the West Wind

I

O wild West Wind[1], thou breath of Autumn's being[2];

Thou, from whose unseen presence the leaves dead
Are driven, like ghosts from an enchanter fleeing,

Yellow, and black, and pale, and hectic red[3],
Pestilence-stricken multitudes[4]: O thou,
Who chariotest[5] to their dark wintry bed

The winged seeds, where they lie cold and low[6],
Each like a corpse within its grave, until
Thine azure sister of the Spring shall blow[7]

Her clarion o'er the dreaming earth, and fill
(Driving sweet buds like flocks to feed in air[8])
With living hues and odours plain and hill:

Wild Spirit, which art moving everywhere;
Destroyer and Preserver; hear, oh, hear!

II

Thou on whose stream[9], 'mid[10] the steep sky's commotion,
Loose clouds like earth's decaying leaves are shed,
Shook from the tangled boughs of Heaven and Ocean,

Angels of rain and lightning[11]: there are spread
On the blue surface of thine aery surge,
Like the bright hair uplifted from the head

Of some fierce Maenad[12], even from the dim verge
Of the horizon to the zenith's height,
The locks[13] of the approaching storm. Thou dirge

Of the dying year, to which this closing night
Will be the dome of a vast sepulchre,
Vaulted with all thy congregated might

Of vapours, from whose solid atmosphere
Black rain, and fire, and hail will burst: oh, hear!

III

Thou who didst waken from his summer dreams

The blue Mediterranean, where he lay,
Lulled by the coil of his crystalline streams,

Beside a Pumice Isle[14] in Baiae's[15] bay,
And saw in sleep old palaces and towers
Quivering within the wave's intenser day,

All overgrown with azure moss and flowers
So sweet, the sense faints picturing them! Thou
For whose path the Atlantic's level powers[16]

Cleave themselves into chasms, while far below
The sea-blooms and the oozy woods which wear
The sapless foliage of the ocean, know

Thy voice, and suddenly grow gray with fear,
And tremble and despoil themselves[17]: oh, hear!

IV

If I were a dead leaf thou mightest bear;
If I were a swift cloud to fly with thee;
A wave to pant beneath thy power, and share

The impulse of thy strength, only less free
Than thou, O uncontrollable! If even
I were as in my boyhood, and could be

The comrade of thy wanderings over Heaven,
As then, when to outstrip thy skiey speed
Scarce[18] seemed a vision; I would ne'er have striven

As thus with thee in prayer in my sore need[19].
Oh, lift me as a wave, a leaf, a cloud!
I fall upon the thorns of life! I bleed!

A heavy weight of hours has chained and bowed
One too like thee: tameless, and swift, and proud.

V

Make me thy lyre, even as the forest is:
What if my leaves are falling like its own[20]!

The tumult of thy mighty harmonies

Will take from both a deep, autumnal tone,
Sweet though in sadness. Be thou, Spirit fierce,
My spirit! Be thou me, impetuous one!

Drive my dead thoughts over the universe
Like withered leaves to quicken a new birth!
And, by the incantation of this verse,

Scatter, is from an unextinguished hearth
Ashes and sparks, my words among mankind!
Be through my lips to unawakened earth

The trumpet of a prophecy! O, Wind[21],
If Winter comes, can Spring be far behind?

Notes

1. O wild West Wind: pay attention to the grammatical structure of the whole stanza. It is an invocation to the west wind.
2. Autumn's being: Autumn's life
3. hectic red: morbidly red caused by hectic fever
4. Pestilence-stricken multitudes: referring to the dead leaves. The leaves are like human beings hit by epidemic disease.
5. chariotest: carry
6. lie cold and low: The seeds are compared to the dead bodies in the grave.
7. Thine azure sister of the Spring shall blow: The west wind that will blow in the spring.
8. Driving sweet buds like flocks to feed in air: as if the new seeds being shepherded to pastures after winter
9. stream: flow of the wind
10. 'mid: amid
11. Angels of rain and lightning: "Angels" refer to the loose clouds.
12. Maenad: a frenzied priestess to Bacchus, the god of wine and vegetation in Greek mythology
13. locks: the hair of the head, here referring to the loose clouds
14. Pumice Isle: the name of an isle near Naples
15. Baiae: an ancient city and a famous resort near Naples where Roman emperors built luxurious palaces
16. the Atlantic's level powers: the Atlantic's surging waves
17. And tremble and despoil themselves: Shelley's notes: "The phenomenon alluded to at the conclusion of the third stanza is well known to naturalists. The vegetation at the bottom of the sea, of rivers,

and of lakes, sympathizes with that of the land in the change of seasons, and is consequently influenced by the winds which announce it." "despoil themselves" means "to deprive themselves of their own foliage by force".

18. Scarce: Here means scarcely.
19. in my sore need: in my painful need
20. What if my leaves are falling like its own: What does it matter if I feel depressed? "its" here refers to the "forest's".
21. Wind: Here it is pronounced [waind] to rhyme with "mankind" and "behind".

Questions

1. Where is the West Wind in each of the first three stanzas? And what is the West Wind doing?
2. What does the poet want to express in the last two stanzas?
3. What major stylistic devices are used in the poem?
4. The West Wind in the poem is generally considered as a symbol. What does it symbolize?

John Keats
1795—1821

John Keats

Along with Byron and Shelley, John Keats was one of the main figures of the second generation of English Romantic poets. But unlike Byron and Shelley, Keats was born in a poor family in London on October 31, 1795. His father was a hostler and stable keeper, and married his employer's daughter. His parents were unable to afford some celebrated schools, so in the summer of 1803 he was sent to board at John Clarke's school in Enfield, close to his grandparents' house. The small school had a liberal outlook and a progressive curriculum more modern than the larger, more prestigious schools. In the family atmosphere at Clarke's, Keats developed an interest in classics and history, which would stay with him throughout his short life. The headmaster's son, Charles Cowden Clarke, also became an important mentor and friend, introducing Keats to Renaissance literature. When Keats was eight years old his father died, and his mother re-married a few months later. In March of 1810, when Keats was 14, his mother died of tuberculosis, leaving him in the custody of his grandmother, who appointed a guardian to take care of him. That autumn, his guardian forced him to leave Clarke's school and bound him to apprentice to a surgeon. For five years Keats lodged in the attic above the surgery and served his apprenticeship, and then worked as a surgeon's helper in the hospital in London for two more years. Cowden Clarke, who remained a close friend of Keats, described this period as "the most placid time in Keats's life".

Disliking his work, Keats decided to abandon his profession in 1817 and devote himself entirely to poetic writing.

With the help of Shelley, Keats published his first collection of poems in 1817. In 1818, he published his long allegorical poem *Endymion*, "inscribed to the memory of Thomas Chatterton", the young forerunner of the Romantic Movement. The two collections were severely attacked by conservative magazines. In June of 1818, Keats left London and started on a walking tour of Scotland, Ireland, and the Lake District with his friend Charles Armitage Brown. During his travels he became acquainted with the life of small towns and villages and witnessed the poverty and privations of the people. By the end of July, he found it necessary to leave his companion and take a ship back to London because of his poor health. There Keats worked harder instead of putting down his pen. In 1821, Keats was invited by Shelley to Italy for the medical treatment, but his health was in such a hopeless state that shortly after his arrival in Rome he died of consumption there. His grave in Rome bears the epigraph: "Here lies one whose name is writ on water."

Keats is an outstanding Romantic poet. He wrote a large number of magnificent poems in his short life. Of his poems the best known are *Isabella* (1819), *The Eve of St. Agnes* (1820), *On the Grasshopper and Cricket* (1816), *Ode to a Nightingale, To Autumn,* and *Ode on a Grecian Urn.* (These Odes were written in 1819 and published in 1820.) His poems reveal the innovation in form, poetic style, and contents. Keats is also a great singer of beauty. He believed "Beauty is truth, truth beauty". The artistic aim of his poetry is to create a beautiful world of imagination as opposed to the sordid reality under capitalism. He found beauty in Greek mythology, in nature, in art, in literature, especially poetry, and in human struggle for liberty.

On the Grasshopper and Cricket

The poetry of earth[1] is never dead:
    When all the birds are faint with the hot sun,
    And hide in cooling trees, a voice[2] will run
From hedge to hedge about the new-mown mead[3];
That is the Grasshopper's—he takes the lead
    In summer luxury[4],—he has never done
    With his delights[5]; for when tired out with fun
He rests at ease beneath some pleasant weed.
The poetry of earth is ceasing never:
    On a lone winter evening, when the frost
        Has wrought[6] a silence, from the stove there shrills
The Cricket's song, in warmth increasing ever,
    And seems to one in drowsiness half lost[7],
        The Grasshopper's among some grassy hills.

Notes

1. The poetry of earth: The music of nature
2. a voice: referring to the sound produced by the vibrations of the wings of the grasshopper
3. the new-mown mead: the new-cut meadow
4. he takes the lead / In summer luxury: his music plays the leading role in the ease and pleasure that summer offers
5. he has never done / With his delights: he has never finished his music with his delight
6. wrought: made or done
7. to one in drowsiness half lost: to one who is half-asleep

Questions

1. What do you think is the theme of the poem?
2. Why does the poet single out the grasshopper and cricket instead of other animals to represent the poetry of earth?
3. Translate the poem into Chinese.

Ode to Autumn[1]

I[2]

Season of mists and mellow fruitfulness,
Close bosom-friend of the maturing sun[3];
Conspiring with him how to load and bless
With fruit the vines that round the thatch-eves[4] run;
To bend with apples the moss'd cottage-trees,
And fill all fruit with ripeness to the core;
To swell the gourd, and plump the hazel shells
With a sweet kernel; to set budding more,
And still more, later flowers for the bees,
Until they think warm days will never cease,
For Summer has o'er-brimm'd their clammy cells.

II

Who hath not seen thee[5] oft amid thy store?
Sometimes whoever seeks abroad[6] may find
Thee sitting careless[7] on a granary floor,
Thy hair soft-lifted by the winnowing wind;
Or on a half-reap'd furrow sound asleep,
Drows'd[8] with the fume of poppies, while thy hook

Spares the next swath and all its twined flowers.
And sometimes like a gleaner thou dost keep
Steady thy laden head across a brook;
Or by a cyder-press, with patient look,
Thou watchest the last oozings hours by hours.

III

Where are the songs of Spring? Ay, where are they?
Think not of them, thou hast thy music too, —
While barred clouds⁹ bloom the soft-dying day,
And touch the stubble-plains with rosy hue;
Then in a wailful choir the small gnats mourn
Among the river sallows¹⁰, borne aloft
Or sinking as the light wind lives or dies;
And full-grown lambs loud bleat from hilly bourn¹¹;
Hedge-crickets sing; and now with treble soft
The red-breast whistles from a garden-croft;
And gathering swallows twitter in the skies.

Notes

1. In a letter written to his friend J.H. Reynolds from Winchester, in September, 1819, Keats says, "How beautiful the season is now—How fine the air.... I never liked stubble-fields so much as now—Aye better than the chilly green of the spring. Somehow, a stubble-field looks warm—in the same way that some pictures look warm. This struck me so much in my Sunday's walk that I composed upon it." Enclosed in the letter was "Ode to Autumn".
2. Notice the grammatical structure of the first stanza. It has only one sentence. Syntactically it is a sentence with a subject but without a predicate.
3. the maturing sun: the sun that matures the fruit
4. eves: eaves
5. thee: Here autumn is personified as a farm labourer.
6. whoever seeks abroad: no matter who goes out to the open field
7. careless: Here means carefree.
8. Drows'd: fallen in half sleep
9. barred clouds: clouds in the shape of bars
10. sallow: willow
11. bourn: a boundary between fields

Questions

1. What is the structure merit of this poem? What specific aspect is described in each of the three stanzas?

2. What is the theme of the poem?
3. Discuss the rhetorical devices used in the poem.

Robert Louis Stevenson
1850—1894

Robert Louis Stevenson

Robert Louis Stevenson, a novelist, poet, short-story writer and essayist, was born in Edinburgh, Scotland. His father was a leading lighthouse engineer. A sickly boy in his childhood, Stevenson could not receive very regular education. At the age of 7, he entered Mr. Henderson's school, but because of his poor health he stayed there only a few weeks and did not return until two years later. Fortunately, Alison Cunningham, his nurse, cared for him tenderly in illness, reading to him from Bunyan and the *Bible* as he lay sick in bed and telling tales, which made him interested in literature. Stevenson recalled this time of sickness in "The Land of Counterpane" in *A Child's Garden of Verses* (1885), one of the best known and most beloved collections of children's poetry in the English language, and dedicated the book to his nurse.

In November 1867, Stevenson entered the Edinburgh University to study engineering for his family business, but he showed little enthusiasm for his studies and devoted much energy to avoiding lectures. Finally he abandoned the study of engineering for law, and determined to be a writer. In 1873, Stevenson's health failed. He suffered from a chronic bronchial condition and frequent hemorrhages and had to spend much of his time travelling in search of health. During his stay in France, he met a married woman Mrs. Fanny Osbourne, ten years his senior, and fell in love with her. They got married in May 1880, although, as he said, he was "a mere complication of cough and bones, much fitter for an emblem of mortality than a bridegroom". Stevenson spent his last years with his wife on an island in Samoa in the South Pacific. On 3 December 1894, Stevenson was talking to his wife and straining to open a bottle of wine when he suddenly exclaimed, "What's that!" asking his wife "Does my face look strange?" and collapsed. He died within a few hours, probably of a cerebral hemorrhage. At that time he was forty-four years old.

Stevenson was a literary celebrity during his lifetime, a famous representative of New Romanticism in the late nineteenth century. During the early period of his writing career, he wrote many essays and travel pieces, as *An Inland Voyage* (1878), *Travel with a Donkey in the Cevennes* (1879), and *Familiar Studies of Men and Books* (1882). His later works are mainly fictions and short stories. *Treasure Island* (1883), a tale of piracy, buried treasure, and adventure, is his first major success. *The Strange Case of Dr. Jekyll and Mr Hyde* (1886) is a famous novella about a dual personality much depicted in plays and films. It is also influential in the growth of understanding of the subconscious mind through its treatment of a kind and intelligent physician who turns into a psychopathic monster after imbibing a drug intended to separate good from evil in a personality. *Kidnapped* (1886) is a historical novel that tells of the boy David Balfour's pursuit of his inheritance and his alliance with Alan Breck in the intrigues of Jacobite troubles in Scotland. In these works, Stevenson shows his new romantic spirit: he does not depict the reality of his time, avoids making comments on the morality and ethics of his contemporaries, but just tries to show his dissatisfaction towards the society through nature and adventure.

The essay "A Night among the Pines" is taken from *Travels with a Donkey in the Cevennes*, a pioneering classic of outdoor literature. The book recounts Stevenson's 12-day, 120-mile solo hiking journey through the sparsely populated and impoverished areas of the Cevennes mountains in south-central France in 1878. The character of Modestine, a stubborn, manipulative donkey he could never quite get the better of, is memorable.

A Night among the Pines

From Bleymard[1] after dinner, although it was already late, I set out to scale[2] a portion of the Lozere[3]. An ill-marked stony drove-road guided me forward; and I met nearly half-a-dozen bullock-carts descending from the woods, each laden with a whole pine-tree for the winter's firing. At the top of the woods, which do not climb very high upon this cold ridge, I struck leftward by a path among the pines, until I hit on a dell of green turf, where a streamlet made a little spout over some stones to serve me for a water-tap. "In a more sacred or sequestered bower... nor nymph nor faunus haunted."[4] The trees were not old, but they grew thickly round the glade[5]: there was no outlook, except north-eastward upon distant hill-tops, or straight upward to the sky; and the encampment felt secure and private like a room. By the time I had made my arrangements and fed Modestine[6], the day was already beginning to decline. I buckled myself to the knees into my sack[7] and made a hearty meal; and as soon as the sun went down, I pulled my cap over my eyes and fell asleep.

Night is a dead monotonous period under a roof; but in the open world it passes lightly, with its stars and dews and perfumes, and the hours are marked by changes in the face of Nature. What seems a kind of temporal death to people choked between walls and curtains, is only a light and living slumber[8] to the man who sleeps afield[9]. All night long he can hear Nature breathing deeply and freely; even as she takes her rest, she turns and smiles; and there is one stirring hour[10] unknown to those who dwell in houses, when a wakeful influence goes abroad over the sleeping hemisphere[11], and all the outdoor world are on their feet[12]. It is then that the cock first crows, not this time to announce the dawn, but like a cheerful watchman speeding the course of night. Cattle awake on the meadows; sheep break their fast[13] on dewy hillsides, and change to a new lair[14] among the ferns; and houseless men, who have lain down with the fowls, open their dim eyes and behold the beauty of the night.

At what inaudible summons, at what gentle touch of Nature, are all these sleepers thus recalled in the same hour to life? Do the stars rain down an influence, or do we share some thrill of mother earth below our resting bodies? Even shepherds and old country-folk, who are the deepest read in these arcana, have not a guess as to the means or purpose of this nightly resurrection. Towards two in the

Stevenson's Tomb

morning they declare the thing takes place; and neither know nor inquire further. And at least it is a pleasant incident. We are disturbed in our slumber only, like the luxurious Montaigne[15], "that we may the better and more sensibly relish it." We have a moment to look upon the stars. And there is a special pleasure for some minds in the reflection that we share the impulse with all outdoor creatures in our neighbourhood, that we have escaped out of the Bastille of civilisation[16], and are become, for the time being, a mere kindly animal and a sheep of Nature's flock.

When that hour came to me among the pines, I wakened thirsty. My tin was standing by me half full of water. I emptied it at a draught; and feeling broad awake after this internal cold aspersion, sat upright to make a cigarette. The stars were clear, coloured, and jewel-like, but not frosty. A faint silvery vapour stood for the Milky Way. All around me the black fir-points stood upright and stock-still. By the whiteness of the pack-saddle, I could see Modestine walking round and round at the length of her tether; I could hear her steadily munching at the sward; but there was not another sound, save the indescribable quiet talk of the runnel over the stones. I lay lazily smoking and studying the colour of the sky, as we call the void of space, from where it showed a reddish grey behind the pines to where it showed a glossy blue-black between the stars. As if to be more like a pedlar[17], I wear a silver ring. This I could see faintly shining as I raised or lowered the cigarette; and at each whiff the inside of my hand was illuminated, and became for a second the highest light in the landscape.

A faint wind, more like a moving coolness than a stream of air, passed down the glade from time to time; so that even in my great chamber the air was being renewed all night long. I thought with horror of the inn at Chasserades and the congregated nightcaps; with horror of the nocturnal[18] prowesses[19] of clerks and students, of hot theatres and pass-keys and close rooms. I have not often enjoyed a more serene possession of myself, nor felt more independent of material aids. The outer world, from which we cower into our houses, seemed after all a gentle habitable place; and night after night a man's bed, it seemed, was laid and waiting for him in the fields, where God keeps an open house. I thought I had rediscovered one of those truths which are revealed to savages and hid from political economists: at the least, I had discovered a new pleasure for myself. And yet even while I was exulting in my solitude I became aware of a strange lack. I wished a companion to lie near me in the starlight, silent and not moving, but ever within touch. For there is a fellowship more quiet even than solitude, and which, rightly understood, is solitude made perfect. And to live out of doors with the woman a man loves is of all lives the most complete and free.

As I thus lay, between content and longing, a faint noise stole towards me through the pines. I thought, at first, it was the crowing of cocks or the barking of dogs at some very distant farm; but steadily and gradually it took articulate shape in my ears[20], until I became aware that a passenger was going by upon the high-road in the valley, and singing loudly as he went. There was more of good-will than grace in his performance; but he trolled with ample lungs; and the sound of his voice took hold upon the hillside and set the air shaking in the leafy glens. I have heard people passing by night in sleeping cities; some of them sang; one, I remember, played loudly on the bagpipes[21]. I have heard the rattle of a cart or carriage spring up suddenly after hours of stillness, and pass, for some minutes, within the range of my hearing as I lay abed. There is a romance about all who are abroad in the black hours, and with something of a thrill we try to guess their business. But here the romance was double: first, this glad passenger, lit internally with wine, who sent up his voice in music through the night; and then I, on the other hand, buckled into my sack, and smoking alone in the pine-woods between four and five thousand feet towards the stars.

When I awoke again (Sunday, 29th September), many of the stars had disappeared; only the stronger companions of the night still burned visibly overhead; and away towards the east I saw a faint haze of light upon the horizon, such as had been the Milky Way when I was last awake. Day was at hand. I lit my lantern, and by its glow-worm light put on my boots and gaiters; then I broke up some bread for Modestine, filled my can at the water-tap, and lit my spirit-lamp[22] to boil myself some chocolate. The blue darkness lay long in the glade where I had so sweetly slumbered; but soon there was a broad streak of orange melting into gold along the mountain-tops of Vivarais[23]. A solemn glee possessed my mind at this gradual and lovely coming in of day. I heard the runnel with delight; I looked round me for something beautiful and unexpected; but the still black pine-trees, the hollow glade, the munching ass, remained unchanged in figure. Nothing had altered but the light, and that, indeed, shed over all a spirit of life and of breathing peace, and moved me to a strange exhilaration.

I drank my water-chocolate, which was hot if it was not rich, and strolled here and there, and up and down about the glade. While I was thus delaying, a gush of steady wind, as long as a heavy sigh, poured direct out of the quarter of the morning. It was cold, and set me sneezing. The trees near at hand tossed their black plumes in its passage; and I could see the thin distant spires of pine along the edge of the hill rock slightly to and fro against the golden east. Ten minutes after, the sunlight spread at a gallop along the hillside, scattering shadows and sparkles, and the day had come completely.

I hastened to prepare my pack, and tackle the steep ascent that lay before me; but I had something on my mind. It was only a fancy; yet a fancy will sometimes be importunate. I had been most hospitably received and punctually served in my green caravanserai. The room was airy, the water excellent, and the dawn had called me to a moment. I say nothing of the tapestries or the inimitable ceiling, nor yet of the view which I commanded from the windows; but I felt I was in some one's debt for all this liberal entertainment. And so it pleased me, in a half-laughing way, to leave pieces of money on the turf as I went along, until I had left enough for my night's lodging. I trust they did not fall to some rich and churlish drover.

Notes

1. Bleymard: Le Bleymard, a town in Lozere province, France
2. scale: climb up
3. Lozere: referring to Lozere Mt. in France, a famous mountain for hiking tour
4. "In a more sacred or sequestered bower... nor nymph nor faunus haunted.": It is taken from "The First Love of Adam and Eve" from John Milton's masterpiece *Paradise Lost*. The original lines are "In shadier bower / More sacred and sequestered, though but feigned / Pan or Sylvanus never slept, nor nymph, / Nor Faunus haunted." Faunus is an ancient Italian deity of pastures and forests, later

identified with the Greek Pan. Stevenson uses these lines to describe the calm and tranquility of the night among the pines.

5. glade: a grassy space without trees in a wood or forest
6. Modestine: the name of Stevenson's donkey
7. sack: referring to the sleep bag
8. slumber: a natural and periodic state of rest during which consciousness of the world is suspended
9. afield: in the open field far away from home or one's usual surroundings
10. stirring hour: exciting moment
11. when a wakeful influence goes abroad over the sleeping hemisphere: when the sleeping earth wakes up
12. all the outdoor world are on their feet: all the living creatures in the open air straighten up
13. break their fast: take their breakfast
14. lair: a place where a wild animal lives
15. Montaigne: Michel Eyquem de Montaigne (1533—1592), one of the most influential writers of the French Renaissance, known for popularizing the essay as a literary genre, and commonly thought of as the father of modern skepticism.
16. the Bastille of civilisation: the Bastille was a fortress built in Paris in the fourteenth century and used as a prison in the seventeenth and eighteenth centuries; it was destroyed July 14, 1789 at the start of the French Revolution. civilisation: civilization.
17. pedlar: peddler, someone who goes from place to place in order to sell something
18. nocturnal: occurring at night
19. prowess: great skill at doing something
20. it took articulate shape in my ears: I could hear the sound very clearly.
21. bagpipe: a musical instrument that is traditionally played in Scotland
22. spirit-lamp: a lamp that burns methylated or other spirits instead of oil
23. Vivarais: the mountain in the south-east of France

Questions

1. Can you summarize the beauty of night that Stevenson experienced among the pines?
2. What are the differences between the night under a roof and the night in Nature according to the author?
3. Why does the author leave pieces of money on the turf when he leaves? What does he want to show through this behaviour?

Chapter Four Human Race and Natural World

Raymond Williams
1921—1988

Raymond Williams, a progressive academic, critic, and novelist, was born in the Welsh border village of Pandy. His father was a railway signalman. He was educated at King Henry VIII Grammar School in Abergavenny. His teenage years were overshadowed by the rise of Nazism and the threat of war. Later, Williams attended Trinity College, Cambridge, but his study was interrupted by World War II. In the winter of 1940, he enlisted in the British army as an anti-tank soldier and attended the fighting from Normandy in 1944 through Belgium and Holland to Germany in 1945. In 1946, he received his M.A. from Cambridge and then served as a tutor in adult education at the University of Oxford for several years.

Raymond Williams

In 1958, Williams published the book *Culture and Society*, exploring how the notion of culture developed in the West, especially Great Britain, from the eighteenth century to twentieth century. The book won him an immediate success for it overturned conventional social and historical thinking about culture. Because of his success, Williams was invited to return to Cambridge in 1961 and became Professor of Drama from 1974 until his retirement in 1983. After the retirement from Cambridge, Williams spent his last years in Saffron Walden, where he continued his writing and made active links with debates in feminism, peace, and ecology social movements.

Raymond Williams is the most influential British Marxist literary and cultural critic after World War II. He is the famous representative of the School of Cultural Studies in Britain and sets out his own approach to cultural studies which he called "cultural materialism" in the book *Marxism and Literature* (1977). Williams joined the Communist Party when he studied at Cambridge, and as an active and committed socialist, he was greatly interested in the relationship between literature and society from an increasingly Marxist point of view. He explored this relationship in his novels as *Border Country* (1960), *Second Generation* (1964), and *The Volunteers* (1978), and also in his critical works as *Reading and Criticism, Man and Society Series* (1950), *The Long Revolution* (1961), *Modern Tragedy* (1966), *The Country and the City* (1973), and *Socialism and Ecology* (1982).

The Country and the City is a highly-acclaimed survey of English literature in terms of changing attitudes towards country and city. By chapters about literature alternating with chapters of social history in the book Williams analyzes the shifting images and associations between the country and the city in English literature since the sixteenth century, and how these images become central symbols for conceptualizing the social and economic changes associated with capitalist development in England. For him, "the contrast of the country and city is one of the major forms in which we become conscious of a central part of our experience and of the crises of our society."

The Country and the City[1]

Chapter One

'Country' and 'city' are very powerful words, and this is not surprising when we remember how much they seem to stand for in the experience of human communities. In English, 'country' is both a nation and a part of a 'land'; 'the country' can be the whole society or its rural area. In the long history of human settlements, this connection between the land from which directly or indirectly we all get our living and the achievements had been the city: the capital, the large town, a distinctive form of civilisation.

On the actual settlements, which in the real history have been astonishingly varied, powerful feelings have gathered and have been generalized. On the country has gathered the idea of a natural way of life: of peace, innocence, and simple virtue. On the city has gathered the idea of an achieved centre: of learning, communication, light. Powerful hostile associations have also developed: on the city as a place of noise, worldliness and ambition; on the country as a place of backwardness, ignorance, limitation. A contrast between country and city, as fundamental ways of life, reaches back into classical times.

Yet the real history, throughout, has been astonishingly varied. The 'country way of life' has included the very different practices of hunters, pastoralists[2], farmers and factory farmers, and its organization has varied from the tribe and the manor[3] to the feudal estate, from the small peasantry and tenant farmers to the rural commune, from the *latifundia*[4] and the plantation to the large capitalist enterprise and the state farm. The city, no less, has been of many kinds: state capital, administrative base, religious centre, market-town, port and mercantile depot, military barracks, industrial concentration. Between the cities of ancient and medieval times and the modern metropolis or conurbation[5] there is connection of name and in part of function, but nothing like identity. Moreover, in our own world, there is a wide range of settlements between the traditional poles of country and city: suburb, dormitory town, shanty town, industrial estate. Even the idea of the village, which seems simple, shows in actual history a wide variation: as to size and character, and internally in its variation between dispersed and nuclear settlements, in Britain as clearly as anywhere.

In and through these differences, all the same, certain images and associations persist; and it is the purpose of this book to describe and analyse them, to see them in relation to the historically varied experience. For practical reasons I take most of my examples English writing, though my interests go much wider. It ought in any case to be clear that the English experience is especially significant, in that one of the decisive transformations, in the relations between country and city, occurred there very early and with a thoroughness which is still in some ways unapproached. The Industrial Revolution[6] not only transformed both city and country; it was based on a highly developed agrarian capitalism, with a very early disappearance of the traditional

Country

peasantry. In the imperialist phase of our history the nature of the rural economy, in the Britain and in its colonies, was again transformed very early: dependence on a domestic agriculture dwindled to very low proportions, with no more than four per cent of economically active men now engaged in farming, and this in a society which had already become the first predominantly urban-dwelling people in the long history of human settlements. Since much of the dominant subsequent development, indeed the very idea of 'development' in the world generally, has been in these decisive directions, the English experience remains exceptionally important: not only symptomatic but in some ways diagnostic; in its intensity still memorable; whatever may succeed. For it is a critical fact that in and through these transforming experiences English attitudes to the country, and to ideas of rural life, persisted with extraordinary power, so that even after the society was predominantly urban its literature, for a generation, was still predominantly rural; and even in the twentieth century, in an urban and industrial land, forms of the older ideas and experience and interpretation of the country and the city a permanent though of course not exclusive importance.

This importance can be stated, and will have to be assessed, as a general problem. But it is as well to say at the outset that this has been for me a personal issue, for as long as I remember. It happened that in a predominantly urban and industrial Britain I was born in a remote village, in a very old settled countryside, on the border between England and Wales. Within twenty miles, indeed at the end of a bus route, was in one direction an old cathedral city, in the other an old frontier market town but only a few miles beyond it the first industrial towns and villages of the great coal and steel area of South Wales. Before I had read any descriptions and interpretations of the changes and variations of settlements and ways of life, I saw them on the ground, and working, in unforgettable clarity. In the course of education I moved to another city, built round a university, and since then, living and travelling and working, I have come to visit, and to need to visit, so many great cities, of different kinds, and to look forward and back, in space and time, knowing and seeking to know this relationship, as an experience and as a problem. I have written about it in other ways but also I have been slowly collecting the evidence to write about it explicitly, as a matter of social, literary and intellectual history.

This book is the result, but through it often and necessarily follows impersonal procedures, in description and analysis, there is behind it, all the time, this personal pressure and commitment. And since the relation of country and city is not only an objective problem and history, but has been and still is for many millions of people a direct and intense preoccupations and experience, I feel no need to justify, though it is as well to mention, this personal cause.

Thus at once, for me, before the argument starts, country life has many meanings. It is the elms, the may[7], the white horse, in the field beyond the window where I am writing. It is the men in the November evening, walking back from pruning, with their hands in the pockets of their khaki coats; and the women in headscarves, outside their cottages, waiting for the blue bus that will take them, inside school hours, to work in the harvest. It is the tractor on the road, leaving its tracks of serrated pressed mud; the light in the small hours, in the pig-farm across the road, in the crisis of a litter; the slow brown van met at the difficult corner, with the crowded sheep jammed to its slatted sides; the heavy smell, on still evenings, of the silage[8] ricks fed with molasses[9]. It is also the sour land, on the thick boulder clay, not far up the road, that is selling for housing, for a speculative development, at twelve thousand pounds an acre.

City

As I said, I was born in a village, and I still live in a village. But where I was born was under the Black Mountains[10], on the Welsh border, where the meadows are bright green against the red earth of the ploughland, and the first trees, beyond the window, are oak and holly. Where I live now is in the flat country, on a headland of boulder clay, towards the edge of the dikes and sluices, the black earth of the Fens, under the high East Anglian skies[11].

That physical contrast is continually present to me, but it is not the only contrast. Within that Black Mountain village, as again here, there is a deep contrast in which so much feeling is held: between what seems an unmediated nature—a physical awareness of trees, birds, the moving of the nature is in fact being produced. Both kinds of hedgerow[12], there on its earthbank, here on the flat or with a lining ditch, together with the oaks and hollies or the elms and thorns that follow their lines, have been seen and planted and tended by men. At the end of the lane by the cottage where I was a child, there is now a straight wide motor road where the lorries race. But the lane also has been set, stoned, driven over: it is a mark on the land of no more than two generations, since a young builder married the daughter of a farmer and was given a corner of a field on which to build their house, and then his workshop with the lane to it, and then neighbouring houses, and then successive workshops converted to new houses; the first workshop was my parents' first home. In the field with the elms and the white horse, behind my own present home, there are faint marks of a ninth-century building, and a foot below the grass there is a cobbled road, that resists the posts being driven, today, for a new wire fence.

This country life then has many meanings: in feeling and activity; in region and in time. The cobbles[13] under the field are older than the university to which the bridletrack[14] leads, five miles under thin thorn hedges, across the open and windy fields, past Starvegoose Wood. The foot of earth over them is a millennium, in one kind of reckoning. But the lane in that Black Mountain village, now so different both from the motor road and from the shaded lane I remember, is recent: about as far back as when my father, at twelve, went to work as a boy on a farm. I have the farmer's reference when he left: the shaky, rounded writing that he was honest and willing; and what he left for was to be a boy porter on the railway: that line of four through the valley, old road, tramroad, new road, railway: the cuttings and embankments moving like foothills; settled and familiar, laid a hundred years ago. When I was born he was a signalman, in the box in the village, with his gardens and his bees, taking procedure to market on a bicycle: a different network, but it was a bicycle he went on, to a market where the farmers came in cars and the dealers in lorries: our own country. He had been as much born to the land as his own father, yet, like him, he could not live by it. That man, Joseph, my grandfather, was a farmworker until middle age, when he lost his job and with it his cottage, and became a roadman: cutting and clearing along a length of the road that led away to the Midlands, to other cities. One uncle lived in London; another in Birmingham; we moved, as a family, on visits and holidays, between country and city, in our own direct relationships. We were a dispersed family, along the road, the railway, and now letters and print. These were the altering communications, the altering connections, between country and city, and between all the intermediate places and communities, the intermediate or temporary jobs and settlements.

So this country life had its meanings, but these changed in themselves and changed in relation to others. In the south-west, at nights, we used to watch the flare, over the black ridge of Brynarw, of the iron furnaces of industrial South Wales. In the east now, at nights, over the field with the elms and the white horse, I watch the glow of Cambridge: a white tinged with orange; and in the autumn, here, the stubble fields are burned, sometimes catching the thorn hedges, and when I saw this first at night I took it as strange accidental fire. My own network, from where I sit writing at the window, is to Cambridge and London, and beyond them to the postmark places, the unfamiliar stamps and the distant cities: Rome, Moscow, New York.

The lights of the city. I go out in the dark, before bed, and look at that glow in the sky: a look at the city while remembering Hardy's Jude[15], who stood and looked at the distant, attainable and unattainable. Christminster[16]. Or I remember Wordswoth coming from high country to London, and saying from Westminster Bridge:

> Earth has not anything to show more fair:
> Dull would he be of soul who could pass by
> A sight so touching in its majesty:
> This City now doth, like a garment, wear
> The beauty of the morning; silent, bare,
> Ships, towers, domes, theatres, and temples lie
> Open unto the fields, and to the sky;
> All bright and glittering in the smokeless air.[17]

It is true that this was the city before the rush and noise of the working day, but the pulse of the recognition is still unmistakable, and I know that I have felt it again and again: the great buildings of civilisation; the meeting-places; the libraries and theatres, the towers ad domes; and often more moving than these, the houses, the streets, the press and excitement of so many people, with so many purposes. I have stood in many cities and felt this pulse in the physical differences of Stockholm and Florence, Pairs and Milan: this identifiable and moving quality: the centre, the activity, the light. Like everyone else I have felt also the chaos of the metro and the traffic jam; the monotony of the ranks of houses, the aching press of strange crowds. But this is not an experience at all, not an adult experience, until it has come to include also the dynamic movement, in these centres of settled and often magnificent achievement. H. G. Wells[18] once said, coming out of a political meeting where they had been discussing social change, that this great towering city was a measure of the obstacle, of how much must be moved if there was to be any change. I have known this feeling, looking up at great buildings that are the centres of power, but I find I do not say 'There is your city, your great bourgeois monument, your towering structure of this still precarious civilisation' or I do not only say that; I say also 'This is what men have built, so often magnificently, and is not everything then possible?' indeed this sense of possibility, of meeting and of movement, is a permanent element of my sense of cities: as permanent a feeling as those other feelings, when I look from the mountain at the great coloured patchwork of fields

that generation of my own people have cleared and set in hedges; or the known living places, the isolated farms, the cluster of cottages by castle or church, the lines made. So that while country and city have this profound importance, in their different ways, my feelings are held, before any argument starts.

But then also, specifically, I came from a village to a city: to be taught, to learn: to submit personal facts, the incidents of a family, to a total record; to learn evidence and connection and altering perspectives. If the walls of the colleges were like the walls of parks, that as children we had walked round, unable to enter, yet now there was a gate, an entry, and a library at the end of it: a direct record, if I could learn to read it. It is ironic to remember that it was only after I came that I heard, from townsmen, academics, an influential version of what country life, country literature, really meant: a prepared and persuasive cultural history. I read related things still, in academic books and in books by men who left private schools to go farming, and by others who grew up in villages and are now country writers: a whole set of books, periodicals, notes in the newspapers: country life. And I find I keep asking the same question, because of the history: where do I stand in relation to these writers; in another country or in this valuing city? That problem is sharp and ironic in its cultural persistence.

But there are more to Cambridge than that. An ambivalence certainly: a university of scholars and teachers but also of coaches and placemen, on their way to higher places; a world of men extending human knowledge and bringing light to nature and to the lives of others; a world other men contracted in sympathy, telling their qualifying paradigms inside the walls, in an idle and arrogant observation and consumption. The university, to my family, had been equally foreign, whether it was Cambridge of Stourbridge Fair[19], once the leading market of the country: 'the prodigious resort of the trading people of all parts of England' as Defoe described it in the 1720s; 'a prodigious complex of people' and also a model, to Bunyan[20], for Vanity Fair. When I returned much later, as a Fellow of a College, I found I was by virtue or default of an intellectual appointment an aspect, an unwilling member, of a collective and perpetual landlord, and I was asked, politely, to attend tenants' lunches, which I could never stomach. I remembered Arthur Young[21] on the University of Cambridge:

> its revenue £16000 a year and for is 6d a member can sit down to a dinner such as gentleman with £1000 a year cannot often give with prudence.

Defoe had followed one road out:

> on the edge of the Fenns, to Huntington, where it joins the great north road; on this side it is all an agreeable corn country, as above, adorned with several seats of gentlemen.

Young, in 1792, had followed another:

> Taking the road from Cambridge to St Neot's, view six or seven miles of the worst husbandry, I hope, in Great Britain.... There seems somewhat of a coincidence between the state of cultivation within sight of the venerable spires of Cambridge and the utter neglect of agriculture in the establishment of that University.

That is the road I now drive on, coming home from the university. The fields are well farmed now. but in the next village west, Cobbett[22] saw, in 1822, something which very much resembles almost a village of the same size in Picardy, where I saw the women dragging harrows to harrow in the corn.

Certainly this village resembles nothing English except some of the rascally rotten boroughs in Cornwall and Devonshire, on which a just Province seems to have entailed its curse. The just about here does seem to be really bad. The face of the country is naked. The few scrubbed trees that now and then meet the eye, and even the quick-sets, are covered with a yellow moss. All is bleak and comfortless; and, just on the most dreary part of this most dreary scene, stands almost opportunely, 'Caxton Gibbet'[23], tendering its one friendly arm to the passer-by. It has recently been fresh-painted, and written on in conspicuous characters, for the benefit, I suppose, of those who cannot exist under the thought of wheat at four shillings a bushel.

That, too, is different now, but whenever I consider the relations between country and city, and between birth and learning, I find this history active and continuous: the relations are not only of ideas and experience, but of rent and interest, of situation and power; a wider system.

This then is where I am, and as I settle to work I find I have to resolve, step by slow step, experiences and questions that once moved like light. The life of country and city is moving and present: moving in time, through the history of a family and a people; moving in feeling and ideas, through a network of relationships and decisions.

A dog is barking—that chained bark—behind the asbestos barn. It is now and then: here and many places. When there are questions to put, I have to push back my chair, look down at my papers, and feel the change.

Notes

1. The selection is the first chapter of the book in which Raymond Williams studies and examines the contradiction, along with the contrasting idea of the city, which in the U.K. has never been separated from the countryside.
2. pastoralist: a grazier or land-holder raising sheep, cattle, etc. on a large scale
3. manor: (in medieval Europe) the manor house of a lord and the lands attached to it
4. latifundia: the plural form of latifundium, a large agricultural estate, esp. one worked by slaves in Latin America
5. conurbation: a large densely populated urban sprawl formed by the growth and coalescence of individual towns or cities
6. the Industrial Revolution: the transformation in the 18th and 19th centuries of first Britain and then other European countries and the US into industrial nations
7. may: the white or pink flowers of hawthorn
8. silage: food for cattle that is made by cutting a crop such as grass or corn when it is green and then keeping it covered
9. molasses: a thick, dark brown syrup which is produced when sugar is processed. It is used in cooking.
10. the Black Mountains: a group of hills spread across parts of Powys and Monmouthshire in southeast Wales, and extending across the national border into Herefordshire, England
11. East Anglian skies: skies in a region of eastern England that was formerly a kingdom
12. hedgerow: a row of bushes, trees, and plants, usually growing along a bank bordering a country

road or between fields
13. cobble: the same as cobblestone, stone with a rounded upper surface which used to be used for making streets
14. bridletrack: bridle path, a path intended for people riding horses
15. Hardy's Jude: Thomas Hardy (1840—1928) is an outstanding poet and novelist in English literature. Jude is the protagonist in his famous novel *Jude the Obscure* (1895).
16. Christminster: cathedral or large church of Christ
17. The fragments are taken from William Wordsworth's famous sonnet *Composed upon Westminster Bridge* written in 1802.
18. H. G. Wells (1866—1946): an English writer, now best known for his work in the science fiction genre. His most notable science fiction works include *The War of the Worlds* (1898), *The Time Machine* (1895), and *The Invisible Man* (1879).
19. Stourbridge Fair: an annual fair held on Stourbridge Common in Cambridge, England
20. Bunyan: John Bunyan (1628—1688) is an English Christian writer and preacher. Stourbridge Fair is the largest fair in Europe and is the inspiration for Bunyan's "Vanity Fair" in his masterpiece *The Pilgrim's Progress* (1678), arguably the most famous published Christian allegory.
21. Arthur Young (1741—1820): an English writer on agriculture, economics, social statistics, and campaigner for the rights of agricultural workers
22. Cobbett: William Cobbett (1762—1835), an English pamphleteer, farmer and journalist
23. Caxton Gibbet: a small knoll on Ermine Street (now the A1198) in England, running between London and Huntingdon, near its crossing with the road (now the A428) between Oxford and Cambridge. There are tales of murderers being hanged and displayed at the nearby village of Caxton in the 1670s, and records in a court case that the gibbet was still there in 1745.

Questions

1. According to Raymond Williams, "country" and "city" are two powerful words. Why? What are the different connotations of these two words?
2. The author tells about his own family stories in great details. What does he want to express through the stories?
3. Raymond Williams uses his own life experience to show his knowing and seeking to know the relationship between country and city. Can you use what you have experienced to explain this relationship?

Chapter Five Faith and Skepticism

    Faith and Skepticism, a theme often covered in realms of religion and philosophy, has also been given extensive exploration and elaboration in literature, though in a relatively general sense. If faith can be defined as a "confident belief in the truth, value, or trustworthiness of a person, an idea, or a thing", skepticism then urges people to make inquiry into and challenge such a belief. In reality, social and cultural upheavals impact on man's thinking about life and the world, so a faith that once was so unshakeable can become weakened and shattered. Writers, who are, more often than not, sensitive to the loss of beliefs and drastic social changes, are also endowed with a gift to convey implicitly or explicitly their doubts hereby arising. They tend to scrutinize the world with a mind unclouded by current opinions, and show a keen observation and unique understanding and critique of human nature in their works.

    In different social contexts, the focus of faith and skepticism might fall on different issues like religious beliefs, social doctrines, or morality. For instance, English literary works, especially after the Restoration, began to introspect about the value of man; the faith in reason in the eighteenth century inspired a more satirical and doubtful look at what had happened and what was happening. When time came to the Victorian age, the multitudinousness caused by industrialization and religious reformation, and the development of science, especially that of geology and Darwinism, brought more confusion to the public and greatly kindled writers' skeptical spirit. The outbreak of the two world wars and the rising of various philosophical and theoretical ideas in the twentieth century broadened writers' skeptical scope and provided more momentum for doubting and subverting the conventional faiths. The fast-changing and conflicting modern period characterized by consumerism, high-technology, and international disputes has also proved a profound source of literary expression of faith and skepticism in today's world.

    Faith and skepticism, is often found expression in literary classics. Shakespeare's *Hamlet* can be acclaimed as a remarkable rendering of man's struggle and agony on this score. The skeptical and melancholy prince vacillates between action and thinking; his doubts about life and death represent man's inquiring mind and symbolize the forever difficult situation man has to confront. Matthew Arnold's *Dover Beach*, an elegy on the loss of religious faith and the fear of the "darkling plain", demonstrates his apprehension about the religious conviction endangered by evolutionary beliefs. Thackeray, in *Vanity Fair*, presents a world that excites readers' doubts about the prevailing morality. Hardy in his poems relates the religious faith with peasant "fancies", and chants his regret, lament and loss at the passing of a securer world of legend, tradition, and faith. Muriel Spark's *The Prime of Miss Jean Brodie* expresses her skepticism about dangerous liaisons among knowledge, power, and loyalty, and Kazuo Ishiguro's *Never Let Me Go* questions the issue of clone technology and modern civilization. These may well exemplify that writers have long been reflecting on and making unremitting efforts to render the tension between faith and skepticism, an endeavor of ideological, philosophical, empirical as well as aesthetic value and significance.

William Shakespeare
1564—1616

Hamlet

Hamlet, Othello, King Lear, and *Macbeth* are universally acknowledged as Shakespeare's greatest tragedies, among which, *Hamlet (The Tragical History of Hamlet, Prince of Denmark)* was written first and published in about 1601. It is a play that "best exemplifies Shakespeare's ability to express the universal awareness of human existence."

This play, with its origin in a legend of northern Europe, dramatizes Hamlet, the young prince of Denmark, and his revenge. Summoned back home from his university, Hamlet is filled with grief for the recent death of his father. His uncle Claudius has crowned himself King and married Hamlet's mother Gertrude. Confronted with his father's ghost, Hamlet comes to know Claudius' murdering of his father, and he vows to avenge his death. But Hamlet does not take immediate action, since he is always skeptical of the rightness of his revenge.

In order to confirm his suspicion and prepare for the revenge, he acts like a madman, even before his sweet heart Ophelia, the advisor Polonius' daughter. Hamlet manages to have an acting company reenact his father's death before Claudius, in the hope of finding out the real murderer. In vain, he has a quarrel with his mother and kills Polonius through the curtain, assuming the person behind it is Claudius. Ophelia reacts to her father's death with utter madness and eventually drowns in a stream. In fear of Hamlet's revenge, Claudius sends Hamlet abroad and intrigues to kill him. When it fails, Claudius arranges a sword duel between Hamlet and Laertes, Ophelia's brother. Both Laertes and Hamlet are stabbed by the poisoned sword, and the dying Hamlet gets his revenge by killing Claudius with the same sword. Finally, Fortinbras, the prince of Norway, becomes the new King of Denmark as Hamlet wishes.

Hamlet, an epitome of the intellectuals—sensitive, speculative, contemplative, humanistic, hesitant and skeptical, may represent their deep emotional uncertainty and insecurity of values in the Elizabethan age. His hesitations have been among the most discussed subjects in criticism. "To be, or not to be: that's a question", an excerpt from Act III of *Hamlet* and perhaps the most famous soliloquy in literary history, is the embodiment of man's skepticism, anxiety, and confusion.

Act III

Hamlet.
To be, or not to be[1]: that is the question:
Whether 'tis nobler in the mind to suffer

The slings[2] and arrows of outrageous fortune,
Or to take arms against a sea of troubles,
And by opposing end them? To die: to sleep;
No more; and by a sleep to say we end[3]
The heart-ache and the thousand natural shocks
That flesh is heir to, 'tis a consummation
Devoutly to be wish'd. To die, to sleep;
To sleep: perchance[4] to dream: ay, there's the rub[5];
For in that sleep of death what dreams may come
When we have shuffled off this mortal coil[6],
Must give us pause: there's the respect
That makes calamity of so long life;
For who would bear the whips and scorns of time,
The oppressor's wrong, the proud man's contumely,
The pangs of despised love, the law's delay,
The insolence of office[7] and the spurns
That patient merit of the unworthy takes,
When he himself might his quietus make[8]
With a bare bodkin[9]? who would these fardels[10] bear,
To grunt and sweat under a weary life,
But that the dread of something after death,
The undiscover'd country from whose bourn
No traveller returns, puzzles the will
And makes us rather bear those ills we have
Than fly to others that we know not of?
Thus conscience does make cowards of us all;
And thus the native hue of resolution
Is sicklied o'er with[11] the pale cast of thought,
And enterprises of great pith and moment[12]
With this regard their currents turn awry[13],
And lose the name of action.

Notes

1. To be, or not to be: To live, or to die. Hamlet calls into question the plight life and death brings, not merely for himself but for all humanity.
2. sling: a simple weapon in the form of a strap or loop, used to hurl stones
3. by a sleep to say we end...: by a sleep it is to say we end....
4. perchance: by chance, perhaps
5. there's the rub: that is the obstacle

6. mortal coil: turmoil of mortality
7. The insolence of office: The insulting behavior of officials
8. he himself might his quietus make: he himself might make his quietus; he himself might settle his own account
9. a bare bodkin: a mere dagger
10. fardel: burden
11. Is sicklied o'er with: Is covered with
12. of great pith and moment: of great importance
13. their currents turn awry: turn away from their course

Questions

1. According to this passage, what makes a person "lose the name of action"?
2. What's the question "To be, or not to be" for? Is it a personal question for Hamlet or a question with general philosophical significance? What do you think of the absence of the first person "I" or "me" in this passage of soliloquy?

William Makepeace Thackeray
1811—1863

William Makepeace Thackeray, the author of a massive body of lyric, dramatic, narrative and expository works, was born in 1811 in Calcutta, India. His father was an English official in the East India Company and died when he was 5. Then, he was sent to London for schooling. With the support of his mother and his step-father, Thackeray had a conventional upper-class education at Charterhouse School and Trinity College, Cambridge, which he left in 1830 without taking a degree. At the university, his chief interest was reading modern literature. He wrote verses, edited a student newspaper, and also had an active social life. Out of the university, he traveled in Germany and France for self-education and art studies.

William Makepeace Thackeray

Thackeray began to study for the bar in London in 1831, but soon gave it up in 1832. Due to bad investments, he lost his money and left for Paris, where he married and had his first article published in *The Constitutional*. Back to London in 1837, he made a living as an illustrator and journalist, contributing to *Fraser's Magazine* and *Punch*. The former published his first series of tales "The Yellowplush Correspondence", and the latter his masterpiece *Vanity Fair*. In 1859—1862, he took up the editorship of *Cornhill Magazine*. In 1863, he died of heart trouble in London.

Most of Thackeray's novels were published serially in journals, describing the worldly, materialistic society of his time. *The Book of Snobs* (entitled *Snob Papers* published in *Punch* from 1846 to 1847), which gives satirical and humorous studies of London manners, established his reputation as a leading satirist of his day. His masterpiece is *Vanity Fair*, published in *Punch* from 1847 to 1848 and in book form in 1848. *Pendennis* (1848—1850) and *The Newcomes* (1853—1855) are novels in similar style. *The Rose and the Ring*, a popular mock fairy tale, appeared in 1854 (dated 1855). Thackeray also wrote two historical novels about the eighteenth century England—*The History of Henry Esmond* (1852) and *The Virginians* (1857—1859), in addition to many essays and lectures which he delivered in England, Scotland, and USA.

Thackeray was a man of doubts, hesitation, and struggles, and his works are full of pathos, humor, love, and charity. By his own peculiar style of characterization and narration, he sought, in his own words, "to convey as strongly as possible the sentiment of reality," and thus he challenged readers' assumptions about human life and has been hailed as a representative of critical realism like Charles Dickens.

Vanity Fair

Thackeray's previous writings had been published either anonymously or under pseudonyms; *Vanity Fair* was the first work under his real name. *Vanity Fair* takes its title from the town designated as the centre of human corruption in *Pilgrim's Progress*, a prose allegory by the seventeenth-century writer John Bunyan. While Bunyan presents the pleasure-loving worldliness of society under the reign of Charles II, Thackeray presents social manners and human frailties in an impressive panorama of the nineteenth-century upper class society. This novel, with a keen, sardonic humor, opens in the Regency England, and traces the fortunes of its characters in England and post-Napoleonic Europe. It gives a penetrating satirical observation of Thackeray's time and is regarded as his most successful work.

On the first monthly installment, this novel bore the heading *Vanity Fair: Pen and Pencil Sketches of English Society*; however, the subtitle was changed to *A Novel Without a Hero* when it came out in one-volume form in 1848. This revision shows Thackeray's "disinterest in creating a romantic hero or in narrating the adventures of a central personage", and the five main characters, Becky Sharp, Amelia, George Osborne, William Dobbin, and Rawdon Crawley, are all presented with certain flaws in personality.

Becky Sharp perhaps is the most memorable character Thackeray ever created. She is an adventuress of poor parentage in contrast with her friend, the wellborn and weakly sentimental Amelia Sedley. Becky contrives unscrupulously to gain a better life by marriage. When failing to ensnare Amelia's wealthy brother Joseph Sedley, she marries Rawdon Crawley, a young officer, son of Sir Pitt Crawley, who is also asking for her hand. Though married, Becky keeps flirting with men. Rawdon, a playboy as he is, is disillusioned and finally leaves Becky when he comes to know her relation with the rich old Lord Steyne. Rawdon dies of fever in West Indies, and Becky manages to control Joseph Sedley and settles down by living on the latter's insurance money after his death. Amelia marries

George Osborne, her childhood sweetheart, despite the objection from George's snobbish father for the financial ruin of her family. George has an affair with Becky behind Amelia's back, and even proposes elopement with Becky. He loses his life in the Battle of Waterloo. Amelia remains infatuated with George until Becky reveals George's betrayal years later. Amelia finally marries her lifelong admirer, Captain William Dobbin, an honest character not much consumed by vanity in this novel.

With a panoramic and critical view of the early nineteenth century society, Thackeray criticized those people in the modern vanity fair, and questioned the value and mores of his society as well as the essence of human nature. He made it one of the most influential novels of its time. Awed by the novel's satirical power, Charlotte Brontë dedicated the second edition of *Jane Eyre* to Thackeray.

Chapter VI of *Vanity Fair* centers on the prospective marriage between Becky and Joseph, and its comic, satirical narrative is most remarkable to question the vanity of the society and its inhabitants.

Chapter VI
Vauxhall

I know that the tune I am piping is a very mild one (although there are some terrific chapters coming presently), and must beg the good-natured reader to remember that we are only discoursing at present about a stockbroker's family in Russell Square[1], who are taking walks, or luncheon, or dinner, or talking and making love as people do in common life, and without a single passionate and wonderful incident to mark the progress of their loves. The argument stands thus—Osborne, in love with Amelia, has asked an old friend to dinner and to Vauxhall[2]—Jos Sedley is in love with Rebecca. Will he marry her? That is the great subject now in hand.

[...]

Let us then step into the coach with the Russell Square party, and be off to the Gardens. There is barely room between Jos[3] and Miss Sharp, who are on the front seat. Mr. Osborne sitting bodkin[4] opposite, between Captain Dobbin and Amelia.

Every soul in the coach agreed, that on that night Jos would propose to make Rebecca Sharp Mrs. Sedley. The parents at home had acquiesced in the arrangement, though, between ourselves, old Mr. Sedley had a feeling very much akin to contempt for his son. He said he was vain, selfish, lazy, and effeminate. He could not endure his airs as a man of fashion, and laughed heartily at his pompous braggadocio stories. "I shall leave the fellow half my property," he said; "and he will have, besides, plenty of his own; but as I am perfectly sure that if you, and I, and his sister were to die to-morrow, he would say 'Good Gad!' and eat his dinner just as well as usual, I am not going to make myself anxious about him. Let him marry whom he likes. It's no affair of mine."

Amelia, on the other hand, as became a young woman of her prudence and temperament, was quite enthusiastic for the match. Once or twice Jos had been on the point of saying something very important to her, to which she was most willing to lend an ear, but the fat fellow could not be brought to unbosom himself of his great secret, and very much to his sister's disappointment he only rid himself of a large sigh and turned away.

This mystery served to keep Amelia's gentle bosom in a perpetual flutter of excitement. If she did not speak with Rebecca on the tender subject, she compensated herself with long and intimate conversations with Mrs. Blenkinsop, the housekeeper, who dropped some hints to the lady's-maid, who may have cursorily mentioned the matter to the cook, who carried the news, I have no doubt, to all the tradesmen, so that Mr. Jos's marriage was now talked of by a very considerable number of persons in the Russell Square world.

It was, of course, Mrs. Sedley's opinion that her son would demean himself by a marriage with an artist's daughter. "But, lor', Ma'am," ejaculated Mrs. Blenkinsop, "we was[5] only grocers when we married Mr. S., who was a stock-broker's clerk, and we hadn't five hundred pounds among us, and we're rich enough now." And Amelia was entirely of this opinion, to which, gradually, the good-natured Mrs. Sedley was brought.

Mr. Sedley was neutral. "Let Jos marry whom he likes," he said; "it's no affair of mine. This girl has no fortune; no more had Mrs. Sedley. She seems good-humoured and clever, and will keep him in order, perhaps. Better she, my dear, than a black Mrs. Sedley, and a dozen of mahogany grandchildren[6]."

So that everything seemed to smile upon Rebecca's fortunes. She took Jos's arm, as a matter of course, on going to dinner; she had sate by him on the box of his open carriage (a most tremendous "buck" he was, as he sat there, serene, in state, driving his greys), and though nobody said a word on the subject of the marriage, everybody seemed to understand it. All she wanted was the proposal, and ah! how Rebecca now felt the want of a mother!—a dear, tender mother, who would have managed the business in ten minutes, and, in the course of a little delicate confidential conversation, would have extracted the interesting avowal from the bashful lips of the young man!

Such was the state of affairs as the carriage crossed Westminster bridge.

The party was landed at the Royal Gardens in due time. As the majestic Jos stepped out of the creaking vehicle the crowd gave a cheer for the fat gentleman, who blushed and looked very big and mighty, as he walked away with Rebecca under his arm. George, of course, took charge of Amelia. She looked as happy as a rose-tree in sunshine.

"I say, Dobbin," says George, "just look to the shawls and things, there's a good fellow." And so while he paired off with Miss Sedley, and Jos squeezed through the gate into the gardens with Rebecca at his side, honest Dobbin contented himself by giving an arm to the shawls, and by paying at the door for the whole party.

[...]

It is to be understood, as a matter of course, that our young people, being in parties of two and two, made the most solemn promises to keep together during the evening, and separated in ten minutes afterwards. Parties at Vauxhall always did separate, but 'twas only to meet again at supper-time, when they could talk of their mutual adventures in the interval.

What were the adventures of Mr. Osborne and Miss Amelia? That is a secret. But be sure of this—they were perfectly happy, and correct in their behaviour; and as they had been in the habit of being together any time these fifteen years, their *tête-à-tête* offered no particular novelty.

But when Miss Rebecca Sharp and her stout companion lost themselves in a solitary walk, in which there were not above five score more of couples similarly straying, they both felt that the situation was extremely tender and critical, and now or never was the moment Miss Sharp thought, to provoke that declaration which was trembling on the timid lips of Mr. Sedley. They had previously been to the panorama of Moscow, where a rude fellow, treading on Miss Sharp's foot, caused her to fall back with a little shriek into the arms of Mr. Sedley, and this little incident increased the tenderness and confidence of that gentleman to such a degree, that he told her several of his favourite Indian stories over again for, at least, the sixth time.

"How I should like to see India!" said Rebecca.

"*Should* you?" said Joseph, with a most killing tenderness; and was no doubt about to follow up this artful interrogatory by a question still more tender (for he puffed and panted a great deal, and Rebecca's hand, which was placed near his heart, could count the feverish pulsations of that organ), when, oh, provoking! the bell rang for the fireworks, and, a great scuffling and running taking place, these interesting lovers were obliged to follow in the stream of people.

Captain Dobbin had some thoughts of joining the party at supper: as, in truth, he found the Vauxhall amusements not particularly lively—but he paraded twice before the box where the now united couples were met, and nobody took any notice of him. Covers were laid for four. The mated pairs were prattling away quite happily, and Dobbin knew he was as clean forgotten as if he had never existed in this world.

"I should only be *de trop*[7]," said the Captain, looking at them rather wistfully. "I'd best go and talk to the hermit,"—and so he strolled off out of the hum of men, and noise, and clatter of the banquet, into the dark walk, at the end of which lived that well-known pasteboard Solitary. It wasn't very good fun for Dobbin—and, indeed, to be alone at Vauxhall, I have found, from my own experience, to be one of the most dismal sports ever entered into by a bachelor.

The two couples were perfectly happy then in their box: where the most delightful and intimate conversation took place. Jos was in his glory, ordering about the waiters with great majesty. He made the salad; and uncorked the Champagne; and carved the chickens; and ate and drank the greater part of the refreshments on the tables. Finally, he insisted upon having a bowl of rack-punch[8]; everybody had rack-punch at Vauxhall. "Waiter, rack-punch."

That bowl of rack-punch was the cause of all this history. And why not a bowl of rack-punch as well as any other cause? Was not a bowl of prussic acid the cause of Fair Rosamond[9]'s retiring from the world? Was not a bowl of wine the cause of the demise of Alexander the Great[10], or, at least, does not Dr. Lempriere say so?—so did this bowl of rack-punch influence the fates of all the principal characters in this "Novel without a Hero," which we are now relating. It influenced their life, although most of them did not taste a drop of it.

The young ladies did not drink it; Osborne did not like it; and the consequence was that Jos, that fat *gourmand*, drank up the whole contents of the bowl; and the consequence of his drinking up the whole contents of the bowl was a liveliness which at first was astonishing, and then became almost painful; for he talked and laughed so loud as to bring scores of listeners round the box, much to the confusion of the innocent party within it; and, volunteering to sing a song (which he did in that maudlin high key peculiar to gentlemen in an inebriated state), he almost drew away the audience who were gathered round the musicians in the gilt scollop-shell, and received from his hearers a great deal of applause.

"Brayvo, Fat un!" said one; "Angcore,[11] Daniel Lambert![12]" said another; "What a figure for the tight-rope!" exclaimed another wag, to the inexpressible alarm of the ladies, and the great anger of Mr. Osborne.

"For Heaven's sake, Jos, let us get up and go," cried that gentleman, and the young women rose.

"Stop, my dearest diddle-diddle-darling," shouted Jos, now as bold as a lion, and clasping Miss Rebecca round the waist.

Rebecca started, but she could not get away her hand. The laughter outside redoubled. Jos continued to drink, to make love, and to sing; and, winking and waving his glass gracefully to his audience, challenged all or any to come in and take a share of his punch.

Mr. Osborne was just on the point of knocking down a gentleman in top-boots, who proposed to take advantage of this invitation, and a commotion seemed to be inevitable, when by the greatest good luck a gentleman of the name of Dobbin, who had been walking about the gardens, stepped up to the box. "Be off, you fools!" said this gentleman—shouldering off a great number of the crowd, who vanished presently before his cocked hat and fierce appearance—and he entered the box in a most agitated state.

"Good Heavens! Dobbin, where have you been?" Osborne said, seizing the white cashmere shawl from his friend's arm, and huddling up Amelia in it.—"Make yourself useful, and take charge of Jos here, whilst I take the ladies to the carriage."

Jos was for rising to interfere—but a single push from Osborne's finger sent him puffing back into his seat again, and the lieutenant was enabled to remove the ladies in safety. Jos kissed his hand to them as they retreated, and hiccupped out "Bless you! Bless you!" Then, seizing Captain Dobbin's hand, and weeping in the most pitiful way, he confided to that gentleman the secret of his loves. He adored that girl who had just gone out; he had broken her heart, he knew he had, by his conduct; he would marry her next morning at St. George's, Hanover Square; he'd knock up the Archbishop of Canterbury at Lambeth[13]: he would, by Jove! and have him in readiness; and, acting on this hint, Captain Dobbin shrewdly induced him to leave the gardens and hasten to Lambeth Palace, and, when once out of the gates, easily conveyed Mr. Jos Sedley into a hackney-coach, which deposited him safely at his lodgings.

George Osborne conducted the girls home in safety: and when the door was closed upon them, and as he walked across Russell Square, laughed so as to astonish the watchman. Amelia looked very ruefully at her friend, as they went up stairs, and kissed her, and went to bed without any more talking.

"He must propose to-morrow," thought Rebecca. "He called me his soul's darling, four times; he squeezed my hand in Amelia's presence. He must propose to-morrow." And so thought Amelia, too. And I dare say she thought of the dress she was to wear as bridesmaid, and of the presents which she should make to her nice little sister-in-law, and of a subsequent ceremony in which she herself might play a principal part, etc., and etc., and etc., and etc.

Oh, ignorant young creatures! How little do you know the effect of rack-punch! What is the rack in the punch, at night, to the rack in the head of a morning?[14] To this truth I can vouch as a man; there is no headache in the world like that caused by Vauxhall punch. Through the lapse of twenty years, I can remember the consequence of two glasses! —two wine-glasses! —but two, upon the honour of a gentleman; and Joseph Sedley, who had a liver complaint, had swallowed at least a quart of the abominable mixture.

That next morning, which Rebecca thought was to dawn upon her fortune, found Sedley groaning in agonies which the pen refuses to describe. Soda-water was not invented yet. Small beer[15]—will it be believed!—was the only drink with which unhappy gentlemen soothed the fever of their previous night's potation. With this mild beverage before him, George Osborne found the ex-Collector of Boggley Wollah groaning on the sofa at his lodgings. Dobbin was already in the room, good-naturedly tending his patient of the night before. The two officers, looking at the prostrate Bacchanalian[16], and askance at each other, exchanged the most frightful sympathetic grins. Even Sedley's valet, the most solemn and correct of gentlemen, with the muteness and gravity of an undertaker, could hardly keep his countenance in order, as he looked at his unfortunate master.

"Mr. Sedley was uncommon wild last night, sir," he whispered in confidence to Osborne, as the latter mounted the stair. "He wanted to fight the 'ackney-coachman, sir. The Capting was obliged to bring him upstairs in his harms like a babby." A momentary smile flickered over Mr. Brush's features as he spoke; instantly, however, they relapsed into their usual unfathomable calm, as he flung open the drawing-room door, and announced "Mr. Hosbin[17]."

"How are you, Sedley?" that young wag began, after surveying his victim. "No bones broke? There's a hackney-coachman downstairs with a black eye, and a tied-up head, vowing he'll have the law of you."

"What do you mean—law?" Sedley faintly asked.

"For thrashing him last night—didn't he, Dobbin? You hit out, sir, like Molyneux[18]. The watchman says he never saw a fellow go down so straight. Ask Dobbin."

"You did have a round with the coachman," Captain Dobbin said, "and showed plenty of fight too."

"And that fellow with the white coat at Vauxhall! How Jos drove at him! How the women screamed! By Jove, sir, it did my heart good to see you. I thought you civilians had no pluck[19]; but I'll never get in your way when you are in your cups, Jos."

"I believe I'm very terrible, when I'm roused," ejaculated Jos from the sofa, and made a grimace so dreary and ludicrous, that the Captain's politeness could restrain him no longer, and he and Osborne fired off a ringing volley of laughter.

Osborne pursued his advantage pitilessly. He thought Jos a milksop. He had been revolving in his mind the marriage question pending between Jos and Rebecca, and was not over well pleased that a member of a family into which he, George Osborne, of the —th, was going to marry, should make a *mésalliance* with a little nobody—a little upstart governess. "You hit, you poor old fellow!" said Osborne. "You terrible! Why, man, you couldn't stand—you made everybody laugh in the Gardens, though you were crying yourself. You were maudlin, Jos. Don't you remember singing a song?"

"A what?" Jos asked.

"A sentimental song, and calling Rosa, Rebecca, what's her name, Amelia's little friend—your dearest diddle-diddle-darling?" And this ruthless young fellow, seizing hold of Dobbin's hand, acted over the scene, to the horror of the original performer, and in spite of Dobbin's good-natured entreaties to him to have mercy.

"Why should I spare him?" Osborne said to his friend's remonstrances, when they quitted the invalid, leaving him under the hands of Doctor Gollop. "What the deuce right has he to give himself his patronizing airs, and make fools of us at Vauxhall? Who's this little schoolgirl that is ogling and making love to him? Hang it, the family's low enough already, without her. A governess is all very well, but I'd rather have a lady for my sister-in-law. I'm a liberal man; but I've proper pride, and know my own station: let her know hers. And I'll take down that great hectoring Nabob, and prevent him from being made a greater fool than he is. That's why I told him to look out, lest she brought an action against him."

"I suppose you know best," Dobbin said, though rather dubiously. "You always were a Tory, and your family's one of the oldest in England. But—"

"Come and see the girls, and make love to Miss Sharp yourself," the lieutenant here interrupted his friend; but Captain Dobbin declined to join Osborne in his daily visit to the young ladies in Russell Square.

As George walked down Southampton Row, from Holborn, he laughed as he saw, at the Sedley Mansion, in two different stories two heads on the look-out.

The fact is, Miss Amelia, in the drawing-room balcony, was looking very eagerly towards the opposite side of the Square, where Mr. Osborne dwelt, on the watch for the lieutenant himself; and Miss Sharp, from her little bed-room on the second floor, was in observation until Mr. Joseph's great form should heave in sight.

"Sister Anne is on the watch-tower[20]," said he to Amelia, "but there's nobody coming"; and laughing and enjoying the joke hugely, he described in the most ludicrous terms to Miss Sedley, the dismal condition of her brother.

"I think it's very cruel of you to laugh, George," she said, looking particularly unhappy; but George only laughed the more at her piteous and discomfited mien[21], persisted in thinking the joke a most diverting one, and when Miss Sharp came downstairs, bantered her with a great deal of liveliness upon the effect of her charms on the fat civilian.

"O Miss Sharp! if you could but see him this morning," he said—"moaning in his flowered dressing-gown—writhing on his sofa; if you could but have seen him lolling out his tongue to Gollop the apothecary."

"See whom?" said Miss Sharp.

"Whom? O whom? Captain Dobbin, of course, to whom we were all so attentive, by the way, last night."

"We were very unkind to him," Emmy said, blushing very much. "I—I quite forgot him."

"Of course you did," cried Osborne, still on the laugh.

"One can't be *always* thinking about Dobbin, you know, Amelia. Can one, Miss Sharp?"

"Except when he overset the glass of wine at dinner," Miss Sharp said, with a haughty air and a toss of the head, "I never gave the existence of Captain Dobbin one single moment's consideration."

"Very good, Miss Sharp, I'll tell him," Osborne said; and as he spoke Miss Sharp began to have a feeling of distrust and hatred towards this young officer, which he was quite unconscious of having inspired. "*He* is to make fun of me, is he?" thought Rebecca. "Has he been laughing about me to Joseph? Has he frightened him? Perhaps he won't come."—A film passed over her eyes, and her heart beat quite quick.

"You're always joking," said she, smiling as innocently as she could. "Joke away, Mr. George; there's nobody to defend *me*." And George Osborne, as she walked away—and Amelia looked reprovingly at him—felt some little manly compunction for having inflicted any unnecessary unkindness upon this helpless creature. "My dearest Amelia," said he, "you are too good—too kind. You don't know the world. I do. And your little friend Miss Sharp must learn her station."

"Don't you think Jos will—"

"Upon my word, my dear, I don't know. He may, or may not. I'm not his master. I only know he is a very foolish vain fellow, and put my dear little girl into a very painful and awkward position last night. My dearest diddle-diddle-darling!" He was off laughing again, and he did it so drolly that Emmy laughed too.

All that day Jos never came. But Amelia had no fear about this; for the little schemer had actually sent away the page, Mr. Sambo's aide-de-camp[22], to Mr. Joseph's lodgings, to ask for some book he had promised, and how he was; and the reply through Jos's man, Mr. Brush, was, that his master was ill in bed, and had just had the doctor with him. He must come to-morrow, she thought, but she never had the courage to speak a word on the subject to Rebecca; nor did that young woman herself allude to it in any way during the whole evening after the night at Vauxhall.

The next day, however, as the two young ladies sate on the sofa, pretending to work, or to write letters, or to read novels, Sambo came into the room with his usual engaging grin, with a packet under his arm, and a note on a tray. "Note from Mr. Jos, Miss," says Sambo.

How Amelia trembled as she opened it!

So it ran:

Dear Amelia,

I send you the *Orphan of the Forest*. I was too ill to come yesterday. I leave town to-day for Cheltenham[23]. Pray excuse me, if you can, to the amiable Miss Sharp, for my conduct at Vauxhall, and entreat her to pardon and forget every word I may have uttered when excited by that fatal supper. As soon as I have recovered, for my health is very much shaken, I shall go to Scotland for some months, and am

Truly yours,

Jos. Sedley

It was the death-warrant. All was over. Amelia did not dare to look at Rebecca's pale face and burning eyes, but she dropt the letter into her friend's lap; and got up, and went upstairs to her room, and cried her little heart out.

Blenkinsop, the housekeeper, there sought her presently with consolation, on whose shoulder Amelia wept confidentially, and relieved herself a good deal. "Don't take on, Miss. I didn't like to tell you. But none of us in the house have liked her except at fust[24]. I sor her with my own eyes reading your Ma's letters. Pinner says she's always about your trinket-box and drawers, and everybody's drawers, and she's sure she's put your white ribbing into her box."

"I gave it her, I gave it her," Amelia said.

But this did not alter Mrs. Blenkinsop's opinion of Miss Sharp. "I don't trust them governesses, Pinner," she remarked to the maid. "They give themselves the hairs and hupstarts of ladies, and their wages is no better than you nor me."

It now became clear to every soul in the house, except poor Amelia, that Rebecca should take her departure, and high and low (always with the one exception) agreed that that event should take place as speedily as possible. Our good child ransacked all her drawers, cupboards, reticules, and gimcrack-boxes—passed in review all her gowns, fichus, tags, bobbins, laces, silk stockings, and fallals—selecting this thing and that and the other, to make a little heap for Rebecca. And going to her Papa, that generous British merchant, who had promised to give her as many guineas as she was years old—she begged the old gentleman to give the money to dear Rebecca, who must want it, while she lacked for nothing.

She even made George Osborne contribute, and nothing loth (for he was as free-handed a young fellow as any in the army), he went to Bond Street[25], and bought the best hat and spencer that money could buy.

"That's George's present to you, Rebecca, dear," said Amelia, quite proud of the bandbox conveying these gifts. "What a taste he has! There's nobody like him."

"Nobody[26]," Rebecca answered. "How thankful I am to him!" She was thinking in her heart, "It was George Osborne who prevented my marriage."—And she loved George Osborne accordingly.

She made her preparations for departure with great equanimity; and accepted all the kind little Amelia's presents, after just the proper degree of hesitation and reluctance. She vowed eternal gratitude to Mrs. Sedley, of course; but did not intrude herself upon that good lady too much, who was embarrassed, and evidently wishing to avoid her. She kissed Mr. Sedley's hand, when he presented her with the purse; and asked permission to consider him for the future as her kind, kind friend and protector. Her behaviour was so affecting that he was going to write her a cheque for twenty pounds more; but he restrained his feelings: the carriage was in waiting to take him to dinner, so he tripped away with a "God bless you, my dear, always come here when you come to town, you know.—Drive to the Mansion House, James."

Finally came the parting with Miss Amelia, over which picture I intend to throw a veil. But after a scene in which one person was in earnest and the other a perfect performer—after the tenderest caresses, the most pathetic tears, the smelling-bottle[27], and some of the very best feelings of the heart, had been called into requisition[28]—Rebecca and Amelia parted, the former vowing to love her friend for ever and ever and ever.

Notes

1. Russell Square: a garden square in Bloomsbury, in the London Borough of Camden. In the novel, it is the residence of the Sedleys.
2. Vauxhall: an inner city area of south London in the London Borough of Lambeth

3. Jos: Joseph
4. sitting bodkin: sitting between two others with almost no room spared
5. we was: we were. Mrs. Blenkinsop often speak with incorrect grammar.
6. mahogany grandchildren: dark reddish-brown grandchildren; mahogany here is used in a derogative sense to suggest that his grandchildren might be the offspring of parents of different races if Joseph marries some black woman.
7. de trop: not wanted or needed
8. rack punch: a kind of alcoholic drink
9. Fair Rosamond: Rosamund Clifford, often called "The Fair Rosamund" or the "Rose of the World", was a mistress of King Henry II. The legend says she was hidden in a labyrinth and discovered by the queen, and the queen poisoned her to death.
10. Alexander the Great (356BC—323BC): the king of Macedonia that conquered the Persian empire. He is considered one of the greatest military geniuses of all times. It is assumed that Alexander was poisoned with arsenic by his possibly illegitimate half-brother.
11. "Brayvo, Fat un!" "Angcore,⋯": cockney accent for "Bravo, Fat one!" "Encore,⋯", which means "Well-done, Fat guy!" "Again,⋯"
12. Daniel Lambert (1770—1809): famed as the heaviest known person of his day
13. the Archbishop of Canterbury at Lambeth: the Archbishop of Canterbury is the senior bishop and principal leader of the Church of England. Lambeth Palace has been a historic London residence of Archbishops of Canterbury since the 13th century.
14. What is the rack in the punch, at night, to the rack in the head of a morning?: A pun is used here. The first "rack" means intoxication; the second suggests pain.
15. Small beer: mild beer
16. Bacchanalian: Bacchanalia is the ancient Roman festival in honor of Bacchus, also known as Dionysus, a god of wine and fertility of the nature. Here it refers to the riotously drunken Joseph.
17. Mr. Hosbin: Mr. Osborne. Sedley's valet speaks with a cockney accent. His "'ackney" "Capting" "harms" "babby" should be "hackney" "Captain" "arms" "baby".
18. Molyneux: Thomas Molyneux (1784—1818), an African-American boxer. He has been recognized as the first world boxing champion from the United States.
19. pluck: courage
20. Sister Anne is on the watch-tower: Sister Anne is a character from the French folktale "Bluebeard". Bluebeard marries several times and kills his wives mercilessly. His newly-wedded wife Ariadne discovers his secret. She and her sister Anne manage to lock themselves in a high tower, and Anne is sent to the top of the tower to watch for their two brothers, who arrive in time and put an end to Bluebeard's life.
21. discomfited mien: embarrassed bearing or manner
22. aide-de-camp: French for field assistant, a personal assistant, secretary, or adjutant to a person of high rank
23. Cheltenham: a town about a hundred miles from London
24. at fust: at first. Mrs. Blenkinsop's cockney accent and poor grammar. Her "sor" "ribbing" "hairs"

and hupstarts" should be "saw" "ribbon" "airs and upstarts".

25. Bond Street: a major shopping street in London, known throughout the world for its wealth of elegant stores, exclusive brands, designer fashion, luxury goods, fine jewels, art and antiques
26. Nobody: Amelia's use of "nobody" and Rebecca's repetition of "nobody" are used in different mood. Amelia is proud of her sweetheart George while Rebecca shows her hatred in a sarcastic tone, for she realizes it is George who scares away Joseph from her.
27. smelling-bottle: a bottle that contains smelling salts, used for arousing consciousness
28. had been called into requisition: had been demanded for use

Questions

1. What is the narrative role of "I" in this chapter of the novel?
2. How are the characters paired and contrasted in this chapter?
3. What are the linguistic features and how are they used by the author to achieve his thematic purpose?

Matthew Arnold
1822—1888

Matthew Arnold

Matthew Arnold, a Victorian poet, critic, and educationist, was born at Laleham-on-Thames in Middlesex. He was the eldest son of Thomas Arnold, headmaster of Rugby School and educationalist in the Victorian Age.

Arnold received instruction under private tutors at home after certain schooling in Laleham. After spending a year in Winchester College in 1836, he went to Rugby School in 1837. There he received literary recognition by winning the Rugby Poetry prize. A carefree, mischievous student as he was, he won an open scholarship to Balliol College, Oxford in 1841, and graduated in 1844. Before holding the position of Her Majesty's Inspector of Schools from 1851 to 1886, Arnold had been Private Secretary to Lord President of the Privy Council, during which period he wrote some of his finest poems and published them in two volumes: *The Strayed Reveller and Other Poems* (1849), and *Empedocles on Etna and Other Poems* (1852). At the age of thirty-four, Arnold was elected to the Poetry Chair at Oxford. As the Chair, he delivered his lectures in English rather than Latin as tradition required, and he was re-elected in 1862.

Arnold believed that poetry is the highest literature and expresses a philosophy, and that great art can function as a civilizing agent to enrich the intellectual and spiritual life of man. During his 35-year inspectorship, he kept on writing poetry and paid more and more attention to literary, social, and cultural criticism, urged by the sordid condition he observed while surveying education system across England and Europe. In his literary critical works *Essays in Criticism* (1865) and *Essays in Criticism, Second Series* (1888), he considered the most important criteria used to judge the value of a poem were "high truth" and "high seriousness". He also showed social and religious criticism in *Culture and Anarchy* (1869). and *Literature and Dogma* (1873). His critical thinking has been influential on critics like T. S. Eliot and F.R.Leavis.

Arnold's poetry and critical works concern issues which are still in question in the modern world, such as "social injustice, unequal educational opportunity, religious doubt, the uncertain role of the arts in the modern world, the restlessness and confusion of modern man". He explored all these issues with a critical mind, and his works constantly have scholarly attention lavished upon them. His prose is distinguished by its open-minded, receptive, and inspiring critical method in a polished style, and his poetry is fastidious, lucid, elevated with sparing use of aureate words, especially marked by a mood of plaintive reflection on "the corrosion of 'Faith' by 'Doubt'".

Among his poems, "Memorial Verses" (1850), "Sohrab and Rustum" (1853), "The Scholar Gypsy" (1853), and "Dover Beach" (1867) are most well-known. "Dover Beach" was first published in the collection *New Poems*. It describes, with a mournful tone, the nightscape of the beach at Dover, and suggests a nightmarish world from which the old religious verities have receded. The cadence in the poem is accompanied by various meters and rhymes as well as various rhetorical devices.

Dover Beach[1]

The sea is calm to-night
The tide is full, the moon lies fair
Upon the straits; on the French coast the light
Gleams and is gone; the cliffs of England stand,
Glimmering and vast, out in the tranquil bay.
Come to the window, sweet is the night-air!
Only, from the long line of spray
Where the sea meets the moon-blanched land,
Listen! you hear the grating roar[2]
Of pebbles which the waves draw back, and fling,
At their return, up the high strand,
Begin, and cease, and then again begin,
With tremulous cadence slow, and bring
The eternal note of sadness in.

Sophocles[3] long ago
Heard it on the Agaean, and it brought
Into his mind the turbid[4] ebb and flow

Of human misery; we
Find also in the sound a thought,
Hearing it by this distant northern sea.

The Sea of Faith
Was once, too, at the full, and round earth's shore
Lay like the folds of a bright girdle furled.
But now I only hear
Its melancholy, long, withdrawing roar,
Retreating, to the breath
Of the night-wind, down the vast edges drear
And naked shingles[5] of the world.

Ah, love, let us be true
To one another! for the world, which seems
To lie before us like a land of dreams,
So various, so beautiful, so new,
Hath really neither joy, nor love, nor light,
Nor certitude[6], nor peace, nor help for pain;
And we are here as on a darkling plain
Swept with confused alarms of struggle and flight,
Where ignorant armies clash by night.[7]

Notes

1. Dover Beach lies in the shore of the Strait of Dover, the narrowest part of the English Channel. The town of Dover is closer to France than any other port city in England. It is generally believed that Arnold went there for honeymoon in 1851 and composed this poem.
2. grating roar: harsh, grinding, or scraping roar. "grating roar" is caused by the conflict between the sea and the land, which might suggest the conflict between long-held religious beliefs and the challenges against them.
3. Sophocles: one of three great ancient Greek tragedians. Arnold alludes here to a passage in the ancient Greek play *Antigone*, by Sophocles, in which Sophocles says the gods can visit ruin on people from one generation to the next, like a swelling tide driven by winds.
4. turbid: muddy, cloudy
5. shingles: water-worn small stones and pebbles on the beach
6. certitude: absolute certainty or conviction
7. Where... night: This line is an allusion to Greek historian Thucydides' account of the Battle of Epipolae (413 BC). In that battle, Athenians fought an army of Syracusans at night. In the darkness, the combatants lashed out blindly at one another. It indicates the chaotic and meaningless battles in human history.

Questions

1. What visual and auditory images are used in this poem? What are their relation to illusion and reality?
2. What's "The Sea of Faith" like? How is the decline of religious faith lamented?
3. What are the rhetorical devices used in this poem? How does the shift of the point of view help to develop the theme of this poem?

Thomas Hardy
1840—1928

Thomas Hardy, novelist and poet, was born on June 2, 1840 in Dorset, a rural region of southwestern England. It has become Wessex in his novels of Character and Environment. His father was a village builder, and his mother was well-read, who educated him until he went to his first school at Bockhampton at eight. His primary school education lasted until he was sixteen, at which time he was apprenticed to a local church architect. Hardy went to London in 1862, and enrolled as a student at King's College, Cambridge. Though he won the prizes from the Royal Institute of British Architects in 1863, he took more interest in Greek and Latin classics and became familiar with the works by such writers as John Stuart Mill, and Auguste Comte.

Thomas Hardy

In 1867, Hardy returned to Dorset and worked as an architect. He also tried his hand at writing then. *Desperate Remedies* (1871) was his first published novel. Then he gave up architecture and devoted himself to literature with a contract for 11 monthly installments of a tale, *A Pair of Blue Eyes*, in the *Cornhill Magazine*. His Wessex novels began with *Far from the Maddening Crowd* (1874). This novel, together with *Under the Greenwood Tree* (1872), *The Return of the Native* (1878), *The Mayor of Casterbridge* (1886), *The Woodlanders* (1887), *Tess of the D'Urbervilles* (1891), and *Jude the Obscure* (1895) made up Hardy's "Novels of Character and Environment", and established him as a formidable writer. The other two groups of his novels, named by Hardy himself as well, are comparatively obscure, i.e. "Novels of Ingenuity" and "Romances and Fantasies". He also was the author of five short-story collections.

In the second half of the nineteenth century, a loss of faith was common among intellectuals in England, and Hardy rendered, in his novels, a certain pessimistic philosophy that mankind is subjected to the rule of some hostile mysterious fate. *Tess of the D'Urbervilles* and *Jude the Obscure* were his last long fictions. Issues like immoral sex, murder, and illegitimate children in these novels challenged the sensibilities of Victorian readers, and aroused heated debate and criticism. Due to the hostile reception, Hardy stopped writing novels and turned entirely to poetry when he was about 60 years old till his last days. Hardy died at Max Gate in January 1928; his heart was buried at Stinsford with his first wife Emma, and his ashes in Poets' Corner in Westminster Abbey.

Hardy began his literary career with writing poetry, but his best poetic works were produced only after he abandoned novels. In 1898 Hardy published his first volume of poetry, *Wessex Poems*, a collection of poems written over 30 years. Throughout his life, he created more than 1000 poems and one epic drama in verse: *The Dynasts* (1907). Among the most admired are some that he wrote to his first deceased wife, which are collected in *Satires and Circumstances* (1914). Though Hardy's verse appears traditional with a balladic and folksong touch, it is unique in its choice of diction, dramatic sharpness, and the sincerity it expresses. His poems, like his novels, often deal with disappointment in love and life, and mankind's struggle against indifference to human sufferings. In 1910, he was awarded the Order of Merit. Hardy is now recognized as one of the greatest poets of the twentieth century.

In "The Oxen", the speaker, in the style of a traditional ballad, recalls from his childhood a naive folk belief in the kneeling of the oxen on Christmas Eve. In this poem, Hardy contrasts piety in the past and loss of faith at present, and there is a pervading sense of regret, loss, and disillusionment throughout the lines. "Ah, Are You Digging on My Grave?" sounds like a folk song in ironic tone. The woman-corpse addresses all the people who she believes are mourning her and would be digging on her grave, and finally she realizes that it is her dog who is burying a bone against future hunger. The poem mocks at the confident belief in human relationship, being a humorous and mildly cynical reminder that life goes on with no regard to the dead.

The Oxen[1]

Christmas Eve, and twelve of the clock.
   "Now they are all on their knees,"
An elder said as we sat in a flock
   By the embers in hearthside ease.

We pictured the meek mild creatures where
   They dwelt in their strawy pen.
Nor did it occur to one of us there
   To doubt they were kneeling then.

So fair a fancy few would weave
   In these years! Yet, I feel,
If someone said on Christmas Eve
   "Come; see the oxen kneel

Thomas Hardy's Study

"In the lonely barton² by yonder coomb³
  Our childhood used to know,"
I should go with him in the gloom,
  Hoping it might be so.

Notes

1. Oxen: The image is an icon in the older sense of that word—a pictorial representation of an article of faith, something in which to place one's trust. It is believed that the oxen in the cowshed would kneel to show respect to Jesus Christ at midnight on Christmas Eve.
2. barton: farm
3. yonder coomb: "yonder" means "over there". It can work as an adjective, as in the poem, or an adverb. "coomb" means "a valley". These words are of Celtic origin.

Questions

1. What are "these years"? How do they contrast with the years of the poet's boyhood?
2. What's the significance of the image of oxen in this poem?
3. This poem is in the form of a traditional ballad with a simple, abab rhyme and four-beat line. How does the form contribute to the anti-traditional theme of the poem?

Ah, Are You Digging on My Grave?

"Ah, are you digging on my grave
        My loved one?—planting rue¹?"
—"No, yesterday he went to wed
One of the brightest wealth has bred.
'It cannot hurt her now,' he said,
        'That I should not be true.'"

"Then who is digging on my grave?
        My nearest dearest kin?"
—"Ah, no; they sit and think, 'What use!
What good will planting flowers produce?
No tendance² of her mound³ can loose
        Her spirit from Death's gin⁴.'"

"But some one digs upon my grave?
        My enemy?—prodding sly?"
—"Nay: when she heard you had passed the Gate

That shuts on all flesh soon or late,
　　She thought you no more worth her hate,
　　　　And cares not where you lie."

"Then, who is digging on my grave?
　　　　Say—since I have not guessed!"
—"O it is I, my mistress dear,
Your little dog, who still lives near,
And much I hope my movements here
　　　　Have not disturbed your rest?"

"Ah yes! You dig upon my grave...
　　　　Why flashed it not on me[5]
That one true heart was left behind!
What feeling do we ever find
To equal among human kind
　　　　A dog's fidelity!"

"Mistress, I dug upon your grave
　　　　To bury a bone, in case
I should be hungry near this spot
When passing on my daily trot.
I am sorry, but I quite forgot
　　　　It was your resting-place."

Notes

1. rue: rue is a shrub and symbolizes sorrow, so the corpse's question suggests double meanings. She is asking her lover if he is planting flowers on her grave and if he is feeling sorrow about her death.
2. tendance: care
3. mound: a raised mass of earth, stones, or other compacted material, sometimes created artificially for purposes of burial; grave
4. gin: a type of snare or trap used to catch animals
5. Why flashed it not on me: Why was I not aware of it?

Questions

1. Who is the speaker and who is the audience? What is the effect of their dialogue?
2. What imagery does the poet use? What is the irony of the poem?
3. Is there any romanticized notion of society revealed in the poem?

Chapter Six Female Individuality and Fulfillment

Historically speaking, it has been a long and unremitting struggle for women to assert their individuality and attain self-fulfillment. In traditional views, women are the second sex and the other to men—where they belong is the household, and school education is beyond their reach. Consequently, few women were granted the "privilege" of engaging in literary creation. And women in men writers' works are often portrayed with prejudice or sympathy, or as some feminist critics have noted, women are often stereotyped either as monsters or angels. Notwithstanding the generally warped women images in literary creation, readers still can find, to their great relief, that flesh-and-blood women characters are not totally absent from men's writings, such as Ophelia in Shakespeare's *Hamlet*, the Wife of Bath in Chaucer's *Canterbury Tales*, Moll in Defoe's *Moll Flanders*, and Mrs. Morel in Lawrence's *Sons and Lovers*. These characters can shed some light on public opinions of women and their place in society throughout different ages.

More zest and concern for women's self-expression and fulfillment can be found in women's own writing. As asserted by critics like Ellen Showalter, before the nineteenth century, there was no possibility for a woman to plan her career as a professional writer, but the eighteenth century did witness some literary creations by a handful of talented women, though they had to publish their works anonymously. The development of industrial revolution and the idea of enlightenment aroused women's awareness of their own rights and freedom. In 1792, Mary Wollstonecraft published *A Vindication of the Rights of Women,* and along with the suffragette movement and women's liberation movement in the 1960s, women began more actively and distinctively to express their actual experience in a way that empowers them as artists. Women writers, such as Jane Austen, the Brontë sisters, George Eliot, Elizabeth Gaskell, Mary Shelley, Virginia Woolf, Sylvia Plath, G.B.Stern, Muriel Spark, A.S.Byatt, and Doris Lessing, have continuously stimulated a rich and diverse intellectual culture and had women's voice and desire more functionally uttered on wider social issues—issues no longer exclusively limited to their own gender. Their creations provide readers with new perspectives to gain a better understanding of women's individuality and fulfillment.

As reflected in their works, women are confronted with the conflicts of work, sex, love, maternity, and politics, and to which extent women can show their individuality or how much they can fulfill themselves is affected by many factors like their legal status, education, and employment. These issues are still problematic and even more complicated nowadays. Contemporary writers, male or female, are trying to give more pertinent and diverse expressions about women in various literary writings.

Geoffrey Chaucer
c.1340—1400

Geoffrey Chaucer was one of the most brilliant writers in medieval times. He was born circa 1340 in a wealthy family in London. His father, a successful wine importer, afforded him an education sufficient for the work in which he later became engaged. He might have studied civil law and business procedure, acquired a good knowledge of Latin, French, and Italian, and became acquainted with the influential writings of Virgil and Ovid.

In 1357 Chaucer became a public servant to Countess Elizabeth of Ulster and started his whole-life service to the court, variously as page-boy, valet, esquire, soldier, diplomat, customs officer, supervisor of public works, Justice of the Peace, Member of Parliament, and royal forester. His career in the British court spared him from relying on the support of patrons, which was a common practice for writers lacking resources then. In 1366 Chaucer married Philippa Roet from a noble family, and the marriage conveniently helped further Chaucer's career in the English court.

The preoccupation with diplomatic missions and court service during the Hundred Years War brought Chaucer into close contact with royal families and distinguished people home and abroad, and meanwhile assisted him in gaining more knowledge and inspiration from foreign literature as an indefatigable reader and writer. He drew his first poetic inspiration from French poetry, and his diplomatic visits to Italy enriched his readings of famous Italian writers of the Renaissance and enhanced his creativeness. He translated the French poem *Romance of the Rose,* and his longest complete poem *Troilus and Criseyde* (1386?) was adapted from Boccaccio's Italian work *Il Filostrato,* a narrative poem about a tragic love story in the context of the Trojan War. Chaucer also completed a prose translation of the sixth-century Latin *Consolation of Phiolosophy*. Another well-known work is The *Parliament of Fowls* (1380?), which ridicules the inauthentic quality of courtly love. *The Canterbury Tales,* written from about 1387 to 1400, is his best-known and most acclaimed work. Chaucer died in 1400 in London and was the first to be buried in Westminster Abbey's Poet's Corner.

As Chaucer scholar Charles W. Dunn remarks from the perspective of literary history: "Chaucer's paramount achievement...lies in his rejection of all that is lifeless and merely formal, in favor of the immediacy and actuality of life as he knew it." Chaucer drew literary nourishment from his observation of life and various sources of knowledge. He had a good knowledge of the idiom and the passions of contemporary men and women, and wrote about them with ease and sincerity. Concerning the portrayal of women, he peopled his stories with contrasting women characters, ranging from fictional queens, maidens to whores. His works present us what it meant to be a woman in then England, as shown in his *The Legend of Good Women* (1385?), and in *The Canterbury Tales.*

Chaucer greatly expanded the writing of his French and Italian predecessors and contemporaries, and significantly enriched English poetry. The eloquence, morality, wit, and originality in his writings are always well admired and discussed. What's more, Chaucer established the East Midland dialect of Middle English as the medium of later major English literature. He is hailed as the founder of English poetry.

Wife of Bath's Prologue in *The Canterbury Tales*

The Canterbury Tales is a monumental work written in Middle English. In this work, the poet and narrator Chaucer joins a body of pilgrims at the Tabard Inn who are ready for a pilgrimage to Canterbury. At the suggestion of the host of the inn, they decide to beguile the time by tale-telling; each pilgrim is to tell four stories, two on the way to Canterbury and two more on the way back. Chaucer initially intended to write about 120 stories, but only 24 tales were written.

The Canterbury Tales consists of the General Prologue, tales, and link passages. Most of the work is written in heroic couplets. The General Prologue provides a framework of the tales, offering vivid sketches of the miscellaneous body of the pilgrims, who can be deemed as representatives of the society of the time. The tales, different in topics and styles, together with the Prologue, produce an extraordinary representation of the mediaeval England. With an underlying comic tone, *The Canterbury Tales* touches such subjects as the role of women, marriage, the truth or deception of art, the nature of death, the function of evil in the Creator's plan, and the hidden mystery of God's being, among which the tales of and by Wife of Bath are of the best-known ones.

The Wife of Bath, in her lengthy biographic prologue, describes her married life with five men. A childless widow and owner of a weaving business, she has managed to use her verbal and sexual power to bring her husbands to submission and their property to her use. Among them, three have been "good" and two have been "bad". She keeps mastery over the first three good ones who are rich, old, and submissive, but she has difficulties with the lively young ones, who must have married her for the wealth she gets from the first three. In her narration, she doesn't much portray the first three as the latter two who might have given her genuine delight from marriage. Even though the fifth husband destroys her hearing by a blow on the ear, she cannot stop herself from loving him, and finally she also succeeds in bringing his meager estate under her control.

Wife of Bath is criticized for her numerous marriages against the doctrines of religion, but in retort, she imitates the ways of churchmen and scholars by backing up her claims with quotations from the Scripture and works of antiquity. Her voluble argument defies the medieval assumption that women are essentially evil because they are the daughters of Eve, the agent of man's fall from Paradise. Feminist critics have often tried to portray the Wife of Bath as an early precursor of feminist thought, while some scholars view her Prologue as anti-feminist rhetoric. This is a

The Canterbury Tales

testimony to Chaucer's artistry; he succeeded in advancing her argument so powerfully and skillfully that "the reader is compelled to admire it even if he does not agree".

The following section is a middle English version of lines 1-51 from *Wife of Bath's Prologue*, and the corresponding modern prose version is attached to it for reference.

    Experience, though noon auctoritee[1]
Were in this world, is right ynogh for me
To speke of wo that is in mariage;
For, lordynges, sith[2] I twelve yeer was of age,
Thonked be God that is eterne on lyve[3],
Housbondes at chirche dore I have had fyve, —
If I so ofte myghte han wedded be, —
And alle were worthy men in hir[4] degree.
But me was told, certeyn, noght longe agon is,
That sith that Crist ne wente nevere but onys
To weddyng in the Cane[5] of Galilee,
That by the same ensample taughte he me
That I ne sholde wedded be but ones.
Herke eek, lo, which a sharp word for the nones,
Bisyde a welle Jesus, God and man,
Spak in repreeve of the Samaritan:
"Thou hast y-had fyve housbondes," — quod he,
"And that ilke man that now hath thee
Is nat thyn housbonde." Thus he seyde, certeyn.
What that he mente ther-by, I kan nat seyn,
But that I axe why that the fifthe man
Was noon housbonde to the Samaritan?
How manye myghte she have in mariage?
Yet herde I nevere tellen in myn age
Upon this nombre diffinicioun.
Men may dyvyne and glosen, up and doun,
But wel I woot, expres, withoute lye,
God bad us for to wexe and multiplye;
That gentil text kan I wel understonde.
Eek wel I woot, he seyde myn housbonde
Sholde lete fader and moder, and take to me.
But of no nombre mencioun made he,
Of bigamye, or of octogamye;
Why sholde men thanne speke of it vileynye[6]?
    Lo, here the wise kyng, daun Salomon;

I trowe he hadde wyves mo than oon⁷.
As wolde God it leveful were to me
To be refresshed half so ofte as he!
Which yifte⁸ of God hadde he for alle his wyvys!
No man hath swich⁹ that in this world alyve is.
God woot, this noble kyng, as to my wit,
The firste nyght had many a murye fit
With ech of hem, so wel was hym on lyve.
Blessed be God that I have wedded five,
Of whiche I have pyked out the beste
Bothe of here nether purs and of here cheste¹⁰.
Diverse scloes maken parfyt clerkes,
And diverse practyk in many sundry werkes
Maken the werkman parfit, sekirly¹¹.
Of Fyve husbondes scoleiyng¹² am I.
Welcome the sixte whan that evere he shal.

Modern prose version of the selected part:

My experience gives me sufficient right to speak of the trouble there is in marriage, even if there were no other authority in the world; for, ladies and gentlemen, since I was twelve years old I have had five husbands, eternal God be thanked—if it is legal to have been married so often—and all were fine men in their way. But not long ago I was certainly told that since Christ attended only one wedding, in Cana of Galilee, He therefore taught me by example to be married only once. And listen also to the sharp words Jesus, God and men, spoke beside the well to scold the Samaritan about this matter: "You have had five husbands," he said, "and that men whom you now have is not your husband." Certainly He said this; what He meant by it I can't say. But I ask why the fifth man was not husband to the Samaritan? How many was she allowed to marry? In my time I never yet heard of a limitation of number. Men can interpret and gloss the text up and down, but I know surely without doubt that God expressly told us to increase and multiply; that pleasant text I can easily understand. I also know very well that He said my husband should leave his father and mother and live with me. But He made no mention of number, of bigamy, or of octogamy. Why then should men call it wickedness?

Look at the wise King, Lord Solomon: I believe he had more than one wife. I wish to God it were possible for me to be refreshed half as often as he was! What a gift from God he had for all his wives! No man now living has the same. God knows, this noble King must have had many a merry bout with each of them the first night, to my thinking. He was well fixed for a lifetime! Thank God that I married five! The sixth, whenever he comes, shall be welcome.

Notes

1. noon auctoritee: no (scholarly) authority
2. sith: since
3. eterne on lyve: eternally alive
4. hir: their
5. Cane: Cana
6. vileynye: reproach
7. oon: one
8. Which yifte: What a gift
9. swich: such
10. cheste: money-chest
11. sekirly: certainly
12. scoleiyng: schooling

Questions

1. What view of marriage does the Wife of Bath hold?
2. How does the Wife of Bath justify her five marriages? Does she mean to contradict the misogynist ideas of her time?

Jane Austen
1775—1817

Jane Austen

One of the top-ranking and the most widely-read English writers, Jane Austen was born in a rural rector's family in 1775 at Steventon, Hampshire. In a house full of lively conversation unspoiled by disagreeable arguments, Jane grew up happily with her six brothers and her elder sister Cassandra. She and her sister were taught at home by their parents. Her mother was the daughter of a clergyman with aristocratic connections, and her father the Reverend George Austen was educated in Oxford. Jane and Cassandra were sent to a small Oxford boarding school and then to a school in Reading for some years. When Jane was eleven, they went back home and continued their education on an informal basis. Jane became acquainted with many literary works, and enjoyed the domesticity of local gentry life. Traveling little, she kept herself apart from the contemporary literary world.

Due to her father's retirement from rectorship, she moved with the family to Bath in 1801. In 1808, three years after her father's death, she moved with her sister and mother to Chawton, where she spent her most creative years and lived until her final days. In 1816, her health began to fail, and she died in July 1817.

Jane Austen started writing in her teens, and in 1796 she began her first book *First Impressions,* which was revised and published sixteen years later as *Pride and Prejudice*. In all, she made herself the author of six novels, *Sense and Sensibility* (1811), *Pride and Prejudice* (1813), *Mansfield Park* (1814), *Emma* (1816), *Northanger Abbey* (1817) and *Persuasion* (1818). She managed to publish the first four anonymously after she settled down in Chawton, and the last two were published posthumously.

With virtuosic techniques, Austen's novels delve into the life of rural middle class people, and display a realistic world of rural felicity. Love, marriage, loyalty and betrayal are favorite subjects in her novels. Though she never got married and seldom traveled, Austen made her descriptions of love and domestic affairs quite smart and poignant, together with a sharp observation of human weaknesses. Moreover, her ironic stance honed her insight into contemporary mores, especially the dependence of women on marriage to secure social standing and economic security. Her concern about women's fate in society is much related to the social milieu that women had to acquire self-improvement through successful marriage.

Pride and Prejudice

When Jane Austen first submitted the manuscript of *Pride and Prejudice*, finished in 1796, to her publisher, it was flatly rejected. No one anticipated that sixteen years later, the revised novel would turn out to be Austen's most popular work and one of the masterpieces in women's writing.

The novel portrays the life in the genteel rural society of the day, and tells of the story of a Bennet family. For Mr. and Mrs. Bennet, the marriage of their five daughters is their central concern, since the father's estate is to be entailed on the nearest male relative, a clergyman named Collins. The Bennet girls, Jane, Elizabeth, Mary, Kitty, and Lydia, are thus pushed to make their fortune by speculating on the marriage market.

The novel, while unfolding itself around the love-affairs of Jane, Elizabeth and Lydia, foregrounds the relationship between the intelligent Elizabeth and the haughty Darcy. At a local ball, Elizabeth and Darcy meet for the first time. Elizabeth overhears Darcy's arrogant talk and refuses to dance with him. Also on this occasion, her elder sister Jane and Darcy's friend Binley begin to form an attachment.

As Darcy grows more interested in Elizabeth, Elizabeth continues to despise him. The rumor

Jane Austen's house

spread by the young officer George Wickham increases her prejudice against him. She is expected to accept the proposal of marriage from Mr. Collins, the inheritor of her father's estate. However she turns it down, and Mr. Collins, stunned by her refusal, soon marries Elizabeth's friend, Charlotte Lucas, who wants to marry for security rather than love. Elizabeth meets Darcy again while visiting Charlotte and Collins. Darcy is living on the estate of his aunt, Lady Catherine De Bourgh. Elizabeth feels uncomfortable with the snobbish Lady and is surprised by Darcy's sudden proposal. Still repelled by Darcy's arrogance, the perspicacious Elizabeth turns him down, accusing him of separating Bingley and Jane and treating Wickham unjustly. The next day, Darcy sends her a letter explaining his conducts. Though reluctant to believe, Elizabeth finally finds out that Darcy is innocent of wrongdoing. All misunderstandings are now cleared up. Happily, Jane and Bingley resume their relationship, and Elizabeth accepts Darcy's proposal, regardless of Lady Catherine De Bourgh's rude interference.

Through Austen's vivid characterization, skillful narrative and idiosyncratic witticism, the life of the rural gentry of the time is exceptionally well rendered. All characters in the novel are glamorous, even those minor ones such as the Bennets, Mr. Collins and Lady Catherine, especially with their laughably specious views and remarks. Social issues like marriage and property inheritance are also explored in an apparently humorous manner. However, the irony veiled in humor clearly reveals women's social plight in the nineteenth century—Women's position in a "marriage mart" and their choice of marriage adequately reflect the social restraints imposed on women and their somewhat "desperate" fight for an ideal life.

Chapter I is well known for its opening sentence which becomes one of the most famous and memorable quotations from her novels. This chapter brings forward the theme of the entire novel, and presents a lively portrait of the members of the Bennet family. In Chapter LVI (or Chapter XIV, Volume 3), the arrogant Lady Catherine visits Elizabeth and rudely asks her not to accept Darcy's proposal. Elizabeth very cleverly parries this verbal inquisition.

Chapter I

It is a truth universally acknowledged, that a single man in possession of a good fortune, must be in want of[1] a wife.

However little known the feelings or views of such a man may be on his first entering a neighbourhood, this truth is so well fixed in the minds of the surrounding families, that he is considered the rightful property of some one or other of their daughters.

"My dear Mr. Bennet," said his lady to him one day, "have you heard that Netherfield Park is let[2] at last?"

Mr Bennet replied that he had not.

"But it is," returned she; "for Mrs Long has just been here, and she told me all about it."

Mr Bennet made no answer.

"Do not you want to know who has taken it?" cried his wife impatiently.

"*You* want to tell me, and I have no objection to hearing it."

This was invitation enough.

"Why, my dear, you must know, Mrs. Long says that Netherfield is taken by a young man of large fortune from the north of England; that he came down on Monday in a chaise and four[3] to see the place, and was so much delighted with it, that he agreed with Mr. Morris immediately; that he is to take possession before Michaelmas[4], and some of his servants are to be in the house by the end of next week."

"What is his name?"

"Bingley."

"Is he married or single?"

"Oh! single, my dear, to be sure! A single man of large fortune; four or five thousand a year. What a fine thing for our girls!"

"How so? How can it affect them?"

"My dear Mr. Bennet," replied his wife, "how can you be so tiresome! You must know that I am thinking of his marrying one of them."

"Is that his design[5] in settling here?"

"Design! nonsense, how can you talk so! But it is very likely that he *may* fall in love with one of them, and therefore you must visit him as soon as he comes."

"I see no occasion for that. You and the girls may go, or you may send them by themselves, which perhaps will be still better, for as you are as handsome as any of them, Mr. Bingley may like you the best of the party."

"My dear, you flatter me. I certainly *have* had my share of beauty, but I do not pretend to be anything extraordinary now. When a woman has five grown-up daughters, she ought to give over thinking of her own beauty."

"In such cases, a woman has not often much beauty to think of."

"But, my dear, you must indeed go and see Mr. Bingley when he comes into the neighbourhood."

"It is more than I engage for[6], I assure you."

"But consider your daughters. Only think what an establishment[7] it would be for one of them. Sir William and Lady Lucas are determined to go, merely on that account, for in general you know, they visit no new comers. Indeed you must go, for it will be impossible for us to visit him, if you do not."

"You are over-scrupulous surely. I dare say Mr. Bingley will be very glad to see you; and I will send a few lines by you to assure him of my hearty consent to his marrying which ever he chuses of the girls; though I must throw in a good word for my little Lizzy."

"I desire you will do no such thing. Lizzy is not a bit better than the others; and I am sure she is not half so handsome as Jane, nor half so good humoured[8] as Lydia. But you are always giving *her* the preference."

"They have none of them much to recommend them," replied he; "they are all silly and ignorant like other girls; but Lizzy has something more of quickness than her sisters."

"Mr. Bennet, how can you abuse your own children in such a way? You take delight in vexing[9] me. You have no compassion on my poor nerves."

"You mistake me, my dear. I have a high respect for your nerves. They are my old friends. I have heard you mention them with consideration these twenty years at least."

"Ah! you do not know what I suffer."

"But I hope you will get over it, and live to see many young men of four thousand a year come into the neighbourhood."

"It will be no use to us, if twenty such should come since you will not visit them."

"Depend upon it, my dear, that when there are twenty, I will visit them all."

Mr. Bennet was so odd a mixture of quick parts[10], sarcastic humour, reserve, and caprice, that the experience of three and twenty years had been insufficient to make his wife understand his character. *Her* mind was less difficult to develop. She was a woman of mean understanding, little information, and uncertain temper. When she was discontented she fancied herself nervous. The business of her life was to get her daughters married; its solace was visiting and news.

Chapter LVI

One morning, about a week after Bingley's engagement with Jane had been formed, as he and the females of the family were sitting together in the dining-room, their attention was suddenly drawn to the window, by the sound of a carriage; and they perceived a chaise and four driving up the lawn. It was too early in the morning for visitors, and besides, the equipage did not answer to[11] that of any of their neighbours. The horses were post[12]; and neither the carriage, nor the livery of the servant who preceded it, were familiar to them. As it was certain, however, that somebody was coming, Bingley instantly prevailed on Miss Bennet to avoid the confinement of such an intrusion, and walk away with him into the shrubbery. They both set off, and the conjectures of the remaining three continued, though with little satisfaction, till the door was thrown open, and their visitor entered. It was Lady Catherine De Bourgh.

They were of course all intending to be surprised; but their astonishment was beyond their expectation; and on the part of Mrs. Bennet and Kitty, though she was perfectly unknown to them, even inferior to what Elizabeth felt.

She entered the room with an air more than usually ungracious, made no other reply to Elizabeth's salutation, than a slight inclination of the head, and sat down without saying a word. Elizabeth had mentioned her name to her mother, on her ladyship's entrance, though no request of introduction had been made.

Mrs. Bennet, all amazement, though flattered by having a guest of such high importance, received her with the utmost politeness. After sitting for a moment in silence, she said very stiffly to Elizabeth,

"I hope you are well, Miss Bennet. That lady I suppose is your mother."

Elizabeth replied very concisely that she was.

"And *that* I suppose is one of your sisters?"

"Yes, madam," said Mrs. Bennet, delighted to speak to a Lady Catherine. "She is my youngest girl but one. My youngest of all, is lately married, and my eldest is somewhere about the grounds, walking with a young man, who I believe will soon become a part of the family."

"You have a very small park here," returned Lady Catherine after a short silence.

"It is nothing in comparison of Rosings[13], my lady, I dare say; but I assure you it is much larger than Sir William Lucas's."

"This must be a most inconvenient sitting room for the evening, in summer; the windows are full west."

Mrs. Bennet assured her that they never sat there after dinner; and then added,

"May I take the liberty of asking your ladyship whether you left Mr. and Mrs. Collins well?"

"Yes, very well. I saw them the night before last."

Elizabeth now expected that she would produce a letter for her from Charlotte, as it seemed the only probable motive for her calling. But no letter appeared, and she was completely puzzled.

Mrs. Bennet, with great civility, begged her ladyship to take some refreshment; but Lady Catherine very resolutely, and not very politely, declined eating any thing; and then rising up, said to Elizabeth,

"Miss Bennet, there seemed to be a prettyish kind of a little wilderness[14] on one side of your lawn. I should be glad to take a turn in it, if you will favour me with your company."

"Go, my dear," cried her mother, "and shew her ladyship about the different walks. I think she will be pleased with the hermitage."

Elizabeth obeyed, and running into her own room for her parasol, attended her noble guest down stairs. As they passed through the hall, Lady Catherine opened the doors into the dining-parlour and drawing-room, and pronouncing them, after a short survey, to be decent looking rooms, walked on.

Her carriage remained at the door, and Elizabeth saw that her waiting-woman was in it. They proceeded in silence along the gravel walk that led to the copse; Elizabeth was determined to make no effort for conversation with a woman, who was now more than usually insolent and disagreeable.

"How could I ever think her like her nephew?" said she, as she looked in her face.

As soon as they entered the copse[15], Lady Catherine began in the following manner: —

"You can be at no loss, Miss Bennet, to understand the reason of my journey hither. Your own heart, your own conscience, must tell you why I come."

Elizabeth looked with unaffected astonishment.

"Indeed, you are mistaken, Madam. I have not been at all able to account for the honour of seeing you here."

"Miss Bennet," replied her ladyship, in an angry tone, "you ought to know, that I am not to be trifled with. But however insincere you may choose to be, you shall not find me so. My character has ever been celebrated for its sincerity and frankness, and in a cause of such moment as this, I shall certainly not depart from it[16]. A report of a most alarming nature, reached me two days ago. I was told, that not only your sister was on the point of being most advantageously married, but that *you*, that Miss Elizabeth Bennet, would, in all likelihood, be soon afterwards united to my nephew, my own nephew, Mr. Darcy. Though I *know* it must be a scandalous falsehood; though I would not injure him so much as to suppose the truth of it possible, I instantly resolved on setting off for this place, that I might make my sentiments known to you."

"If you believed it impossible to be true," said Elizabeth, colouring with astonishment and disdain, "I wonder you took the trouble of coming so far. What could your ladyship propose by it?"

"At once to insist upon having such a report universally contradicted."

"Your coming to Longbourn, to see me and my family," said Elizabeth, coolly, "will be rather a confirmation of it; if, indeed, such a report is in existence."

"If! Do you then pretend to be ignorant of it? Has it not been industriously circulated by yourselves? Do you not know that such a report is spread abroad?"

"I never heard that it was."

"And can you likewise declare, that there is no *foundation* for it?"

"I do not pretend to possess equal frankness with your ladyship. You may ask questions, which I shall not choose to answer."

"This is not to be borne. Miss Bennet, I insist on being satisfied[17]. Has he, has my nephew, made you an offer of marriage?"

"Your ladyship has declared it to be impossible."

"It ought to be so; it must be so, while he retains the use of his reason. But your arts and allurements may, in a moment of infatuation, have made him forget what he owes to himself and to all his family. You may have drawn him in."

"If I have, I shall be the last person to confess it."

"Miss Bennet, do you know who I am? I have not been accustomed to such language as this. I am almost the nearest relation he has in the world, and am entitled to know all his dearest concerns."

"But you are not entitled to know *mine*; nor will such behaviour as this, ever induce me to be explicit."

"Let me be rightly understood. This match, to which you have the presumption to aspire, can never take place. No, never. Mr. Darcy is engaged to *my daughter*. Now what have you to say?"

"Only this; that if he is so, you can have no reason to suppose he will make an offer to me."

Lady Catherine hesitated for a moment, and then replied.

"The engagement between them is of a peculiar kind. From their infancy, they have been intended for each other. It was the favourite wish of his mother, as well as of her's[18]. While in their cradles, we planned the union: and now, at the moment when the wishes of both sisters would be accomplished, in their marriage, to be prevented by a young woman of inferior birth, of no importance in the world, and wholly unallied to the family! Do you pay no regard to the wishes of his friends? To his tacit engagement with Miss De Bourgh[19]? Are you lost to every feeling of propriety and delicacy? Have you not heard me say, that from his earliest hours he was destined for his cousin?"

"Yes, and I had heard it before. But what is that to me? If there is no other objection to my marrying your nephew, I shall certainly not be kept from it, by knowing that his mother and aunt wished him to marry Miss De Bourgh. You both did as much as you could, in planning the marriage; its completion depended on others. If Mr. Darcy is neither by honour nor inclination confined to his cousin, why is not he to make another choice? And if I am that choice, why may not I accept him?"

"Because honour, decorum, prudence, nay[20], interest, forbid it. Yes, Miss Bennet, interest; for do not expect to be noticed by his family or friends, if you wilfully act against the inclinations of all. You will be censured, slighted, and despised, by every one connected with him. Your alliance will be a disgrace; your name will never even be mentioned by any of us."

"These are heavy misfortunes," replied Elizabeth. "But the wife of Mr. Darcy must have such extraordinary sources of happiness necessarily attached to her situation, that she could, upon the whole, have no cause to repine."

"Obstinate, headstrong girl! I am ashamed of you! Is this your gratitude for my attentions to you last spring? Is nothing due to me on that score?"[21]

"Let us sit down. You are to understand, Miss Bennet, that I came here with the determined resolution of carrying my purpose; nor will I be dissuaded from it. I have not been used to submit to any person's whims. I have not been in the habit of brooking disappointment."

"*That* will make your ladyship's situation at present more pitiable; but it will have no effect on *me*."

"I will not be interrupted. Hear me in silence. My daughter and my nephew are formed for each other. They are descended on the maternal side, from the same noble line; and, on the father's, from respectable, honourable, and ancient, though untitled families. Their fortune on both sides is splendid. They are destined for each other by the voice of every member of their respective houses; and what is to divide them? The upstart pretensions of a young woman without family, connections, or fortune. Is this to be endured! But it must not, shall not be. If you were sensible of your own good, you would not wish to quit the sphere in which you have been brought up."

"In marrying your nephew, I should not consider myself as quitting that sphere. He is a gentleman; I am a gentleman's daughter; so far we are equal."

"True. You *are* a gentleman's daughter. But who was your mother? Who are your uncles and aunts? Do not imagine me ignorant of their condition."

"Whatever my connections may be," said Elizabeth, "if your nephew does not object to them, they can be nothing to *you*."

"Tell me, once for all, are you engaged to him?"

Though Elizabeth would not, for the mere purpose of obliging Lady Catherine, have answered this question, she could not but say, after a moment's deliberation,

"I am not."

Lady Catherine seemed pleased.

"And will you promise me, never to enter into such an engagement?"

"I will make no promise of the kind."

"Miss Bennet, I am shocked and astonished. I expected to find a more reasonable young woman. But do not deceive yourself into a belief that I will ever recede. I shall not go away, till you have given me the assurance I require."

"And I certainly *never* shall give it. I am not to be intimidated into anything so wholly unreasonable. Your ladyship wants Mr. Darcy to marry your daughter; but would my giving you the wished-for promise, make *their* marriage at all more probable? Supposing him to be attached to me, would my refusing to accept his hand make him wish to bestow it on his cousin? Allow me to say, Lady Catherine, that the arguments with which you have supported this extraordinary application[22], have been as frivolous as the application was ill judged. You have widely mistaken my character, if you think I can be worked on by such persuasions as these. How far your nephew might approve of your interference in *his* affairs, I cannot tell; but you have certainly no right to concern yourself in mine. I must beg, therefore, to be importuned no farther on the subject."

"Not so hasty, if you please. I have by no means done."[23] To all the objections I have already urged,

I have still another to add. I am no stranger to the particulars of your youngest sister's infamous elopement. I know it all; that the young man's marrying her, was a patched-up business, at the expence of your father and uncles. And is *such* a girl to be my nephew's sister? Is her husband, is the son of his late father's steward, to be his brother? Heaven and earth!—of what are you thinking! Are the shades of Pemberley to be thus polluted?"

"You can *now* have nothing farther to say," she resentfully answered. "You have insulted me, in every possible method. I must beg to return to the house."

And she rose as she spoke. Lady Catherine rose also, and they turned back. Her ladyship was highly incensed.

"You have no regard, then, for the honour and credit of my nephew! Unfeeling, selfish girl! Do you not consider that a connection with you, must disgrace him in the eyes of everybody?"

"Lady Catherine, I have nothing farther to say. You know my sentiments."

"You are then resolved to have him?"

"I have said no such thing. I am only resolved to act in that manner, which will, in my own opinion, constitute my happiness, without reference to *you*, or to any person so wholly unconnected with me."

"It is well. You refuse, then, to oblige me. You refuse to obey the claims of duty, honour, and gratitude. You are determined to ruin him in the opinion of all his friends, and make him the contempt of the world."

"Neither duty, nor honour, nor gratitude," replied Elizabeth, "have any possible claim on me, in the present instance. No principle of either, would be violated by my marriage with Mr. Darcy. And with regard to the resentment of his family, or the indignation of the world, if the former *were* excited by his marrying me, it would not give me one moment's concern—and the world in general would have too much sense to join in the scorn."

"And this is your real opinion! This is your final resolve! Very well. I shall now know how to act. Do not imagine, Miss Bennet, that your ambition will ever be gratified. I came to try you. I hoped to find you reasonable; but depend upon it I will carry my point."

In this manner Lady Catherine talked on, till they were at the door of the carriage, when, turning hastily round, she added,

"I take no leave of you, Miss Bennet. I send no compliments to your mother. You deserve no such attention. I am most seriously displeased."

Elizabeth made no answer, and without attempting to persuade her ladyship to return into the house, walked quietly into it herself. She heard the carriage drive away as she proceeded up stairs. Her mother impatiently met her at the door of the dressing room, to ask why Lady Catherine would not come in again and rest herself.

"She did not choose it," said her daughter; "she would go."

"She is a very fine-looking woman! and her calling here was prodigiously civil! For she only came, I suppose, to tell us the Collinses were well. She is on her road somewhere, I dare say, and so passing through Meryton[24], thought she might as well call on you. I suppose she had nothing particular to say to you, Lizzy?"

Elizabeth was forced to give into a little falsehood here; for to acknowledge the substance of their conversation was impossible[25].

Notes

Chapter I

1. in want of: lack; in need of
2. let: rented
3. a chaise and four: a four-wheeled closed carriage usually drawn by two or four horses. An income of at least £800, and preferably £1,000 a year was needed to keep a carriage.
4. Michaelmas: the festival of Saint Michael, held on September 29
5. design: purpose; deliberate intention
6. more than I engage for: more than I can promise
7. what an establishment: what a marriage
8. good humoured: good natured
9. vex: annoy
10. quick parts: talents, capacities, abilities

Chapter LVI

11. did not answer to: was not similar to
12. The horses were post: post-horse. It suggests that the guest comes from afar by riding post-horse.
13. Rosings: the name of Lady Catherine's estate
14. a prettyish kind of a little wilderness: somewhat pretty wild scenery
15. copse: a thicket of small trees or shrubs
16. it: my character
17. I insist on being satisfied: I insist that you give me a satisfying answer
18. her's: hers
19. Miss De Bourgh: the daughter of Lady Catherine
20. nay: no
21. Is nothing due to me on that score?: Lady Catherine gives Elizabeth a treat last spring, and she asks Elizabeth why not repay her kindness.
22. application: request
23. I have by no means done.: I have not finished at all.
24. Meryton: the area where the Bennets live
25. for to acknowledge the substance of their conversation was impossible: for Elizabeth considers it impossible for her to reveal their talk to her mother.

Questions

1. What have you learned from the novel about the life of women in the early nineteenth century?
2. What methods are used to characterize the Bennet family in Chapter I?

3. How does Jane Austen set up the tension between Lady Catherine and Elizabeth? Is it in a comic manner and what is satirized?

Charlotte Brontë
1816—1855

Charlotte Brontë

Charlotte Brontë, Emily Brontë, and Anne Brontë made up the famous "Brontë sisters". Among the three, Charlotte Brontë is the eldest. She was born on 21 April 1816 at Thornton in Yorkshire, the third of six children in a family of Irish origin. The Brontë family moved to Haworth in 1820 since her father Patrick was appointed perpetual curate there. Her mother died not long after the settlement in 1821, and left her children in the care of their aunt. The harsh and inhospitable environment ruined the health of the Brontë children. Charlotte's sister Emily, author of *Wuthering Heights*, died at the age of thirty, and Anne, author of *Agnes Grey*, died at twenty-nine, both unmarried. Charlotte married at thirty-eight, but nine months after her marriage she died from pregnancy and chronically weak constitution.

In her youth, Charlotte, together with her sisters, was sent to Clergy Daughters' School, where her two elder sisters died of tuberculosis due to its unhealthy conditions. Charlotte's account of the "Lowood Institution" in *Jane Eyre* is essentially a representation of the harshness of life in that school. After the death of the two girls, the rest Brontë girls and their brother Branwell were mainly educated at home by their father for the next six years. They read books voraciously, and learned much about writing. In 1831, Charlotte studied at a private school Roe Head for a year and a half, and she returned there in 1835 as an assistant teacher. She made two good friends in Roe Head and corresponded with them regularly for over twenty years; they later provided lengthy reminiscences for her biographer Mrs. Gaskell in *The Life of Charlotte Brontë*.

For some time, Charlotte worked as a governess under the pressure of her family's financial difficulties. Though failing to open their own school and frustrated by their brother's scandal and increasingly irrational behavior, Charlotte and the other two sisters made some achievements in writing. In 1845, they published anonymously a volume of poetry entitled *Poems by Currer, Ellis and Acton Bell,* but it received little attention. However, their literary endeavors continued. Charlotte's first novel *The Professor* was rejected by the publisher of Emily's *Wuthering Heights* and Anne's *Agnes Grey*. But her second one, *Jane Eyre,* won immediate and widespread acclaim in 1847 and made her a welcome figure in London, where she met well-established writers like Thackeray, G. H. Lewis, Matthew Arnold, and Mrs. Gaskell. From 1848 to 1849, Charlotte lost her brother and sisters one after another, and writing became an anodyne for her sufferings. Her next important novel *Shirley,* a work concerning the industrial troubles, came out in 1849, and her much acclaimed autobiographical novel *Villette* appeared in 1853.

In her works, Charlotte often delineates the plights of a lonely young intelligent woman who is cast out into the world to struggle for self-realization and emotion fulfillment against socially repressive circumstances. The powerful penetration into her heroines' struggling mentality and the unique employment of subjective narration, in addition to a tinge of gothic horror, make her writing innovative and emotionally intense. Her novels more often than not bear some autobiographic features, which adds to their conviction and coherence. They also present a sober understanding of life and social issues through portraying the pains and pleasures of her middle-class characters. Charlotte's creative writings thus partake of a strong touch of realism, and her much individualized female characters become classic images in world literature.

Jane Eyre

Jane Eyre was published in October, 1847 in three volumes under Charlotte's pen name Currer Bell. It became one of the most popular and important novels of the Victorian age. The *Edinburgh Review* called it "a book of singular fascination".

This novel, in the first person narration, relates how Jane Eyre matures from an orphaned and isolated girl to a self-fulfilled intelligent woman. It begins with the ten-year-old Jane's miserable childhood with her aunt Mrs. Reed and cousins at Gateshead. Locked up in a room where her deceased uncle lived, she has hallucinations and passes out. Under the advice of Mr. Lloyd, the physician, she is sent to Lowood School, a charity school. In the school, Jane suffers from its harsh conditions and the humiliation of being called a liar. Fortunately she can find refuge in Miss Temple and Helen Burns' friendship. After six years' hard study there, Jane takes up two years' teaching in the school. When Miss Temple marries, she decides to leave Lowood and takes up a governess position in Thornfield.

In Thornfield Hall, she meets the master of the house, Edward Rochester, due to a horse accident. Jane is attracted by Rochester, a Byronic hero with a mysterious and passionate nature. But she is made uneasy by odd things in the house, such as a strange laughter, a mysterious fire in Rochester's room, or a sudden attack at Richard Mason, an old acquaintance of Rochester. Rochester blames all these on a certain eccentric maid Grace Poole, but Jane is not fully convinced. After a temporary absence for her dying aunt, Jane returns to Thornfield only to find that Rochester intends to marry a beautiful Blanche Ingram. Not knowing this is a charade by Rochester, Jane confesses her love to Rochester, and he proposes. Happiness is soon hindered by weird events. Two nights before the wedding, a frightening woman enters her room and rips her wedding veil in two. Rochester again levels the accusation at that weird servant Grace. On the wedding day, when Jane and Rochester stand before the altar, ready for their marriage vows, they are stopped by Mr. Mason and a lawyer. They announce Rochester cannot marry because he is still married to Mason's sister Bertha Antoinetta Mason. The truth is out: Bertha, not Grace (Bertha's keeper), is responsible for the eccentricities at Thornfield. Rochester explains that he does marry Bertha but soon finds her insane and locks her up in the house. Jane, out of dignity, refuses his offer to leave for France, and sneaks away in the middle of the night.

Wandering alone, she stops at Moor House and comes to know St. John Rivers and his two sisters, who offer her shelter and a job. During her stay there, Jane receives 20,000 pounds from her uncle, and it turns out that she and the Rivers are cousins. Jane splits her inheritance with the Rivers. The earnest but stubborn St. John, intending to be a missionary in India, tries to convince Jane to accompany him as his wife. Jane almost agrees, but one night she suddenly hears Rochester's disembodied voice calling out to her. Jane soon leaves Moor House for Thornfield only to find a burned wreck. Bertha burns the house down one night, and Rochester loses an eye and a hand in trying to save her. On hearing this, Jane immediately goes for him, who lives in seclusion at Ferndean, and soon marries him. Ten years later, Jane writes this narrative.

Jane Eyre calls into question most of society's major issues, including education, family, social class, and Christianity. Its particular appeal to female identity touches the right chord with readers now and then. In *Wide Sargasso Sea* (1966), a prequel novel to *Jane Eyre*, Jean Rhys re-imagines Bertha Mason's story and casts a new light on the madwoman in the attic.

The following excerpts are from Chapter II and XXIII. In the first excerpt, Jane is put into the red-room for her offense to Mrs. Reed. In the second, Jane confronts Mr. Rochester and declares her love and her pursuit of equality.

Chapter II

[...]

The red-room was a square chamber, very seldom slept in: I might say never, indeed, unless when a chance[1] influx of visitors at Gateshead Hall rendered it necessary to turn to account all the accommodation it contained: yet it was one of the largest and stateliest chambers in the mansion. A bed supported on massive pillars of mahogany, hung with curtains of deep red damask, stood out like a tabernacle in the centre, the two large windows, with their blinds always drawn down, were half shrouded in festoons and falls of similar drapery; the carpet was red; the table at the foot of the bed was covered with a crimson cloth; the walls were a soft fawn colour with a blush of pink in it; the wardrobe, the toilet-table, the chairs, were of darkly-polished old mahogany. Out of these deep surrounding shades rose high, and glared white, the piled-up mattresses and pillows of the bed, spread with a snowy Marseilles counterpane. Scarcely less prominent was an ample cushioned easy-chair near the head of the bed, also white, with a footstool before it; and looking, as I thought, like a pale throne.

This room was chill, because it seldom had a fire; it was silent, because remote from the nursery and kitchens; solemn, because it was known to be so seldom entered. The housemaid alone came here on Saturdays, to wipe from the mirrors and the furniture a week's quiet dust; and Mrs Reed herself, at far intervals, visited it to review the contents of a certain secret drawer in the wardrobe, where were stored divers parchments[2], her jewel-casket, and a miniature of her deceased husband; and in those last words lies the secret of the red-room—the spell which kept it so lonely in spite of its grandeur.

Mr Reed had been dead nine years: it was in this chamber he breathed his last; here he lay in state; hence his coffin was borne by the undertaker's men; and, since that day, a sense of dreary consecration had guarded it from frequent intrusion.

My seat, to which Bessie and the bitter Miss Abbot had left me riveted, was a low ottoman near the marble chimney-piece; the bed rose before me; to my right hand there was the high, dark wardrobe, with subdued, broken reflections varying the gloss of its panels; to my left were the muffled windows; a great looking-glass between them repeated the vacant majesty of the bed and room. I was not quite sure whether they had locked the door; and, when I dared move, I got up and went to see. Alas, yes! no jail was ever more secure. Returning, I had to cross before the looking-glass; my fascinated glance involuntarily explored the depth it revealed. All looked colder and darker in that visionary hollow than in reality: and the strange little figure there gazing at me with a white face and arms specking the gloom, and glittering eyes of fear moving where all else was still, had the effect of a real spirit: I thought it like one of the tiny phantoms, half fairy, half imp[3], Bessie's evening stories represented as coming out of lone, ferny dells in moors, and appearing before the eyes of belated travellers. I returned to my stool.

Superstition was with me at that moment: but it was not yet her hour for complete victory: my blood was still warm; the mood of the revolted slave was still bracing me with its bitter vigour; I had to stem a rapid rush of retrospective thought before I quailed to the dismal present.

[…]

"Unjust!—unjust!" said my reason, forced by the agonizing stimulus into precocious though transitory power: and Resolve, equally wrought up, instigated some strange expedient to achieve escape from insupportable oppression—as running away, or, if that could not be effected, never eating or drinking more, and letting myself die.

What a consternation of soul was mine that dreary afternoon! How all my brain was in tumult, and all my heart in insurrection! Yet in what darkness, what dense ignorance, was the mental battle fought! I could not answer the ceaseless inward question—why I thus suffered; now, at the distance of—I will not say how many years, I see it clearly.

I was a discord in Gateshead Hall: I was like nobody there; I had nothing in harmony with Mrs Reed or her children, or her chosen vassalage. If they did not love me, in fact, as little did I love them. They were not bound to regard with affection a thing that could not sympathize with one amongst them; a heterogeneous thing, opposed to them in temperament, in capacity, in propensities; a useless thing, incapable of serving their interest, or adding to their pleasure; a noxious thing, cherishing the germs of indignation at their treatment, of contempt of their judgment. I know that had I been a sanguine, brilliant, careless, exacting, handsome, romping child—though equally dependent and friendless—Mrs Reed would have endured my presence more complacently; her children would have entertained for me more of the cordiality of fellow-feeling; the servants would have been less prone to make me the scapegoat of the nursery.

Daylight began to forsake the red-room; it was past four o'clock, and the beclouded afternoon was tending to drear twilight. I heard the rain still beating continuously on the staircase window, and the wind howling in the grove behind the hall; I grew by degrees cold as a stone, and then my courage sank. My habitual mood of humiliation, self-doubt, forlorn depression, fell damp on the embers of my decaying ire. All said I was wicked, and perhaps I might be so: what thought had I been but just conceiving of starving myself to death? That certainly was a crime: and was I fit to die? Or was the vault under the chancel of Gateshead Church an inviting bourne? In such vault I had been told did Mr Reed lie buried; and led by this thought to recall his idea, I dwelt on it with gathering dread. I could not remember him; but I knew that he was my own uncle—my mother's brother—that he had taken me when a parentless infant to his house; and that in his last moments he had required a promise of Mrs Reed that she would rear and maintain me as one of her own children. Mrs Reed probably considered she had kept this promise; and so she had, I dare say, as well as her nature would permit her; but how could she really like an interloper not of her race, and unconnected with her, after her husband's death, by any tie? It must have been most irksome to find herself bound by a hard-wrung pledge to stand in the stead of a parent to a strange child she could not love, and to see an uncongenial alien permanently intruded on her own family group.

A singular notion dawned upon me. I doubted not—never doubted—that if Mr Reed had been alive he would have treated me kindly; and now, as I sat looking at the white bed and overshadowed walls—occasionally also turning a fascinated eye towards the dimly gleaming mirror—I began to recall what I had heard of dead men, troubled in their graves by the violation of their last wishes, revisiting the earth to punish the perjured and avenge the oppressed; and I thought Mr Reed's spirit, harassed by the wrongs of his sister's child, might quit its abode—whether in the church vault or in the unknown world of the departed—and rise before me in this chamber. I wiped my tears and hushed my sobs, fearful lest any sign of violent grief might waken a preternatural voice to comfort me, or elicit from the gloom some haloed face, bending over me with strange pity. This idea, consolatory in theory, I felt would be terrible if realized: with all my might I endeavoured to stifle it—I endeavoured to be firm. Shaking my hair from my eyes, I lifted my head and tried to look boldly round the dark room; at this moment a light gleamed on the wall. Was it, I asked myself, a ray from the moon penetrating some aperture in the blind? No; moonlight was still, and this stirred; while I gazed, it glided up to the ceiling and quivered over my head. I can now conjecture readily that this streak of light was, in all likelihood, a gleam from a lantern carried by some one across the lawn; but then, prepared as my mind was for horror, shaken as my nerves were by agitation, I thought the swift-darting beam was a herald of some coming vision from another world. My heart beat thick, my head grew hot; a sound filled my ears, which I deemed the rushing of wings; something seemed near me; I was oppressed, suffocated: endurance broke down; I rushed to the door and shook the lock in desperate effort. Steps came running along the outer passage; the key turned, Bessie and Abbot entered.

"Miss Eyre, are you ill?" said Bessie.

"What a dreadful noise! It went quite through me!" exclaimed Abbot.

"Take me out! Let me go into the nursery!" was my cry.

"What for? Are you hurt? Have you seen something?" again demanded Bessie.

"Oh! I saw a light, and I thought a ghost would come." I had now got hold of Bessie's hand, and she did not snatch it from me.

"She has screamed out on purpose," declared Abbot, in some disgust. "And what a scream! If she had been in great pain one would have excused it, but she only wanted to bring us all here; I know her naughty tricks."

"What is all this?" demanded another voice peremptorily; and Mrs Reed came along the corridor, her cap flying wide, her gown rustling stormily. "Abbot and Bessie, I believe I gave orders that Jane Eyre should be left in the red-room till I came to her myself."

"Miss Jane screamed so loud, ma'am," pleaded Bessie.

"Let her go," was the only answer. "Loose Bessie's hand, child: you cannot succeed in getting out by these means, be assured. I abhor artifice, particularly in children; it is my duty to show you that tricks will not answer; you will now stay here an hour longer, and it is only on condition of perfect submission and stillness that I shall liberate you then."

"O aunt! have pity! Forgive me! I cannot endure it—let me be punished some other way! I shall be killed if—"

"Silence! This violence is all most repulsive:" and so, no doubt, she felt it. I was a precocious actress in her eyes: she sincerely looked on me as a compound of virulent passions, mean spirit, and dangerous duplicity.

Bessie and Abbot having retreated, Mrs Reed, impatient of my now frantic anguish and wild sobs, abruptly thrust me back and locked me in, without farther parley. I heard her sweeping away; and soon after she was gone, I suppose I had a species of fit: unconsciousness closed the scene.

Chapter XXIII

[...]

"Jane," he recommenced, as we entered the laurel walk and slowly strayed down in the direction of the sunk fence and the horse-chestnut, "Thornfield is a pleasant place in summer, is it not?"

"Yes, sir."

"You must have become in some degree attached to the house—you, who have an eye for natural beauties, and a good deal of the organ of Adhesiveness[4]?"

"I am attached to it, indeed."

"And though I don't comprehend how it is, I perceive you have acquired a degree of regard for that foolish little child Adèle, too; and even for simple Dame Fairfax?"

"Yes, sir; in different ways, I have an affection for both."

"And would be sorry to part with them?"

"Yes."

"Pity!" he said, and sighed and paused.

"It is always the way of events in this life," he continued presently: "no sooner have you got settled in a pleasant resting-place, than a voice calls out to you to rise and move on, for the hour of repose is expired."

"Must I move on, sir?" I asked. "Must I leave Thornfield?"

"I believe you must, Jane. I am sorry, Janet, but I believe indeed you must."

This was a blow: but I did not let it prostrate me.

"Well, sir, I shall be ready when the order to march comes."

"It is come now—I must give it to-night."

"Then you are going to be married, sir?"

"Ex-act-ly - pre-cise-ly: with your usual acuteness, you have hit the nail straight on the head."

"Soon, sir?"

"Very soon, my—that is, Miss Eyre: and you'll remember, Jane, the first time I, or Rumour, plainly intimated to you that it was my intention to put my old bachelor's neck into the sacred noose, to enter into the holy estate of matrimony—to take Miss Ingram to my bosom, in short (she's an extensive armful: but that's not to the point—one can't have too much of such a very excellent thing as my beautiful Blanche): well, as I was saying—listen to me, Jane! You're not turning your head to look after more moths, are you? That was only a lady-clock, child, 'flying away home'. I wish to remind you that it was you who first said to me, with that discretion I respect in you—with that foresight, prudence, and humility which befit your responsible and dependent position—that in case I married Miss Ingram, both you and little Adèle had better trot forthwith. I pass over the sort of slur conveyed in this suggestion on the character of my beloved; indeed, when you are far away, Janet, I'll try to forget it: I shall notice only its wisdom; which is such that I have made it my law of action. Adèle must go to school; and you, Miss Eyre, must get a new situation."

"Yes, sir, I will advertise immediately: and meantime, I suppose—" I was going to say, "I suppose I may stay here, till I find another shelter to betake myself to": but I stopped, feeling it would not do to risk a long sentence, for my voice was not quite under command.

"In about a month I hope to be a bridegroom," continued Mr Rochester; "and in the interim, I shall myself look out for employment and an asylum for you."

"Thank you, sir; I am sorry to give—"

"Oh, no need to apologize! I consider that when a dependent does her duty as well as you have done yours, she has a sort of claim upon her employer for any little assistance he can conveniently render her; indeed, I have already, through my future mother-in-law, heard of a place that I think will suit: it is to undertake the education of the five daughters of Mrs Dionysius O'Gall of Bitternutt Lodge, Connaught, Ireland. You'll like Ireland, I think: they're such warm-hearted people there, they say."

"It is a long way off, sir."

"No matter—a girl of your sense will not object to the voyage or the distance."

"Not the voyage, but the distance: and then the sea is a barrier — "

"From what, Jane?"

"From England and from Thornfield: and—"

"Well?"

"From you, sir."

I said this almost involuntarily, and with as little sanction of free will, my tears gushed out. I did not cry so as to be heard, however; I avoided sobbing. The thought of Mrs O'Gall and Bitternutt Lodge struck cold to my heart; and colder the thought of all the brine and foam destined, as it seemed, to rush between me and the master at whose side I now walked; and coldest the remembrance of the wider ocean—wealth, caste, custom—intervened between me and what I naturally and inevitably loved.

"It is a long way," I again said.

"It is, to be sure; and when you get to Bitternutt Lodge, Connaught, Ireland, I shall never see you again, Jane: that's morally certain. I never go over to Ireland, not having myself much of a fancy for the country. We have been good friends, Jane; have we not?"

"Yes, sir."

"And when friends are on the eve of separation, they like to spend the little time that remains to them close to each other. Come! We'll talk over the voyage and the parting quietly, half an hour or so, while the stars enter into their shining life up in heaven yonder: here is the chestnut-tree; here is the bench at its old roots. Come, we will sit there in peace to-night, though we should never more be destined to sit there together."

He seated me and himself.

"It is a long way to Ireland, Janet, and I am sorry to send my little friend on such weary travels; but if I can't do better, how is it to be helped? Are you anything akin to me, do you think, Jane?"

I could risk no sort of answer by this time: my heart was still.

"Because," he said, "I sometimes have a queer feeling with regard to you—especially when you are near me, as now: it is as if I had a string somewhere under my left ribs, tightly and inextricably knotted to a similar string situated in the corresponding quarter of your little frame. And if that boisterous Channel and two hundred miles or so of land, come broad between us, I am afraid that cord of communion will be snapped; and then I've a nervous notion I should take to bleeding inwardly. As for you—you'd forget me."

"That I never should, sir: you know—" Impossible to proceed.

"Jane, do you hear that nightingale singing in the wood? Listen!"

In listening, I sobbed convulsively; for I could repress what I endured no longer; I was obliged to yield, and I was shaken from head to foot with acute distress. When I did speak, it was only to express an impetuous wish that I had never been born, or never come to Thornfield.

"Because you are sorry to leave it?"

The vehemence of emotion, stirred by grief and love within me, was claiming mastery, and struggling for full sway, and asserting a right to predominate, to overcome, to live, rise, and reign at last: yes—and to speak.

"I grieve to leave Thornfield: I love Thornfield: I love it, because I have lived in it a full and delightful life—momentarily at least. I have not been trampled on. I have not been petrified. I have not been buried with inferior minds, and excluded from every glimpse of communion with what is bright and energetic and high. I have talked, face to face, with what I reverence, with what I delight in—with an original, a vigorous, an expanded mind. I have known you, Mr Rochester; and it strikes me with terror and anguish to feel I absolutely must be torn from you for ever. I see the necessity of departure; and it is like looking on the necessity of death."

"Where do you see the necessity?" he asked suddenly.

"Where? You, sir, have placed it before me."

"In what shape?"

"In the shape of Miss Ingram; a noble and beautiful woman—your bride."

"My bride! What bride? I have no bride!"

"But you will have."

"Yes—I will!—I will!" he set his teeth.

"Then I must go—you have said it yourself."

"No: you must stay! I swear it—and the oath shall be kept."

"I tell you I must go!" I retorted, roused to something like passion. "Do you think I can stay to become nothing to you? Do you think I am an automaton?—a machine without feelings? And can bear to have my morsel of bread snatched from my lips, and my drop of living water dashed from my cup? Do you think, because I am poor, obscure, plain, and little, I am soulless and heartless? You think wrong!—I have as much soul as you—and full as much heart! And if God had gifted me with some beauty and much wealth, I should have made it as hard for you to leave me as it is now for me to leave you. I am not talking to you now through the medium of custom, conventionalities, nor even of mortal flesh: it is my spirit that addresses your spirit; just as if both had passed through the grave, and we stood at God's feet, equal,—as we are!"

"As we are!" repeated Mr. Rochester—"so," he added, enclosing me in his arms, gathering me to his breast, pressing his lips on my lips: "so, Jane!"

"Yes, so, sir," I rejoined: "and yet not so: for you are a married man—or as good as a married man, and wed to one inferior to you—to one with whom you have no sympathy—whom I do not believe you truly love; for I have seen and heard you sneer at her. I would scorn such a union: therefore I am better than you—let me go!"

"Where, Jane? To Ireland?"

"Yes—to Ireland. I have spoken my mind, and can go anywhere now."

"Jane, be still; don't struggle so, like a wild frantic bird that is rending its own plumage in its desperation."

"I am no bird; and no net ensnares me; I am a free human being with an independent will, which I now exert to leave you."

Another effort set me at liberty, and I stood erect before him.

"And your will shall decide your destiny," he said. "I offer you my hand, my heart, and a share of all my possessions."

"You play a farce, which I merely laugh at."

"I ask you to pass through life at my side—to be my second self, and best earthly companion."

"For that fate you have already made your choice, and must abide by it."

"Jane, be still a few moments: you are over-excited: I will be still too."

A waft of wind came sweeping down the laurel-walk, and trembled through the boughs of the chestnut: it wandered away—away—to an indefinite distance—it died. The nightingale's song was then the only voice of the hour: in listening to it, I again wept. Mr Rochester sat quiet, looking at me gently and seriously. Some time passed before he spoke; he at last said—

"Come to my side, Jane, and let us explain and understand one another."

"I will never again come to your side: I am torn away now, and cannot return."

"But, Jane, I summon you as my wife: it is you only I intend to marry."

I was silent: I thought he mocked me.

"Come, Jane—come hither."

"Your bride stands between us."

He rose, and with a stride reached me.

"My bride is here," he said, again drawing me to him, "because my equal is here, and my likeness. Jane, will you marry me?"

Still I did not answer, and still I writhed myself from his grasp: for I was still incredulous.

"Do you doubt me, Jane?"

"Entirely."

"You have no faith in me?"

"Not a whit."

"Am I a liar in your eyes?" he asked passionately. "Little sceptic, you shall be convinced. What love have I for Miss Ingram? None: and that you know. What love has she for me? None: as I have taken pains to prove: I caused a rumour to reach her that my fortune was not a third of what was supposed; and after that I presented myself to see the result; it was coldness both from her and her mother. I would not—I could not—marry Miss Ingram. You—you strange, you almost unearthly thing!—I love as my own flesh. You—poor and obscure, and small and plain as you are—I entreat to accept me as a husband."

"What, me!" I ejaculated, beginning in his earnestness—and especially in his incivility—to credit his sincerity: "me who have not a friend in the world but you—if you are my friend: not a shilling but what you have given me?"

"You, Jane, I must have you for my own—entirely my own. Will you be mine? Say yes, quickly."

"Mr Rochester, let me look at your face: turn to the moonlight."

"Why?"

"Because I want to read your countenance—turn!"

"There! You will find it scarcely more legible than a crumpled, scratched page. Read on: only make haste, for I suffer."

His face was very much agitated and very much flushed, and there were strong workings in the features, and strange gleams in the eyes.

"Oh, Jane, you torture me!" he exclaimed. "With that searching and yet faithful and generous look, you torture me!"

"How can I do that? If you are true, and your offer real, my only feelings to you must be gratitude and devotion—they cannot torture."

"Gratitude!" he ejaculated; and added wildly—"Jane accept me quickly. Say, Edward—give me my name—Edward—I will marry you."

"Are you in earnest? Do you truly love me? Do you sincerely wish me to be your wife?"

"I do; and if an oath is necessary to satisfy you, I swear it."

"Then, sir, I will marry you."

"Edward—my little wife!"

"Dear Edward!"

"Come to me—come to me entirely now," said he; and added, in his deepest tone, speaking in my ear as his cheek was laid on mine, "Make my happiness—I will make yours."

"God pardon me!" he subjoined ere long; "and man meddle not with me: I have her, and will hold her."

"There is no one to meddle, sir. I have no kindred to interfere."

"No—that is the best of it," he said. And if I had loved him less I should have thought his accent and look of exultation savage; but, sitting by him, roused from the nightmare of parting—called to the paradise of union—I thought only of the bliss given me to drink in so abundant a flow. Again and again he said, "Are you happy, Jane?" And again and again I answered, "Yes." After which he murmured, "It will atone—it will atone. Have I not found her friendless, and cold, and comfortless? Will I not guard, and cherish, and solace her? Is there not love in my heart, and constancy in my resolves? It will expiate at God's tribunal. I know my Maker sanctions what I do. For the world's judgment—I wash my hands thereof. For man's opinion—I defy it."

But what had befallen the night? The moon was not yet set, and we were all in shadow: I could scarcely see my master's face, near as I was. And what ailed the chestnut tree? it writhed and groaned; while wind roared in the laurel walk, and came sweeping over us.

Notes

Chapter II:

1. chance: random; unexpected
2. divers parchments: various paper documents
3. imp: a small, magical creature that often causes trouble in a playful way

Chapter XXIII:

4. the organ of Adhesiveness: a metonymy for the ability to form attachments to people and places

Questions

1. In Chapter II, why is Jane so scared of staying in the red-room?
2. In Chapter XXIII, what do you think of the conversation between Jane and Rochester?
3. Discuss Jane as a narrator and as a character. Is she a trustworthy storyteller?
4. Jean Rhys's best-selling fiction *Wide Sargasso Sea* (1966) brings into the light a most mysterious character in *Jane Eyre*: the madwoman in the attic. It has the madwoman as its heroine and tells what happens before Jane Eyre's encounter with Rochester. Read both novels and discuss about the two heroines.

Chapter Six Female Individuality and Fulfillment

Virginia Woolf
1882—1941

Virginia Woolf, a formidable figure in modern literature, was born in a scholarly puritan family in Hyde Park Gate, London in July, 1882. She was the third of her parents' four children. In her youth, her family often went on summer vacation in Cornwall, and it became the setting for many of her novels. Unlike her brothers, Virginia was educated, for the most part, at home. Her father Sir Leslie Stephen, biographer, scholar, and editor of the *Dictionary of National Biography,* instructed her in the use of his library. She read Carlyle, Lamb, and Montaigne with passion and developed interest in history, biography, essay, as well as novels. In the summer of 1892, Virginia, elder sister Vanessa, and brother Thoby collaborated on their weekly family newspaper, *The Hyde Park Gate News,* and in the autumn of 1897, Woolf started classes in Greek and Latin with private tutors.

Virginia Woolf

Virginia began serious writing when the family moved from Hyde Park Gate to Gordon Square in Bloomsbury in 1904 after her father's death. From then on, Virginia, together with her sister Vanessa Bell, became the hostess to and a central figure in Bloomsbury gatherings. The celebrated participants include Clive Bell, Roger Fry, Lytton Strachey, John Maynard Keynes, and E. M. Forster. Virginia married Leonard Woolf, a member of the Bloomsbury group, in 1912. They together established Hogarth Press in 1917, and published many contemporary pioneer writings. Virginia Woolf drowned herself in the River Ouse, at Rodmell in March 1941, during a period of depression.

During her writing career, Virginia often suffered from mental breakdown, which might be related to her childhood experience, as revealed in *Moments of Being*, a collection of her four previously unpublished autobiographical writings. Though frequently troubled by mental illness, she kept a productive life and created prodigious writings. She held that a writer should be skillful at grasping the moments of being and the change of human nature, and such belief brought about her works experimental in narrative technique as well as controversial in ideas. That might explain why her writings continue to be the source for scholarly studies.

Her first novel *The Voyage Out* was published in 1915, followed by nine more. *Mrs Dalloway* (1925), *To the Lighthouse* (1927) and *The Waves* (1931) established and solidified her position as an experimental writer, and a foremost modernist of the twentieth century. The use of the stream-of-consciousness technique and the subversion of the traditional chronological narrative are most admirable, among other things. Her novels *Orlando* (1928) and *Flush* (1933) shed new light on fictional biography writing. She also wrote short stories like "The Mark on the Wall" and "A Haunted House".

In addition to fictions, Woolf wrote a great number of letters, diaries, and essays. Her essays, elegants and flexible in style, combine the art of literary criticism and fictional narration. Her perceptive comments on classical and contemporary writers and works exhibit her unique understanding of literary tradition and innovation. Her important criticism on modern fictions can be found in essays like "Mr Bennett and Mrs Brown" and "The Narrow Bridge of Art".

In her writings of different genres, Woolf embedded her thinking about women's condition and women's writing, and has been hailed as a pioneer of feminist thinking. Some of her essays in this aspect are particularly explicit and insightful. In 1929, "A Room of One's Own" was published with its famous dictum, "A woman must have money and a room of her own if she is to write fiction." This essay, like Mary Wollstonecraft's *A Vindication of the Rights of Woman* (1792), and Simone de Beauvoir's *The Second Sex* (1949), has exerted pervasive influence on feminism, gender and culture studies. In 1938, Woolf published "Three Guineas", also a formidable book-length essay that presented a more general protest against the presumed inferiority of women in contemporary political and social life. "Professions for Women" is another famous essay. To some extent, it is a sequel to "A Room of One's Own" and a prelude to "Three Guineas", and is probably most known for Woolf's declaration to kill the "Angel in the House".

Professions for Women[1]

When your secretary invited me to come here, she told me that your Society is concerned with the employment of women and she suggested that I might tell you something about my own professional experiences. It is true I am a woman; it is true I am employed; but what professional experiences have I had? It is difficult to say. My profession is literature; and in that profession there are fewer experiences for women than in any other, with the exception of the stage—fewer, I mean, that are peculiar to women. For the road was cut many years ago—by Fanny Burney[2], by Aphra Behn[3], by Harriet Martineau[4], by Jane Austen, by George Eliot—many famous women, and many more unknown and forgotten, have been before me, making the path smooth, and regulating my steps. Thus, when I came to write, there were very few material obstacles in my way. Writing was a reputable and harmless occupation. The family peace was not broken by the scratching of a pen. No demand was made upon the family purse. For ten and sixpence one can buy paper enough to write all the plays of Shakespeare—if one has a mind that way. Pianos and models, Paris, Vienna and Berlin, masters and mistresses, are not needed by a writer. The cheapness of writing paper is, of course, the reason why women have succeeded as writers before they have succeeded in the other professions.

But to tell you my story—it is a simple one. You have only got to figure to yourselves a girl in a bedroom with a pen in her hand. She had only to move that pen from left to right—from ten o'clock to one. Then it occurred to her to do what is simple and cheap enough after all—to slip a few of those pages into an envelope, fix a penny stamp in the corner, and drop the envelope into the red box at the corner. It was thus that I became a journalist; and my effort was rewarded on the first day of the following month—a very glorious day it was for me—by a letter from an editor containing a cheque for one pound ten shillings and sixpence. But to show you how little I deserve to be called a professional woman, how little I know of the struggles and difficulties of such lives, I have to admit that instead of spending that sum upon bread and butter, rent, shoes and stockings, or butcher's bills, I went out and bought a cat—a beautiful cat, a Persian cat, which very soon involved me in bitter disputes with my neighbours.

What could be easier than to write articles and to buy Persian cats with the profits? But wait a moment. Articles have to be about something. Mine, I seem to remember, was about a novel by a famous man. And while I was writing this review, I discovered that if I were going to review books I should need to do battle with a certain phantom[5]. And the phantom was a woman, and when I came to know her better I called her after the heroine of a famous poem, The Angel in the House[6]. It was she who used to come between me and my paper when I was writing reviews. It was she who bothered me and wasted my time and so tormented me that at last I killed her. You who come of a younger and happier generation may not have heard of her—you may not know what I mean by the Angel in the House. I will describe her as shortly as I can. She was intensely sympathetic. She was immensely charming. She was utterly unselfish. She excelled in the difficult arts of family life. She sacrificed herself daily. If there was chicken, she took the leg; if there was a draught she sat in it—in short she was so constituted that she never had a mind or a wish of her own, but preferred to sympathize always with the minds and wishes of others. Above all—I need not say it—she was pure. Her purity was supposed to be her chief beauty—her blushes, her great grace. In those days—the last of Queen Victoria—every house had its Angel. And when I came to write I encountered her with the very first words. The shadow of her wings fell on my page; I heard the rustling of her skirts in the room. Directly, that is to say, I took my pen in hand to review that novel by a famous man, she slipped behind me and whispered: "My dear, you are a young woman. You are writing about a book that has been written by a man. Be sympathetic; be tender; flatter; deceive; use all the arts and wiles of our sex. Never let anybody guess that you have a mind of your own. Above all, be pure." And she made as if to guide my pen. I now record the one act for which I take some credit to myself, though the credit rightly belongs to some excellent ancestors of mine who left me a certain sum of money—shall we say five hundred pounds a year?—so that it was not necessary for me to depend solely on charm for my living. I turned upon her and caught her by the throat. I did my best to kill her. My excuse, if I were to be had up in a court of law, would be that I acted in self-defence. Had I not killed her she would have killed me. She would have plucked the heart out of my writing. For, as I found, directly I put pen to paper, you cannot review even a novel without having a mind of your own, without expressing what you think to be the truth about human relations, morality, sex. And all these questions, according to the Angel in the House, cannot be dealt with freely and openly by women; they must charm, they must conciliate[7], they must—to put it bluntly—tell lies if they are to succeed. Thus, whenever I felt the shadow of her wing or the radiance of her halo upon my page, I took up the inkpot and flung it at her. She died hard. Her fictitious nature was of great assistance to her. It is far harder to kill a phantom than a reality. She was always creeping back when I thought I had dispatched[8] her. Though I flatter myself that I killed her in the end, the struggle was severe; it took much time that had better have been spent upon learning Greek grammar; or in roaming the world in search of adventures. But it was a real experience; it was an experience that was bound to befall all women writers at that time. Killing the Angel in the House was part of the occupation of a woman writer.

But to continue my story. The Angel was dead; what then remained? You may say that what remained was a simple and common object—a young woman in a bedroom with an inkpot. In other words, now that she had rid herself of falsehood, that young woman had only to be herself. Ah, but what is "herself"? I mean, what is a woman? I assure you, I do not know. I do not believe that you know. I do not believe that anybody can know until she has expressed herself in all the arts and professions open to human skill. That indeed is one of the reasons why I have come here—out of respect for you, who are in process of showing us by your experiments what a woman is, who are in process of providing us, by your failures and successes, with that extremely important piece of information.

But to continue the story of my professional experiences. I made one pound ten and six by my first review; and I bought a Persian cat with the proceeds. Then I grew ambitious. A Persian cat is all very well, I said; but a Persian cat is not enough. I must have a motor car. And it was thus that I became a novelist—for it is a very strange thing that people will give you a motor car if you will tell them a story. It is a still stranger thing that there is nothing so delightful in the world as telling stories. It is far pleasanter than writing reviews of famous novels. And yet, if I am to obey your secretary and tell you my professional experiences as a novelist, I must tell you about a very strange experience that befell me as a novelist. And to understand it you must try first to imagine a novelist's state of mind. I hope I am not giving away professional secrets if I say that a novelist's chief desire is to be as unconscious as possible. He has to induce in himself a state of perpetual lethargy. He wants life to proceed with the utmost quiet and regularity. He wants to see the same faces, to read the same books, to do the same things day after day, month after month, while he is writing, so that nothing may break the illusion in which he is living—so that nothing may disturb or disquiet the mysterious nosings about, feelings round, darts, dashes and sudden discoveries of that very shy and illusive spirit, the imagination. I suspect that this state is the same both for men and women. Be that as it may, I want you to imagine me writing a novel in a state of trance. I want you to figure to yourselves a girl sitting with a pen in her hand, which for minutes, and indeed for hours, she never dips into the inkpot. The image that comes to my mind when I think of this girl is the image of a fisherman lying sunk in dreams on the verge of a deep lake with a rod held out over the water. She was letting her imagination sweep unchecked round every rock and cranny of the world that lies submerged in the depths of our unconscious being. Now came the experience, the experience that I believe to be far commoner with women writers than with men. The line raced through the girl's fingers. Her imagination had rushed away. It had sought the pools, the depths, the dark places where the largest fish slumber[9]. And then there was a smash. There was an explosion. There was foam and confusion. The imagination had dashed itself against something hard. The girl was roused from her dream. She was indeed in a state of the most acute and difficult distress. To speak without figure she had thought of something, something about the body, about the passions which it was unfitting for her as a woman to say. Men, her reason told her, would be shocked. The consciousness of what men will say of a woman who speaks the truth about her passions had roused her from her artist's state of unconsciousness. She could write no more. The trance[10] was over. Her imagination could work no longer. This I believe to be a very common experience with women writers—they are impeded by the extreme conventionality of the other sex. For though men sensibly allow themselves great freedom in these respects, I doubt that they realize or can control the extreme severity with which they condemn such freedom in women.

These then were two very genuine experiences of my own. These were two of the adventures of my professional life. The first—killing the Angel in the House—I think I solved. She died. But the second, telling the truth about my own experiences as a body, I do not think I solved. I doubt that any woman has solved it yet. The obstacles against her are still immensely powerful—and yet they are very difficult to define. Outwardly, what is simpler than to write books? Outwardly, what obstacles are there for a woman rather than for a man? Inwardly, I think, the case is very different; she has still many ghosts to fight, many prejudices to overcome. Indeed it will be a long time still, I think, before a woman can sit down to write a book without finding a phantom to be slain, a rock to be dashed against. And if this is so in literature, the freest of all professions for women, how is it in the new professions which you are now for the first time entering?

Those are the questions that I should like, had I time, to ask you. And indeed, if I have laid stress upon these professional experiences of mine, it is because I believe that they are, though in different forms, yours also. Even when the path is nominally open—when there is nothing to prevent a woman from being a doctor, a lawyer, a civil servant—there are many phantoms and obstacles, as I believe, looming in her way. To discuss and define them is I think of great value and importance; for thus only can the labour be shared, the difficulties be solved. But besides this, it is necessary also to discuss the ends and the aims for which we are fighting, for which we are doing battle with these formidable obstacles. Those aims cannot be taken for granted; they must be perpetually questioned and examined. The whole position, as I see it—here in this hall surrounded by women practising for the first time in history I know not how many different professions—is one of extraordinary interest and importance. You have won rooms of your own in the house hitherto exclusively owned by men. You are able, though not without great labour and effort, to pay the rent. You are earning your five hundred pounds a year. But this freedom is only a beginning; the room is your own, but it is still bare. It has to be furnished; it has to be decorated; it has to be shared. How are you going to furnish it, how are you going to decorate it? With whom are you going to share it, and upon what terms? These, I think are questions of the utmost importance and interest. For the first time in history you are able to ask them; for the first time you are able to decide for yourselves what the answers should be. Willingly would I stay and discuss those questions and answers—but not tonight. My time is up; and I must cease.

Notes

1. In 1931, Woolf was invited to address the London branch of the National Society for Women's Service, and her speech was collected and revised in *The Death of Moth*.
2. Fanny Burney (1752—1840): an English novelist, diarist and playwright. She published her first novel, *Evelina*, anonymously in 1778, and foreshadowed the development of the novel of manners.
3. Aphra Behn (1640—1689): a prolific dramatist, fiction writer, and poet of the English Restoration and one of the first English professional female writers. Her works include *The Rover* and *Oroonoko*.
4. Harriet Martineau (1802—1876): essayist, novelist, journalist, and economic and historical writer,

often cited as the first female sociologist. Perhaps her most scholarly work is *The Positive Philosophy of Auguste Comte, Freely Translated and Condensed* (1853).

5. phantom: a ghost or an apparition
6. The Angel in the House: This term is taken from Coventry Patmore's poem of that name.
7. conciliate: regain or try to regain (friendship or goodwill) by pleasant behavior
8. dispatch: put to death summarily; kill
9. slumber: be dormant or not active
10. trance: dreamy state in which one concentrates on one's thoughts and does not notice what is happening around one

Questions

1. Why does Woolf take action to kill the Angel in the House? Do you agree on her reasoning?
2. How does Woolf illustrate her second experience and what is her point?
3. Woolf says, "Indeed it will be a long time still, I think, before a woman can sit down to write a book without finding a phantom to be slain, a rock to be dashed against. And if this is so in literature, the freest of all professions for women, how is it in the new professions which you are now for the first time entering?" What's your response to this question?

Chapter Seven   Mythology and Reality

According to some critics, mythology is an essential medium, which carries the essence of early notions explaining how our human ancestors viewed the world and interpreted it through observation, experiences, and how they managed to deal with both, and construe a rational meaning to themselves and to their offsprings. For centuries, following the appearance of monotheistic religions and in many parts of the world, the ancient fairy-tales, and myths became viewed as superstitious stories containing evil ideas opposing religion. Myths did survive as oral tradition passing from a generation to the next; however, the significant symbols enclosed have lost their implication to humanity. It was not until the late nineteenth and beginning of the twentieth century that scholars began to realize myths unfold a reality and a series of sophisticated ideas that belong to the ancient world; it became more evident that mythology, in all its forms, leads us to understand the reason for our existence as perceived since time immemorial.

Although mythology is said to be a religion in which we no longer believe, writers have persisted in using the myths of Venus, Prometheus, Hercules, and Ulysses for their plots, episodes, and allusions. By employing invented myths, writers project their philosophical speculation toward life. The ancient Greek myths, especially Homer's *Iliad* and *Odyssey*, are rich resources of literary creation. Dante once depicted Odyssey (the Greek name for Ulysses) as a hero, who never returned to his home place, Ithaca, but urged his men to go on exploring westward. Tennyson revised that version and endowed the protagonist with the courage to set sail to pursue a new world and new knowledge. Through the recreation of Greek myth, Tennyson expresses not only his own determination and courage to brave the struggle of life, but also the restlessness and aspiration of that age.

It is true that mythology provides people with abundant resources of imagination and emotional consolation, but it is somewhat away from the problems of the real world, especially after the industrialization. The advancement of science in the late nineteenth century and the early twentieth century leads to the accumulation of wealth, and the gap between the rich and poor is deepened. This tendency gives rise to realism, a literary trend representing the life as it really is. The theme of the realistic works may be diverse depending on the objects they describe. One of the striking features of the realistic works at that time is to criticize rather than praise. For example, George Bernard Shaw, the best-known English dramatist since Shakespeare, takes the contemporary social issue as his subjects with the aim of directing social reforms. Most of his plays are concerned with political, economic, moral, or religious problems. Similar to Shaw, W. H. Auden also depicts social problems in his poems. Much of his poetry is concerned with moral issues and evidences a strong political, social, and psychological context. Some critics have called Auden an "anti-romantic"—a poet of analytical clarity who sought for order, for universal patterns of human existence.

No matter how different they are, mythology and reality are permanent resources for writers to explore the significance of the physical and spiritual world.

Alfred Tennyson
1809—1892

Alfred Tennyson

The poet Alfred Tennyson was born on August 5, 1809 in Somersby, Lincolnshire. His father was a clergyman and rector.

Tennyson began to write poetry at an early age and in 1872, he and his brother published *Poems by Two Brothers,* the theme of which was influenced by Byron and oriental cultures. After spending four unhappy years in school he was tutored at home. Tennyson then studied at Trinity College, Cambridge. During his life in the college, he joined in a circle of brilliant young men, known as "the Apostles" and became an intimate friend of the leader, Arthur Henry Hallam. During these years, Tennyson published his first signed work *Poems, Chiefly Lyrical* (1830). In 1833, Hallam died suddenly in Vienna, which was a heavy blow to him.

In 1842, Tennyson's *Poems* came out, which was well received by readers. Collected in the book are the dramatic monologue "Ulysses", the epic narrative "Morte d'Arthur" and the exquisite idyll "The Gardener's Daughter", etc. In the year 1850, Tennyson was appointed the Poet Laureate after Wordsworth. This year also witnessed the publication of his greatest work *In Memoriam*, which he began to write immediately after Hallam's death. An elegy for his lost friend, this work is also an elaborate and powerful expression of Tennyson's philosophical and religious thoughts, his doubts about the meaning of life, the existence of the soul and the afterlife. Such thoughts and doubts were shared by most people in an age when the old Christian belief was challenged by new scientific discoveries. It was also this year that Tennyson was married to Emily Sellwood after a prolonged ten-year engagement. After the marriage, the Tennysons settled in Farringford in 1853. During these later years he produced some of his best poems like *Maud*, a collection of short lyrics. *Enoch Arden* (1864) was based on a true story of a sailor thought drowned at sea who returned home after several years. *Idylls of the King* (1859—1885) dealt with the Celtic legends of King Arthur and his knights of the Round Table. Tennyson reproduced the old legend and portrayed King Arthur as a hero trying to restore order and harmony out of chaos. In the 1870s Tennyson wrote several plays, among them the poetic dramas *Queen Mary* (1875) and *Harold* (1877) were remarkable. In 1884 he was created a baron. Tennyson died at Aldwort on October 6, 1892 and was buried in the Poets' Corner in Westminster Abbey.

Tennyson's poetry is rich in poetic images and melodious language. Those images are borrowed from mythology but endowed with modern interpretation to reflect the spirit of Victorian Age.

Ulysses[1]

This poem is written as a dramatic monologue: the entire poem is spoken by a single character. The lines are in blank verse, or unrhymed iambic pentameter, which serves to impart a fluid and natural quality to Ulysses' speech. The poem is divided into four paragraph-like stanzas: In the first stanza, Ulysses declares that there is little point in his staying home "by this still hearth" with his old wife, doling out rewards and punishments for the unnamed masses who live in his kingdom. Then he proclaims, in the second stanza, that he "cannot rest from travel" but feels compelled to live to the fullest and swallow every last drop of life. In the third stanza, Ulysses speaks to an unidentified audience concerning his son Telemachus, who will act as his successor while he resumes his travels. He speaks highly of his son's capabilities as a ruler, praising his prudence, dedication, and devotion to the gods. In the final stanza, Ulysses addresses the mariners with whom he has worked, traveled, and weathered life's storms over many years. Although Ulysses and his mariners are not as strong as they were in youth, they are "strong in will" and are sustained by their resolve to push onward relentlessly: "To strive, to seek, to find, and not to yield."

It little profits that an idle king,
By this still hearth[2], among these barren crags[3],
Matched with an aged wife, I mete and dole[4]
Unequal laws[5] unto a savage race,
That hoard, and sleep, and feed, and know not me.
  I cannot rest from travel; I will drink
life to the lees[6]. All times I have enjoyed
Greatly, have suffered greatly, both with those
that loved me, and alone; on shore, and when
Through scudding drifts the rainy Hyades[7]
Vexed the dim sea. I am become a name;
For always roaming with a hungry heart
Much have I seen and known——cities of men
And manners, climates, councils, governments,
Myself not least, but honored of them all—
And drunk delight of battle with my peers,
Far on the ringing plains of windy Troy[8].
I am part of all that I have met;
Yet all experience is an arch where-through[9]
Gleams that untraveled world whose margin fades
Forever and forever when I move.
How dull it is to pause, to make an end.
To rust unburnished, not to shine in use!
As though to breathe were life! Life piled on life

Were all too little, and of one to me
Little remains; but every hour is saved
From that eternal silence, something more,
A bringer of new things; and vile it were
For some three suns[10] to store and hoard myself,
And this gray spirit yearning in desire
To follow knowledge like a sinking star,
Beyond the utmost bound of human thought.

   This is my son, my own Telemachus,
To whom I leave the scepter and the isle—
Well-loved of me, discerning to fulfill
This labor, by slow prudence to make mild
A rugged people, and through soft degrees
Subdue them to the useful and the good.
Most blameless is he, centered in the sphere
Of common duties, decent not to fail
In offices of tenderness, and pay
Meet adoration to my household gods[11],

   When I am gone. He works his work, I mine.
There lies the port; the vessel puffs her sail;
There gloom the dark, broad seas. My mariners,
Souls that have toiled, and wrought, and thought with me—
That ever with a frolic welcome took
The thunder and the sunshine, and opposed
Free hearts, free foreheads—you and I are old;
Old age hath yet his honor and his toil.
Death closes all; but something ere[12] the end,
Some work of noble note, may yet be done,
Not unbecoming[13] men that strove with gods.
The lights begin to twinkle from the rocks;
The long day wanes; the slow moon climbs; the deep
Moans round with many voices. Come, my friends.
'Tis not too late to seek a newer world.
Push off, and sitting well in order smite[14]
the sounding furrows; for my purpose holds
To sail beyond the sunset, and the baths
Of all the western stars, until I die.
It may be that the gulfs will wash us down;
It may be that we shall touch the Happy Isles[15],
And see the great Achilles[16], whom we knew.

Though much is taken, much abides; and though
We are not now that strength which in old days
Moved earth and heaven, that which we are, we are—
One equal temper of heroic hearts,
Made weak by time and fate, but strong in will
To strive, to seek, to find, and not to yield.

Notes

1. Ulysses: He is the king of the Ithaca Island in Greek mythology. In Homer's *Odessey*, Ulysses arrives home after the Trojan War and ten years' adventure at sea. But according to Dante, he never returns home, but goes on exploration westward. In this poem, Tennyson combines these two versions. Ulysses is now three years in his island, reunited with his wife Penelope and his son Telemachus. But he will not endure the peaceful life every day. Instead, he persuades his followers to set sail again to pursue a new world and new knowledge. The poem is written in the form of dramatic monologue.
2. still hearth: the tranquil family life
3. barren crags: Here referring to the Ithaca island
4. mete and dole: measure and give, the object is unequal laws.
5. Unequal laws: different laws, rewards and punishments
6. I will drink/life to the lees: I will keep traveling and exploring till the end of my life.
7. Hyades: a cluster of stars indicating the coming of rains
8. Troy: the city in which the ten-year Trojan war happened
9. where-through: through which
10. three suns: three years
11. household gods: the ancestors
12. ere: before
13. unbecoming: unfit
14. smite: strike hard
15. the Happy Isles: the paradise for immortal heroes in Greek myth
16. Achilles: a Greek hero of the Trojan War and the central character and greatest warrior of Homer's *Iliad*. He died in the war and became immortal after death.

Questions

1. In what way does Tennyson's Ulysses differ from that of Homer's?
2. What does Ulysses try to express in the dramatic monologue?
3. How does dramatic monologue, a poetic technique, contribute to the theme of the poem?

George Bernard Shaw
1856—1950

George Bernard Shaw

George Bernard Shaw was born in Dublin, Ireland, the son of a civil servant. At the age of 14, he left school and started to work in an estate agent's office. In 1876 Shaw gave up his job and moved to London, where he established himself as a leading music and theatre critic in the eighties and nineties and became a prominent member of the Fabian Society, for which he composed many pamphlets. Together with his fellow Fabians, he regarded the establishment of socialism by the emancipation of land and industrial capital from individual and class ownership as the final goal.

Shaw began his literary career as a novelist. Between 1876 and 1883, he wrote 5 novels but none of them brought him profit or fame. Then he served as a critic of music and drama for a number of magazines and newspapers. His career as a dramatist began in 1892 with his first play *Widower's House* and gained success quickly. After this, his wonderful plays came out one after another. In his life, Shaw wrote more than 50 plays of different subjects. His early plays are called appropriately Plays Pleasant and Unpleasant. These plays are mainly concerned with social problems. *Widower's House*, for instance, is to expose slum landlordism. *Mrs. Warren's Profession* (1893) savagely attacks social hypocrisy and the economic oppression of women, *Candida* (1895) is a comedy about the wife of a clergyman, and what happens when a weak, young poet wants to rescue her from her dull family life. In this period, Shaw's radical rationalism, his utter disregard of conventions and his keen verbal wit often turn the stage into a forum of ideas, and nowhere more openly than in the famous discourses on the Life Force, which is the power to create superior beings to be equal to God and to solve all the social, moral, and metaphysical problems of human society. *Man and Superman* (1903) is a typical example of this group.

Other important plays by Shaw are *Caesar and Cleopatra* (1901), a historical play filled with allusions to modern times, *The Doctor's Dilemma* (1906), a comedy about the ignorance, incompetence, and arrogance of the medical profession, *Pygmalion* (1912), a witty study of phonetics as well as a clever treatment of middle-class morality and class distinction. Because of his success in drama, Shaw is regarded as "a second Shakespeare" who has revolutionized the British theatre. Shaw was awarded the Nobel Prize for Literature in 1925. He accepted the honor but refused the money. On November 2, 1950, Shaw died at Ayot St. Lawrence, Hertfordshire at the age of 94.

Shaw followed the tradition of realism in his literary creation. His plays, the plots of which may be borrowed from mythology, are concerned with such realistic issues as politics, economy, morality, and religion in modern society. In his plays, Shaw shows his passion of indignation against various social evils like oppression, exploitation, hypocrisy, and poverty. Readers can easily have access to such traces in his works.

Pygmalion

According to Greek mythology, Pygmalion, king of Cyprus and famous sculptor, is a legendary figure. He carved a woman out of ivory and named her Galatea, with whom he fell in love. Pygmalion said his prayers at the altar of Aphrodite, the goddess of beauty and love. He quietly wished for a bride who would be "the living likeness of my ivory girl". Aphrodite granted Pygmalion's wish and gave life to Galatea, making her his wife.

The basic Pygmalion story has been widely transmitted and re-presented in the arts through the centuries, among which Shaw's play might be one of the most prominent. The play *Pygmalion* was originally written for the actress Mrs. Patrick Campbell. Later it became the basis for two films and a musical entitled *My Fair Lady*. Based on classical myth, this play is about the complex business of human relationships in a social world. Henry Higgins, a Phonetics Professor tutors a Cockney Eliza Doolittle, not only in the refinement of speech, but also in the refinement of her manner. When the end result produces a very ladylike Miss Doolittle, the lessons learned become much more far reaching. The play is a sharp irony of the rigid British class system of the day and a commentary on women's independence. The following excerpts are about the way Henry Higgins teaches the flower girl to refine her accent and conversation and conduct herself with upper-class manners in social situations.

Pygmalion

Act II (Excerpt)

HIGGINS: [as he shuts the last drawer] Well, I think that's the whole show.

PICKERING: It's really amazing. I haven't taken half of it in, you know.

HIGGINS: Would you like to go over any of it again?

PICKERING: [rising and coming to the fireplace, where he plants himself with his back to the fire] No, thank you; not now. I'm quite done up for this morning.

HIGGINS: [following him, and standing beside him on his left] Tired of listening to sounds?

PICKERING: Yes. It's a fearful strain. I rather fancied myself because I can pronounce twenty-four distinct vowel sounds; but your hundred and thirty beat me. I can't hear a bit of difference between most of them.

HIGGINS: [chuckling, and going over to the piano to eat sweets] Oh, that comes with practice. You hear no difference at first; but you keep on listening, and presently you find they're all as different as A from B. [Mrs. Pearce looks in: she is Higgins's housekeeper] What's the matter?

MRS. PEARCE: [hesitating, evidently perplexed] A young woman wants to see you, sir.

HIGGINS: A young woman! What does she want?

MRS. PEARCE: Well, sir, she says you'll be glad to see her when you know what she's come about. She's quite a common girl, sir. Very common indeed. I should have sent her away, only I thought perhaps you wanted her to talk into your machines¹. I hope I've not done wrong; but really you see such queer people sometimes—you'll excuse me, I'm sure, sir—

HIGGINS: Oh, That's all right, Mrs. Pearce. Has she an interesting accent?

MRS. PEARCE: Oh, something dreadful, sir, really. I don't know how you can take an interest in it.

HIGGINS: [to Pickering] Let's have her up. Shew² her up, Mrs. Pearce [he rushes across to his working table and picks out a cylinder to use on the phonograph].

MRS. PEARCE: [only half resigned to it] Very well, sir. It's for you to say. [She goes downstairs].

HIGGINS: This is rather a bit of luck. I'll shew you how I make records. We'll set her talking; and I'll take it down first in Bell's visible Speech; then in broad Romic; and then we'll get her on the phonograph so that you can turn her on as often as you like with the written transcript before you.

MRS. PEARCE: [returning] This is the young woman, sir.

[The flower girl enters in state. She has a hat with three ostrich feathers, orange, sky-blue, and red. She has a nearly clean apron, and the shoddy coat has been tidied a little. The pathos of this deplorable figure, with its innocent vanity and consequential air, touches Pickering, who has already straightened himself in the presence of Mrs. Pearce. But as to Higgins, the only distinction he makes between men and women is that when he is neither bullying nor exclaiming to the heavens against some featherweight cross, he coaxes women as a child coaxes its nurse when it wants to get anything out of her.]

HIGGINS: [brusquely, recognizing her with unconcealed disappointment, and at once, babylike, making an intolerable grievance of it] Why, this is the girl I jotted down last night. She's no use: I've got all the records I want of the Lisson Grove lingo³; and I'm not going to waste another cylinder on it. [To the girl] Be off with you: I don't want you.

THE FLOWER GIRL: Don't you be so saucy⁴. You ain't heard what I come for yet. [To Mrs. Pearce, who is waiting at the door for further instruction] Did you tell him I come in a taxi?

MRS. PEARCE: Nonsense, girl! what do you think a gentleman like Mr. Higgins cares what you came in?

THE FLOWER GIRL: Oh, we are proud! He ain't above giving lessons, not him: I heard him say so. Well, I ain't come here to ask for any compliment; and if my money's not good enough I can go elsewhere.

HIGGINS: Good enough for what?

THE FLOWER GIRL: Good enough for ye-oo⁵. Now you know, don't you? I'm come to have lessons, I am. And to pay for em⁶ too: make no mistake.

HIGGINS: [stupent⁷] Well ! ! ! [Recovering his breath with a gasp] What do you expect me to say to you?

THE FLOWER GIRL: Well, if you was a gentleman, you might ask me to sit down, I think. Don't I tell you I'm bringing you business?

HIGGINS: Pickering: shall we ask this baggage[8] to sit down or shall we throw her out of the window?
THE FLOWER GIRL: [running away in terror to the piano, where she turns at bay[9]] Ah-ah-ah- ow-ow-ow-oo! [Wounded and whimpering] I won't be called a baggage when I've offered to pay like any lady.
[Motionless, the two men stare at her from the other side of the room, amazed.]
PICKERING: [gently] What is it you want, my girl?
THE FLOWER GIRL: I want to be a lady in a flower shop stead of[10] selling at the corner of Tottenham Court Road. But they won't take me unless I can talk more genteel. He said he could teach me. Well, here I am ready to pay him—not asking any favor—and he treats me as if I was dirt.
MRS. PEARCE: How can you be such a foolish ignorant girl as to think you could afford to pay Mr. Higgins?
THE FLOWER GIRL: Why shouldn't I? I know what lessons cost as well as you do; and I'm ready to pay.
HIGGINS: How much?
THE FLOWER GIRL: [coming back to him, triumphant] Now you're talking! I thought you'd come off it when you saw a chance of getting back a bit of what you chucked at[11] me last night. [Confidentially] You'd had a drop in[12], hadn't you?
HIGGINS: [peremptorily] Sit down.
THE FLOWER GIRL: Oh, if you're going to make a compliment of it—
HIGGINS: [thundering at her] Sit down.
MRS. PEARCE: [severely] Sit down, girl. Do as you're told. [She places the stray chair near the hearthrug between Higgins and Pickering, and stands behind it waiting for the girl to sit down].
THE FLOWER GIRL: Ah-ah-ah-ow-ow-oo! [She stands, half rebellious, half bewildered].

PICKERING: [very courteous] Won't you sit down?
LIZA: [coyly] Don't mind if I do. [She sits down. Pickering returns to the hearthrug].

HIGGINS: What's your name?
THE FLOWER GIRL: Liza Doolittle.
HIGGINS: [declaiming gravely] Eliza, Elizabeth, Betsy and Bess, They went to the woods to get a bird nes': PICKERING. They found a nest with four eggs in it: HIGGINS. They took one apiece, and left three in it.
[They laugh heartily at their own wit.]
LIZA: Oh, don't be silly.
MRS. PEARCE: You mustn't speak to the gentleman like that.
LIZA: Well, why won't he speak sensible to me?
HIGGINS: Come back to business. How much do you propose to pay me for the lessons?
LIZA: Oh, I know what's right. A lady friend of mine gets French lessons for eighteen pence

an hour from a real French gentleman. Well, you wouldn't have the face to ask me the same for teaching me my own language as you would for French; so I won't give more than a shilling. Take it or leave it.

HIGGINS: [walking up and down the room, rattling his keys and his cash in his pockets] You know, Pickering, if you consider a shilling, not as a simple shilling, but as a percentage of this girl's income, it works out as fully equivalent to sixty or seventy guineas from a millionaire.

PICKERING: How so?

HIGGINS: Figure it out. A millionaire has about £150 a day. She earns about half-a-crown[13].

LIZA: [haughtily] Who told you I only—

HIGGINS: [continuing] She offers me two-fifths of her day's income for a lesson. Two-fifths of a millionaire's income for a day would be somewhere about £60. It's handsome. By George, it's enormous! It's the biggest offer I ever had.

LIZA: [rising, terrified] Sixty pounds! What are you talking about? I never offered you sixty pounds. Where would I get—

HIGGINS: Hold your tongue.

LIZA: [weeping] But I ain't got sixty pounds. Oh—

MRS. PEARCE: Don't cry, you silly girl. Sit down. Nobody is going to touch your money.

HIGGINS: Somebody is going to touch you, with a broomstick, if you don't stop snivelling. Sit down.

LIZA: [obeying slowly] Ah-ah-ah-ow-oo-o! One would think you was my father.

HIGGINS: If I decide to teach you, I'll be worse than two fathers to you. Here [he offers her his silk handkerchief]!

LIZA: What's this for?

HIGGINS: To wipe your eyes. To wipe any part of your face that feels moist. Remember: that's your handkerchief; and that's your sleeve. Don't mistake the one for the other if you wish to become a lady in a shop.

[Liza, utterly bewildered, stares helplessly at him.]

MRS. PEARCE: It's no use talking to her like that, Mr. Higgins: she doesn't understand you. Besides, you're quite wrong: she doesn't do it that way at all [she takes the handkerchief].

LIZA: [snatching it] Here! You give me that handkerchief. He give it to me, not to you.

PICKERING: [laughing] He did. I think it must be regarded as her property, Mrs. Pearce.

MRS. PEARCE: [resigning herself] Serve you right, Mr. Higgins.

PICKERING: Higgins: I'm interested. What about the ambassador's garden party? I'll say you're the greatest teacher alive if you make that good[14]. I'll bet you all the expenses of the experiment you can't do it. And I'll pay for the lessons.

LIZA: Oh, you are real good. Thank you, Captain.

HIGGINS: [tempted, looking at her] It's almost irresistible. She's so deliciously low—so horribly dirty—

LIZA: [protesting extremely] Ah-ah-ah-ah-ow-ow-oo-oo!!! I ain't dirty: I washed my face and hands afore[15] I come, I did.

PICKERING: You're certainly not going to turn her head with flattery, Higgins.

MRS. PEARCE: [uneasy] Oh, don't say that, sir: There's more ways than one of turning a girl's head; and nobody can do it better than Mr. Higgins, though he may not always mean it. I do hope, sir, you won't encourage him to do anything foolish.

HIGGINS: [becoming excited as the idea grows on him] What is life but a series of inspired follies? The difficulty is to find them to do. Never lose a chance: it doesn't come every day. I shall make a duchess of this draggle-tailed guttersnipe[16].

LIZA: [strongly deprecating this view of her] Ah-ah-ah-ow-ow-oo!

HIGGINS: [carried away] Yes: in six months—in three if she has a good ear and a quick tongue—I'll take her anywhere and pass her off as[17] anything. We'll start today: now! this moment! Take her away and clean her, Mrs. Pearce. Monkey Brand, if it won't come off any other way. Is there a good fire in the kitchen?

MRS. PEARCE: [protesting]. Yes; but—

HIGGINS: [storming on] Take all her clothes off and burn them. Ring up Whiteley or somebody for new ones. Wrap her up in brown paper till they come.

LIZA: You're no gentleman, you're not, to talk of such things. I'm a good girl, I am; and I know what the like of you are, I do.

HIGGINS: We want none of your Lisson Grove prudery here, young woman. You've got to learn to behave like a duchess. Take her away, Mrs. Pearce. If she gives you any trouble wallop[18] her.

Act III (Excerpt)

THE PARLOR-MAID: [opening the door] Miss Doolittle. [She withdraws].

HIGGINS: [rising hastily and running to Mrs. Higgins] Here she is, mother. [He stands on tiptoe and makes signs over his mother's head to Eliza to indicate to her which lady is her hostess].

[Eliza, who is exquisitely dressed, produces an impression of such remarkable distinction and beauty as she enters that they all rise, quite fluttered. Guided by Higgins's signals, she comes to Mrs. Higgins with studied grace.]

LIZA: [speaking with pedantic[19] correctness of pronunciation and great beauty of tone] How do you do, Mrs. Higgins? [She gasps slightly in making sure of the H in Higgins, but is quite successful]. Mr. Higgins told me I might come.

MRS. HIGGINS: [cordially] Quite right: I'm very glad indeed to see you.

PICKERING: How do you do, Miss Doolittle?

LIZA: [shaking hands with him] Colonel Pickering, is it not?

MRS. EYNSFORD HILL: I feel sure we have met before, Miss Doolittle. I remember your eyes.

LIZA: How do you do? [She sits down on the ottoman[20] gracefully in the place just left vacant by Higgins].

MRS. EYNSFORD HILL: [introducing] My daughter Clara.

LIZA: How do you do?

CLARA: [impulsively] How do you do? [She sits down on the ottoman beside Eliza, devouring her with her eyes].

FREDDY: [coming to their side of the ottoman] I've certainly had the pleasure.

MRS. EYNSFORD HILL: [introducing] My son Freddy.

LIZA: How do you do?

[Freddy bows and sits down in the Elizabethan chair, infatuated[21].]

HIGGINS: [suddenly] By George[22], yes: it all comes back to me! [They stare at him]. Covent Garden! [Lamentably] What a damned thing!

MRS. HIGGINS: Henry, please! [He is about to sit on the edge of the table]. Don't sit on my writing-table: you'll break it.

HIGGINS: [sulkily] Sorry.

[He goes to the divan[23], stumbling into the fender and over the fire-irons on his way; extricating himself with muttered imprecations; and finishing his disastrous journey by throwing himself so impatiently on the divan that he almost breaks it. Mrs. Higgins looks at him, but controls herself and says nothing.]

[A long and painful pause ensues.]

MRS. HIGGINS: [at last, conversationally] Will it rain, do you think?

LIZA: The shallow depression in the west of these islands is likely to move slowly in an easterly direction. There are no indications of any great change in the barometrical situation.

FREDDY: Ha! ha! how awfully funny!

LIZA: What is wrong with that, young man? I bet I got it right.

FREDDY: Killing[24]!

MRS. EYNSFORD HILL: I'm sure I hope it won't turn cold. There's so much influenza about. It runs right through our whole family regularly every spring.

LIZA: [darkly[25]] My aunt died of influenza: so they said.

MRS. EYNSFORD HILL: [clicks her tongue sympathetically]!!!

LIZA: [in the same tragic tone] But it's my belief they done the old woman in.

MRS. HIGGINS: [puzzled] Done her in?

LIZA: Y-e-e-e-es, Lord love you! Why should she die of influenza? She come through diphtheria right enough the year before. I saw her with my own eyes. Fairly blue with it, she was. They all thought she was dead; but my father he kept ladling gin[26] down her throat till she came to so sudden that she bit the bowl off the spoon.

MRS. EYNSFORD HILL: [startled] Dear me!

LIZA: [piling up the indictment] What call would a woman with that strength in her have to die of influenza? What become of her new straw hat that should have come to me? Somebody pinched[27] it; and what I say is, them as pinched it done her in.

MRS. EYNSFORD HILL: What does doing her in mean?

HIGGINS: [hastily] Oh, That's the new small talk. To do a person in means to kill them.

MRS. EYNSFORD HILL: [to Eliza, horrified] You surely don't believe that your aunt was killed?

LIZA: Do I not! Them she lived with would have killed her for a hat-pin, let alone a hat.

MRS. EYNSFORD HILL: But it can't have been right for your father to pour spirits down her throat

	like that. It might have killed her.
LIZA:	Not her. Gin was mother's milk to her. Besides, he'd poured so much down his own throat that he knew the good of it.
MRS. EYNSFORD HILL:	Do you mean that he drank?
LIZA:	Drank! My word! Something chronic[28].
MRS. EYNSFORD HILL:	How dreadful for you!
LIZA:	Not a bit. It never did him no harm what I could see. But then he did not keep it up regular. [Cheerfully] On the burst, as you might say, from time to time. And always more agreeable when he had a drop in. When he was out of work, my mother used to give him four pence and tell him to go out and not come back until he'd drunk himself cheerful and loving-like. There's lots of women has to make their husbands drunk to make them fit to live with. [Now quite at her ease] You see, it's like this. If a man has a bit of a conscience, it always takes him when he's sober; and then it makes him low-spirited. A drop of booze just takes that off and makes him happy. [To Freddy, who is in convulsions of suppressed laughter] Here! what are you sniggering at?
FREDDY:	The new small talk. You do it so awfully well.
LIZA:	If I was doing it proper, what was you laughing at? [To Higgins] Have I said anything I oughtn't?
MRS. HIGGINS:	[interposing] Not at all, Miss Doolittle.
LIZA:	Well, That's a mercy, anyhow. [Expansively] What I always say is—
HIGGINS:	[rising and looking at his watch] Ahem!
LIZA:	[looking round at him; taking the hint; and rising] Well: I must go. [They all rise. Freddy goes to the door]. So pleased to have met you. Good-bye. [She shakes hands with Mrs. Higgins].
MRS. HIGGINS:	Good-bye.
LIZA:	Good-bye, Colonel Pickering.
PICKERING:	Good-bye, Miss Doolittle. [They shake hands].
LIZA:	[nodding to the others] Good-bye, all.
FREDDY:	[opening the door for her] Are you walking across the Park, Miss Doolittle? If so—
LIZA:	Walk! Not bloody likely. [Sensation]. I am going in a taxi. [She goes out].

Act V (Excerpt)

LIZA:	Every girl has a right to be loved.
HIGGINS:	What! By fools like that?
LIZA:	Freddy's not a fool. And if has weak and poor and wants me, may be had make me happier than my betters that bully me and don't want me.
HIGGINS:	Can he make anything of you?[29] That's the point.
LIZA:	Perhaps I could make something of him. But I never thought of us making anything of one another; and you never think of anything else. I only want to be natural.
HIGGINS:	In short, you want me to be as infatuated about you as Freddy? Is that it?

LIZA: No I don't. That's not the sort of feeling I want from you. And don't you be too sure of yourself or of me. I could have been a bad girl if I'd liked. I've seen more of some things than you, for all[30] your learning. Girls like me can drag gentlemen down to make love to them easy enough. And they wish each other dead the next minute.

HIGGINS: Of course they do. Then what in thunder are we quarrelling about?

LIZA: [much troubled] I want a little kindness. I know I'm a common ignorant girl, and you a book-learned gentleman; but I'm not dirt under your feet. What I done [correcting herself] what I did was not for the dresses and the taxis: I did it because we were pleasant together and I come—came—to care for you; not to want you to make love to me, and not forgetting the difference between us, but more friendly like.

HIGGINS: Well, of course. That's just how I feel. And how Pickering feels. Eliza: you're a fool.

LIZA: That's not a proper answer to give me [she sinks on the chair at the writing-table in tears].

HIGGINS: It's all you'll get until you stop being a common idiot. If you're going to be a lady, you'll have to give up feeling neglected if the men you know don't spend half their time snivelling over you and the other half giving you black eyes[31]. If you can't stand the coldness of my sort of life, and the strain of it, go back to the gutter. Work till you are more a brute than a human being; and then cuddle and squabble and drink till you fall asleep. Oh, it's a fine life, the life of the gutter. It's real: it's warm: it's violent: you can feel it through the thickest skin: you can taste it and smell it without any training or any work. Not like Science and Literature and Classical Music and Philosophy and Art. You find me cold, unfeeling, selfish, don't you? Very well: be off with you to the sort of people you like. Marry some sentimental hog or other with lots of money, and a thick pair of lips to kiss you with and a thick pair of boots to kick you with. If you can't appreciate what you've got, you'd better get what you can appreciate.

LIZA: [desperate] Oh, you are a cruel tyrant. I can't talk to you: you turn everything against me: I'm always in the wrong. But you know very well all the time that you're nothing but a bully. You know I can't go back to the gutter, as you call it, and that I have no real friends in the world but you and the Colonel. You know well I couldn't bear to live with a low common man after you two; and it's wicked and cruel of you to insult me by pretending I could. You think I must go back to Wimpole Street because I have nowhere else to go but father's. But don't you be too sure that you have me under your feet to be trampled on and talked down[32]. I'll marry Freddy, I will, as soon as he's able to support me.

HIGGINS: [sitting down beside her] Rubbish! you shall marry an ambassador. You shall marry the Governor-General of India or the Lord-Lieutenant of Ireland, or somebody who wants a deputy-queen. I'm not going to have my masterpiece[33] thrown away on Freddy.

LIZA: You think I like you to say that. But I haven't forgot what you said a minute ago; and I won't be coaxed[34] round as if I was a baby or a puppy. If I can't have kindness, I'll have independence.

HIGGINS:	Independence? That's middle class blasphemy[35]. We are all dependent on one another, every soul of us on earth.
LIZA:	[rising determinedly] I'll let you see whether I'm dependent on you. If you can preach, I can teach. I'll go and be a teacher.
HIGGINS:	What'll you teach, in heaven's name?
LIZA:	What you taught me. I'll teach phonetics.
HIGGINS:	Ha! Ha! Ha!
LIZA:	I'll offer myself as an assistant to Professor Nepean.
HIGGINS:	[rising in a fury] What! That impostor[36]! that humbug[37]! that toadying ignoramus[38]! Teach him my methods! my discoveries! You take one step in his direction and I'll wring your neck. [He lays hands on her]. Do you hear?
LIZA:	[defiantly non-resistant] Wring away. What do I care? I knew you'd strike me some day. [He lets her go, stamping with rage at having forgotten himself, and recoils so hastily that he stumbles back into his seat on the ottoman]. Aha! Now I know how to deal with you. What a fool I was not to think of it before! You can't take away the knowledge you gave me. You said I had a finer ear than you. And I can be civil and kind to people, which is more than you can. Aha! That's done you, Henry Higgins, it has. Now I don't care that [snapping her fingers] for your bullying and your big talk. I'll advertize it in the papers that your duchess is only a flower girl that you taught, and that she'll teach anybody to be a duchess just the same in six months for a thousand guineas. Oh, when I think of myself crawling under your feet and being trampled on and called names, when all the time I had only to lift up my finger to be as good as you, I could just kick myself.
HIGGINS:	[wondering at her] You damned impudent slut, you! But it's better than snivelling; better than fetching slippers and finding spectacles, isn't it? [Rising] By George, Eliza, I said I'd make a woman of you; and I have. I like you like this.
LIZA:	Yes: you turn round and make up to[39] me now that I'm not afraid of you, and can do without you.
HIGGINS:	Of course I do, you little fool. Five minutes ago you were like a millstone round my neck. Now you're a tower of strength: a consort battleship. You and I and Pickering will be three old bachelors together instead of only two men and a silly girl.

[Mrs. Higgins returns, dressed for the wedding. Eliza instantly becomes cool and elegant.]

MRS. HIGGINS:	The carriage is waiting, Eliza. Are you ready?
LIZA:	Quite. Is the Professor coming?
MRS. HIGGINS:	Certainly not. He can't behave himself in church. He makes remarks out loud all the time on the clergyman's pronunciation.
LIZA:	Then I shall not see you again, Professor. Good bye. [She goes to the door].
MRS. HIGGINS:	[coming to Higgins] Good-bye, dear.
HIGGINS:	Good-bye, mother. [He is about to kiss her, when he recollects something]. Oh, by the way, Eliza, order a ham and a Stilton cheese, will you? And buy me a pair of reindeer gloves, number eights, and a tie to match that new suit of mine, at Eale & Binman's.

                    You can choose the color. [His cheerful, careless, vigorous voice shows that he is incorrigible].
LIZA: [disdainfully] Buy them yourself. [She sweeps out].
MRS. HIGGINS: I'm afraid You've spoiled that girl, Henry. But never mind, dear: I'll buy you the tie and gloves.
HIGGINS: [sunnily] Oh, don't bother. She'll buy em all right enough. Good-bye.
[They kiss. Mrs. Higgins runs out. Higgins, left alone, rattles his cash in his pocket; chuckles; and disports himself in a highly self-satisfied manner.]

Notes

Act II

1. ...talk into your machines: to be recorded by recorder for academic research (Higgins is a Phonetics professor).
2. Shew: Show
3. Lisson Grove lingo: local accent of Lisson Grove
4. saucy: impolite
5. ye-oo: you
6. em: them
7. stupent: surprised
8. baggage: derogatory term for woman
9. at bay: be confined in despair like an animal
10. stead of: instead of
11. chuck at: throw at
12. had a drop in: had been drunk
13. half-a-crown: two and a half shilling; crown: a coin of five shilling
14. make that good: carry out the promise
15. afore: before
16. draggle-tailed guttersnipe: ragged beggar
17. pass her off as: pretend to be
18. wallop: beat violently

Act III

19. pedantic: excessively concerned with minor details or with displaying academic learning
20. ottoman: a low upholstered seat without a back or arms
21. infatuated: be inspired with an intense passion or admiration
22. By George: Indeed
23. divan: a bed consisting of a base and mattress but no footboard or headboard
24. Killing: interesting, attractive
25. darkly: mysteriously
26. gin: a clear alcoholic spirit distilled from grain

27. pinch: rob, steal
28. chronic: persisting for a long time or constantly recurring

Act V
29. Can he make anything of you? : Is he useful for you? make something of...: give or ascribe a specified amount of attention or importance to...
30. for all: despite
31. give you black eyes: beat you
32. talk down: bully
33. masterpiece: Here referring to Liza
34. coax: persuade someone gradually or by flattery to do something
35. blasphemy: the action offence of speaking irreverently about God or sacred things
36. impostor: a person who pretends to be someone else in order to deceive others
37. humbug: hypocrite
38. ignoramus: stupid person
39. make up to: attempt to win the favor of someone by being pleasant

Questions

1. What is the difference between Eliza as a flower girl and a duchess as far as her accent is concerned?
2. What does Eliza mean by saying "Buy them yourself" when Higgins asks her to buy him something?
3. Does Eliza finally become independent? Why or why not?

Wystan Hugh Auden
1907—1973

Wystan Hugh Auden, an English poet, playwright, critic, and librettist, was born in York, England in 1907. His father was a prominent physician with an extensive knowledge of mythology and folklore, and his mother was a strict Anglican. Both of them exerted strong influences on Auden's poetry creation.

When he was young, Auden showed strong interest in science and engineering, which earned him a scholarship to Oxford University, where his fascination with poetry led him to change his field of study to English. At Oxford, Auden became familiar with modernist poetry, particularly that of T. S. Eliot. It was also at Oxford that Auden became member of a group of writers called the "Oxford Group" or the "Auden

Wystan Hugh Auden

Generation," which included Stephen Spender, C. Day Lewis, and Louis MacNeice. The group adhered to various Marxist and anti-fascist doctrines and addressed social, political, and economic concerns in their writings.

Auden's poems from the second half of the 1930s witness his many travels during that period of political turmoil. "Spain," one of his most famous and widely anthologized pieces, is based on his experiences in that country during its civil war of 1936 to 1939. In 1938, he went to China together with novelist Christopher Isherwood to visit the Sino-Japanese War and produced the book *Journey to a War* in 1939. The book is in three parts: a series of poems by Auden describing his and Isherwood's journey to China in 1938; a "Travel-Diary" by Isherwood about their travels in China itself, and their observations of the Sino-Japanese War; and "In Time of War: A Sonnet Sequence with a Verse Commentary" (Auden later renamed it "Sonnets from China") by Auden, with reflections on the contemporary world and their experiences in China.

Just before World War II broke out, Auden immigrated to the United States. His first book written in America, *Another Time*, contains some of his best-known poems, such as "September 1, 1939" and "Musee des Beaux Arts," the latter of which was inspired by a Breughel painting. The volume also contains elegies to poets A. E. Housman, Matthew Arnold, and William Butler Yeats, whose careers and aesthetic concerns had influenced the development of Auden's artistic credo. Stylistically, these poems are fragmentary and terse, relying on concrete images and colloquial language to convey Auden's political and psychological concerns. Auden won the Pulitzer Prize in 1948 for *The Age of Anxiety: A Baroque Eclogue,* which explores the attempts of the protagonists to comprehend themselves and the world in which they live.

In his later years, Auden wrote three major volumes: *City Without Walls and Other Poems, Epistle to a Godson and Other Poems,* and the posthumously published *Thank You, Fog: Last Poems.* All these works are noted for their lexical range and humanitarian content. He won the National Book Award in Poetry for "The Shield of Achilles" in 1956 and the National Medal for Literature in 1967. In 1972, he moved his winter home from New York to Oxford, but he continued to spend summer in Austria. He died in Vienna in 1973 and was buried in Kirchstetten.

Musee des Beaux Arts[1]

"Musee des Beaux Arts", which means "Museum of Fine Arts" in French, is a poem Auden composed after he visited that museum in Paris. The poem is a reflection on the old paintings which depict the reality of life. Auden mentions three of the paintings which show the place of suffering in human life. According to the poet, disasters, tragedies and sufferings are a part of life; they happen any time. But life has to go on. The poem also indirectly shows human beings' indifference towards their fellow beings. The language of the poem is simple and its description is the basis for meditation, which is the poem's theme.

About suffering they were never wrong,
The Old Masters[2]; how well, they understood
Its human position; how it takes place
While someone else is eating or opening a window or just walking dully along;
How, when the aged are reverently, passionately waiting
For the miraculous birth, there always must be
Children who did not specially want it to happen[3], skating
On a pond at the edge of the wood:
They never forgot
That even the dreadful martyrdom[4] must run its course[5]
Anyhow in a corner, some untidy spot
Where the dogs go on with their doggy life and the torturer's horse
Scratches its innocent behind on a tree.

In Breughel's Icarus[6], for instance: how everything turns away
Quite leisurely from the disaster; the ploughman may
Have heard the splash, the forsaken cry,
But for him it was not an important failure[7]; the sun shone
As it had to on the white legs disappearing into the green
Water; and the expensive delicate ship that must have seen
Something amazing, a boy falling out of the sky,
had somewhere to get to and sailed calmly on.

Notes

1. This poem is written in free verse. It can be divided into two parts, the first of which describes scenes of "suffering" and "dreadful martyrdom". The second half of the poem refers to the painting *Landscape with the Fall of Icarus*. Auden's description allows us to visualize this specific moment and instance of the indifference of the world to suffering.
2. The Old Masters: Here referring to the masters of the art world
3. For the miraculous birth...want it to happen: In Matthew 2:16-18, Herod the Great was told that a king would be born to the Jews and ordered the Magi to alert him when the king was found. The Magi, warned by an angel, did not do so. When Herod realized that he had been outwitted by the Magi, he was furious, and he gave orders to kill all the boys in Bethlehem and its vicinity who were two years old and under. That is why the children of Auden's poem "did not specially want it (the miraculous birth) to happen."
4. martyrdom: the death or suffering of a martyr. The innocent boys of Herod's wrath are traditionally considered the first of the Christian martyrs.
5. run its course: complete its natural development without interference
6. Breughel's Icarus: Peter Breughel is a painter who lived in the first half of the 16th century in Belgium. His paintings, in general, have allegorical or moralizing significance. The "Fall of Icarus"

was his only mythological subject. Icarus, the son of Daedalus, was a Greek mythological figure. He and his dad were stuck in Crete, because the King of Crete wouldn't let them leave. Daedalus made some wings for both of them and gave his son instruction on how to fly. Icarus, however, flied too close to the sun. This caused the wax that held his wings to his body to melt. Icarus crashed into the sea and died.

7. the ploughman ... not an important failure: In Breughel's painting, he portrays several men and a ship performing daily activities in a charming landscape peacefully. While this occurs, Icarus is visible in the bottom right hand corner of the picture; his legs splayed at absurd angles, drowning in the water. From this sharp contrast, reader can detect the ignorance of people to their fellow men's suffering.

Questions

1. What kind of picture can you visualize from Auden's description? Briefly illustrate it.
2. What does Auden try to convey in this poem?

Chapter Eight Civilization and Alienation

Civilization, a term opposed to barbarism or rudeness, embodies the progress of human beings. However, with the advancement of modern science and technology, the estrangement between people is becoming increasingly apparent. Consequently, though more rational and more successful concerning material progress, civilization is seen as unnatural, and leads to "vices of social life" such as guile, hypocrisy, envy, and avarice. Many sociologists were concerned about the alienating effects of civilization and put forward various theories, the renowned of which was the theory of scientific socialism initiated by Karl Marx and Friedrich Engels. Marx believed that alienation is a systematic result of capitalism. His theory of alienation was based upon his observation that in emerging industrial production under capitalism, workers inevitably lose control of their lives and selves by not having any control of their work. Marx's theory and the like have exerted profound influence on many western intellectuals.

Many English writers of the 20th century launch fierce attack on the decay of west civilization from different aspects, with the colonization being the first to bear the brunt. For a long time, colonization has done great damage to the underdeveloped countries. Although its form has changed, the disastrous effect can never be ignored. Joseph Conrad, in his *Heart of Darkness*, reveals the residual influence of colonialism on Africans through the life experience of a white men, Kurtz, who is not only a pioneer in colonization but a symbol of western civilization. Different from Conrad, T. S. Eliot focuses, through his poems, on the spiritual world of western people, especially the post-war generation. In "The Hollow Man", Eliot presents the despair of the hollow man waiting for death. But even death can never give them tranquility. The state of the hollow man is a true portrayal of modern man under the influence of western civilization. Wars, especially the Second World War, have great impact on the physical as well as spiritual aspect of human beings. It aggravates the alienation of modern people. In this respect, William Golding illustrates profoundly in his masterpiece *Lord of the Flies*. Superficially, the novel is just an adventure story of children under isolated circumstances; fundamentally, it is a novel for readers to consider the truth about human nature. Similar to Golding, the playwright Harold Pinter is good at presenting the estranged condition of human being in his plays, among which *The Dumb Waiter* is undoubtedly an outstanding one. As a representative writer of the Theater of Absurd, Pinter writes about human beings living a meaningless life in an alien, decaying world as what the two hit-men do in the above mentioned play.

Alienation is becoming more and more serious with the advancement of the civilization, and modern writers tend to focus more on the dark side and hardly find any solution to the problem. But it goes without saying that human beings begin to realize the issue through their efforts and may try to avoid the negative effects as much as possible.

Joseph Conrad
1857—1924

Joseph Conrad

Joseph Conrad, a novelist and short-story writer, was born in Berdichev, a region that had once been a part of Poland, but was then under Russian rule. His father was an aristocrat without lands, a poet and translator of Shakespeare and Dickens and French literature. As a boy, young Joseph read Polish and French versions of English novels. English was his third language; he learned to read and write in French before he knew English. By 1869 Conrad's parents had died of tuberculosis, and he was sent to Switzerland to his maternal uncle who was to be a continuing influence on his life. In the mid-1870s he joined the French merchant marine as an apprentice, and made between 1875 and 1878 three voyages to the West Indies. He then began to work aboard British ships, learning English from his shipmates. He was made a Master Mariner, and served more than sixteen years, during which he was once hired to take a steamship into Africa, and according to him, the experience of seeing firsthand the horrors of colonial rule left him a changed man. In 1886 he was given British citizenship and he changed officially his name to Joseph Conrad. By 1894 Conrad's sea life was over and he decided to devote himself entirely to literature. The year 1894 was a landmark year for Conrad: his first novel was published; he met Edward Garnett, who would become a lifelong friend; and he met Jessie George, his future wife. He continued writing in various houses in Kent but lived in near poverty until the popular success of *Chance* (1913). He was offered a knighthood in America in 1924, but he declined. Conrad died of a heart attack in 1924 at the age of 67 at his home in Canterbury, England.

During his life, Conrad sailed to many parts of the world including Australia, various ports of the Indian Ocean, the Malay states, South America, and the South Pacific Island. In 1890 he sailed in Africa up the Congo River, which provided much material for his novel *Heart of Darkness* (1902). His condemnation of colonialism is well documented in the journal he kept during this visit. The major productive period of Conrad's career spanned from 1897 to 1911, during which time he composed *The Nigger of the Narcissus* (1897), *Youth* (1902), *Heart of Darkness, Lord Jim* (1900), *Nostromo* (1904), *The Secret Agent* (1907), and *Under Western Eyes* (1911), among other works. Over the last two decades of his life, Conrad produced more autobiographical writings and novels, including *The Arrow of Gold* (1919) and *The Rescue* (1920). His final novel, *The Rover* (1923), was published in 1923.

Conrad's writing is known for its dense and almost poetic prose, the use of hauntingly dark metaphors and his ambiguous characters that rarely represent either good or evil, which is a typical expression of alienation in modern people. His literary works have a profound impact on the Modernist movement, influencing a long list of writers including T.S. Eliot, Virginia Woolf, Thomas Mann, Ernest Hemingway, F. Scott Fitzgerald, and William Faulkner.

The following excerpt is from chapter one, in which the narrator Marlow started his journey along the Congo River in a steamboat. During his trip, he witnessed the wretched living situation of the local people, especially the black laborers. Meanwhile, he also encountered white colonists, who had an apparent superiority over the African people.

Heart of Darkness

Heart of Darkness, partly based on Conrad's four-month command of a Congo River steamboat, was written in 1899. The narrator of the novel, Marlow, who perhaps is not so reliable, depicts to his friends a trip into Africa. Marlow works for a company that is only interested in ivory and during his journey he witnesses the suffering of the native workers. Meanwhile, he finds Kurtz, a prosperous ivory agent with deteriorating health. Kurtz represents a type of personality: one that is intelligent, ambitious and capable. But at the sight

of money, he turns into an evil genius and finally he goes insane and before dying, Marlow hears him weakly whisper: "The horror! The horror!" Upon his return to Europe, Marlow visits Kurtz's fiancée, who is dressed in black and still deep in mourning. She presses Marlow for information, asking him to repeat Kurtz's final words. Marlow lies and tells her that Kurtz's final word was her name. To some extent, Marlow's journey to meet Kurtz and bring him home to Europe is symbolic of his journey to the heart of darkness, the subconscious mind. As for the title of the book, different interpretations are suggested. But generally speaking, *Heart of Darkness* is interpreted as a journey to the dark soul of mankind. It exposes the myth of colonization whilst exploring three levels of darkness: the darkness of the Congo wildness, the darkness of the European's cruel treatment of the natives, and the unfathomable darkness within every human being for committing heinous acts of evil.

Chapter One (Excerpt)

"It was upward of thirty days before I saw the mouth of the big river[1]. We anchored off the seat of the government. But my work would not begin till some two hundred miles farther on. So as soon as I could I made a start for a place thirty miles higher up.

"I had my passage on a little sea-going steamer. Her captain was a Swede, and knowing me for a seaman, invited me on the bridge." He was a young man, lean, fair, and morose, with lanky hair and a shuffling gait. As we left the miserable little wharf, he tossed his head contemptuously at the shore. 'Been living there?' he asked. I said, 'Yes.' 'Fine lot these government chaps—are they not?'[2] he went on, speaking English with great precision and considerable bitterness. 'It is funny what some people will do for a few francs a month. I wonder what becomes of that kind when it goes up country?' I said to him I expected to see that soon. 'So-o-o!' he exclaimed. He shuffled athwart, keeping one eye ahead vigilantly. 'Don't be too sure,' he continued. 'The other day I took up a man who hanged himself on the road. He was a Swede, too.' 'Hanged himself! Why, in God's name?' I cried. He kept on looking out watchfully. 'Who knows? The sun too much for him, or the country perhaps.'

"At last we opened a reach[3]. A rocky cliff appeared, mounds of turned-up earth by the shore, houses on a hill, others, with iron roofs, amongst a waste of excavations, or hanging to the declivity[4]. A continuous noise of the rapids above hovered over this scene of inhabited devastation. A lot of people, mostly black and naked, moved about like ants. A jetty[5] projected into the river. A blinding sunlight drowned all this at times in a sudden recrudescence of glare. 'There's your Company's station,' said the Swede, pointing to three wooden barrack-like structures on the rocky slope. 'I will send your things up. Four boxes did you say? So. Farewell.'

"I came upon a boiler wallowing in the grass, then found a path leading up the hill. It turned aside for the boulders, and also for an undersized railway-truck lying there on its back with its wheels in the air. One was off. The thing looked as dead as the carcass of some animal. I came upon more pieces of decaying machinery, a stack of rusty rails. To the left a clump of trees made a shady spot, where dark things seemed to stir feebly. I blinked, the path was steep. A horn tooted to the right, and I saw the black people run. A heavy and dull detonation shook the ground, a puff of smoke came out of the cliff, and that was all. No change appeared on the face of the rock. They were building a railway. The cliff was not in the way or anything; but this objectless blasting was all the work going on.

"A slight clinking behind me made me turn my head. Six black men advanced in a file, toiling up the path. They walked erect and slow, balancing small baskets full of earth on their heads, and the clink kept time with their footsteps. Black rags were wound round their loins[6], and the short ends behind waggled to and fro like tails. I could see every rib, the joints of their limbs were like knots in a rope; each had an iron collar on his neck, and all were connected together with a chain whose bights swung between them, rhythmically clinking. Another report[7] from the cliff made me think suddenly of that ship of war I had seen firing into a continent. It was the same kind of ominous[8] voice; but these men could by no stretch of imagination be called enemies. They were called criminals, and the outraged law, like the bursting shells, had come to them, an insoluble mystery from the sea. All their meagre breasts panted together, the violently dilated[9] nostrils quivered, the eyes stared stonily uphill. They passed me within six inches, without a glance, with that complete, deathlike indifference of unhappy savages. Behind this raw matter one of the reclaimed[10], the product of the new forces at work, strolled despondently[11], carrying a rifle by its middle. He had a uniform jacket with one button off, and seeing a white man on the path, hoisted his weapon to his shoulder with alacrity[12]. This was simple prudence, white men being so much alike at a distance that he could not tell who I might be. He was speedily reassured, and with a large, white, rascally grin, and a glance at his charge, seemed to take me into partnership in his exalted trust. After all, I also was a part of the great cause of these high and just proceedings.[13]

"Instead of going up, I turned and descended to the left. My idea was to let that chain-gang get out of sight before I climbed the hill. You know I am not particularly tender; I've had to strike and to fend off. I've had to resist and to attack sometimes — that's only one way of resisting — without counting the exact cost, according to the demands of such sort of life as I had blundered into. I've seen the devil of violence, and the devil of greed, and the devil of hot desire; but, by all the stars![14] these were strong, lusty, red-eyed devils, that swayed and drove men—men, I tell you. But as I stood on this hillside, I foresaw that in the blinding sunshine of that land I would become acquainted with a flabby, pretending, weak-eyed devil of a rapacious[15] and pitiless folly. How insidious he could be, too, I was only to find out several months later and a thousand miles farther. For a moment I stood appalled, as though by a warning. Finally I descended the hill, obliquely, towards the trees I had seen.

"I avoided a vast artificial hole somebody had been digging on the slope, the purpose of which I found it impossible to divine. It wasn't a quarry or a sandpit, anyhow. It was just a hole. It might have been connected with the philanthropic[16] desire of giving the criminals something to do. I don't know. Then I nearly fell into a very narrow ravine[17], almost no more than a scar in the hillside. I discovered that a lot of imported drainage-pipes for the settlement had been tumbled in there. There wasn't one that was not broken. It was a wanton smash-up. At last I got under the trees. My purpose was to stroll into the shade for a moment; but no sooner within than it seemed to me I had stepped into the gloomy circle of some Inferno[18]. The rapids[19] were near, and an uninterrupted, uniform, headlong, rushing noise filled the mournful stillness of the grove, where not a breath stirred, not a leaf moved, with a mysterious sound—as though the tearing pace of the launched earth had suddenly become audible.

"Black shapes crouched, lay, sat between the trees leaning against the trunks, clinging to the earth, half coming out, half effaced within the dim light, in all the attitudes of pain, abandonment, and despair. Another mine on the cliff went off, followed by a slight shudder of the soil under my feet. The work was going on. The work! And this was the place where some of the helpers had withdrawn to die.

"They were dying slowly — it was very clear. They were not enemies, they were not criminals, they were nothing earthly now — nothing but black shadows of disease and starvation, lying confusedly in the greenish gloom. Brought from all the recesses of the coast in all the legality of time contracts, lost in uncongenial surroundings, fed on unfamiliar food, they sickened, became inefficient, and were then allowed to crawl away and rest. These moribund[20] shapes were free as air — and nearly as thin. I began to distinguish the gleam of the eyes under the trees. Then, glancing down, I saw a face near my hand. The black bones reclined at full length with one shoulder against the tree, and slowly the eyelids rose and the sunken eyes looked up at me, enormous and vacant, a kind of blind, white flicker in the depths of the orbs, which died out slowly. The man seemed young — almost a boy — but you know with them it's hard to tell. I found nothing else to do but to offer him one of my good Swede's ship's biscuits I had in my pocket. The fingers closed slowly on it and held — there was no other movement and no other glance. He had tied a bit of white worsted[21] round his neck — Why? Where did he get it? Was it a badge — an ornament — a charm — a propitiatory act? Was there any idea at all connected with it? It looked startling round his black neck, this bit of white thread from beyond the seas.

"Near the same tree two more bundles of acute angles sat with their legs drawn up. One, with his chin propped on his knees, stared at nothing, in an intolerable and appalling manner: his brother phantom rested its forehead, as if overcome with a great weariness; and all about others were scattered in every pose of contorted collapse, as in some picture of a massacre or a pestilence. While I stood horror-struck, one of these creatures rose to his hands and knees, and went off on all-fours towards the river to drink. He lapped out of his hand, then sat up in the sunlight, crossing his shins in front of him, and after a time let his woolly head fall on his breastbone.

"I didn't want any more loitering in the shade, and I made haste towards the station. When near the buildings I met a white man, in such an unexpected elegance of get-up[22] that in the first moment I took him for a sort of vision. I saw a high starched[23] collar, white cuffs[24], a light alpaca jacket, snowy trousers, a clean necktie, and varnished boots. No hat. Hair parted, brushed, oiled, under a green-lined parasol held in a big white hand. He was amazing, and had a penholder behind his ear.

"I shook hands with this miracle, and I learned he was the Company's chief accountant, and that all the book-keeping was done at this station. He had come out for a moment, he said, 'to get a breath of fresh air.' The expression sounded wonderfully odd, with its suggestion of sedentary desk-life. I wouldn't have mentioned the fellow to you at all, only it was from his lips that I first heard the name of the man who is so indissolubly connected with the memories of that time. Moreover, I respected the fellow. Yes; I respected his collars, his vast cuffs, his brushed hair. His appearance was certainly that of a hairdresser's dummy; but in the great demoralization of the land he kept up his appearance. That's backbone. His starched collars and got-up shirt-fronts were achievements of character. He had been out nearly three years; and, later, I could not help asking him how he managed to sport such linen. He had just the faintest blush, and said modestly, 'I've been teaching one of the native women about the station. It was difficult. She had a distaste for the work.' Thus this man had verily accomplished something. And he was devoted to his books, which were in apple-pie order.

"Everything else in the station was in a muddle—heads, things, buildings. Strings of dusty niggers with splay feet arrived and departed; a stream of manufactured goods, rubbishy cottons, beads, and brass-wire set into the depths of darkness, and in return came a precious trickle of ivory.

"I had to wait in the station for ten days—an eternity. I lived in a hut in the yard, but to be out of the chaos I would sometimes get into the accountant's office. It was built of horizontal planks, and so badly put together that, as he bent over his high desk, he was barred from neck to heels with narrow strips of sunlight. There was no need to open the big shutter to see. It was hot there, too; big flies buzzed fiendishly, and did not sting, but stabbed. I sat generally on the floor, while, of faultless appearance (and even slightly scented), perching on a high stool, he wrote, he wrote. Sometimes he stood up for exercise. When a truckle-bed with a sick man (some invalid agent from upcountry) was put in there, he exhibited a gentle annoyance. 'The groans of this sick person,' he said, 'distract my attention. And without that it is extremely difficult to guard against clerical errors in this climate.'

"One day he remarked, without lifting his head, 'In the interior you will no doubt meet Mr. Kurtz[25].' On my asking who Mr. Kurtz was, he said he was a first-class agent; and seeing my disappointment at this information, he added slowly, laying down his pen, 'He is a very remarkable person.' Further questions elicited[26] from him that Mr. Kurtz was at present in charge of a trading-post, a very important one, in the true ivory-country, at 'the very bottom of there. Sends in as much ivory as all the others put together ...' He began to write again. The sick man was too ill to groan. The flies buzzed in a great peace.

"Suddenly there was a growing murmur of voices and a great tramping of feet. A caravan[27] had come in. A violent babble of uncouth sounds burst out on the other side of the planks. All the carriers were speaking together, and in the midst of the uproar the lamentable voice of the chief agent was heard 'giving it up' tearfully for the twentieth time that day.... He rose slowly. 'What a frightful row,' he said. He crossed the room gently to look at the sick man, and returning, said to me, 'He does not hear.' 'What! Dead?' I asked, startled. 'No, not yet,' he answered, with great composure. Then, alluding with a toss of the head to the tumult in the station-yard, 'When one has got to make correct entries, one comes to hate those savages—hate them to the death.' He remained thoughtful for a moment. 'When you see Mr. Kurtz' he went on, 'tell him from me that everything here' — he glanced at the deck — 'is very satisfactory. I don't like to write to him — with those messengers of ours you never know who may get hold of your letter — at that Central Station.' He stared at me for a moment with his mild, bulging eyes. 'Oh, he will go far, very far,' he began again. 'He will be a somebody in the Administration before long. They, above — the Council in Europe, you know — mean him to be.'

"He turned to his work. The noise outside had ceased, and presently in going out I stopped at the door. In the steady buzz of flies the homeward-bound agent was lying finished and insensible; the other, bent over his books, was making correct entries of perfectly correct transactions; and fifty feet below the doorstep I could see the still tree-tops of the grove of death.

"Next day I left that station at last, with a caravan of sixty men, for a two-hundred-mile tramp.

"No use telling you much about that. Paths, paths, everywhere; a stamped-in network of paths spreading over the empty land, through the long grass, through burnt grass, through thickets, down and up chilly ravines, up and down stony hills ablaze with heat; and a solitude, a solitude, nobody, not a hut. The population had cleared out a long time ago. Well, if a lot of mysterious niggers armed with all kinds of fearful weapons suddenly took to travelling on the road between Deal and Gravesend, catching the yokels[28] right and left to carry heavy loads for them, I fancy every farm and cottage thereabouts would get empty very soon. Only here the dwellings were gone, too. Still I passed through several abandoned villages. There's something pathetically childish in the ruins of grass walls. Day after day, with the stamp and shuffle of sixty pair of bare feet behind me, each pair under a 60-lb.[29] load. Camp, cook, sleep, strike camp, march. Now and then a carrier dead in harness, at rest in the long grass near the path, with an empty water-gourd and his long staff lying by his side. A great silence around and above. Perhaps on some quiet night the tremor of far-off drums, sinking, swelling, a tremor vast, faint; a sound weird, appealing, suggestive, and wild—and perhaps with as profound a meaning as the sound of bells in a Christian country. Once a white man in an unbuttoned uniform, camping on the path with an armed escort of lank Zanzibaris, very hospitable and festive—not to say drunk. Was looking after the upkeep of the road, he declared. Can't say I saw any road or any upkeep, unless the body of a middle-aged negro, with a bullet-hole in the forehead, upon which I absolutely stumbled three miles farther on, may be considered as a permanent improvement. I had a white companion, too, not a bad chap, but rather too fleshy and with the exasperating habit of fainting on the hot hillsides, miles away from the least bit of shade and water. Annoying, you know, to hold your own coat like a parasol[30] over a man's head while he is coming to. I couldn't help asking him once what he meant by coming there at all. 'To make money, of course. What do you think?' he said, scornfully. Then he got fever, and had to be carried in a hammock slung under a pole. As he weighed sixteen stone I had no end of rows with the carriers. They jibbed, ran away, sneaked off with their loads in the night—quite a mutiny. So, one evening, I made a speech in English with gestures, not one of which was lost to the sixty pairs of eyes before me, and the next morning I started the hammock off in front all right. An hour afterwards I came upon the whole concern wrecked in a bush—man, hammock, groans, blankets, horrors. The heavy pole had skinned his poor nose. He was very anxious for me to kill somebody, but there wasn't the shadow of a carrier near. I remembered the old doctor—'It would be interesting for science to watch the mental changes of individuals, on the spot.' I felt I was becoming scientifically interesting. However, all that is to no purpose. On the fifteenth day I came in sight of the big river again, and hobbled into the Central Station. It was on a back water surrounded by scrub and forest, with a pretty border of smelly mud on one side, and on the three others enclosed by a crazy fence of rushes. A neglected gap was all the gate it had, and the first glance at the place was enough to let you see the flabby devil was running that show. White men with long staves in their hands appeared languidly from amongst the buildings, strolling up to take a look at me, and then retired out of sight somewhere....

Notes

1. the big river: Here referring to the Congo River
2. Fine lot these government chaps—are they not?: These fellows in government are fine, aren't they?
3. reach: a continuous extent of water, especially a stretch of river between two bend
4. declivity: a downward slope
5. jetty: a landing stage at which boats can dock or be moored
6. loins: waist
7. report: a sudden loud noise of an explosion
8. ominous: giving the worrying impression that something bad is going to happen
9. dilated: make or become larger
10. the reclaimed: redeem someone from a state of vice; reform
11. despondently: in low spirits from loss of hope or courage
12. alacrity: brisk and cheerful readiness
13. This paragraph describes the life of Africans.
14. by all the stars!: an expression of astonishment
15. rapacious: aggressively greedy or grasping
16. philanthropic: generous and kind
17. ravine: a deep, narrow gorge with steep sides
18. Inferno: Hell
19. rapid: a fast-flowing and turbulent part of a river
20. moribund: (of a person) at the point of death
21. worsted: a fine smooth yarn spun from combed lone-staple wool
22. get-up: a style of dress, especially an elaborate one
23. starched: stiffen (fabric or clothing) with starch
24. cuff: the end part of a sleeve
25. Kurtz: a central fictional character in the novella, who is a trader of ivory in Africa and commander of a trading post. He monopolizes his position as a demigod among native Africans.
26. elicit: draw out (a response, answer, or fact) from someone

27. caravan: a group of people, especially traders, travelling together across a desert in Asia or North Africa
28. yokel: an uneducated person from countryside
29. 60-lb.: 60 pounds
30. parasol: a light umbrella used to give shade from the sun

Questions

1. How does Conrad describe the situation of the black people in the excerpt? How about the white man? What do you think is the cause for all of this?
2. In paragraph 9 of the excerpt, Conrad illustrates his encounter with an African boy, whose white worsted round the neck leaves him a deep impression. What do you think is the symbolic meaning of it?
3. In what way does this excerpt embody the theme of the novel?

William Golding
1911—1993

William Golding

William Golding was born in 1911 in Cornwall, England. His father was a schoolmaster and his mother was a suffragette. When Golding was young, his parents expected him to be a scientist, but he revolted. After two years at Oxford, he became devoted to English literature. In 1934, a year before graduation, he published his first work, a book of poetry, which was largely overlooked by critics.

After college, Golding worked in settlement houses and theater for a time. Eventually, he decided to follow in his father's footsteps. In 1935 Golding took a position teaching English and philosophy at Bishop Wordsworth's School in Salisbury. Golding's experience of teaching unruly young boys would later serve as inspiration for his novel *Lord of the Flies*. In 1940 Golding temporarily abandoned the teaching profession to join the Royal Navy and fight in World War II, during which he fought battleships at the sinking of the Bismarck, and also fended off submarines and planes. And he was promoted as Lieutenant because of his bravery in the war. Like his teaching experience, Golding's participation in the war would prove to be fruitful materials for his fiction. In 1945, after World War II had ended, Golding went back to teaching and writing. In 1954, he published his first and most acclaimed novel, *Lord of the Flies*. Since its publication, the novel has been widely regarded as a classic, worthy of in-depth analysis and discussion around the world. Among the most successful novels of Golding's writing career were *Rites of Passage* (winner of the 1980 Booker McConnell Prize), *Pincher Martin* (1956), *Free Fall* (1959) and *The*

Pyramid (1967). While Golding was mainly a novelist, his body of work also includes poetry, plays, essays and short stories. At the age of 73, Golding was awarded the 1983 Nobel Prize for Literature. In 1988 he was knighted by England's Queen Elizabeth II. Golding spent the last few years of his life quietly living with his wife at their house near Falmouth, Cornwall, where he continued to toil at his writing. On June 19, 1993, Golding died of a heart attack.

In his fictions, Golding allegorically makes broad use of allusion to classical literature, mythology, and Christian symbolism, tinted with a color of darkness and devil, and mixed with a faint pessimism. Many of his novels emphasize the brutal and violent human impulses that arise in the absence of political order. *Lord of the Flies* is just a good example.

Lord of the Flies

Composed shortly after the end of WWII, the novel *Lord of the Flies* tells a gripping story of a group of adolescent boys stranded on a deserted island after a plane wreck.

The story happens under the circumstance that some English children who survive in an airplane accident wait for the rescue from adults on an isolated island during the war in the planned future. At first, the boys scatter about in different directions on the island until Ralph, a blond-hair boy blows the conch under the guidance and encouragement of another boy, Piggy. After hearing the sound of conch, the other boys gather together and attempt to set up a normal society on the island. Ralph lights a fire with Piggy's spectacles and makes the smoke on the mountains in order to create SOS signal for a passing ship to rescue them. Jack, leader of a choir-school group, acts as the leading hunter for pigs. The children miss a precious opportunity to be rescued by the ship passing by due to Jack's fault. Moreover, they feel the terrible beast haunting around on the island. Jack makes a fly-infested pig's head struck on a pole and intent to worship it as the Lord of the Flies. Gradually, Jack's followers become much crazier. They take Piggy's glasses for making fire to roast meat and even smash him to death. Almost all the boys change into barbaric children. Accidentally, boys make the island on fire, the smoke of which is finally observed by the naval officers. All the boys, especially Ralph who ultimately escapes from the chase, are rescued.

Although the characters are mainly children, the book explores the savage side of human nature as the boys, let loose from the constraints of society, brutally turn against one another in the face of an imagined enemy. This book sets the tone for Golding's future work, in which he continues to examine man's internal struggle between good and evil. There are several conflicts depicted in the novel: civilization vs. savagery, individualism vs. community, and man vs. nature. And of course, the book can be read allegorically, such as the nature of evil, the loss of innocence, and the negative consequences of war. According to Golding, the aim of the narrative is "to trace the defects of society back to the defects of human nature"; the moral illustrated is that "the shape of society must depend on the ethical nature of the individual and not on any political system however apparently logical or respectable." And since the lost children are the inheritors of the same defects of nature which doomed their fathers, the tragedy on the island is bound to repeat the actual pattern of human history.

The following excerpt is from Chapter Eight, in which Piggy suggests that they start a fire down by the beach and he organizes the new fire area by the beach. Far off along the beach, Jack, with some boys, says that they might go later to the castle rock, but now they will kill a pig and have a feast to celebrate their independence. They find a group of pigs, and Jack kills a large sow. They cut off the pig's head and leave it on a stick as a gift for the beast at the mountaintop.

Chapter Eight (Excerpt)
Gift for the Darkness

[...]

The greatest ideas are the simplest. Now there was something to be done they worked with passion. Piggy was so full of delight and expanding liberty in Jack's departure, so full of pride in his contribution to the good of society that he helped to fetch wood. The wood he fetched was close at hand, a fallen tree on the platform that they did not need for the assembly, yet to the others the sanctity of the platform had protected even what was useless there. Then the twins realized they would have a fire near them as a comfort in the night and this set a few littluns[1] dancing and clapping hands.

The wood was not so dry as the fuel they had used on the mountain. Much of it was damply rotten and full of insects that scurried; logs had to be lined from the soil with care or they crumbled into sodden powder. More than this, in order to avoid going deep into the forest the boys worked near at hand on any fallen wood no matter how tangled with new growth. The skirts of the forest and the scar were familiar, near the conch and the shelters and sufficiently friendly in daylight. What they might become in darkness nobody cared to think. They worked therefore with great energy and cheerfulness, though as time crept by there was a suggestion of panic in the energy and hysteria in the cheerfulness. They built a pyramid of leaves and twigs, branches and togs, on the bare sand by the platform. For the first time on the island, Piggy himself removed his one glass, knelt down and focused the sun on tinder. Soon there was a ceiling of smoke and a bush of yellow flame.

The littluns who had seen few fires since the first catastrophe became wildly excited. They danced and sang and there was a partyish air about the gathering.

At last Ralph stopped work and stood up, smudging the sweat from his face with a dirty forearm.

"We'll have to have a small fire. This one's too big to keep up."

Piggy sat down carefully on the sand and began to polish his glass.

"We could experiment. We could find out how to make a small hot fire and then put green branches on to make smoke. Some of them leaves must be better for that than the others."

As the fire died down so did the excitement. The littluns stopped singing and dancing and drifted away toward the sea or the fruit trees or the shelters.

Ralph flopped down in the sand.

"We'll have to make a new list of who's to took after the fire."

"If you can find 'em."

He looked round. Then for the first time he saw how few biguns[2] there were and understood why the work had been so hard.

"Where's Maurice?"

Piggy wiped his glass again.

"I expect ... no, he wouldn't go into the forest by himself, would he?"

Ralph jumped up, ran swiftly round the fire and stood by Piggy, holding up his hair.

"But we've got to have a list! There's you and me and Samneric and—"

He would not look at Piggy but spoke casually.

"Where's Bill and Roger?"

Piggy leaned forward and put a fragment of wood on the fire.

"I expect they've gone. I expect they won't play either."

Ralph sat down and began to poke little holes in the sand. He was surprised to see that one had a drop of blood by it. He examined his bitten nail closely and watched the little globe of blood that gathered where the quick[3] was gnawed away.

Piggy went on speaking.

"I seen them stealing off[4] when we was gathering wood. They went that way. The same way as he went himself."

Ralph finished his inspection and looked up into the air. The sky, as if in sympathy with the great changes among them, was different today and so misty that in some places the hot air seemed white. The disc of the sun was dull silver as though it were nearer and not so hot, yet the air stifled.

"They always been making trouble, haven't they?"

The voice came near his shoulder and sounded anxious.

"We can do without 'em. We'll be happier now, won't we?"

Ralph sat. The twins came, dragging a great log and grinning in their triumph. They dumped the log among the embers[5] so that sparks flew.

"We can do all right on our own, can't we?"

For a long time while the log dried, caught fire and turned red hot, Ralph sat in the sand and said nothing. He did not see Piggy go to the twins and whisper with them, nor how the three boys went together into the forest.

"Here you are."

He came to himself with a jolt. Piggy and the other two were by him. They were laden with[6] fruit.

"I thought perhaps," said Piggy, "we ought to have a feast, kind of."

The three boys sat down. They had a great mass of the fruit with them and all of it properly ripe. They grinned at Ralph as he took some and began to eat.

"Thanks," he said. Then with an accent of pleased surprise—"Thanks!"

"Do all right on our own," said Piggy. "It's them that haven't no common sense that make trouble on this island. We'll make a little hot fire—"

Ralph remembered what had been worrying him.

"Where's Simon?"

"I don't know."

"You don't think he's climbing the mountain?"

Piggy broke into noisy laughter and took more fruit.

"He might be." He gulped[7] his mouthful. "He's cracked."

Simon had passed through the area of fruit trees but today the littluns had been too busy with the fire on the beach and they had not pursued him there. He went on among the creepers until he reached the great mat that was woven by the open space and crawled inside. Beyond the screen of leaves the sunlight pelted down and the butterflies danced in the middle their unending dance. He knelt down and the arrow of the sun fell on him. That other time the air had seemed to vibrate with heat; but now it threatened. Soon the sweat was running from his long coarse hair. He shifted restlessly but there was no avoiding the sun. Presently he was thirsty, and then very thirsty.

He continued to sit.

Far off alone the beach, Jack was standing before a small group of boys. He was looking brilliantly happy.

"Hunting," he said. He sized them up. Each of them wore the remains of a black cap and ages ago they had stood in two demure rows and their voices had been the song of angels.

"We'll hunt. I'm going to be chief."

They nodded, and the crisis passed easily.

"And then—about the beast."

They moved, looked at the forest.

"I say this. We aren't going to bother about the beast."

He nodded at them.

"We're going to forget the beast."

"That's right!"

"Yes!"

"Forget the beast!"

If Jack was astonished by their fervor[8] he did not show it.

"And another thing. We shan't dream so much down here. This is near the end of the island."

They agreed passionately out of the depths of their tormented private lives.

"Now listen. We might go later to the castle rock. But now I'm going to get more of the biguns away from the conch and all that we'll kill a pig and give a feast." He paused and went on more slowly. "And about the beast when we kill we'll leave some of the kill for it. Then it won't bother us, maybe."

He stood up abruptly.

"We'll go into the forest now and hunt."

He turned and trotted away and after a moment they followed him obediently.

They spread out, nervously, in the forest. Almost at once Jack found the dung and scattered roots that told of pig and soon the track was fresh. Jack signaled the rest of the hunt to be quiet and went forward by himself. He was happy and wore the damp darkness of the forest like his old clothes. He crept down a slope to rocks and scattered trees by the sea.

The pigs lay, bloated bags of fat, sensuously enjoying the shadows under the trees. There was no wind and they were unsuspicious; and practice had made Jack silent as the shadows. He stole away again and instructed his hidden hunters. Presently they all began to inch forward sweating in the silence and heat. Under the trees an ear flapped idly. A little apart from the rest, sunk in deep maternal bliss, lay the largest sow[9] of the lot. She was black and pink; and the great bladder of her belly was fringed with a row of piglets that slept or burrowed and squeaked.

Fifteen yards from the drove Jack stopped, and his arm, straightening, pointed at the sow. he looked round in inquiry to make sure that everyone understood and the other boys nodded at him. The row of right arms slid back.

"Now!"

The drove of pigs started up; and at a range of only ten yards the wooden spears with fire-hardened points flew toward the chosen pig. One piglet, with a demented shriek, rushed into the sea trailing Roger's spear behind it. The sow gave a gasping squeal and staggered up, with two spears sticking in her fat flank. The boys shouted and rushed forward, the piglets scattered and the sow burst the advancing line and went crashing away through the forest.

"After her!"

They raced along the pig-track, but the forest was too dark and tangled so that Jack, cursing, stopped them and cast among the trees. Then he said nothing for a time but breathed fiercely so that they were awed by him and looked at each other in uneasy admiration. Presently he stabbed down at the ground with his finger.

"There—"

Before the others could examine the drop of blood, Jack had swerved off, judging a trace, touching a bough that gave. So he followed, mysteriously right and assured, and the hunters trod behind him.

He stopped before a covert.

"In there."

They surrounded the covert but the sow got away with the sting of another spear in her flank. The trailing butts hindered her and the sharp, cross-cut points were a torment. She blundered into a tree, forcing a spear still deeper; and after that any of the hunters could follow her easily by the drops of vivid blood. The afternoon wore on, hazy and dreadful with damp heat; the sow staggered her way ahead of them, bleeding and mad, and the hunters followed, wedded to her in lust, excited by the long chase and the dropped blood. They could see her now, nearly got up with her, out she spurted with her last strength and held ahead of them again. They were just behind her when she staggered into an open space where bright flowers grew and butterflies danced round each other and the air was hot and still.

Here, struck down by the heat, the sow fell and the hunters hurled themselves at her. This dreadful eruption from an unknown world made her frantic; she squealed and bucked and the air was full of sweat and noise and blood and terror. Roger ran round the heap, prodding with his spear whenever pigflesh appeared. Jack was on top of the sow, stabbing downward with his knife. Roger found a lodgment for his point and began to push till he was leaning with his whole weight. The spear moved forward inch by inch and die terrified squealing became a high-pitched scream. Then Jack found the throat and the hot blood spouted over his hands. The sow collapsed under them and they were heavy and fulfilled upon her. The butterflies still danced, preoccupied in the center of die clearing.

At last the immediacy of the kill subsided. The boys drew back, and Jack stood up, holding out his hands.

"Look."

He giggled and flicked them while the boys laughed at his reeking palms. Then Jack grabbed Maurice and rubbed the stuff over his cheeks. Roger began to withdraw his spear and the boys noticed it for the first time. Robert stabilized the thing in a phrase which was received uproariously.

"Right up her ass!"

"Did you hear?"

"Did you hear what he said?"

"Right up her ass!"

This time Robert and Maurice acted the two parts; and Maurice's acting of the pig's efforts to avoid the advancing spear was so funny that the boys cried with laughter.

At length[10] even this palled[11]. Jack began to clean his bloody hands on the rock. Then he started work on the sow and paunched her, lugging out the hot bags of colored guts, pushing them into a pile on the rock while the others watched him. He talked as he worked.

"We'll take the meat along the beach. I'll go back to the platform and invite them to a feast. That should give us time."

Roger spoke.

"Chief—"

"Uh—?"

"How can we make a fire?"

Jack squatted back and frowned at the pig.

"We'll raid them and take fire. There must be four of you; Henry and you, Bill and Maurice. We'll put on paint and sneak up; Roger can snatch a branch while I say what I want. The rest of you can get this back to where we were. We'll build the fire there. And after that—"

He paused and stood up, looking at the shadows under the trees. His voice was lower when he spoke again.

"But we'll leave part of the kill for ..."

He knelt down again and was busy with his knife. The boys crowded round him. He spoke over his shoulder to Roger.

"Sharpen a stick at both ends."

Presently he stood up, holding the dripping sow's head in his hands.

"Where's that stick?"

"Here."

"Ram one end in the earth. Oh—it's rock. Jam it in that crack. There."

Jack held up the head and jammed the soft throat down on the pointed end of the stick which pierced through into the mouth. He stood back and the head hung there, a little blood dribbling down the stick.

Instinctively the boys drew back too; and the forest was very still. They listened, and the loudest noise was the buzzing of flies over the spilled guts.

Jack spoke in a whisper.

"Pick up the pig."

Maurice and Robert skewered the carcass, lifted the dead weight, and stood ready. In the silence, and standing over the dry blood, they looked suddenly furtive.

Jack spoke loudly.

"This head is for the beast. It's a gift."

The silence accepted the gift and awed them. The head remained there, dim-eyed, grinning faintly, blood blackening between the teeth. All at once they were running away, as fast as they could, through the forest toward the open beach.

Simon stayed where he was, a small brown image, concealed by the leaves. Even if he shut his eyes the sow's head still remained like an after-image. The half-shut eyes were dim with the infinite cynicism of adult life. They assured Simon that everything was a bad business.

"I know that."

Simon discovered that he had spoken aloud. He opened his eyes quickly and there was the head grinning amusedly in the strange daylight, ignoring the flies, the spilled guts, even ignoring the indignity of being spiked on a stick.

He looked away, licking his dry lips.

A gift for the beast. Might not the beast come for it? The head, he thought, appeared to agree with him. Run away, said the head silently, go back to the others. It was a joke really—why should you bother? You were just wrong, that's all. A little headache, something you ate, perhaps. Go back, child, said the head silently.

Simon looked up, feeling the weight of his wet hair, and gazed at the sky. Up there, for once, were clouds, great bulging towers that sprouted away over the island, grey and cream and copper-colored. The clouds were sitting on the land; they squeezed, produced moment by moment this close, tormenting heat. Even the butterflies deserted the open space where the obscene thing grinned and dripped. Simon lowered his head, carefully keeping his eyes shut, then sheltered them with his hand. There were no shadows under the trees but everywhere a pearly stillness, so that what was real seemed illusive and without definition. The pile of guts was a black blob of flies that buzzed like a saw. After a while these flies found Simon. Gorged, they alighted by his runnels of sweat and drank. They tickled under his nostrils and played leap-frog on his thighs. They were black and iridescent green and without number; and in front of Simon, the Lord of the Flies hung on his stick and grinned. At last Simon gave up and looked back; saw the white teeth and dim eyes, the blood—and his gaze was held by that ancient, inescapable recognition. In Simon's right temple[12], a pulse began to beat on the brain.

Notes

1. littluns: small children from roughly 6 years old. They symbolize a sense of innocence and almost a need to be protected from the savagery of the uncivilized older "biguns".
2. biguns: older boys in the island, as represented by Jack, Ralph, Piggy, Simon, etc.
3. quick: the soft tender flesh below the growing part of a fingernail or toenail
4. steal off: move somewhere quietly
5. embers: small pieces of burning coal or wood in a dying fire
6. laden with: loaded with
7. gulp: swallow (food or drink) quickly or in large mouthfuls
8. fervor: intense and passionate feeling
9. sow: adult female pig
10. At length: In detail; fully

11. pall: become less appealing or interesting through familiarity
12. temple: the flat part of either side of the head between the forehead and the ear

Questions

1. How did the boys make a fire? What does the fire symbolize?
2. Why did Jack want to hunt? What role did Jack play in the process of hunting?
3. Describe Simon's feeling when he stayed with the gift for the beast alone. How to interpret the image of the pig head surrounded by flies? Why does Golding call it Lord of the flies?

Thomas Stearns Eliot
1888—1965

Thomas Stearns Eliot, poet, critic, and editor, was born in Missouri, USA. He lived in St. Louis during the first eighteen years of his life and attended Harvard University. In 1910, he left the United States for France, where he earned both undergraduate and masters' degrees. Later he studied literature and philosophy in Germany and England. Then he returned to Harvard to pursue a doctorate in philosophy, but returned to Europe and settled in England in 1914. The following year, he got married and began working in London, first as a teacher, and later for Lloyd's Bank.

Thomas Stearns Eliot

It was in London that Eliot came under the influence of his contemporary Ezra Pound, who recognized his poetic genius at once, and assisted in the publication of his work in a number of magazines, most notably "The Love Song of J. Alfred Prufrock" in 1915. Eliot became the editor of the *Criterion,* one of the most influential literary reviews at that time. And in the same year, his most famous poem, *The Waste Land,* appeared in the first number of the *Criterion.* By 1930, and for the next thirty years, he was the most dominant figure in poetry and literary criticism in the English-speaking world. After 1923, Eliot's family and career experienced a succession of misfortunes: his wife nearly died; he nearly lost his job in the bank. So, at about the same time, Eliot turned to Anglican Church for religious support. The conversion of his future faith can be found in "The Hollow Men", a poem read as a sequel to *The Waste Land*'s philosophical despair when it appeared in *Poems 1909—1925* (1925). In 1927, Eliot took British citizenship and became conservative both politically and literarily. He published a group of essays, considering himself as a "classicist in literature, royalist in politics, and Anglo-catholic in religion." His major later poems include *Ash Wednesday* (1930) and *Four Quartets* (1943). Eliot was also an important playwright, whose verse dramas include *Murder in the Cathedral* (1935), *The Family Reunion* (1939), and *The Cocktail Party* (1950). After an unhappy first marriage, Eliot separated from his first wife in 1933, and was remarried in 1956. Because of his great achievements in poetry, Eliot received the Nobel Prize for Literature in 1948. In 1965, he died in London and according to his own instructions his ashes were interred in the church of St. Michael's in East Coker.

Eliot's poems in many respects articulate the disillusionment of a younger post-World-War-I generation with the values and conventions—both literary and social—of the Victorian era. They explore the decay of culture in the modern Western world, expressing a sense of the disintegration of life. His most representative poem, *The Waste Land,* is hailed as a landmark of the twentieth century English poem. With bold technical innovations in versification and style, the poem not only presents a panorama of physical disorder and spiritual desolation in the modern Western world, but also reflects the prevalent mood of disillusionment and despair of a whole post-war generation.

The following selected poem is "The Hollow Men", which has similar theme to *The Waste Land* and it is generally regarded as the darkest of Eliot's poems. In this poem, the hollow men were in early hell and must wait for death to liberate them into a kind of purgatory. But they cannot find salvation even in it.

The Hollow Men

Mistah Kurtz[1]—he dead.[2]
A penny for the Old Guy[3]

I

We are the hollow men[4]
We are the stuffed men[4]
Leaning together
Headpiece filled with straw[4]. Alas!
Our dried voices, when
We whisper together
Are quiet and meaningless
As wind in dry grass
Or rats' feet over broken glass
In our dry cellar

Shape without form, shade without colour,
Paralysed force, gesture without motion;

Those who have crossed
With direct eyes, to death's other Kingdom[5]
Remember us—if at all—not as lost
Violent souls, but only
As the hollow men
The stuffed men.

II

Eyes I dare not meet in dreams
In death's dream kingdom
These do not appear:
There, the eyes are
Sunlight on a broken column[6]
There, is a tree swinging
And voices are
In the wind's singing
More distant and more solemn
Than a fading star.

Let me be no nearer
In death's dream kingdom
Let me also wear
Such deliberate disguises
Rat's coat, crowskin, crossed staves[7]
In a field
Behaving as the wind behaves
No nearer—

Not that final meeting
In the twilight kingdom

III

This is the dead land
This is cactus land
Here the stone images
Are raised, here they receive
The supplication of a dead man's hand
Under the twinkle of a fading star.

Is it like this
In death's other kingdom
Waking alone
At the hour when we are
Trembling with tenderness
Lips that would kiss
Form prayers to broken stone.

IV

The eyes are not here
There are no eyes here
In this valley of dying stars
In this hollow valley
This broken jaw of our lost kingdoms

In this last of meeting places
We grope together
And avoid speech
Gathered on this beach of the tumid river[8]

Sightless, unless
The eyes reappear
As the perpetual star
Multifoliate rose[9]
Of death's twilight kingdom
The hope only
Of empty men.

V

Here we go round the prickly pear[10]
Prickly pear prickly pear
Here we go round the prickly pear
At five o'clock in the morning.[11]

Between the idea
And the reality
Between the motion
And the act[12]
Falls the Shadow
　　　　For Thine is the Kingdom[13]

Between the conception
And the creation
Between the emotion
And the response
Falls the Shadow
　　　　Life is very long

Between the desire
And the spasm
Between the potency
And the existence
Between the essence
And the descent
Falls the Shadow
For Thine is the Kingdom

For Thine is
Life is
For Thine is the

This is the way the world ends[14]
This is the way the world ends
This is the way the world ends
Not with a bang but a whimper.[15]

Notes

1. Mistah Kurtz: a character in Joseph Conrad's *Heart of Darkness*
2. Mistah Kurtz—he dead: These are the words spoken by a servant to announce Kurtz's death. They signal the end of an evil presence, but also the end of one who was formerly a great man.
3. A penny for the Old Guy: This is a cry of English children on the streets on Guy Fawkes Day, November 5, when they beg for money for fireworks to celebrate the day. Guy Fawkes was a traitor who attempted with conspirators to blow up both houses of Parliament in 1605. After the conspiracy was discovered and Guy Fawkes revealed the names of his co-conspirators, they were soon executed. Now the British celebrate November 5 with bonfires, fireworks, and by burning effigies of Guy.
4. The "hollow men" and "stuffed men", "filled with straw" are a combination of the effigies burned on Guy Fawkes Day. More profoundly, they are Eliot's modern man, empty and corrupt.
5. Those... Kingdom: Those who have left behind a state of spiritual nothingness (or, alternatively, hell or purgatory) and entered into knowledge and recognition of that state (or heaven). They are the ones who are capable of looking directly at life and the universe and seeing the inner truth. The idea of crossing refers to a transition from one state to the other.
6. broken column: a traditional graveyard memorial for a premature death
7. crossed staves: Here referring to scarecrows
8. tumid river: swollen river, the River Acheron in Hell in Dante's "Inferno". The damned must cross this river to get to the land of the dead.
9. Multifoliate rose: In Dante's "Divine Comedy", paradise is described as a rose of many leaves.
10. prickly pear: cactus

11. five o'clock in the morning: the traditional time of Christ's resurrection. These lines parody a children's song "Here we go round the mulberry bush", which is derived from a dance around a mulberry bush on a cold and frosty morning. According to Eliot, by performing an infertility dance at the moment of resurrection, we are in effect blocking and rejecting the salvation it can bring.
12. Between... act: a reference to *Julius Caesar*, "Between the acting of a dreadful thing/And the first motion, all the interim is/Like a phantasma or a hideous dream."
13. For Thine is the Kingdom: These are the beginning of the closing words of the Lord's Prayer.
14. This is the way the world ends: Here, Eliot is again parodying the line in children's song mentioned in note 11, specifically the line "this is the way we clap our hands".
15. Not with a bang but a whimper: "whimper" can be understood in many ways according to the context of the poem. The whimper is what Guy Fawkes exhaled when he gave up his co-conspirators; it is what Brutus and Cassius in *Julius Caesar* spoke when their plans to rule crumbled; it is Kurtz's last utterance in *Heart of Darkness* when he finally realizes the truth of the world he lives in. And it is also the end for all hollow men.

Questions

1. Eliot claimed to have made up the title "The Hollow Men" from combining "The Hollow Land", the title of a romance by William Morris with Joseph Rudyard Kipling's title, "The Broken Men". What is the symbolic meaning of the hollow man judging from the context of the modern world?
2. "The Hollow Men" is full of allusions from many resources including the above mentioned two poems. What other resources can you find out?

Harold Pinter
1930—2008

Harold Pinter

The playwright Harold Pinter was born on October 10, 1930, in a lower middle-class neighborhood in London. His father was a tailor specializing in women's clothing and his mother, a homemaker. The Pinters were part of a wave of Jewish emigration to the UK at the turn of the last century. When World War II broke out, young Pinter saw some of the bombing of his city by the Germans and was evacuated from London to Cornwall with other children. This firsthand experience of war and destruction left a lasting impression on him. He once said that his encounter with anti-Semitism was the fuse that ignited the organic process leading him to becoming a playwright.

After the war, Pinter studied acting at the Royal Academy of

Dramatic Art and the Central School of Speech and Drama. Then he worked in regional theater as an actor in the 1950s. He wrote his first play, *The Room,* in 1957. In the same year, he wrote a second one-act play, *The Dumb Waiter,* an absurdist drama concerning two hit men employed by a secret organization to kill an unknown victim. It was with this play that Pinter added an element of black comedy through his brilliant use of dialogue to portray the absurdity of the characters' situation. After this, he went on to create his first full-length drama, *The Birthday Party,* which was staged in the following year but received dissenting reviews from critics. Pinter had his first taste of success in 1960 with *The Caretaker.* The play, like many of Pinter's works, conveyed "a world of perplexing menace". Judging from the theme and technique employed, Pinter's early plays were rooted in the absurdism that became the major theatrical paradigm on the European stage in the end of the 20th century after the horrors of the war and the Holocaust. Plays of this kind include *The Homecoming, No Man's Land,* and so on. After the great plays of his early and mid-period, Pinter became more overtly political. His later plays typically addressed political subjects and often were allegories on oppression. The short play *Mountain Language,* for instance, was written to highlight the mistreatment of the Kurdish people in Turkey.

Pinter was diagnosed with cancer in 2001 but he continued writing, and especially expressed condemnation on war. In 2005, Pinter was honored with the Nobel Prize for Literature. He died of cancer on December 24, 2008. His work has inspired and informed generations of playwrights.

Pinter's plays have some unique features, which are usually dark and claustrophobic. His language is full of menacing pauses and the lives of Pinter's characters usually are revealed to be stunted by guilt and horror. All these give rise to a term "Pinteresque".

The following excerpt is from Part Two. In this part, Gus reenters the room and starts to ask Ben a question. Ben does not tell anything to Gus, instead pushing for him to go make tea. When Gus comes back, Ben tells Gus that they'll have to wait for Wilson to show up, and Gus reminds him that sometimes Wilson sends a message instead of coming in person. He says he's been thinking about the last person who came to them as a target. Suddenly, the two men hear a clatter. Gus finds the rim of the dumb waiter, opens it, and finds a piece of paper that has been sent down from above. Then, the dumb waiter clatters again as another note is sent down. The men move around in indecision, looking up the dumb waiter's hatch and touching one another on the shoulder, wondering whether they should send something up.

The Dumb Waiter

The Dumb Waiter, a representative of Pinteresque play, depicts two hit-men, Ben and Gus, who are waiting in a basement room for their assignment to kill someone. During the boredom of waiting, they talk about a lot of things, such as the semantics of "light the kettle" and "put on the kettle". A dumb waiter is in the back of the room, which delivers occasional food

orders. Gus leaves the room to get a drink of water. Just at this moment, Ben receives order from the dumb waiter that their victim is on his way to the room. Ben shouts for Gus, but in vain. The play ends when the two stare at each other before the curtain comes down.

Excerpt

GUS: I wonder who it'll be tonight.

[Silence]

Eh, I've been wanting to ask you something.

BEN: [putting his legs on the bed] Oh, for Christ's sake.

GUS: No. I was going to ask you something.

[He rises and sits on Ben's bed]

BEN: What are you sitting on my bed for?

[Gus sits]

What's the matter with you? You're always asking me questions. What's the matter with you?

GUS: Nothing.

BEN: You never used to ask me so many damn questions. What's come over[1] you?

GUS: No, I was just wondering.

BEN: Stop wondering. You've got a job to do. Why don't you just do it and shut up?

GUS: That's what I was wondering about.

BEN: What?

GUS: The job.

BEN: What job?

GUS: [tentatively] I thought perhaps you might know something.

[Ben looks at him.]

I thought perhaps you — I mean — have you got any idea — who's it going to be tonight?

BEN: Who what's going to be?

[They look at each other]

GUS: [at length] Who it's going to be.

[Silence]

BEN: Are you feeling all right?

GUS: Sure.

BEN: Go and make the tea.

GUS: Yes, sure.

[Gus exits, Ben looks after him. He then takes his revolver from under the pillow and checks it for ammunition. Gus re-enters]

The gas has gone out.

BEN: Well, what about it?

GUS: There's a meter.

BEN: I haven't got any money.

GUS: Nor have I.

BEN: You'll have to wait.

GUS: What for?

BEN: For Wilson.

GUS: He might not come. He might just send a message. He doesn't always come.

BEN: Well, you'll have to do without it, won't you?

GUS: Blimey[2].

BEN: You'll have a cup of tea afterwards. What's the matter with you?

GUS: I like to have one before.

[Ben holds the revolver up to the light and polishes it]

BEN: You'd better get ready anyway.

GUS: Well, I don't know, that's a bit much, you know, for my money. [He picks up a packet of tea from the bed and throws it into the bag] I hope he's got a shilling, anyway, if he comes. He's entitled to[3] have. After all, it's his place, he could have seen there was enough gas for a cup of tea.

BEN: What do you mean, it's his place?

GUS: Well, isn't it?

BEN: He's probably only rented it. It doesn't have to be his place.

GUS: I know it's his place. I bet the whole house is. He's not even laying on[4] any gas now either. [Gus sits on his bed] It's his place all right. Look at all the other places. You go to this address, there's a key there, there's a teapot, there's never a soul in sight — [He pauses] Eh, nobody ever hears a thing, have you ever thought of that? We never get any complaints, do we, too much noise or anything like that? You never see a soul, do you? — except the bloke who comes. You ever noticed that? I wonder if the walls are sound-proof. [He touches the wall above his bed] Can't tell. All you do is wait, eh? Half the time he doesn't even bother to put in an appearance, Wilson.

BEN: Why should he? He's a busy man.

GUS: I find him hard to talk to, Wilson. Do you know that, Ben?

BEN: Scrub round it[5], will you?

[Pause]

GUS: There are a number of things I want to ask him. But I can never get round to it[6], when I see him.

[Pause]

I've been thinking about the last one.

BEN: What last one?

GUS: That girl.

[Ben grabs the paper, which he reads. Gus rises, looking down at Ben] How many times have you read that paper?

[Ben slams down the paper and rises]

BEN: [angrily] What do you mean?

GUS: I was just wondering how many times you'd —

BEN: What are you doing, criticizing me?

GUS: No, I was just —

BEN: You'll get a swipe[7] round your earhole if you don't watch your step.

GUS: Now look here, Ben —

BEN: I'm not looking anywhere! [He addresses the room] How many times have I — ! A bloody[8] liberty!

GUS: I didn't mean that.

BEN: You just get on with it, mate. Get on with it[9], that's all.

[Ben gets back on the bed]

GUS: I was just thinking about that girl, that's all.

[Gus sits on the bed]

She wasn't much to look at, I know, but still. It was a mess though, wasn't it? What a mess. Honest, I can't remember a mess like that one. They don't seem to hold together[10] like men, women. A looser texture[11], like. Didn't she spread[12], eh? She didn't half spread. Kaw! I've been meaning to ask you.

[Ben sits up and clenches his eyes]

Who clears up after we're gone? I'm curious about that. Who does the clearing up? Maybe they don't clear up. Maybe they just leave them there, eh? What do you think? How many jobs have we done? Blimey, I can't count them. What if they never clear anything up after we've gone.

BEN: [pityingly] You mutt. Do you think we're the only branch of this organization? Have a bit of common.[13] They got departments for everything.

GUS: What cleaners and all?

BEN: You birk[14]!

GUS: No, it was that girl made me start to think —

[There is a loud clatter and racket in the bulge[15] of wall between the beds, of something descending. They grab their revolvers, jump up and face the wall. The noise comes to a stop. Silence. They look at each other. Ben gestures sharply towards the wall. Gus approaches the wall slowly. He bangs it with his revolver. It is hollow. Ben moves to the head of the bed, his revolver cocked[16]. Gus puts his revolver on his bed and pats along the bottom of the center panel. He finds a rim. He lifts the panel. Disclosed is a serving-hatch, a "dumb waiter[17]". A wide box is held by pulleys. Gus peers into the box. He brings out a piece of paper.]

BEN: What is it?

GUS: You have a look at it.

BEN: Read it.

GUS: [reading] Two braised steak and chips. Two sago puddings. Two teas without sugar.

BEN: Let me see that. [He takes the paper]

GUS: [to himself] Two teas without sugar.

BEN: Mmmmm.

GUS: What do you think of that?

BEN: Well —

[The box goes up. Ben levels his revolver]

GUS: Give us a chance! They're in a hurry, aren't they?

[Ben re-reads the note. Gus looks over his shoulder]

That's a bit — that's a bit funny, isn't it?

BEN: No. It's not funny. It probably used to be a cafe here, that's all. Upstairs. These places change hands very quickly.

GUS: A cafe?

BEN: Yes.

GUS: What, you mean this was the kitchen, down here?

BEN: Yes, they change hands overnight, these places. Go into liquidation[18]. The people who run it, you know, they don't find it a going concern[19], they move out.

GUS: You mean the people who ran this place didn't find it a going concern and moved out?

BEN: Sure.

GUS: WELL, WHO'S GOT IT NOW?

[Silence]

BEN: What do you mean, who's got it now?

GUS: Who's got it now? If they moved out, who moved in?

BEN: Well, that all depends —

[The box descends with a clatter and bang. Ben levels his revolver. Gus goes to the door and brings out a piece of paper.]

GUS: [reading] Soup of the day[20]. Liver and onions. Jam tart.

[A pause. Gus looks at Ben. Ben takes the note and reads it. He walks slowly to the hatch. Gus follows. Ben looks into the hatch but not up it. Gus puts his hand on Ben's shoulder. Ben throws it off. Gus puts a finger to his mouth. He leans on the hatch and swiftly looks up it. Ben flings him away in alarm. Ben looks at the note. He throws his revolver on the bed and speaks with decision.]

BEN: We'd better send something up.

GUS: Eh?

BEN: We'd better send something up.

GUS: Oh! Yes. Yes. Maybe you're right.

Notes

1. come over: (of a feeling or manner) begin to affect (someone)
2. Blimey: a word used to express one's surprise, excitement, or alarm
3. be entitled to: give a legal right or a just claim to receive or do something
4. lay on: provide a service
5. Scrub round it: Avoid or disregard something
6. get round to it: deal successfully with (a problem)
7. swipe: hit or try to hit with a swinging blow
8. bloody: used to express anger, annoyance, or shock, or simply for emphasis
9. Get on with it: Nonsense
10. hold together: remain united, here means as strong as man.
11. looser texture: a body not so strong
12. Didn't she spread: Wasn't she shot apart?
13. Have a bit of common. : Have common sense.
14. birk: a word commonly used to refer to someone who is a bit silly or has done something stupid

15. bulge: a rounded projection, bend, or protruding part
16. cock: ready to be released by the trigger
17. dumb waiter: a small lift for carrying thing, especially food, between the floors of a building
18. liquidation: the process by which a company is brought to an end, and the assets and property of the company are redistributed
19. a going concern: a business that functions without the worry of liquidation
20. Soup of the day: Soup of the present time

Questions

1. According to their conversation, who do you think is the junior member of the team? And who is the senior one? Why?
2. How to interpret the messages delivered by the dumb waiter?
3. Some critic points out, "a Pinter drama is dark and claustrophobic. His language is full of menacing pauses." Can you find these features in the play?

Chapter Nine Cultural Diversity

Culture, with its long and dynamic history, is a term most difficult to be defined in a universally accepted way. In the 2001 *UNESCO Universal Declaration on Cultural Diversity,* culture is described as "the set of spiritual, material, intellectual and emotional features of society or a social group", consisting of "art and literature, lifestyles, ways of living together, value systems, traditions and beliefs". Among all the characteristics of culture, cultural diversity is the most self-evident one, stemming from the varied and varying physical and social environments that nurture cultures of various types in human history. Culture, on the whole, has always taken different forms all the way through time and space.

Literature, an integral part of culture, bears the characteristics of plurality and uniqueness, two attributes inherent in culture as a broader concept. As an aesthetic way for man to approach the outside world, literature is, in a sense, a reflection of the rich and varied world which man inhabits and of his unremitting exertions in the pursuit of material, intellectual, emotional and spiritual well-being and contentment. The same is true of English literature. Fostered under the influence of differing historical, political and cultural forces, miscellaneous English literary works give insight into cultural constituents such as laws, customs, institutions, ethics, and values of the specific stretches of time and places in which they were written or in which they are set in. On the other hand, English, the linguistic medium for literary creation, has in itself always been bursting with vitality and variety in the evolution of English literature. The individual endeavors on the part of all the great writers vary significantly from one to another, adding to the diversity of English literature. By engaging readers in fresh human experiences of others, English literature, along with other parts of world literature, can be conducive to helping readers out of the limitations imposed by the time and place they live in and fostering the awareness of unity and harmony, which is indispensable to the sustainable subsistence and prosperity of all human beings.

The three selected works in this chapter are merely glimpses into the essentially diverse world. All the three writers, with distinction in their background, experience and vision, and literary explorations, have approached various issues typical of the historical and sociological conditions in which they have been through and their literary worlds are constructed. Edward Morgan Forster, living in an age witnessing England on the wane, consistently imbues his works with liberal humanism. His novels include a strong measure of social comment, rooted in his keen observation of the British middle class he himself is from and inspired by his extensive travels abroad. In *A Passage to India,* he describes the social and political realities of India several decades before the end of British rule, with the British and the Indian fundamentally uncommunicative and incompatible, and suggests that goodwill and sincerity alone are far from being able to resolve the conflicts of the colonial society, the embodiment of the universe perplexed by conflicting forces. Doris May Lessing, an accomplished woman writer with a comprehensive worldview, focuses on a wide range of interest, including racism, feminism, communism, and mysticism, which on the whole elucidates part of the changes English women's literature has undergone. In *The Grass Is Singing,* she delineates how devastating the apartheid system can be, to both the oppressor and the oppressed, and aims at a profound transformation of the world and of human relationships. Kazuo Ishiguro, the Japanese-born English writer, rose to fame when both English nation and its literary world grew multiracial and multicultural. Despite his unique cultural identity, Ishiguro aspires to write international novels, those with a vision of life important to the people worldwide. "Malvern Hills", a story about how music brings a young British guitarist and a Swiss musician couple much closer, echoes part of Ishiguro's defining themes like unfulfilled dreams, choices, passing of time, exemplifying the writer's commitment to concerns of universal interest.

Chapter Nine　Cultural Diversity

Edward Morgan Forster
1879—1970

Edward Morgan Forster, an English novelist, short story writer and essayist, was born in London on January 1, 1879. When he was still an infant, his father, an architect, died and consequently he was brought up by his mother and female relatives from both sides of the family. The two distinct family traditions gave him a good insight into tensions between differing forces. Forster first attended a preparatory school at Eastbourne and later Tonbridge School. Yet it was during the years at King's College, Cambridge University that he tremendously broadened his horizons. There he met a group of unconventional and talented intellectuals, whom later became members of the Bloomsbury Group. The values of the Group, such as "friendship, a testing of moral values, an appreciation of innovation in the arts", were to profoundly influence his literary works. In his last year at Cambridge, Forster began contributing essays to the *Basileona*, the Cambridge undergraduate literary journal. In 1902 he became an instructor at the Working Men's College in London.

Edward Morgan Forster

Living through a historical period marked by England's shaken confidence, people's disillusionment with the state of society, the loss of morality, England's declining status as an empire, Forster included moral degeneracy, rigidity of the upper middle class, the vitality of the working class and foreigners, the consequences of repression, the quest for wholeness, and the renovating power of nature among his dominating subject matters in his creative works. He imbued his works with liberal humanism. Advocating the morality of "a developed heart", he associated "the development of the novel" with "the development of humanity". His four Edwardian classics, *Where Angels Fear to Tread* (1905), *The Longest Journey* (1907), *A Room with a View* (1908), *Howards End* (1910), are all characterized with both his love for and criticism of the English middle class he himself was from. They concern the class differences and examine mores and values of conventional middle class in the early twentieth century England, displaying Forster's contempt for conventionality, his passion for truth, his regard for the individual, his belief in personal relationships and his love for art.

In the nineteenth century numerous educated upper- class and middle- class Europeans visited foreign sites, putting themselves in touch with cultures different from their own. After graduating from Cambridge, Forster traveled in Italy, Austria, Greece, which exposed him to a more liberal and stimulating environment than that of the conventional British middle class. Enchanted and inspired, he wrote short stories "The Story of a Panic" (1903) and "The Road from Colonus" (1904), contrasting different attitudes of travelers facing alien civilizations. In novels *Where Angels Fear to Tread* and *A*

Room with a View, Forster dramatized, at greater length, the sharp conflict between the Italian and English cultures, and presented characters distinguishing themselves in their ways to react to an alternative milieu. Forster's later continual travels brought him closer to more cultures outside England, including Germany, India and Egypt, and offered him even more acute insights which make his works conducive to multicultural understanding. *Alexandria: A History and a Guide* (1922) and *Pharos and Pharillon* (1923), his two Egypt books, and *The Hill of Devi* (1953), a collection of letters recounting his experiences in India, evidence his actual and spiritual journeys to a better understanding of foreign lands, cultures and peoples, which in turn enabled Forster to see, in a different light, his own land, culture and people, and ultimately mankind as a whole. Meanwhile his belief in the significance of personal relationships was enhanced, especially those related with the boundaries of class, culture, race, and gender. In 1912 and 1921 Forster visited India twice, which nurtured *A Passage to India* (1924), a masterpiece confronting the East with the West and illustrating his endeavor to advocate understanding and harmony in human relationships and to search for a more lasting home for humankind.

A Passage to India

Forster dedicated *A Passage to India*, a culmination in his career as a man of letters, to his friendship with Syed Ross Masood who taught Forster much about Indian society. During his two extended stays in India, Forster witnessed the detrimental effects of colonialism on both Indian society and the governing Anglo-Indians. In the novel, he portrays the differences and the conflicts between the British and the Indians in colonial India in order to show his critical insight into the Anglo-Indian colonial society. The depiction of a fictional world unprepared for true and complete understanding and love in human relationships and the revelation of weaknesses of both the British and the Indian characters demonstrate Forster's contemplation about what underlie this drama in miniature of the universe perplexed by conflicting forces.

The novel is set in India under the British rule. A British lady Adela Quested, accompanied by her best friend the elderly Mrs. Moore, comes to the Indian city of Chandrapore to see Ronny Heaslop, Mrs. Moore's son who works as City Magistrate in Chandrapore. Adela is to decide whether or not to marry Ronny, whom she has known in Britain, and to then live an Anglo-Indian life. With a keen interest in real India, Adela is eager to see true Indians. However, at a bridge party arranged by Mr. Turton, the city Collector, Adela observes how arrogantly her countrymen, including Ronny, treat their Indian guests and feels upset about the gulf between her countrymen in India and those local Indians. Unexpectedly, Adela gets to know Mr. Fielding, who is the Principal of the Government College and is as fair-minded as her, and is invited to his house for tea. At Fielding's house, Adela, together with Mrs.

Moore, has a good time and is introduced to and favorably impressed by Aziz, a young Islamic doctor from India's Minto Hospital. The latter warm-heartedly arranges an excursion to Marabar Hills, a local place of interest, for the two decent British ladies. Nevertheless, the excursion unexpectedly ends up in a trial for Aziz. On the excursion day, Mrs. Moore doesn't feel well. After visiting one of Marabar caves, she asks Adela to visit some other caves. In the course, Adela asks Aziz some questions that make Aziz displeased. Within one Cave, Adela was so afflicted by the overwhelming echo that she falsely believes Aziz has assaulted her. Honest, sincere, fair-minded as she is, Adela, obsessed with the illusion in that Marabar Cave, leaves the Hills without any notice and reports alleged assault to the authorities. Aziz is arrested on the train back to Chandrapore. The Marabar Cave case aggravates the tension between the British and the Indians. Mrs. Moore is against Adela this time, declaring Aziz to be innocent. She is arranged to return to Britain by Ronny, who is afraid of her favorable testimony on behalf of Aziz at the trial. Mrs. Moore dies at sea on the way back. Despite Fielding's attempts at defending Aziz, a trial is due. However, during the cross-examination in the courtroom, Adela eventually recovers her composure and withdraws the charge. Aziz is set free yet bears grudge against Adela whereas the latter is abandoned by the majority of her countrymen, including Ronny who breaks off the engagement with Adela. At this time, Mr. Fielding extends a helping hand to Adela and the latter dispels the misgivings within Mr. Fielding after a long talk. Prudish but genuine, Adela writes a letter of apology to Aziz. In dismay, Adela goes back to Britain. When Fielding persuades Aziz not to sue Adela for damages, Aziz is affected by the rumor about Fielding and Adela. The hostility has lingered for a long time until Mr. Fielding reveals the fact responsible for the misunderstanding. The work ends in the scene of Fielding and Aziz riding horses together, somewhat reconciled; yet a perfect accord will remain elusive until India wins complete independence.

The selection below revolves around a bridge party arranged by the collector Mr. Turton for the two new-comers Mrs. Moore and Miss Quested in an effort to bridge the differences between the British and the Indians.

Chapter V

The Bridge Party[1] was not a success — at least it was not what Mrs Moore and Miss Quested were accustomed to consider a successful party. They arrived early, since it was given in their honour, but most of the Indian guests had arrived even earlier, and stood massed at the further side of the tennis lawns, doing nothing.

"It is only just five," said Mrs Turton. "My husband will be up from his office in a moment and start the thing. I have no idea what we have to do. It's the first time we've ever given a party like this at the Club. Mr Heaslop, when I'm dead and gone will you give parties like this? It's enough to make the old type of Burra Sahib[2] turn in his grave."

Ronny laughed deferentially. "You wanted something not picturesque and we've provided it," he remarked to Miss Quested. "What do you think of the Aryan Brother[3] in a topi[4] and spats[5]?"

Neither she nor his mother answered. They were gazing rather sadly over the tennis lawn. No, it was not picturesque; the East, abandoning its secular magnificence, was descending into a valley whose further side no man can see.

"The great point to remember is that no one who's here matters; those who matter don't come. Isn't that so, Mrs Turton?"

"Absolutely true," said the great lady, leaning back. She was "saving herself up," as she called it — not for anything that would happen that afternoon or even that week, but for some vague future occasion when a high official might come along and tax her social strength. Most of her public appearances were marked by this air of reserve.

Assured of her approbation[6], Ronny continued: "The educated Indians will be no good to us if there's a row, it's simply not worth while conciliating[7] them, that's why they don't matter. Most of the people you see are seditious at heart, and the rest'd run squealing. The cultivator — he's another story. The Pathan[8] — he's a man if you like. But these people — don't imagine they're India." He pointed to the dusky line beyond the court, and here and there it flashed a pince-nez[9] or shuffled a shoe, as if aware that he was despising it. European costume had lighted like a leprosy. Few had yielded entirely, but none were untouched. There was a silence when he had finished speaking, on both sides of the court; at least, more ladies joined the English group, but their words seemed to die as soon as uttered. Some kites hovered overhead, impartial, over the kites passed the mass of a vulture, and, with an impartiality exceeding all, the sky, not deeply coloured but translucent, poured light from its whole circumference. It seemed unlikely that the series stopped here. Beyond the sky must not there be something that overarches all the skies[10], more impartial even than they? Beyond which again. . . .

They spoke of *Cousin Kate*[11].

They had tried to reproduce their own attitude to life upon the stage, and to dress up as the middle-class English people they actually were. Next year they would do *Quality Street*[12] or *The Yeomen of the Guard*[13]. Save for[14] this annual incursion, they left literature alone. The men had no time for it, the women did nothing that they could not share with the men. Their ignorance of the arts was notable, and they lost no opportunity of proclaiming it to one another; it was the public-school attitude, flourishing more vigorously than it can yet hope to do in England. If Indians were shop, the arts were bad form, and Ronny had repressed his mother when she inquired after his viola; a viola was almost a demerit, and certainly not the sort of instrument one mentioned in public. She noticed now how tolerant and conventional his judgments had become; when they had seen *Cousin Kate* in London together in the past, he had scorned it; now he pretended that it was a good play, in order to hurt nobody's feelings. An "unkind notice" had appeared in the local paper, "the sort of thing no white man could have written," as Mrs Lesley said. The play was praised, to be sure, and so were the stage management and the performance as a whole, but the notice contained the following sentence: "Miss Derek, though she charmingly looked her part, lacked the necessary experience, and occasionally forgot her words." This tiny breath of genuine criticism had given deep offence, not indeed to Miss Derek[15], who was as hard as nails[16], but to her friends. Miss Derek did not belong to Chandrapore[17]. She was stopping for a fortnight with the McBrydes[18], the police people, and she had been so good as to fill up a gap in the cast at the last moment. A nice impression of local hospitality she would carry away with her.

"To work, Mary, to work," cried the Collector[19], touching his wife on the shoulder with a switch.

Mrs. Turton got up awkwardly. "What do you want me to do? Oh, those purdah[20] women! I never thought any would come. Oh dear!"

A little group of Indian ladies had been gathering in a third quarter of the grounds, near a rustic summer-house, in which the more timid of them had already taken refuge. The rest stood with their backs to the company and their faces pressed into a bank of shrubs. At a little distance stood their male relatives, watching the venture. The sight was significant: an island bared by the turning tide, and bound to grow.

"I consider they ought to come over to me."

"Come along, Mary, get it over."

"I refuse to shake hands with any of the men, unless it has to be the Nawab[21] Bahadur[22]."

"Whom have we so far?" He glanced along the line. "H'm! H'm! Much as one expected. We know why he's here, I think — over that contract — and he wants to get the right side of me for Mohurram[23], and he's the astrologer who wants to dodge the municipal building regulations, and he's that Parsee[24], and he's — hullo! There he goes — smash into our hollyhocks. Pulled the left rein when he meant the right. All as usual."

"They ought never to have been allowed to drive in; it's so bad for them," said Mrs Turton, who had at last begun her progress to the summer-house[25], accompanied by Mrs Moore, Miss Quested, and a terrier. "Why they come at all I don't know. They hate it as much as we do. Talk to Mrs McBryde. Her husband made her give purdah parties until she struck."

"This isn't a purdah party," corrected Miss Quested.

"Oh, really," was the haughty rejoinder.

"Do kindly tell us who these ladies are," asked Mrs. Moore.

"You're superior to them, anyway. Don't forget that. You're superior to everyone in India except one or two of the ranis[26], and they're on an equality."

Advancing, she shook hands with the group and said a few words of welcome in Urdu[27]. She had learnt the lingo[28], but only to speak to her servants, so she knew none of the politer forms, and of the verbs only the imperative mood. As soon as her speech was over, she inquired of her companions, "Is that what you wanted?"

"Please tell these ladies that I wish we could speak their language, but we have only just come to their country."

"Perhaps we speak yours a little," one of the ladies said.

"Why, fancy, she understands!" said Mrs Turton.

"Eastbourne[29], Piccadilly[30], High Park Corner," said another of the ladies.

"Oh yes, they're English-speaking."

"But now we can talk; how delightful!" cried Adela, her face lighting up.

"She knows Paris also," called one of the onlookers.

"They pass Paris on the way, no doubt," said Mrs Turton, as if she was describing the movements of migratory birds. Her manner had grown more distant since she had discovered that some of the group was westernized, and might apply her own standards to her.

"The shorter lady, she is my wife, she is Mrs Bhattacharya," the onlooker explained. "The taller lady, she is my sister, she is Mrs Das."

The shorter and the taller ladies both adjusted their saris, and smiled. There was a curious uncertainty about their gestures, as if they sought for a new formula which neither East nor West could provide. When Mrs Bhattacharya's husband spoke, she turned away from him, but she did not mind seeing the other men. Indeed all the ladies were uncertain, cowering, recovering, giggling, making tiny gestures of atonement or despair at all that was said, and alternately fondling the terrier or shrinking from him. Miss Quested now had her desired opportunity; friendly Indians were before her, and she tried to make them talk, but she failed, she strove in vain against the echoing walls of their civility. Whatever she said produced a murmur of deprecation, varying into a murmur of concern when she dropped her pocket-handkerchief. She tried doing nothing, to see what that produced, and they too did nothing. Mrs Moore was equally unsuccessful. Mrs Turton waited for them with a detached expression; she had known what nonsense it all was from the first.

When they took their leave, Mrs Moore had an impulse, and said to Mrs Bhattacharya, whose face she liked, "I wonder whether you would allow us to call on you some day."

"When?" she replied, inclining charmingly.

"Whenever is convenient."

"All days are convenient."

"Thursday ..."

"Most certainly."

"We shall enjoy it greatly, it would be a real pleasure. What about the time?"

"All hours."

"Tell us which you would prefer. We're quite strangers to your country; we don't know when you have visitors," said Miss Quested.

Mrs Bhattacharya seemed not to know either. Her gesture implied that she had known, since Thursdays began, that English ladies would come to see her on one of them, and so always stayed in. Everything pleased her, nothing surprised. She added, "We leave for Calcutta today."

"Oh, do you?" said Adela, not at first seeing the implication. Then she cried, "Oh, but if you do we shall find you gone."

Mrs Bhattacharya did not dispute it. But her husband called from the distance, "Yes, yes, you come to us Thursday."

"But you'll be in Calcutta."

"No, no, we shall not." He said something swiftly to his wife in Bengali[31]. "We expect you Thursday."

"Thursday ..." the woman echoed.

"You can't have done such a dreadful thing as to put off going for our sake?" exclaimed Mrs Moore.

"No, of course not, we are not such people." He was laughing.

"I believe that you have. Oh, please — it distresses me beyond words."

Everyone was laughing now, but with no suggestion that they had blundered. A shapeless discussion occurred, during which Mrs Turton retired, smiling to herself. The upshot was that they were to come Thursday, but early in the morning, so as to wreck the Bhattacharya plans as little as possible, and Mr Bhattacharya would send his carriage to fetch them, with servants to point out the way. Did he

Chapter Nine Cultural Diversity

know where they lived? Yes, of course he knew, he knew everything; and he laughed again. They left among a flutter of compliments and smiles, and three ladies, who had hitherto taken no part in the reception, suddenly shot out of the summer-house like exquisitely coloured swallows, and salaamed[32] them.

Meanwhile the Collector had been going his rounds[33]. He made pleasant remarks and a few jokes, which were applauded lustily, but he knew something to the discredit of nearly every one of his guests, and was consequently perfunctory. When they had not cheated, it was bhang[34], women, or worse, and even the desirables wanted to get something out of him. He believed that a Bridge Party did good rather than harm, or he would not have given one, but he was under no illusions, and at the proper moment he retired to the English side of the lawn. The impressions he left behind him were various. Many of the guests, especially the humbler and less Anglicized[35], were genuinely grateful. To be addressed by so high an official was a permanent asset. They did not mind how long they stood, or how little happened, and when seven o'clock struck they had to be turned out. Others were grateful with more intelligence. The Nawab Bahadur, indifferent for himself and for the distinction with which he was greeted, was moved by the mere kindness that must have prompted the invitation. He knew the difficulties. Hamidullah[36] also thought that the Collector had played up well. But others, such as Mahmoud Ali[37], were cynical; they were firmly convinced that Turton had been made to give the party by his official superiors and was all the time consumed with impotent rage, and they infected some who were inclined to a healthier view. Yet even Mahmoud Ali was glad he had come. Shrines are fascinating, especially when rarely opened, and it amused him to note the ritual of the English Club, and to caricature[38] it afterwards to his friends.

After Mr. Turton, the official who did his duty best was Mr Fielding, the Principal of the little Government College. He knew little of the District and less against the inhabitants, so he was in a less cynical state of mind. Athletic and cheerful, he romped[39] about, making numerous mistakes which the parents of his pupils tried to cover up, for he was popular among them. When the moment for refreshments came, he did not move back to the English side, but burned his mouth with gram[40]. He talked to anyone and he ate anything. Amid much that was alien, he learnt that the two new ladies from England had been a great success, and that their politeness in wishing to be Mrs Bhattacharya's guests had pleased not only her but all Indians who heard of it. It pleased Mr Fielding also. He scarcely knew the two new ladies, still he decided to tell them what pleasure they had given by their friendliness.

He found the younger of them alone. She was looking through a nick in the cactus hedge at the distant Marabar Hills[41], which had crept near, as was their custom at sunset; if the sunset had lasted long enough, they would have reached the town, but it was swift, being tropical. He gave her his information, and she was so much pleased and thanked him so heartily that he asked her and the other lady to tea.

"I'd like to come very much indeed, and so would Mrs Moore, I know."

"I'm rather a hermit, you know."

"Much the best thing to be in this place."

"Owing to my work and so on, I don't get up much to the Club."

"I know, I know, and we never get down from it. I envy you being with Indians."

"Do you care to meet one or two?"

"Very, very much indeed; it's what I long for. This party today makes me so angry and miserable. I think my countrymen out here must be mad. Fancy inviting guests and not treating them properly! You and Mr Turton and perhaps Mr McBryde are the only people who showed any common politeness. The rest make me perfectly ashamed, and it's got worse and worse."

It had. The Englishmen had intended to play up better, but had been prevented from doing so by their womenfolk, whom they had to attend, provide with tea, advise about dogs, etc. When tennis began, the barrier grew impenetrable. It had been hoped to have some sets between East and West, but this was forgotten, and the courts were monopolized by the usual Club couples. Fielding resented it too, but did not say so to the girl, for he found something theoretical in her outburst. Did she care about Indian music? he inquired; there was an old professor down at the College who sang.

"Oh, just what we wanted to hear. And do you know Doctor Aziz[42]?"

"I know all about him. I don't know him. Would you like him asked too?"

"Mrs Moore says he is so nice."

"Very well, Miss Quested. Will Thursday suit you?"

"Indeed it will, and that morning we go to this Indian lady's. All the nice things are coming Thursday."

"I won't ask the City Magistrate[43] to bring you. I know he'll be busy at that time."

"Yes, Ronny is always hard-worked," she replied, contemplating the hills. How lovely they suddenly were! But she couldn't touch them. In front, like a shutter, fell a vision of her married life. She and Ronny would look into the Club like this every evening, then drive home to dress; they would see the Lesleys and the Callendars and the Turtons and the Burtons, and invite them and be invited by them, while the true India slid by unnoticed. Colour would remain — the pageant of birds in the early morning, brown bodies, white turbans, idols whose flesh was scarlet or blue — and movement would remain as long as there were crowds in the bazaar and bathers in the tanks. Perched up on the seat of a dogcart, she would see them. But the force that lies behind colour and movement would escape her even more effectually than it did now. She would see India always as a frieze[44], never as a spirit, and she assumed that it was a spirit of which Mrs Moore had had a glimpse.

And sure enough they did drive away from the Club in a few minutes, and they did dress, and to dinner came Miss Derek and the McBrydes, and the menu was: Julienne soup full of bullety bottled peas, pseudo-cottage bread, fish full of branching bones, pretending to be plaice, more bottled peas with the cutlets, trifle, sardines on toast: the menu of Anglo-India[45]. A dish might be added or subtracted as one rose or fell in the official scale, the peas might rattle less or more, the sardines and the vermouth be imported by a different firm, but the tradition remained: the food of exiles[46], cooked by servants who did not understand it. Adela thought of the young men and women who had come out before her, P.-and-O.-ful[47] after P.-and-O.-ful, and had been set down to the same food and the same ideas, and been snubbed in the same good-humoured way until they kept to the accredited themes and began to snub others. "I should never get like that," she thought, for she was young herself; all the same, she knew that she had come up against something that was both insidious and tough, and against which she needed allies. She must gather around her at Chandrapore a few people who felt as she did, and she was glad to have met Mr Fielding and the Indian lady with the unpronounceable name. Here at all events was a nucleus[48]; she should know much better where she stood in the course of the next two days.

Miss Derek — she companioned a Maharani[49] in a remote Native State. She was genial and gay and made them all laugh about her leave, which she had taken because she felt she deserved it, not because the Maharani said she might go. Now she wanted to take the Maharajah's[50] motor-car as well; it had gone to a Chiefs' Conference at Delhi, and she had a great scheme for burgling it at the junction as it came back in the train. She was also very funny about the Bridge Party — indeed she regarded the entire peninsula as a comic opera. "If one couldn't see the laughable side of these people one'd be done for[51]," said Miss Derek. Mrs McBryde — it was she who had been the nurse — ceased not to exclaim, "Oh, Nancy, how topping! Oh, Nancy, how killing! I wish I could look at things like that." Mr McBryde did not speak much; he seemed nice.

When the guests had gone, and Adela gone to bed, there was another interview between mother and son. He wanted her advice and support — while resenting interference. "Does Adela talk to you much?" he began. "I'm so driven with work, I don't see her as much as I hoped, but I hope she finds things comfortable."

"Adela and I talk mostly about India. Dear, since you mention it, you're quite right — you ought to be more alone with her than you are."

"Yes, perhaps, but then people'd gossip."

"Well, they must gossip some time! Let them gossip."

"People are so odd out here, and it's not like home — one's always facing the footlights, as the Burra Sahib said. Take a silly little example: when Adela went out to the boundary of the Club compound, and Fielding followed her. I saw Mrs Callendar[52] notice it. They notice everything, until they're perfectly sure you're their sort."

"I don't think Adela'll ever be quite their sort — she's much too individual."

"I know, that's so remarkable about her," he said thoughtfully. Mrs Moore thought him rather absurd. Accustomed to the privacy of London, she could not realize that India, seemingly so mysterious, contains none, and that consequently the conventions have greater force. "I suppose nothing's on her mind," he continued.

"Ask her, ask her yourself, my dear boy."

"Probably she's heard tales of the heat, but of course I should pack her off to the hills every April — I'm not one to keep a wife grilling in the plains."

"Oh, it wouldn't be the weather."

"There's nothing in India but the weather, my dear mother; it's the alpha and omega[53] of the whole affair."

"Yes, as Mr McBryde was saying, but it's much more the Anglo-Indians themselves who are likely to get on Adela's nerves. She doesn't think they behave pleasantly to Indians, you see."

"What did I tell you?" he exclaimed, losing his gentle manner. "I knew it last week. Oh, how like a woman to worry over a side-issue!"

She forgot about Adela in her surprise. "A side-issue, a side-issue?" she repeated. "How can it be that?"

"We're not out here for the purpose of behaving pleasantly!"

"What do you mean?"

"What I say. We're out here to do justice and keep the peace. Them's my sentiments. India isn't a drawing-room."

"Your sentiments are those of a god," she said quietly, but it was his manner rather than his sentiments that annoyed her.

Trying to recover his temper, he said, "India likes gods."

"And Englishmen like posing as gods."

"There's no point in all this. Here we are, and we're going to stop, and the country's got to put up with us, gods or no gods. Oh, look here," he broke out, rather pathetically, "what do you and Adela want me to do? Go against my class, against all the people I respect and admire out here? Lose such power as I have for doing good in this country because my behaviour isn't pleasant? You neither of you understand what work is, or you'd never talk such eyewash[54]. I hate talking like this, but one must occasionally. It's morbidly sensitive to go on as Adela and you do. I noticed you both at the Club today — after the Collector had been at all that trouble to amuse you. I am out here to work, mind, to hold this wretched country by force. I'm not a missionary or a Labour Member or a vague sentimental sympathetic literary man. I'm just a servant of the Government; it's the profession you wanted me to choose myself, and that's that. We're not pleasant in India, and we don't intend to be pleasant. We've something more important to do."

He spoke sincerely. Every day he worked hard in the court trying to decide which of two untrue accounts was the less untrue, trying to dispense justice fearlessly, to protect the weak against the less weak, the incoherent against the plausible, surrounded by lies and flattery. That morning he had convicted a railway clerk of overcharging pilgrims for their tickets, and a Pathan of attempted rape. He expected no gratitude, no recognition for this, and both clerk and Pathan might appeal, bribe their witnesses more effectually in the interval, and get their sentences reversed. It was his duty. But he did expect sympathy from his own people, and except from newcomers he obtained it. He did think he ought not to be worried about Bridge Parties when the day's work was over and he wanted to play tennis with his equals or rest his legs upon a long chair.

He spoke sincerely, but she could have wished with less gusto[55]. How Ronny revelled in the drawbacks of his situation! How he did rub it in that he was not in India to behave pleasantly, and derived positive satisfaction there-from[56]! He reminded her of his public-school days. The traces of young-man humanitarianism had sloughed off[57], and he talked like an intelligent and embittered boy. His words without his voice might have impressed her, but when she heard the self-satisfied lilt of them, when she saw the mouth moving so complacently and competently beneath the little red nose, she felt, quite illogically, that this was not the last word on India. One touch of regret — not the canny substitute but the true regret from the heart — would have made him a different man, and the British Empire a different institution.

"I'm going to argue, and indeed dictate," she said, clinking her rings. "The English are out here to be pleasant."

"How do you make that out, mother?" he asked, speaking gently again, for he was ashamed of his irritability.

"Because India is part of the earth. And God has put us on the earth in order to be pleasant to each other. God ... is ... love." She hesitated, seeing how much he disliked the argument, but something made her go on. "God has put us on earth to love our neighbours and to show it, and He is omnipresent, even in India, to see how we are succeeding."

He looked gloomy, and a little anxious. He knew this religious strain in her, and that it was a symptom of bad health; there had been much of it when his stepfather died. He thought, "She is certainly ageing, and I ought not to be vexed with anything she says."

"The desire to behave pleasantly satisfies God ... The sincere if impotent desire wins His blessing. I think everyone fails, but there are so many kinds of failure. Goodwill and more goodwill and more goodwill. Though I speak with the tongues of ..."

He waited until she had done, and then said gently, "I quite see that. I suppose I ought to get off to my files now, and you'll be going to bed."

"I suppose so, I suppose so." They did not part for a few minutes, but the conversation had become unreal since Christianity had entered it. Ronny approved of religion as long as it endorsed the National Anthem, but he objected when it attempted to influence his life. Then he would say in respectful yet decided tones, "I don't think it does to talk about these things, every fellow has to work out his own religion," and any fellow who heard him muttered, "Hear!"

Mrs Moore felt that she had made a mistake in mentioning God, but she found Him increasingly difficult to avoid as she grew older, and He had been constantly in her thoughts since she entered India, though oddly enough He satisfied her less. She must needs[58] pronounce His name frequently, as the greatest she knew, yet she had never found it less efficacious. Outside the arch there seemed always an arch, beyond the remotest echo a silence. And she regretted afterwards that she had not kept to the real serious subject that had caused her to visit India — namely, the relationship between Ronny and Adela. Would they, or would they not, succeed in becoming engaged to be married?

Notes

1. Bridge Party: "a party to bridge the gulf between East and West" (Chapter III, page 49). This is a phrase invented by the Collector Mr. Turton one day at the Club, where Adela asked him whether it was possible to meet some Indians whom Mr. Turton came across socially. Mr. Turton came up with this idea and kept his word the next day, by sending invitations to quite a few Indian gentlemen for a party to be arranged in the garden of the Club on another day.
2. Burra Sahib: great master; a title used in India in the past to show respect for a European man with some status
3. Aryan Brother: an Indian person speaking an Indo-Iranian language, which is one part of Indo-European language family
4. topi: a hat to protect people from the sun
5. spat: a cloth covering for the instep and ankle, and which was worn by men over the shoe in the past
6. approbation: agreement or praise

7. conciliate: stop somebody from being angry or discontented; pacify
8. Pathan: a member of a people inhabiting Afghanistan and the western Pakistan
9. pince-nez: a pair of glasses, in the past, worn by clipping them on the nose
10. Beyond the sky must not there be something that overarches all the skies: Beyond the sky there must not be something that overarches all the skies
11. *Cousin Kate*: a comedy by Hubert Henry Davies (1876—1917)
12. *Quality Street*: a play created by James Matthew Barrie (1860—1937)
13. *The Yeomen of the Guard:* an opera collaborated by William Schwenck Gilbert (1836—1911) and Arthur Seymour Sullivan (1842—1900). Yeomen of the Guard are bodyguards of the British Monarch.
14. Save for: Except
15. Miss Derek: a companion of a Maharani in Mudkul State, which is a remote Indian state in the novel
16. as hard as nails: showing no fear
17. Chandrapore: the Indian city in the novel, where the story was set in
18. the McBrydes: the police officer Mr. McBryde and his family
19. the Collector: District Collector; a senior officer in one of the Districts into which India, under British rule, was divided
20. purdah: a system, in some Muslim societies, of keeping women out of the sight of men or strangers
21. Nawab: an Indian ruler at the provincial level
22. Bahadur: a title for an officer in British India
23. Mohurram: Muharram, the first month of the Islamic calendar
24. Parsee: a member of a religious group whose ancestors fled from Persia to India and whose religion is Zoroastrianism
25. summer-house: a small building in a garden for sitting in during fine weather
26. rani: a female Indian ruler or the wife of an Indian ruler
27. Urdu: a language widely used in India
28. lingo: a local dialect
29. Eastbourne: a town on the south coast of England
30. Piccadilly: a road in London, where fashionable shops, hotels and restaurants are located
31. Bengali: the language used by people in eastern India
32. salaam: make a gesture of greeting or respect, in some eastern countries, by bending the body deeply and putting the right hand on the forehead
33. round: a sequence of activities
34. bhang: the leaves and flower tops of the cannabis, used as a drug
35. Anglicized: be British in appearance, sound, character, etc.
36. Hamidullah: a lawyer in the novel; a friend of Doctor Aziz, one of the main characters in the novel
37. Mahmoud Ali: a lawyer in the novel; a friend of Doctor Aziz, one of the main characters in the novel
38. caricature: describe or present somebody or something as an object to be laughed at

39. romp: play about happily, energetically and noisily
40. gram: hard round seeds, like chickpeas, cooked and eaten as food
41. Marabar Hills: an indispensable part of the setting for the theme of the novel. Caves of Marabar Hills are twenty miles off the city of Chandrapore and make the city extraordinary, according to the leading sentence of the novel.
42. Doctor Aziz: one of the main characters in the novel, who later is to be involved in the case of so called Marabar Hills Harassment
43. City Magistrate: Heaslop Ronny serves as City Magistrate at Chandrapore.
44: frieze: a horizontal band of decoration with pictures, patterns, etc., near the ceiling of the building
45. Anglo-India: a British person born or living or having lived long in India
46. exile: a person who leaves his or her native country
47. P.-and-O.-ful: in great numbers. Here "P.-and-O." refers to Peninsular and Oriental Steam Navigation Company, which was the principal shipping line between England and India.
48. nucleus: the central part
49. Maharani: the wife of a Maharajah
50. Maharajah: a ruler of one of the states of India in the past
51. be done for: be destroyed or ruined
52. Mrs. Callendar: the wife of Mr. Callendar, the Civil Surgeon who was British and had lived in Indian for a long time
53. alpha and omega: the most important part
54. eyewash: nonsense
55. gusto: enjoyment or enthusiasm
56. there-from: from that
57. slough off: get rid of something unwanted
58. must needs: cannot avoid doing something. "needs" is an adverb, which means "necessarily".

Questions

1. What may account for the flop of the bridge party? Is it possible for people from different cultural backgrounds to be friends with each other?
2. What does Adela feel about Aziz, Fielding, Ronny and others at the party?
3. Marabar Hills appear in this part. What part do the Hills play at this stage of the novel? What role does it play to enhance the strangeness Adela feels at the party?

Doris May Lessing
1919—2013

Doris May Lessing

Doris May Lessing, an English novelist, short story writer, nonfiction writer, dramatist, was born as Doris May Taylor, one of the two children of her English parents, on October 22, 1919 in Kermanshah, Persia (now Iran). Years later the family moved to Rhodesia (now Zimbabwe), the setting of part of her works, and lived in poverty after her father Alfred Taylor failed in his struggles for farming. Doris studied first at the Dominican convent school and then a government school for girls until she had to leave school owing to eye problems and subsequently taught herself at home with the books ordered by her mother from London. An omnivorous reader, she had written two drafts for novels by the age of eighteen and was selling stories to magazines. She had supported herself by doing several secretarial jobs before she eventually settled down to writing. In the early 1940s she joined the Communist Party, from which she resigned afterwards. In 1949 Lessing moved to London and has lived there ever since.

Prolific in many genres and best known for her short stories and novels, Lessing, a woman writer with a comprehensive worldview, has touched on a wide range of issues like racism, women's issues, left-wing politics, psychology, and mysticism, generation gap, the meaning of home, aging throughout her productive literary career. Having grown up in southern Rhodesia, the former British colony, and confronted the tragedies of WWII, Lessing commits herself to social and political responsibilities and conveys what she has observed and contemplated in her creations. It is true that her important works are mostly about women, but her female characters are presented for varied imaginative journeys on behalf of humankind as a whole, seeking to save human civilization. *The Grass Is Singing* (1950), her debut in the literary world, and short stories such as those in *This Was the Old Chief's Country* (1952) deal with racial problems in African settings and evidence the overwhelming impact of social forces upon characters. The novel *The Golden Notebook* (1962), widely esteemed as Lessing's masterpiece and considered autobiographical, recounts the heroine Martha Quest's pursuit of individual identity and values and thus ultimately psychic wholeness. On the other hand, theories of the Freudian and Jungian psycho-analysis, Laingianism and Sufism have further enhanced Lessing's perceptions of mankind and vision of the world. *Landlocked* (1965), the fourth volume of the "Children of Violence" series(1952—1969), displays Lessing's special interest in Sufism, an inner and mystical dimension of Islam, which advocates mystical intuition replacing rational thought as a means of alleviating world problems and purifying one's self. In the 1970s, under the influence of Carl Jung and R. D. Laing, a famous radical psychologist, Lessing took to "inner space fiction", with the novel *Briefing for a Descent into Hell* (1971) representative of this category and centering on the psychic wholeness of the protagonist Charles Watkins, a Cambridge professor of classics.

For Lessing, being a writer is synonymous with being an "architect of soul". To fulfill her commitments as a serious and profound thinker of humankind, she has continually experimented with various writing techniques. She began her career as a realist, setting her fictional characters often in routine interactions with daily objects, employing detailed, realistic descriptions, symbolism and imagery, and consequently achieving tension and immediacy in her works. *The Golden Notebook*, with its complex and disjointed narration, marks a revolution in her literary creation. "Canopus in Argos: Archives" (1979—1982), a science-fiction series, is another instance of Lessing's effort at diversifying the means of demonstrating her critical thinking of the world today. In 2007, she was awarded the Nobel Prize of Literature.

The Grass Is Singing

One of the first books confronting the issue of apartheid, *The Grass Is Singing* was published in 1950 with great success in Britain, America and ten European countries. A white woman as a focal character, it offers a penetrating insight into the dehumanizing effect the historical and political circumstances have upon individuals. A successful colonial novel, the work does not deal with exclusively racism or patriarchy, with a broader view intended by Lessing.

The novel begins with one newspaper report of a case of murder, in which the protagonist Mary Turner, wife of a white farmer in southern Africa, is killed by the black servant Moses, which foreshadows the suffocating tone of a story unfolded in a flashback. Mary Turner, a white woman born and bred in southern Africa, isn't blessed with a happy childhood. Her parents, both South Africans, quarrel very often over monetary problems as a result of her father's habitual drinking, which exerts upon Mary an effect so negative that she despises men and dreads getting married for quite a long time. Her life changes for better when she goes to school, begins to work and finally leads a comfortable life of a single woman in town, working as capable personal secretary of her employer and earning good money. At the age of thirty, she suddenly feels desperate for marriage after overhearing two friends gossiping about her singleness. Soon she accidentally meets Dick, a poor white farmer who happens to be as eager to get married as she is. Their quick marriage frees Mary from the unpleasant social pressure of staying unmarried but throws her into the hard life similar to that imposed upon her mother for ages. Initially, she flings herself into adapting to the new life as a wife of a farmer, she running the house and Dick managing the farm. Nevertheless, the lack of comfort and variety and hope gradually wears her out and she feels the distance between Dick and herself. In dismay, she flees back to the town in an attempt at reverting to the life before marriage, yet in vain. Taken back to their home on the farm by Dick, she eventually succumbs to the stagnant life in the country. In the meantime, her deep-rooted fear and hatred of the black, which stems from the typical upbringing for all women in southern Africa, prompts Mary to willfully cling to her humiliating way of treating the black. Her excessive cruelty to both black servants and laborers earns her a bad name among the black. On the other hand, Dick, in spite of his love for his farm and persistent struggles for farming, fails to make the farm thrive. Their farm is dying due to Dick's inefficiency in farming. With all the hopes crushed, in isolation and despair, Mary secretly involves herself in a relationship with Moses, the black servant, which is to be seen as a shameful breach of color bar by all the white in the district including herself. When the secret was uncovered accidentally by another white man, Mary inflicts her twisted irritation upon Moses in defense of her lost dignity as a white. In his fury Moses kills her, and is arrested soon.

In the selection below, Dick falls ill and Mary has to go to the field to supervise the black laborers working on their farm. The devastating consequences of apartheid are obvious on both sides, the supervisor and the supervised. Then the succeeding part describes how Mary tries to persuade Dick into a new effort for farming.

Chapter VII (Excerpt)

For one thing, Dick had never been ill before, although this was a malaria district and he had lived in it so long. Perhaps he had had malaria in his blood for years and never known it? He always took quinine[1], every night, during the wet season, but not when it grew cold. Somewhere on the farm there must be, he said, a tree trunk filled with stagnant water, in a warm enough spot for mosquitoes to breed; or perhaps an old rusting tin in a shady place where the sun could not reach the water to evaporate it. In any event, weeks after one could expect fever in the usual way, Mary saw Dick come up from the lands one evening, pale and shivering. She offered him quinine and aspirin, which he took, and afterwards fell into bed, without eating his supper. The next morning, angry with himself and refusing to believe he was ill, he was off to work as usual, wearing a heavy leather jacket as a futile prophylactic[2] against violent shivering fits. At ten in the morning, with the fever sweat pouring down his face and neck and soaking his shirt, he crawled up the hill and got between blankets, half-unconscious already.

It was a very sharp attack, and because he was not used to illness, he was querulous[3] and difficult. Mary sent a letter over to Mrs Slatter — though she hated having to ask favours of her — and later that day Charlie brought the doctor in his car; he had driven thirty miles to fetch him. The doctor made the usual pronouncements, and when he had finished with Dick, told Mary the house was dangerous as it was, and should be wired for mosquitoes. Also, he said, the bush should be cut back for another hundred yards about the house. Ceilings should be put in at once, otherwise there was danger of their both getting sunstroke. He looked shrewdly at Mary, informed her she was anaemic[4], run down and in a bad nervous condition and she should go for at least three months to the coast at once. He then left, while Mary stood on the verandah and watched the car drive off, with a grim little smile on her face. She was thinking, with hate, that it was all very well for rich professionals to talk. She hated that doctor, with his calm way of shrugging off their difficulties; when she had said they could not afford a holiday, he had said sharply, 'Nonsense! Can you afford to be really ill?' And he had asked how long it had been since she had been to the coast? She had never seen the sea! But the doctor had understood their position better than she imagined, for the bill she awaited with dread, did not come. After a while she wrote to know how much they owed, and the answer came back: 'Pay me when you can afford it.' She was miserable with frustrated pride; but let it go — they literally did not have the money.

Mrs Slatter sent over a sack of citrus from her orchard for Dick, and many offers of assistance. Mary was grateful for her presence there, only five miles away, but decided not to call her save[5] in an emergency. She wrote one of those dry little notes of hers in thanks for the citrus, and said that Dick was better. But Dick was not at all better. There he lay, in all the helpless terror of a person suffering his first bad illness, with his face turned to the wall and a blanket over his head. 'Just like a nigger!' said Mary in sharp scorn over his cowardice; she had seen sick natives lie just like that, in a kind of stoical apathy[6]. But from time to time Dick roused himself to ask about the farm. Every conscious moment he worried about the things that would be going wrong without his supervision. Mary nursed him like a baby for a week, conscientiously, but with impatience because of his fear for himself. Then the fever left him, and he was weak and depressed, hardly able to sit up. He now tossed and kicked and fretted, talking all the time about his farmwork.

She saw that he wanted her to go down and see to things, but did not like to suggest it. For a while she did not respond to the appeal she saw in his weakened and querulous face; then, realizing he would get out of bed before he was fit to walk, she said she would go.

She had to crush down violent repugnance[7] to the idea of facing the farm natives herself. Even when she had called the dogs to her and stood on the verandah with the car keys in her hand, she turned back again to the kitchen for a glass of water; sitting in the car with her foot resting on the accelerator, she jumped out again, on an excuse that she needed a handkerchief. Coming out of the bedroom she noticed the long sjambok[8] that rested on two nails over the kitchen door, like an ornament: it was a long time since she had remembered its existence. Lifting it down, looping it over her wrist, she went to the car with more confidence. Because of it, she opened the back door of the car and let out the dogs; she hated the way they breathed down the back of her neck as she drove. She left them whining with disappointment outside the house, and drove herself down to the lands where the boys were supposed to be working. They knew of Dick's illness, and were not there, having dispersed, days before, to the compound[9]. She took the car along the rough and rutted road as near as she could get to the compound, and then walked towards it along the native path that was trodden hard and smooth but with a soft littering of glinting slippery grass over it, so that she had to move carefully to save herself from sliding. The long pale grass left sharp needles in her skirts, and the bushes shook red dust into her face.

The compound was built on a low rise above the vlei[10], about half a mile from the house. The system was that a new labourer presenting himself for work was given a day without pay to build a hut for himself and his family before taking his place with the workers. So there were always new huts, and always empty old ones that slowly collapsed and fell down unless somebody thought of burning them. The huts were closely clustered over an acre or two of ground. They looked like natural growths from the ground, rather than man-made dwellings. It was as though a giant black hand had reached down from the sky, picked up a handful of sticks and grass, and dropped them magically on the earth in the form of huts. They were grass-roofed, with pole walls plastered with mud, and single low doors, but no windows. The smoke from the fires inside percolated[11] through the thatch or drifted in clouds from the doorways, so that each had the appearance of smouldering slowly from within. Between the huts were irregular patches of ill-cultivated mealies, and pumpkin vines trailed everywhere through plants and bushes and up over the walls and roofs, with the big amber-coloured pumpkins scattered among the leaves. Some of them were beginning to rot, subsiding into a sour festering ooze of pinky stuff, covered with flies. Flies were everywhere. They hummed round Mary's head in a cloud as she walked, and they were clustered round the eyes of the dozen small black children who were pot-bellied and mostly naked, staring at her as she picked her way through the vines and mealies past the huts. Thin native mongrels[12], their bones ridging through their hides, bared their teeth and cringed. Native women, draped in dirty store-stuff, and some naked above the waist with their slack black breasts hanging down, gazed at her from doorways with astonishment at her queer appearance, commenting on her among themselves, laughing, and making crude remarks. There were some men: glancing through doorways she could see bodies huddled asleep; some sat on their haunches on the ground in groups, talking. But she had no idea which were Dick's labourers, which were merely visiting here, or perhaps passing through the place on their way somewhere else. She stopped before one of them and told him to fetch the headboy, who soon came stooping out of one of the better huts that were ornamented on the walls with patterns of daubed red and yellow clay. His eyes were inflamed: she could see he had been drinking.

She said in kitchen kaffir: 'Get the boys on to the lands in ten minutes.'

'The boss is better?' he asked with hostile indifference.

She ignored the question, and said, 'You can tell them that I will take two and six off the ticket of every one of them that isn't at work in ten minutes.' She held out her wrist and pointed to the watch, showing him the time interval.

The man slouched[13] and stooped in the sunshine, resenting her presence; the native women stared and laughed; the filthy, underfed children crowded around, whispering to each other; the starved dogs slunk in the background among the vines and mealies. She hated the place, which she had never entered before. 'Filthy savages!' she thought vindictively[14]. She looked straight into the reddened, beer-clouded eyes of the headman, and repeated, 'Ten minutes.' Then she turned and walked off down the winding path through the trees, listening for the sounds of the natives turning out of the huts behind her.

She sat in the car waiting, beside the land where she knew they were supposed to be reaping maize. After half an hour a few stragglers arrived, the headboy among them. At the end of an hour not more than half of the labourers were present: some had gone visiting to neighbouring compounds without permission, some lay drunk in their huts. She called the headboy to her, and took down the names of those who were absent, writing them in her big awkward hand on a scrap of paper, spelling the unfamiliar names with difficulty. She remained there the whole morning, watching the straggling[15] line of working boys, the sun glaring down through the old canvas hood on to her bare head. There was hardly any talking among them. They worked reluctantly, in a sullen silence; and she knew it was because they resented her, a woman, supervising them. When the gong rang for the lunch interval, she went up to the house and told Dick what had happened, but toning it down[16] so that he would not worry. After lunch she drove down again, and curiously enough without repugnance for this work from which she had shrunk so long. She was exhilarated[17] by the unfamiliar responsibility, the sensation of pitting her will against the farm. Now she left the car standing on the road, as the gang of natives moved in to the middle of the field where the pale gold maize stood high above their heads, and where she could not see them from outside. They were tearing off the heavy cobs, and putting them into the half-sacks tied round their waists, while others followed, cutting down the pillaged stalks and leaning them in small pyramids that regularly dotted the field. She moved steadily along the land with them, standing in the cleared part among the rough stubble, and watched them ceaselessly. She still carried the long thong of leather looped round one wrist. It gave her a feeling of authority, and braced her against the waves of hatred that she could feel coming from the gang of natives. As she walked steadily along beside them, with the hot yellow sunlight on her head and neck, making her shoulders ache, she began to understand how it was that Dick could stand it, day after day. It was difficult to sit still in the car with the heat filtering through the roof; it was another thing to move along with the workers, in the rhythm of their movement, concentrated on the work they were doing. As the long afternoon passed, she watched, in a kind of alert stupor, the naked brown backs bend, steady and straighten, the ropes of muscle sliding under the dusty skin. Most of them wore pieces of faded stuff as loincloths; some, khaki shorts; but nearly all were naked above the waist. They were a short thin crowd of men, stunted by bad feeding, but muscular and tough. She was oblivious to anything outside of this field, the work to be done, the gang of natives. She forgot about the heat, the beating sun, the glare. She watched the dark hands stripping cobs, and leaning the ragged gold stems together, and thought of nothing else. When one of the men paused for a moment in his work to rest, or to wipe the running sweat from his eyes, she waited one minute by her watch, and then called sharply to him to begin again. He would look slowly round at her, then bend back to the mealies, slowly, as if in protest. She did not know that Dick made a habit of calling a general rest of five minutes each hour; he had learned they worked better for it; it seemed to her an insolence directed against her authority over them when they stopped, without permission, to straighten their backs and wipe off the sweat. She kept them at it until sundown, and went back to the house satisfied with herself, not even tired. She was exhilarated and light-limbed, and swung the sjambok jauntily[18] on her wrist.

 Dick was lying in bed in the low-roofed room that was as chilly in the cool months as soon as the sun went down as it was hot in summer, anxious and restless, resenting his helplessness. He did not like to think of Mary close to those natives all day; it was not a woman's job. And besides, she was so bad with natives, and he was short of labour. But he was relieved and rested when she told him how the work was progressing. She said nothing of how she disliked the natives, of how the hostility that she could feel as something palpable[19] coming from them against her, affected her; she knew he could be in bed for days yet, and that she would have to do it whether she liked it or not. And, really, she liked it. The sensation of being boss over perhaps eighty black workers gave her new confidence; it was a good feeling, keeping them under her will, making them do as she wanted.

 At the week's end it was she who sat behind the small table set out on the verandah among the pot plants while the gangs of boys stood outside, under dark overshadowing trees waiting to be paid. This was the monthly ritual.

 It was already dusk, the first stars coming out in the sky; and on the table was set a hurricane lamp, whose low dull flame looked a doleful bird caught in a glass cage. The bossboy beside her called out the names as she turned them up on her list. As she came to those who had not obeyed her summons that first day, she deducted half a crown, handing over the balance in silver; the average wage was about fifteen shillings, for the month. There were sullen[20] murmurings amongst the natives; and as there was a small storm of protest brewing, the bossboy moved to the low wall and began arguing with them in his own language. She could only understand an odd word here or there, but she disliked the man's attitude and tone; he seemed, from his manner, to be telling them to accept an unalterable evil fate, not scolding them, as she would have liked to do, for their negligence and laziness. After all, for several days they had done no work at all. And if she did what she had threatened, the whole lot of them would be docked[21] two and sixpence, because none had obeyed her and appeared on the lands within the specified ten minutes. They were in the wrong; she was in the right; and the bossboy should be telling them so, not persuasively arguing with them and shrugging his shoulders — and even, once, laughing. At last he turned back to her, told her they were dissatisfied and demanded what was due. She said shortly and finally that she had said she would deduct that amount and she intended to keep her word. She would not change her mind. Suddenly angry, she added, without reflecting, that those who did not like it could leave. She went on with the business of arranging the little piles of notes and silver, taking no notice of the storm of talk outside. Some of them walked off to the compound, accepting the position. Others waited in groups till she had finished the paying, and then came up to the wall. One after another spoke to the bossboy, saying they wanted to leave. She felt a little afraid, because she knew how hard it was to get labour, and how this was Dick's most persistent worry. Nevertheless, even while she turned her head to listen for Dick's movements in the bed that was behind her through one thickness of wall, she was filled with determination and resentment, because they expected to be paid for work they had not done, and had gone visiting when Dick was ill; above all, that they had not come to the lands in that interval of ten minutes. She turned to the waiting group and told them that those of them who were contracted natives could not leave.

These had been recruited by what is the South African equivalent of the old press gang: white men who lie in wait for the migrating bands of natives on their way along the roads to look for work, gather them into large lorries, often against their will (sometimes chasing them through the bush for miles if they try to escape), lure them by fine promises of good employment and finally sell them to the white farmers at five pounds or more per head for a year's contract.

Of these boys she knew that some would be found to have run away from the farm during the next few days; and some would not be recovered by the police, for they would escape through the hills to the border and so out of reach. But she was not going to be swayed now by fear of their going and Dick's labour troubles; she would die rather than show weakness. She dismissed them, using the police as a threat. The others, who were working on a monthly basis, and whom Dick kept with him by a combination of coaxing and good-humoured threats, she said could leave at the month's end. She spoke to them directly — not through the medium of the bossboy — in cold clear tones, explaining with admirable logic how they were in the wrong, and how she was justified in acting as she did. She ended with a short homily[22] on the dignity of work, which is a doctrine bred into the bones of every white South African. They would never be any good, she said (speaking in kitchen kaffir which some of them did not understand, being fresh from their kraals[23]) until they learned to work without supervision, for the love of it, to do as they were told, to do a job for its own sake, not thinking about the money they would be paid for it. It was this attitude towards work that had made the white man what he was: the white man worked because it was good to work, because working without reward was what proved a man's worth.

The phrases of this little lecture came naturally to her lips: she did not have to look for them in her mind. She had heard them so often from her father, when he was lecturing his native servants, that they welled up from the part of her brain that held her earliest memories.

The natives listened to her with what she described to herself as 'cheeky'[24] faces. They were sullen and angry, listening to her (or what they could understand of her speech) with inattention, simply waiting for her to finish.

Then, brushing away their protests, which broke out as soon as her voice stopped, she got up with an abrupt dismissing gesture, lifted the little table with the paper bags of money stacked on it, and carried it reside. After a while she heard them moving off, talking and grumbling among themselves, and looking through the curtains saw their dark bodies mingling with the shadows of the trees before they disappeared. Their voices floated back: angry shouts now and imprecations[25] against her. She was filled with vindictiveness and a feeling of victory. She hated them all, every one of them, from the headboy whose subservience[26] irritated her, to the smallest child; there were some children working among the others who could be no more than seven or eight years old.

She had learned, standing in the sun watching them all day, to hide her hatred when she spoke to them, but she did not attempt to hide it from herself. She hated it when they spoke to each other in dialects she did not understand, and she knew they were discussing her and making what were probably obscene remarks against her — she knew it, though she could only ignore it. She hated their half-naked, thick-muscled black bodies stooping in the mindless rhythm of their work. She hated their sullenness, their averted eyes when they spoke to her, their veiled insolence; and she hated more than anything, with a violent physical repulsion, the heavy smell that came from them, a hot, sour animal smell.

'How they stink,' she said to Dick, in an explosion of anger that was the reaction from setting her will against theirs.

Dick laughed a little. He said, 'They say we stink.'

'Nonsense!' she exclaimed, shocked that these animals should so presume.

'Oh yes,' he said, not noticing her anger, 'I remember talking to old Samson once. He said: "You say we smell. But to us there is nothing worse than a white man's smell."'

'Cheek!' she began indignantly; but then she saw his still pale and hollowed face, and restrained herself. She had to be very careful, because he was liable to be touchy and irritable in his present stage of weakness.

'What were you talking to them about?' he asked.

'Oh, nothing much,' she said warily, turning away. She had decided not to tell him about the boys that were leaving until later, when he was really well.

'I hope you are being careful with them,' he said anxiously. 'You have to go slow with them these days, you know. They are all spoilt.'

'I don't believe in treating them soft,' she said scornfully. 'If I had my way, I'd keep them in order with the whip.'

'That's all very well,' he said irritably, 'but where would you get the labour?'

'Oh, they all make me sick,' she said, shuddering.

During this time, in spite of the hard work and her hatred of the natives, all her apathy and discontent had been pushed into the background. She was too absorbed in the business of controlling the natives without showing weakness, of running the house and arranging things so that Dick would be comfortable when she was out. She was finding out, too, about every detail of the farm: how it was run and what was grown. She spent several evenings over Dick's books when he was asleep. In the past she had taken no interest in this: it was Dick's affair. But now she was analysing figures — which wasn't difficult with only a couple of cash books — seeing the farm whole in her mind. She was shocked by what she found. For a little while she thought she must be mistaken; there must be more to it than this. But there was not. She surveyed what crops were grown, what animals there were, and analysed without difficulty the causes of their poverty. The illness, Dick's enforced seclusion and her enforced activity, had brought the farm near to her and made it real. Before it had been an alien and rather distasteful affair from which she voluntarily excluded herself, and which she made no attempt to understand as a whole, thinking it more complicated than it was. She was now annoyed with herself that she had not tried to appreciate these problems before.

Now, as she followed the gang of natives up the field, she thought continually about the farm, and what should be done. Her attitude towards Dick, always contemptuous, was now bitter and angry. It was not a question of bad luck, it was simply incompetence. She had been wrong in thinking that those outbursts of wishful thinking over turkeys, pigs, etc., had been a kind of escape from the discipline of his work on the farm. He was all of a piece, everything he did showed the same traits. Everywhere she found things begun and left unfinished. Here it was a piece of land that had been half-stumped and then abandoned so that the young trees were growing up over it again; there it was a cowshed made half of brick and iron and half of bush timber and mud. The farm was a mosaic of different crops. A single fifty-acre land had held sunflowers, sun-hemp, maize, monkeynuts and beans. Always he reaped twenty sacks of this and thirty sacks of that with a few pounds profit to show on each crop. There was not a single thing properly done on the whole place, nothing! Why was he incapable of seeing it? Surely he must see that he would never get any further like this?

Sun-dazed, her eyes aching with the glare, but awake to every movement of the boys, she contrived, schemed and planned, deciding to talk to Dick when he was really well, to persuade him to face clearly where he would end if he did not change his methods. It was only a couple of days before he would be well enough to take over the work: she would allow him a week to get back to normal, and then give him no peace till he followed her advice.

But on that last day something happened that she had not foreseen.

Down in the vlei, near the cowsheds, was where Dick stacked his mealiecobs each year. First sheets of tin were laid down, to protect them from white ants; then the sacks of cobs were emptied on to it, and there slowly formed a low pile of white, slippery-sheathed mealies[27]. This was where she remained these days, to supervise the proper emptying of the sacks. The natives unloaded the dusty sacks from the waggon, holding them by the corners on their shoulders, bent double under the weight. They were like a human conveyor-belt. Two natives standing on the waggon swung the heavy sack on to the waiting bent back. The men moved steadily forward in a file, from the waggon's side to the mealie-dump, staggering up its side on the staircase of wedged full sacks, to empty the cobs[28] in white flying shower down the stack. The air was gritty[29] and prickly with the tiny fragments of husk. When Mary passed her hand over her face, she could feel it rough, like fine sacking.

She stood at the foot of the heap, which rose before her in a great shining white mountain against the vivid sky, her back to the patient oxen which were standing motionless with their heads lowered, waiting till the waggon should be emptied and they free to move off on another trip. She watched the natives, thinking about the farm, and swinging the sjambok from her wrist so that it made snaky patterns in the red dust. Suddenly she noticed that one of the boys was not working. He had fallen out of line, and was standing by, breathing heavily, his face shining with sweat. She glanced down at her watch. One minute passed, then two. But still he stood, his arms folded, motionless. She waited till the hand of the watch had passed the third minute, in growing indignation that he should have the temerity to remain idle when he should know by now her rule that no one should exceed the allowed one-minute pause. Then she said, 'Get back to work.' He looked at her with the expression common to African labourers: a blank look, as if he hardly saw her, as if there was an obsequious[30] surface with which he faced her and her kind, covering an invulnerable and secret hinterland. In a leisurely way he unfolded his arms and turned away. He was going to fetch himself some water from the petrol tin that stood under a bush for coolness, nearby. She said again, sharply, her voice rising: 'I said, get back to work.'

At this he stopped still, looked at her squarely and said in his own dialect which she did not understand, 'I want to drink.'

'Don't talk that gibberish[31] to me,' she snapped. She looked around for the bossboy who was not in sight.

The man said, in a halting ludicrous[32] manner, 'I ... want ... water.' He spoke in English, and suddenly smiled and opened his mouth and pointed his finger down his throat. She could hear the other natives laughing a little from where they stood on the mealie-dump. Their laughter, which was good-humoured, drove her suddenly mad with anger: she thought it was aimed at her, whereas these men were only taking the opportunity to laugh at something, anything at all, in the middle of their work; one of themselves speaking bad English and sticking his finger down his throat was as good a thing to laugh at as any other.

But most white people think it is 'cheek' if a native speaks English. She said, breathless with anger, 'Don't speak English to me,' and then stopped. This man was shrugging and smiling and turning his eyes up to heaven as if protesting that she had forbidden him to speak his own language, and then hers — so what was he to speak? That lazy insolence stung her into an inarticulate rage. She opened her mouth to storm at him, but remained speechless. And she saw in his eyes that sullen resentment, and — what put the finishing touch to it — amused contempt. Involuntarily she lifted her whip and brought it down across his face in a vicious swinging blow. She did not know what she was doing. She stood quite still, trembling; and when she saw him put his hand, dazedly to his face, she looked down at the whip she held in stupefaction[33], as if the whip had swung out of its own accord, without her willing it. A thick weal pushed up along the dark skin of the cheek as she looked, and from it a drop of bright blood gathered and trickled down and off his chin, and splashed to his chest. He was a great hulk of a man, taller than any of the others, magnificently built, with nothing on but an old sack trod round his waist. As she stood there, frightened, he seemed to tower over her. On his big chest another red drop fell and trickled down to his waist. Then she saw him make a sudden movement, and recoiled[34], terrified; she thought he was going to attack her. But he only wiped the blood off his face with a big hand that shook a little. She knew that all the natives were standing behind her stock-still, watching the scene. In a voice that sounded harsh from breathlessness, she said, 'Now get back to work.' For a moment the man looked at her with an expression that turned her stomach liquid with fear. Then, slowly, he turned away, picked up a sack and rejoined the conveyor-belt of natives. They all began work again quite silently. She was trembling with fright, at her own action, and because of the look she had seen in the man's eyes.

She thought: he will complain to the police that I struck him? This did not frighten her, it made her angry. The biggest grievance[35] of the white farmer is that he is not allowed to strike his natives, and that if he does, they may — but seldom do — complain to the police. It made her furious to think that this black animal had the right to complain against her, against the behaviour of a white woman. But it is significant that she was not afraid for herself. If this native had gone to the police station, she might have been cautioned, since it was her first offence, by a policeman who was a European, and who came on frequent tours of the district, when he made friends with the farmers, eating with them, staying the night with them, joining their social life. But he, being a contracted native, would have been sent back to this farm; and Dick was hardly likely to make life easy for a native who had complained of his wife. She had behind her the police, the courts, the jails; he, nothing but patience. Yet she was maddened by the thought he had even the right to appeal; her greatest anger was directed against the sentimentalists and theoreticians, whom she thought of as 'They' — the law-makers and the Civil Service — who interfered with the natural right of a white farmer to treat his labour as he pleased.

But mingled with her anger was that sensation of victory, a satisfaction that she had won in this battle of wills. She watched him stagger up the sacks, his great shoulders bowed under his load, taking a bitter pleasure in seeing him subdued thus. And nevertheless her knees were still weak: she could have sworn that he nearly attacked her in that awful moment after she struck him. But she stood there unmoving, locking her conflicting feelings tight in her chest, keeping her face composed and severe; and that afternoon she returned again, determined not to shrink at the last moment, though she dreaded the long hours of facing the silent hostility and dislike.

When night came at last, and the air declined swiftly into the sharp cold of a July night, and the natives moved off, picking up old tins they had brought to drink from, or a ragged coat, or the corpse of some rat or veld creature they had caught while working and would cook for their evening meal, and she knew her task was finished, because tomorrow Dick would be here, she felt as if she had won a battle. It was a victory over these natives, over herself and her repugnance of them, over Dick and his slow, foolish shiftlessness. She had got far more work out of these savages than he ever had. Why, he did not even know how to handle natives!

But that night, facing again the empty days that would follow, she felt tired and used-up. And the argument with Dick, that she had been planning for days, and that had seemed such a simple thing when she was down on the lands, away from him, considering the farm and what should be done with it without him, leaving him out of account, seemed now a weary heartbreaking task. For he was preparing to take up the reins again as if her sovereignty had been nothing, nothing at all. He was absorbed and preoccupied again, that evening, and not discussing his problems with her. And she felt aggrieved and insulted; for she did not care to remember that for years she had refused all his pleas for her help and that he was acting as she had trained him to act. She saw, that evening, as the old fatigue came over her and weighted her limbs, that Dick's well-meaning blunderings would be the tool with which she would have to work. She would have to sit like a queen bee in this house and force him to do what she wanted.

The next few days she bided her time[36], watching his face for the returning colour and the deepening sunburn that had been washed out by the sweats of fever. When he seemed fully himself again, strong, and no longer petulant[37] and irritable, she broached[38] the subject of the farm.

They sat one evening under the dull lamplight, and she sketched for him, in her quick emphatic way, exactly how the farm was running, and what money he could expect in return, even if there were no failures and bad seasons. She demonstrated to him, unanswerably, that they could never expect to get out of the slough[39] they were in, if they continued as they were: a hundred pounds more, fifty pounds less, according to the variations of weather and the prices, would be all the difference they could anticipate.

As she spoke her voice became harsh, insistent, angry. Since he did not speak, but only listened uneasily, she got out his books and supported her contentions with figures. From time to time he nodded, watching her finger moving up and down the long columns, pausing as she emphasized a point, or did rapid calculations. As she went on he said to himself that he ought not to be surprised, for he knew her capacity; had it not been for this reason that he had asked for her help?

For instance, she ran chickens on quite a big scale now, and made a few pounds every month from eggs and table birds; but all the work in connection with this seemed to be finished in a couple of hours. That regular monthly income had made all the difference to them. Nearly all day, he knew, she had nothing to do: yet other women who ran poultry on such a scale found it heavy work. Now she was analysing the farm, and the organization of crops, in a way that made him feel humble, but also provoked him to defend himself. For the moment, however, he remained silent, feeling admiration, resentment and self-pity; the admiration temporarily gaining upper hand. She was making mistakes over details, but on the whole she was quite right: every cruel thing she said was true! While she talked, pushing the roughened hair out of her eyes with her habitual impatient gesture, he felt hurt too; he recognized the justice of her remarks, he was prevented from defensiveness because of the impartiality of her voice; but at the same time the impartiality stung him and wounded him. She was looking at the farm from outside, as a machine for making money: that was how she regarded it. She was critical entirely from this angle. But she left so much out of account. She gave him no credit for the way he looked after his soil, for that hundred acres of trees. And he could not look at the farm as she did. He loved it and was part of it. He liked the slow movement of the seasons, and the complicated rhythm of the 'little crops' that she kept describing with contempt as useless.

When she had finished, his conflicting emotions kept him silent, searching for words. And at last he said, with that little defeated smile of his: 'Well, and what shall we do?' She saw that smile and hardened her heart: it was for the good of them both; and she had won! He had accepted her criticisms. She began explaining, in detail, exactly what it was they should do. She proposed they grew tobacco: people all about them were growing it and making money. Why shouldn't they? And in everything she said, every inflection of her voice, was one implication: that they should grow tobacco, make enough money to pay their debts, and leave the farm as soon as they could.

His realization, at last, of what she was planning, stunned his responses. He said bleakly: 'And when we have made all that money, what shall we do?'

For the first time she looked unconfident, glanced down at the table, could not meet his eyes. She had not really thought of it. She only knew that she wanted him to be a success and make money, so that they would have the power to do what they wanted, to leave the farm, to live a civilized life again. The stinting poverty in which they lived was unbearable; it was destroying them. It did not mean there was not enough to eat: it meant that every penny must be watched, new clothes forgone, amusements abandoned, holidays kept in the never-never-land of the future. A poverty that allows a tiny margin for spending, but which is shadowed always by a weight of debt that nags like a conscience is worse than starvation itself. That was how she had come to feel. And it was bitter because it was a self-imposed poverty. Other people would not have understood Dick's proud self sufficiency. There were plenty of farmers in the district, in fact all over the country, who were as poor as they, but who lived as they pleased, piling up debts, hoping for some windfall in the future to rescue them. (And, in parentheses, it must be admitted that their cheerful shiftlessness[40] was proved to be right: when the war came and the boom in tobacco, they made fortunes from one year to the next — which occurrence made the Dick Turners appear even more ridiculous than ever.) And if the Turners had decided to abandon their pride, to take an expensive holiday and to buy a new car, their creditors, used to these farmers, would have agreed. But Dick would not do this. Although Mary hated him for it, considering he was a fool, it was the only thing in him she still respected: he might be a failure and a weakling[41], but over this, the last citadel[42] of his pride, he was immovable.

Which was why she did not plead with him to relax his conscience and do as other people did. Even then fortunes were being made out of tobacco. It seemed so easy. Even now, looking across the table at Dick's weary, unhappy face, it seemed so easy. All he had to do was to make up his mind to it. And then? That was what he was asking — what was their future to be?

When she thought of that hazy, beautiful time in the future, when they could live as they pleased, she always imagined herself back in town, as she had been, with the friends she had known then, living in the Club for young women. Dick did not fit into the picture. So when he repeated his question, after her long evasive silence, during which she refused to look into his eyes, she was silenced by their inexorably different needs. She shook the hair again from her eyes, as if brushing away something she did not want to think about, and said, begging the question, 'Well, we can't go on like this, can we?'

And now there was another silence. She tapped on the table with the pencil, twirling it around between finger and thumb, making a regular irritating noise that caused him to tauten his muscles against it.

So now it was up to him. She had handed the whole thing over to him again and left him to do as he could — but she would not say towards what goal she wanted him to work. And he began to feel bitter and angry against her. Of course they could not go on like this: had he ever said they should? Was he not working like a nigger to free them? But then, he had got out of the habit of living in the future; this aspect of her worried him. He had trained himself to think ahead to the next season. The next season was always the boundary of his planning. Yet she had soared beyond all that and was thinking of other people, a different life — and without him: he knew it, though she did not say so. And it made him feel panicky, because it was so long now since he had been with other people that he did not need them. He enjoyed an occasional grumble with Charlie Slatter, but if he was denied that outlet, then it did not matter. And it was only when he was with other people that he felt useless, and a failure. He had lived for so many years with the working natives, planning a year ahead, that his horizons had narrowed to fit his life, and he could not imagine anything else. He certainly could not think of himself anywhere but on this farm: he knew every tree on it. This is no figure of speech: he knew the veld he lived from as the natives know it. His was not the sentimental love of the townsman. His senses had been sharpened to the noise of the wind, the song of the birds, the feel of the soil, changes in weather — but they had been dulled to everything else. Off this farm he would wither and die. He wanted to make good so that they continue living on the farm, but in comfort, and so that Mary could have the things she craved. Above all, so that they could have children. Children, for him, were an insistent need. Even now, he had not given up hope that one day... And he had never understood that she visualized a future off the farm, and with his concurrence! It made him feel lost and blank, without support for his life. He looked at her almost with horror, as an alien creature who had no right to be with him, dictating what he should do.

But he could not afford to think of her like that: he had realized, when she ran away, what her presence in his house meant to him. No; she must learn to understand his need for the farm, and when he had made good, they would have children. She must learn that his feeling of defeat was not really caused by his failure as a farmer at all: his failure was her hostility towards him as a man, their being together as they were. And when they could have children even this would be healed, and they would be happy. So he dreamed, his head on his hands, listening to that tap-tap-tap of the pencil.

But in spite of this comfortable conclusion to his meditation, his sense of defeat was overwhelming. He hated the thought of tobacco; he always had, it seemed to him an inhuman crop. His farm would have to be run in a different way; it would mean standing for hours inside buildings in steamy temperatures; it would mean getting up at nights to watch thermometers.

So he fiddled with his papers on the table, pressed his head into his hands, and rebelled miserably against his fate. But it was no good, with Mary sitting opposite him forcing him to do as she willed. At last he looked up, smiled a twisted unhappy smile, and said, 'Well, boss, can I think it over for a few days?' But his voice was strained with humiliation. And when she said irritably, 'I do wish you wouldn't call me boss!' he did not answer, though the silence between them said eloquently what they were afraid to say. She broke it at last by rising briskly from the table, sweeping away the books, and saying, 'I am going to bed.' And left him there, sitting with his thoughts.

Three days later he said quietly, his eyes averted, that he was arranging with native builders to put up two barns.

When he looked at her at last, forcing himself to face her uncontrollable triumph, he saw her eyes bright with new hope, and thought with disquiet what it would mean to her if he failed this time.

Notes

1. quinine: a drug used to treat malaria
2. prophylactic: a medicine or course of action intended to prevent a disease
3. querulous: complaining
4. anaemic: suffering from anaemia, a condition in which there are too few red blood cells in one's blood
5. save: except
6. stoical apathy: the feeling of not being interested but being patient when suffering
7. repugnance: strong dislike
8. sjambok: a long stiff whip usually made of rhinoceros hide in South Africa
9. compound: an enclosed area where a group of buildings stand
10. vlei: a shallow natural pool of water in South Africa
11. percolate: pass gradually through a surface that has small holes in it
12. mongrel: a dog whose parents are of different breeds
13. slouch: sit, stand or walk in a lazy way
14. vindictively: having or showing a strong desire to harm those who, you think, have harmed you
15. straggling: spreading loosely and untidily
16. tone... down: make something less extreme or intense; moderate
17. exhilarated: made somebody feel very excited
18. jauntily: cheerfully and confidently
19. palpable: obvious
20. sullen: showing bad temper without speaking
21. dock: take away (something, especially a sum of money)
22. homily: a tedious talk about how to behave
23. kraal: a traditional African village surrounded by a fence
24. cheeky: rude; disrespectful
25. imprecation: a curse
26. subservience: excessive willingness to obey someone else's wishes
27. mealie: maize
28. cob: or corncob, the long hard part in the center of an ear of corn
29. gritty: containing very small pieces of stone or sand
30. obsequious: too eager to please somebody to gain favor
31. gibberish: words that are meaningless or difficult to understand
32. ludicrous: ridiculous
33. stupefaction: the state of being greatly shocked, unable to think clearly
34. recoil: move back suddenly in fear or disgust
35. grievance: a complaint, especially in the case of unfair treatment

36. bid her time: wait for a good opportunity to do something
37. petulant: childishly bad-tempered and unreasonable
38. broach: begin to talk about a sensitive or difficult subject
39. slough: a bad condition from which one cannot easily free oneself
40. shiftlessness: the quality of being lazy and lacking ambition
41. weakling: a person lacking in physical or mental strength
42. citadel: a fortress built to protect a city in the event of attack

Questions

1. How does Lessing delineate Mary, her first fictional protagonist, in this part? What do you think of Mary?
2. Mary and Dick are different in several ways, like that of treating the black, of viewing and running their farm, of confronting the plight of poverty. Can they justify themselves? How do these differences foreshadow the tragedy in the end?
3. The sjambok is an object standing out in this part. Is it conducive to the progress of the plot in this part?

Kazuo Ishiguro
1954—

Kazuo Ishiguro, a Japanese-born English novelist, short story writer and screenwriter, was born on November 8, 1954 in Nagasaki, one of the two Japanese cities raided by the atomic bomb during the WWII. In 1960, his father was assigned to work in England and the family thus moved there. Ishiguro was first educated at a local state primary school where freedom of choice in study was encouraged and therefore he spent a lot of time inventing spy stories, and then the Woking County Grammar School for Boys in Surrey, where he was provided with a chance to get a taste of the conventional English society. In the meantime, he was exposed to Japanese culture at home. In 1970, the family made the final decision to stay in England. Ishiguro took the British citizenship in the early 1980s. The dual

Kazuo Ishiguro

cultural influence would play an essential role in his brilliant contributions as an immigrant writer to the remaking of English literary landscape since the early 1980s.

At the University of Kent Ishiguro studied philosophy and literature and graduated with honors with a Bachelor of Arts. He then received a Master of Arts in creative writing from the University of East Anglia. He worked as a social worker before concentrating on writing. Ishiguro got three short stories published in an anthology for new writers when he still took creative writing course at the University of East Anglia, and consequently received a contract for his first novel *A Pale View of Hills* (1982). One of most acclaimed novelists among his generation, he has his preeminence verified by the number of awards he has received at a comparatively young age. His works have been translated into numerous languages. Two novels *The Remains of the Day* (1989) and *Never Let Me Go* (2005) have been adapted into films. He also has written screenplays.

Since World War II, massive immigrants from former English colonies and other parts of the world have made English society more multicultural. To seek to establish connections within the pluralistic world, immigrant writers, like V. S. Naipaul, Salman Rushdie and Ishiguro, have examined the social, political, and cultural consequences of historical immigration, adding new dimensions to the contemporary English literature. Ishiguro, with an identity neither entirely English nor fully Japanese, at heart wishes to write international novels. "An international novel," he believes, is one that "contains a vision of life that is of importance to people of varied backgrounds around the world" and "may concern characters who jet across continents, but may just as easily be set firmly in one small locality". His declaration resonates with the status quo of the English literary world which, he thinks, was "turning to the book with the large global theme" as he rose to fame.

In general, Ishiguro's fiction evolves around memories in combination with themes such as social constraints, nostalgia, and loss, guilt, self-deception, self-delusion, duty, choices, passing of time. His characters, with diversified cultural identities, are often forced by external circumstances to review their lives and question their values and ideals. The Japanese woman Etsuko in *A Pale View of Hills*, the Japanese artist Masuji Ono in *An Artist of the Floating World* (1986), and the English butler Stevens in *The Remains of the Day* all try to make sense of the past by virtue of remembrance. Exploring the pressure of historical events on individual life and having human values and ideals tested is part of his commitment to concerns of universal interest. On the other hand, his literary creation is characterized by his keen observation of eastern and western culture in both realistic and surrealistic stories, first-person point of view, and his delicate language style. His characters present themselves through the stories they themselves tell of.

Malvern Hills

In his teens and early twenties Ishiguro dreamed of becoming a singer-songwriter, but then he felt the limits of this career for him and he found writing could take him further. This earlier pursuit has been reflected in his literary creation. His 2009 short story collection *Nocturnes: Five Stories of Music and Nightfall* consists of five stories, all concerning music. They are "Crooner", "Come Rain or Come Shine", "Malvern Hills", "Nocturne" and "Cellists". A departure from his early well-established novels in terms of genre, this collection of stories echoes Ishiguro's identifying international themes, such as unfulfilled dreams, wasted potential, self-deception and choices. Confronted with various external pressures, characters, with varied cultural backgrounds, make their own choices: the fading

American singer Tony in "Crooner" singing for his beloved wife before the breakup, the language teacher and music fan Raymond visiting a couple who are both his friends and for the moment in conflict in "Come Rain or Come Shine", the jazz musician Steve being confined to a Beverly Hills hotel after a plastic surgery for a possible promising future in "Nocturne", and in the last story the Hungarian cellist Tibor being tutored by an older American woman who is convinced of her own music genius but actually has never played cello since the age of eleven. The physical places these stories are set in are as varied: Venice, London, Malvern Hills, Los Angeles and lastly Venice again. The collection earns the writer a literary award as well.

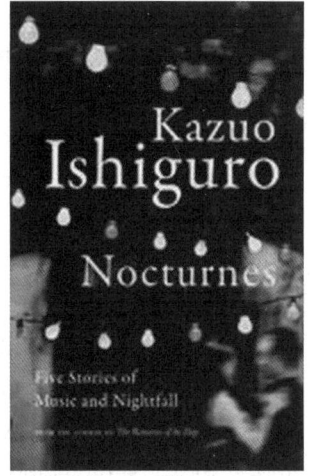

"Malvern Hills" is compared to an interlude by some critics. The third story in sequence, it revolves around the narrator, a young British guitarist who fails in a series of auditions and decides to leave London for a break. Living with his sister and brother-in-law who run a cafe in the Malvern Hills, he encounters a Swiss musician couple who believe in the music though their life does not work out quite as they have hoped. He still works on the song unfinished yet when the story ends.

Malvern Hills[1]

I'd spent the spring in London, and all in all, even if I hadn't achieved everything I'd set out to, it had been an exciting interlude[2]. But with the weeks slipping by and summer getting closer, the old restlessness had started to return. For one thing, I was getting vaguely paranoid[3] about running into any more of my former university friends. Wandering around Camden Town[4], or going through CDs I couldn't afford in West End[5] megastores, I'd already had too many of them come up to me, asking how I was getting on since leaving the course to 'seek fame and fortune'. It's not that I was embarrassed to tell them what I'd been up to. It was just that — with a very few exceptions — none of them was capable of grasping what was or wasn't, for me at this particular point, a 'successful' few months.

As I've said, I hadn't achieved every goal I'd set my sights on, but then those goals had always been more like long-term targets. And all those auditions[6], even the really dreary ones, had been an invaluable experience. In almost every case, I'd taken something away with me, something I'd learned about the scene in London, or else about the music business in general.

Some of these auditions had been pretty professional affairs. You'd find yourself in a warehouse, or a converted garage block, and there'd be a manager, or maybe the girl-friend of a band member, taking your name, asking you to wait, offering you tea, while the sounds of the band, stopping and starting, thundered out from the adjoining space. But the majority of auditions happened at a much more shambolic[7] level. In fact, when you saw the way most bands went about things, it was no mystery why the whole scene in London was dying on its feet. Time and again, I'd walk past rows of anonymous suburban terraces on the city outskirts, carry my acoustic[8] guitar up a staircase, and enter a stale-smelling flat with mattresses and sleeping bags all over the floor, and band members who

235

mumbled and barely looked you in the eye. I'd sing and play while they stared emptily at me, till one of them might bring it to an end by saying something like: 'Yeah, well. Thanks anyway, but it's not quite our genre.'

 I soon worked out that most of these guys were shy or plain awkward about the audition process, and that if I chatted to them about other things, they'd become a lot more relaxed. That's when I'd pick up all kinds of useful info: where the interesting clubs were, or the names of other bands in need of a guitarist. Or sometimes it was just a tip about a new act to check out. As I say, I never came away empty-handed.

 On the whole, people really liked my guitar-playing, and a lot of them said my vocals[9] would come in handy for harmonies[10]. But it quickly emerged there were two factors going against me. The first was that I didn't have equipment. A lot of bands were wanting someone with electric guitar, amps[11], speakers, preferably transport, ready to slot right into their gigging schedule. I was on foot with a fairly crappy acoustic. So no matter how much they liked my rhythm work or my voice, they'd no choice but to turn me away. This was fair enough.

 Much harder to accept was the other main obstacle — and I have to say, I was completely surprised by this one. There was actually a problem about me writing my own songs. I couldn't believe it. There I'd be, in some dingy apartment, playing to a circle of blank faces, then at the end, after a silence that could go on for fifteen, thirty seconds, one of them would ask suspiciously: 'So whose number[12] was that?' And when I said it was one of my own, you'd see the shutters coming down. There'd be little shrugs, shakes of the head, sly smiles exchanged, then they'd be giving me their rejection patter.

 The umpteenth[13] time this happened, I got so exasperated, I said: 'Look, I don't get this. Are you wanting to be a covers band for ever? And even if that's what you want to be, where do you think those songs come from in the first place? Yeah, that's right. Someone writes them!'

 But the guy I was talking to stared at me vacantly, then said: 'No offence, mate. It's just that there are so many wankers[14] going around writing songs.'

 The stupidity of this position, which seemed to extend right across the London scene, was key to persuading me there was something if not utterly rotten, then at least extremely shallow and inauthentic about what was going down here, right at the grass-roots level, and that this was undoubtedly a reflection of what was happening in the music industry all the way up the ladder.

 It was this realisation, and the fact that as the summer came closer I was running out of floors to sleep on, that made me feel for all the fascination of London — my university days looked grey by comparison — it would be good to take a break from the city. So I called up my sister, Maggie, who runs a cafe with her husband up in the Malvern Hills, and that's how it came to be decided I'd spend the summer with them.

 Maggie's four years older and is always worrying about me, so I knew she'd be all for my coming up. In fact, I could tell she was glad to be getting the extra help. When I say her cafe is in the Malvern Hills, I don't mean it's in Great Malvern[15] or down on the A road[16], but literally up there in the hills. It's an old Victorian house standing by itself facing the west side, so when the weather's nice, you can have your tea and cake out on the cafe terrace with a sweeping view over Herefordshire[17].

Maggie and Geoff[18] have to close the place in the winter, but in the summer it's always busy, mainly with the locals — who park their cars in the West of England car park a hundred yards below and come panting up the path in sandals and floral dresses — or else the walking brigade[19] with their maps and serious gear.

Maggie said she and Geoff couldn't afford to pay me, which suited me just fine because it meant I couldn't be expected to work too hard for them. All the same, since I was getting bed and board, the understanding seemed to be that I'd be a third member of staff. It was all a bit unclear, and at the start, Geoff, in particular, seemed torn between giving me a kick up the arse for not doing enough, and apologising for asking me to do anything at all, like I was a guest. But things soon settled down to a pattern. The work was easy enough — I was especially good at making sandwiches — and I sometimes had to keep reminding myself of my main objective in coming out to the country in the first place: that's to say, I was going to write a brand-new batch of songs ready for my return to London in the autumn.

I'm naturally an early riser, but I quickly discovered that breakfast at the cafe was a nightmare, with customers wanting eggs done this way, toast like that, everything getting overcooked. So I made a point of[20] never appearing until around eleven. While all the clatter was going on downstairs, I'd open the big bay window in my room, sit on the broad window sill and play my guitar looking out over miles and miles of countryside. There was a run of really clear mornings just after I arrived, and it was a glorious feeling, like I could see forever, and when I strummed[21] my chords, they were ringing out across the whole nation. Only when I turned and stuck my head right out of the window would I get an aerial view of the cafe terrace below, and become aware of the people coming and going with their dogs and pushchairs.

I wasn't a stranger to this area. Maggie and I had grown up only a few miles away in Pershore[22] and our parents had often brought us for walks on the hills. But I'd never been much up for it in those days, and as soon as I was old enough, I'd refused to go with them. That summer though, I felt this was the most beautiful place in the world; that in many ways I'd come from and belonged to the hills. Maybe it was something to do with our parents having split up, the fact that for some time now, that little grey house opposite the hairdresser was no longer 'our' house. Whatever it was, this time round, instead of the claustrophobia[23] I remembered from my childhood, I felt affection, even nostalgia, about the area.

I found myself wandering in the hills practically every day, sometimes with my guitar if I was sure it wouldn't rain. I liked in particular Table Hill and End Hill, at the north end of the range, which tend to get neglected by day-trippers. There I'd sometimes be lost in my thoughts for hours at a time without seeing a soul. It was like I was discovering the hills for the first time, and I could almost taste the ideas for new songs welling up in my mind.

Working at the cafe, though, was another matter. I'd catch a voice, or see a face coming up to the counter while I was preparing a salad, that would jerk me back to an earlier part of my life. Old friends of my parents would come up and grill[24] me about what I was up to, and I'd have to bluff until they decided to leave me in peace. Usually they'd sign off with something like: 'Well at least you're keeping busy,' nodding towards the sliced bread and tomatoes, before waddling back to their table with their cup and saucer. Or someone I'd known at school would come in and start talking to me in their new 'university' voice, maybe dissecting the latest Batman film in clever-clever language, or else starting on about the real causes of world poverty.

I didn't really mind any of this. In fact, some of these people I was genuinely quite glad to see. But there was one person who came into the cafe that summer, the instant I saw her, I felt myself freezing up, and by the time it occurred to me to escape into the kitchen, she'd already seen me.

This was Mrs Fraser — or Hag Fraser, as we used to call her. I recognised her as soon as she came in with a muddy little bulldog. I felt like telling her she couldn't bring the dog inside, though people always did that when they came to get things. Hag Fraser had been one of my teachers at school in Pershore. Thankfully she retired before I went into the sixth form, but in my memory her shadow falls over my entire school career. Her aside, school hadn't been that bad, but she'd had it in for me from the start, and when you're just eleven years old, there's nothing you can do to defend yourself from someone like her. Her tricks were the usual ones twisted teachers have, like asking me in lessons exactly the questions she sensed I wouldn't be able to answer, then making me stand up and getting the class to laugh at me. Later, it got more subtle. I remember once, when I was fourteen, a new teacher, a Mr Travis, had exchanged jokes with me in class. Not jokes against me, but like we were equals, and the class had laughed, and I'd felt good about it. But a couple of days later, I was going down the corridor and Mr Travis was coming the other way, talking with her, and as I came by she stopped me and gave me a complete bollocking[25] about late homework or something. The point is she'd done this just to let Mr Travis know I was a 'troublemaker'; that if he'd thought for one moment I was one of the boys worthy of his respect, he was making a big mistake. Maybe it was because she was old, I don't know, but the other teachers never seemed to see through her. They all took whatever she said as gospel[26].

When Hag Fraser came in that day, it was obvious she remembered me, but she didn't smile or call me by name. She bought a cup of tea and a packet of Custard Creams, then took them outside to the terrace. I thought that was that. But then a while later, she came in again, put her empty cup and saucer down on the counter and said: 'Since you won't clear the table, I've brought these in myself.' She gave me a look that went on a second or two longer than was normal — her old if-only-I-could-swat[27]-you look — then left.

All my hatred for the old dragon came back, and by the time Maggie came down a few minutes later, I was completely fuming. She saw it straight away and asked what was wrong. There were a few customers out on the terrace, but no one inside, so I started shouting, calling Hag Fraser every filthy name she deserved. Maggie got me to calm down, then said:

'Well, she's not anybody's teacher any more. She's just a sad old lady whose husband's gone and left her.'

'Not surprised.'

'But you have to feel a bit sorry for her. Just when she thought she could enjoy her retirement, she's left for a younger woman. And now she has to run that bed-and-breakfast by herself and people say the place is falling apart.'

This all cheered me up no end. I forgot about Hag Fraser soon after that, because a group came in and I had to make a lot of tuna salads. But a few days later when I was chatting to Geoff in the kitchen,

Chapter Nine Cultural Diversity

I got a few more details from him; like how her husband of forty-odd years had gone off with his secretary; and how their hotel had got off to a reasonable start, but now all the gossip was of guests demanding their money back, or checking out within hours of arrival. I saw the place myself once when I was helping Maggie with the cash-and-carry[28] and we drove past. Hag Fraser's hotel was right there on the Elgar Route[29], a fairly substantial granite house with an outsize sign saying 'Malvern Lodge'.

But I don't want to go on about Hag Fraser too much. I'm not obsessed with her or with her hotel. I'm only putting this all here now because of what happened later, once Tilo and Sonja came in.

Geoff had gone into Great Malvern that day, so it was just me and Maggie holding the fort[30]. The main lunch rush was over, but at the point when the Krauts[31] came in, we still had plenty going on. I'd clocked them in my mind as 'the Krauts' the moment I heard their accents. I wasn't being racist. If you have to stand behind a counter and remember who didn't want beetroot, who wanted extra bread, who gets what put on which bill, you've no choice but to turn all the customers into characters, give them names, pick out physical peculiarities. Donkey Face had a ploughman's[32] and two coffees Tuna mayo[33] baguettes[34] for Winston Churchill and his wife. That's how I was doing it. So Tilo and Sonja were 'the Krauts'.

It was very hot that afternoon, but most of the customers — being English — still wanted to sit outside on the terrace, some of them even avoiding the parasols[35] so they could go bright red in the sun. But the Krauts decided to sit indoors in the shade. They had on loose, camel-coloured trousers, trainers[36] and T-shirts, but somehow looked smart, the way people from the continent often do. I supposed they were in their forties, maybe early fifties — I didn't pay too much attention at that stage. They ate their lunch talking quietly to each other, and they seemed like any pleasant, middle-aged couple from Europe. Then after a while, the guy got up and started wandering about the room, pausing to study an old faded photo Maggie has on the wall, of the house as it was in 1915. Then he stretched out his arms and said:

'Your countryside here is so wonderful! We have many fine mountains in Switzerland. But what you have here is different. They are hills. You call them hills. They have a charm all their own because they are gentle and friendly.'

'Oh, you're from Switzerland,' Maggie said in her polite voice. 'I've always wanted to go there. It sounds so fantastic, the Alps, the cable-cars.'

'Of course, our country has many beautiful features. But here, in this spot, you have a special charm. We have wanted to visit this part of England for so long. We always talked of it, and now finally we are here!' He gave a hearty laugh. 'So happy to be here!'

'That's splendid,' Maggie said. 'I do hope you enjoy it. Are you here for long?'

'We have another three days before we must return to our work. We have looked forward to coming here ever since we observed a wonderful documentary film many years ago, concerning Elgar. Evidently Elgar loved these hills and explored them thoroughly on his bicycle. And now we are finally here!'

Maggie chatted with him for a few minutes about places they'd already visited in England, what they should see in the local area, the usual staff you were supposed to say to tourists. I'd heard it loads of times before, and I could do it myself more or less on automatic, so I started to tune out[37]. I just took

239

in that the Krauts were actually Swiss and that they were travelling around by hired car. He kept saying what a great place England was and how kind everyone had been, and made big laughing noises whenever Maggie said anything halfway jokey. But as I say, I'd tuned out, thinking they were just this fairly boring couple. I only started paying attention again a few moments later, when I noticed the way the guy kept trying to bring his wife into the conversation, and how she kept silent, her eyes fixed on her guidebook and behaving like she wasn't aware of any conversation at all. That's when I took a closer look at them.

They both had even, natural suntans, quite unlike the sweaty lobster looks of the locals outside, and despite their age, they were both slim and fit-looking. His hair was grey, but luxuriant, and he'd had it carefully groomed, though in a vaguely seventies style, a bit like the guys in Abba[38]. Her hair was blonde, almost snowy white, and her face was stern-looking, with little lines etched around the mouth that spoilt what would otherwise have been the beautiful older woman look. So there he was, as I say, trying to bring her into the conversation.

'Of course, my wife enjoys Elgar greatly and so would be most curious to visit the house in which he was born.'

Silence.

Or: 'I am not a great fan of Paris, I must confess. I much prefer London. But Sonja here, she loves Paris.'

Nothing.

Each time he said something like this, he'd turn towards his wife in the corner, and Maggie would be obliged to look over to her, but the wife still wouldn't glance up from her book. The man didn't seem especially perturbed[39] by this and went on talking cheerfully. Then he stretched out his arms again and said: 'If you will excuse me, I think I may for a moment go and admire your splendid scenery!'

He went outside, and we could see him walking around the terrace. Then he disappeared out of our view. The wife was still there in the corner, reading her guidebook, and after a while Maggie went over to her table and began clearing up. The woman ignored her completely until my sister picked up a plate with a tiny bit of roll still left on it. Then suddenly she slammed down her book and said, far more loudly than necessary: 'I have not finished yet!'

Maggie apologised and left her with her piece of roll — which I noticed the woman made no move to touch. Maggie looked at me as she came past and I gave her a shrug. Then a few moments later, my sister asked the woman, very nicely, if there was anything else she'd like.

'No. I want nothing else.'

I could tell from her tone she should be left alone, but with Maggie it was a kind of reflex[40]. She asked, like she really wanted to know: 'Was everything all right?'

For at least five or six seconds, the woman went on reading, like she hadn't heard. Then she put down her book again and glared at my sister.

'Since you ask,' she said, 'I shall tell you. The food was perfectly okay. Better than in many of the awful places you have around here. However, we waited thirty-five minutes simply to be served a sandwich and a salad. Thirty-five minutes.'

I now realised this woman was livid[41] with anger. Not the sort that suddenly hits you, then drains away. No, this woman, I could tell, had been in a kind of white heat for some time. It's the sort of anger that arrives and stays put, at a constant level, like a bad headache, never quite peaking and refusing to find a proper outlet. Maggie's always so even-tempered she couldn't recognise the symptoms, and probably thought the woman was complaining in a more or less rational way. Because she apologised and started to say: 'But you see, when there's a big rush like we had earlier ...'

'Surely you get it every day, no? Is that not so? Every day, in the summer, when the weather is fine, there is just such a big rush? Well? So why can't you be ready? Something that happens every day and it surprises you. Is that what you are telling me?'

The woman had been glaring at my sister, but as I came out from behind the counter to stand beside Maggie, she transferred her gaze to me. And maybe it was to do with the expression I had on my face, I could see her anger go up a couple more notches[42]. Maggie turned and looked at me, and began gently to push me away, but I resisted, and kept gazing at the woman. I wanted her to know it wasn't just her and Maggie in this. God knows where this would have got us, but at that moment the husband came back in.

'Such a marvellous view! A marvellous view, a marvellous lunch, a marvellous country!'

I waited for him to sense what he'd walked into, but if he noticed, he showed no sign of taking it into account. He smiled at his wife and said, presumably for our benefit in English: 'Sonja, you really must go and have a look. Just walk to the end of the little path out there!'

She said something in German, then went back to her book. He came further into the room and said to us:

'We had considered driving on to Wales this afternoon. But your Malvern Hills are so wonderful, I really think we might stay here in this district for the remaining three days of our vacation. If Sonja agrees, I will be overjoyed!'

He looked at his wife, who shrugged and said something else in German, to which he laughed his loud, open laugh.

'Good! She agrees! So it is settled. We will no longer drive to Wales. We will hang out here in your district for the next three days!'

He beamed at us, and Maggie said something encouraging. I was relieved to see the wife putting her book away and getting ready to leave. The man, too, went to the table, picked up a small rucksack and put it on his shoulder. Then he said to Maggie:

'I wonder. Is there by any chance a small hotel you can recommend for us nearby? Nothing too expensive, but comfortable and pleasant. And if possible, with something of the English flavour!'

Maggie was a bit stumped[43] by this and delayed her answer by saying something meaningless like: 'What sort of place did you want?' But I said quickly:

'The best place around here is Mrs Fraser's. It's just down along the road to Worcester. It's called Malvern Lodge.'

'The Malvern Lodge! That sounds just the ticket!'

Maggie turned away disapprovingly and pretended to be clearing away more things while I gave them all the details on how to find Hag Fraser's hotel. Then the couple left, the guy thanking us with big smiles, the woman not giving a backward glance.

My sister gave me a weary look and shook her head. I just laughed and said:

'You've got to admit, that woman and Hag Fraser really deserve one another. It was just too good an opportunity to miss.'

'It's all very well for you to amuse yourself like that,' Maggie said, pushing past me to the kitchen. 'I have to live here.'

'So what? Look, you'll never see those Krauts again. And if Hag Fraser finds out we've been recommending her place to passing tourists, she's hardly going to complain, is she?'

Maggie shook her head, but there was more of a smile about it this time.

The cafe got quieter after that, then Geoff came back, so I went off upstairs, feeling I'd done more than my share for the time being. Up in my room, I sat at the bay window with my guitar and for a while got engrossed in a song I was halfway through writing. But then — and it seemed like no time — I could hear the afternoon tea rush starting downstairs. If it got really mad, like it usually did, Maggie was bound to ask me to come down — which really wouldn't be fair, given how much I'd done already. So I decided the best thing would be for me to slip out to the hills and continue my work there.

I left the back way without encountering anyone, and immediately felt glad to be out in the open. It was pretty warm though, especially carrying a guitar case, and I was glad of the breeze.

I was heading for a particular spot I'd discovered the previous week. To get there you climbed a steep path behind the house, then walked a few minutes along a more gradual incline[44] till you came to this bench. It's one I'd chosen carefully, not just because of the fantastic view, but because it wasn't at one of those junctions in the paths where people with exhausted children come staggering up and sit next to you. On the other hand it wasn't completely isolated, and every now and then, a walker would pass by, saying 'Hi!' in the way they do, maybe adding some quip[45] about my guitar, all without breaking stride. I didn't mind this at all. It was kind of like having an audience and not having one, and it gave my imagination just that little edge it needed.

I'd been there on my bench for maybe half an hour when I became aware that some walkers, who'd just gone past with the usual short greeting, had now stopped several yards away and were watching me. This did rather annoy me, and I said, a little sarcastically:

'It's okay. You don't have to toss me any money.'

This was answered by a big hearty laugh which I recognised, and I looked up to see the Krauts coming back towards the bench.

The possibility flashed through my mind that they'd gone to Hag Fraser's, realised I'd pulled a fast one on them[46], and were now coming to get even with me[47]. But then I saw that not only the guy, but the woman too, was smiling cheerfully. They retraced their steps till they were standing in front of me, and since by this time the sun was falling, they appeared for a moment as two silhouettes, the big afternoon sky behind them. Then they came closer and I could see they were both gazing at my guitar — which I'd continued to play — with a look of happy amazement, the way people gaze at a baby. Even more astonishing, the woman was tapping her foot to my beat. I got self-conscious and stopped.

'Hey, carry on!' the woman said. 'It's really good what you play there.'

'Yes,' the husband said, 'wonderful! We heard it from a distance.' He pointed. 'We were right up there, on that ridge, and I said to Sonja, I can hear music.'

'Singing too,' the woman said. 'I said to Tilo, listen, there is singing somewhere. And I was right, yes? You were singing also a moment ago.'

I couldn't quite accept that this smiling woman was the same one who'd given us such a hard time at lunch, and I looked at them again carefully, in case this was a different couple altogether. But they were in the same clothes, and though the man's Abba-style hair had come undone a bit in the wind, there was no mistaking it. In any case, the next moment, he said:

'I believe you are the gentleman who served us lunch in the delightful restaurant.'

I agreed I was. Then the woman said:

'That melody you were singing a moment ago. We heard it up there, just in the wind at first. I loved the way it fell at the end of each line.'

'Thanks,' I said. 'It's something I'm working on. Not finished yet.'

'Your own composition? Then you must be very gifted! Please do sing your melody again, as you were before.'

'You know,' the guy said, 'when you come to record your song, you must tell the producer this is how you want it to sound. Like this!' He gestured behind him at Herefordshire stretched out before us. 'You must tell him this is the sound, the aural environment you require. Then the listener will hear your song as we heard it today, caught in the wind as we descend the slope of the hill...'

'But a little more clearly, of course,' the woman said. 'Or else the listener will not catch the words. But Tilo is correct. There must be a suggestion of outdoors. Of air, of echo.'

They seemed on the verge of getting carried away, like they'd just come across another Elgar in the hills. Despite my initial suspicions, I couldn't help but warm to them.

'Well,' I said, 'since I wrote most of the song up here, it's no wonder there's something of this place in it,'

'Yes, yes,' they both said together, nodding. Then the woman said: 'You must not be shy. Please share your music with us. It sounded wonderful.'

'All right,' I said, playing a little doodle[48]. 'All right, I'll sing you a song, if you really want me to. Not the one I haven't finished. Another one. But took, I can't do it with you two standing right over me like this.'

'Of course,' Tilo said. 'We are being so inconsiderate. Sonja and I have had to perform in so many strange and difficult conditions, we become insensitive to the needs of another musician.'

He looked around and sat down on a patch of stubbly grass near the path, his back to me and facing the view. Sonja gave me an encouraging smile, then sat down beside him. Immediately, he put an arm around her shoulders, she leaned towards him, then it was almost like I wasn't there any more, and they were having an intimate lovey-dovey[49] moment gazing over the late-afternoon countryside.

'Okay, here goes,' I said, and went into the song I usually open with at auditions. I aimed my voice at the horizon but kept glancing at Tilo and Sonja. Though I couldn't see their faces, the whole way they remained snuggled[50] up to each other with no hint of restlessness told me they were enjoying what they were hearing. When I finished, they turned to me with big smiles and applauded, sending echoes around the hills.

'Fantastic!' Sonja said. 'So talented!'

'Splendid, splendid,' Tilo was saying.

I felt a little embarrassed by this and pretended to be absorbed in some guitar work. When I eventually looked up again, they were still sitting on the ground, but had now shifted their positions so they could see me.

'So you're musicians?' I asked. 'I mean, professional musicians?'

'Yes,' said Tilo, 'I suppose you could call us professionals. Sonja and I, we perform as a duo. In hotels, restaurants. At weddings, at parties. All over Europe, though we like best to work in Switzerland and Austria. We make our living this way, so yes, we are professionals.'

'But first and foremost, Sonja said, we play because we believe in the music. I can see it is the same for you.'

'If I stopped believing in my music,' I said, 'I'd stop, just like that.' Then I added: 'I'd really like to do it professionally. It must be a good life.'

'Oh yes, it's a good life,' said Tilo. 'We're very lucky we are able to do what we do.'

'Look,' I said, maybe a little suddenly. 'Did you go to that hotel I told you about?'

'How very rude of us!' Tilo exclaimed. 'We were so taken by your music, we forgot completely to thank you. Yes, we went there and it is just the ticket. Fortunately there were still vacancies.'

'It's just what we wanted,' said Sonja. 'Thank you.'

I pretended again to become absorbed in my chords. Then I said as casually as I could: 'Come to think of it, There's this other hotel I know. I think it's better than Malvern Lodge. I think you should change.'

'Oh, but we're quite settled now,' said Tilo. 'We have unpacked our things, and besides, it's just what we need.'

'Yeah, but ... Well, the thing is, earlier on, when you asked me about a hotel, I didn't know you were musicians. I thought you were bankers or something.'

They both burst out laughing, like I'd made a fantastic joke. Then Tilo said:

'No, no, we're not bankers. Though there have been many times we wished we were!'

'What I'm saying,' I said, 'is there are other hotels much more geared, you know, to artistic types. It's hard when strangers ask you to recommend a hotel, before you know what sort of people they are.'

'It's kind of you to worry,' said Tilo. 'But please, don't do so any longer. What we have is perfect. Besides, people are not so different. Bankers, musicians, we all in the end want the same things from life.'

'You know, I'm not sure that is so true,' Sonja said. 'Our young friend here, you see he doesn't look for a job in a bank. His dreams are different.'

'Perhaps you are right, Sonja. All the same, the present hotel is fine for us.'

I leant over the strings and practised another little phrase to myself, and for a few seconds nobody spoke. Then I asked: 'So what sort of music do you guys play?'

Tilo shrugged. 'Sonja and I play a number of instruments between us. We both play keyboards. I am fond of the clarinet[51]. Sonja is a very fine violinist, and also a splendid singer. I suppose what we like to do best is to perform our traditional Swiss folk music, but in a contemporary manner. Sometimes even what you might call a radical manner. We take inspiration from great composers who took a similar path. Janáček[52], for instance. Your own Vaughan Williams[53].'

'But that kind of music', Sonja said, 'we don't play so much now.'

They exchanged glances with what I thought was just a hint of tension. Then Tilo's usual smile was back on his face.

'Yes, as Sonja points out, in this real world, much of the time, we must play what our audience is most likely to appreciate. So we perform many hits. Beatles, the Carpenters. Some more recent songs. This is perfectly satisfying.'

'What about Abba?' I asked on an impulse, then immediately regretted it. But Tilo didn't seem to sense any mockery.

'Yes, indeed, we do some Abba. "Dancing Queen". That one always goes down well. In fact, it is on "Dancing Queen" I actually do a little singing myself, a little harmony part. Sonja will tell you I have the most terrible voice. So we must make sure to perform this song only when our customers are right in the middle of their meal, when there is for them no chance of escape!'

He did his big laugh, and Sonja laughed too, though not so loudly. A power-cyclist, kitted out in what looked like a black wetsuit, went speeding by us, and for the next few moments, we all watched his frantic, receding shape.

'I went to Switzerland once,' I said eventually. 'A couple of summers ago. Interlaken[54]. I stayed at the youth hostel there.'

'Ah yes, Interlaken. A beautiful place. Some Swiss people scoff at it. They say it is just for the tourists. But Sonja and I always love to perform there. In fact, to play in Interlaken on a summer evening, to happy people from all over the world, it is something very wonderful. I hope you enjoyed your visit there.'

'Yeah, it was great.'

'There is a restaurant in Interlaken where we play a few nights every summer. For our performance, we position ourselves under the restaurant's canopy, so we are facing the dining tables, which of course are outdoors on such an evening. And as we perform, we are able to see all the tourists, eating and talking together under the stars. And behind the tourists, we see the big field, where during the day the paragliders are landing, but which at night is lit up by the lamps along the Höheweg[55]. And if your eye may travel further, there are the Alps overlooking the field. The outlines of the Eiger[56], the Mönch[57], the Jungfrau[58]. And the air is pleasantly warm and filled with the music we are making. I always feel when we are there, this is a privilege. I think, yes, it is good to be doing this.'

'That restaurant,' Sonja said. 'Last year, the manager made us wear full costumes while we performed, even though it was so hot. It was very uncomfortable, and we said, what difference does it make, why must we have our bulky waistcoats and scarves and hats? In just our blouses, we look neat and still very Swiss. But the restaurant manager tells us, we put on the full costumes or we don't play. Our choice, he says, and walks away, just like that.'

'But Sonja, that is the same in any job. There is always a uniform, something the employer insists you must wear. It is the same for bankers! And in our case, at least it is something we believe in. Swiss culture. Swiss tradition.'

Once again something vaguely awkward hovered between them, but it was just for a second or two, and then they both smiled as they fixed their gazes back on my guitar. I thought I should say something, so I said:

'I think I'd enjoy that. Being able to play in different countries. It must keep you sharp, really aware of your audiences.'

'Yes,' Tilo said, 'it is good that we perform to all kinds of people. And not only in Europe. All in all, we have got to know so many cities so well.'

'Düsseldorf[59], for instance,' said Sonja. There was something different about her voice now — something harder — and I could see again the person I'd encountered back at the cafe. Tilo, though, didn't seem to notice anything and said to me, in a carefree sort of way:

'Düsseldorf is where our son is now living. He is your age. Perhaps a little older.'

'Earlier this year,' Sonja said, 'we went to Düsseldorf. We have an engagement to play there. Not the usual thing, this is a chance to play our real music. So we call him, our son, our only child, we call to say we are coming to his city. He does not answer his phone, so we leave a message. We leave many messages. No reply. We arrive in Düsseldorf, we leave more messages. We say, here we are, we are in your city. Still nothing. Tilo says don't worry, perhaps he will come on the night, to our concert. But he does not come. We play, then we go to another city, to our next engagement.'

Tilo made a chuckling noise. 'I think perhaps Peter heard enough of our music while he was growing up! The poor boy, you see, he had to listen to us rehearsing, day after day.'

'I suppose it can be a bit tricky,' I said. 'Having children and being musicians.'

'We only had the one child,' Tilo said, 'so it was not so bad. Of course we were fortunate. When we had to travel, and we couldn't take him with us, his grandparents were always delighted to help. And when Peter was older, we were able to send him to a good boarding school. Again, his grandparents came to the rescue. We could not afford such school fees otherwise. So we were very fortunate.'

'Yes, we were fortunate,' Sonja said. 'Except Peter hated his school.'

The earlier good atmosphere was definitely slipping away. In an effort to cheer things up, I said quickly: 'Well, anyway, it looks like you both really enjoy your work.'

'Oh yes, we enjoy our work,' said Tilo. 'It's everything to us. Even so, we very much appreciate a vacation. Do you know, this is our first proper vacation in three years.'

This made me feel really bad all over again, and I thought about having another go at persuading them to change hotels, but I could see how ridiculous this would look. I just had to hope Hag Fraser pulled her finger out[60]. Instead, I said:

'Look, if you like, I'll play you that song I was working on earlier. I haven't finished it, and I wouldn't usually do this. But since you heard some of it anyway, I don't mind playing you what I've got so far.'

The smile returned to Sonja's face. 'Yes,' she said, 'please do let us hear. It sounded so beautiful.'

As I got ready to play, they shifted again, so they were facing the view like before, their backs to me. But this time, instead of cuddling, they sat there on the grass with surprisingly upright postures, each with a hand up to the brow to shield away the sun. They stayed like that all the time I played, peculiarly still, and what with the way each of them cast a long afternoon shadow, they looked like matching art exhibits. I brought my incomplete song to a meandering halt, and for a moment they didn't move. Then their postures relaxed, and they applauded, though perhaps not quite as enthusiastically as the last time. Tilo got to his feet, muttering compliments, then helped Sonja up. It was only when you saw how they did this that you remembered they were really quite middle-aged. Maybe they were just tired. For all I know, they might have done a fair bit of walking before they'd come across me. All the same, it seemed to me they found it quite a struggle to get up.

'You've entertained us so marvellously,' Tilo was saying. 'Now we are the tourists, and someone else plays for us! It makes a pleasant change.'

'I would love to hear that song when it is finished,' Sonja said, and she seemed really to mean it. 'Maybe one day I will hear it on the radio. Who knows?'

'Yes,' Tilo said, 'and then Sonja and I will play our cover version to our customers!' His big laugh rang through the air. Then he did a polite little bow and said: 'So today we are in your debt three times over. A splendid lunch. A splendid choice of hotel. And a splendid concert here in the hills!'

As we said our goodbyes, I had an urge to tell them the truth. To confess that I'd deliberately sent them to the worst hotel in the area, and warn them to move out while there was still time. But the affectionate way they shook my hand made it all the harder to come out with this. And then they were going down the hill and I was alone on the bench again.

The cafe had closed by the time I came down from the hills. Maggie and Geoff looked exhausted. Maggie said it had been their busiest day yet and seemed pleased about it. But when Geoff made the same point over supper — which we ate in the cafe from various left-overs — he put it like it was a negative thing, like it was awful they'd been made to work so hard and where had I been to help? Maggie asked how my afternoon had gone, and I didn't mention Tilo and Sonja — that seemed too complicated — but told her I'd gone up to the Sugarloaf[61] to work on my song. And when she asked if I'd made any progress, and I said yes, I was making real headway now, Geoff got up and marched out moodily, even though there was still food on his plate. Maggie pretended not to notice, and fair enough, he came back a few minutes later with a can of beer, and sat there reading his newspaper and not saying much. I didn't want to be the cause of a rift between my sister and brother-in-law, so I excused myself soon after that and went upstairs to work some more on the song.

My room, which was such an inspiration in the daytime, Wasn't nearly so appealing after dark. For a start, the curtains didn't pull all the way across, which meant if I opened a window in the stifling heat, insects from miles around would see my light and come charging in. And the light I had was just this one bare bulb hanging down from the ceiling rose, which cast gloomy shadows all round the room, making it look all the more obviously the spare room it was. That evening, I was wanting light to work by, to jot down lyrics as they occurred to me. But it got far too stuffy, and in the end I switched off the bulb, pulled back the curtains, and opened the windows wide. Then I sat in the bay with my guitar, just the way I did in the day.

I'd been there like that for about an hour, playing through various ideas for the bridge passage, when there was a knock and Maggie stuck her head round the door. Of course everything was in darkness, but outside down on the terrace there was a security light, so I could just about make out her face. She had on this awkward smile, and I thought she was about to ask me to come and help with yet another chore. She came right in, closed the door behind her and said:

'I'm sorry, love. But Geoff's really tired tonight, he's been working so hard. And now he says he wants to watch his movie in peace?'

She said it like that, like it was a question, and it took me a moment to realise she was asking me to stop playing my music.

'But I'm working on something important here,' I said.

'I know. But he's really tired tonight, and he says he can't relax because of your guitar.'

'What Geoff needs to realise,' I said, 'is that just as he's got his work to do, I've got mine.'

My sister seemed to think about this. Then she did a big sigh. 'I don't think I ought to report that back to Geoff.'

'Why not? Why don't you? It's time he got the message.'

'Why not? Because I don't think he'd be very pleased, That's why not. And I don't really think he'd accept that his work and your work are quite on the same level.'

I stared at Maggie, for a moment quite speechless. Then I said: 'You're talking such rubbish. Why are you talking such rubbish?'

She shook her head wearily, but didn't say anything.

'I don't understand why you're talking such rubbish,' I said. 'And just when things are going so well for me.'

'Things are going well for you, are they, love?' She kept looking at me in the half-light. 'Well, all right,' she said in the end. 'I won't argue with you.' She turned away to open the door. 'Come down and join us, if you like,' she said as she left.

Rigid with rage, I stared at the door that had closed behind her. I became aware of muffled sounds from the television downstairs, and even in the state I was in, some detached part of my brain was telling me my fury should be directed not at Maggie, but at Geoff, who'd been systematically trying to undermine me ever since I'd got here. Even so, it was my sister I was livid at. In all the time I'd been in her house, she hadn't once asked to hear a song, the way Tilo and Sonja had done. Surely it wasn't too much to ask of your own sister, and one who'd been, I happened to remember, a big music fan in her teens? And now here she was, interrupting me when I was trying to work and talking all this rubbish. Every time I thought of the way she'd said: 'All right, I won't argue with you,' I felt fresh fury coursing[62] through me.

I came down off the window sill, put away the guitar, and threw myself down on my mattress. Then for the next little while I stared at the patterns on the ceiling. It seemed clear I'd been invited here on false pretences, that this had all been about getting cheap help for the busy season, a mug they didn't even have to pay. And my sister didn't understand what I was trying to achieve any better than did her moron[63] of a husband. It would serve them both right if I left them here in the lurch and went back to London. I kept going round and round with this stuff, until maybe an hour or so later, I calmed down a bit and decided I'd just turn in for the night.

I didn't speak much to either of them when I came down as usual just after the breakfast rush. I made some toast and coffee, helped myself to some left-over scrambled eggs, and settled down in the corner of the cafe. All through my breakfast the thought kept occurring to me I might run into Tilo and Sonja again up in the hills. And though this might mean having to face the music[64] about Hag Fraser's place, even so, I realised I was hoping it would happen. Besides, even if Hag Fraser's was truly awful, they'd never suppose I'd recommended it out of malice. There'd be any number of ways for me to get out of it.

Maggie and Geoff were probably expecting me to help again with the lunch rush, but I decided they needed a lesson about taking people for granted. So after breakfast, I went upstairs, got my guitar and slipped out the back way.

It was really hot again and the sweat was running down my cheek as I climbed the path leading up to my bench. Even though I'd been thinking about Tilo and Sonja at breakfast, I'd forgotten them by this point, and so got a surprise when, coming up the final slope, I looked towards the bench and saw Sonja sitting there by herself. She spotted me immediately and waved.

I was still a bit wary of her, and especially without Tilo around, I wasn't so keen to sit down with her. But she gave me a big smile and did a shifting movement, like she was making room for me, so I didn't have much choice.

We said our hellos, then for a time we just sat there side by side, not speaking. This didn't seem so odd at first, partly because I was still getting my breath back, and partly because of the view. There was more haze and cloud than the previous day, but if you concentrated, you could still see beyond the Welsh borders to the Black Mountains. The breeze was quite strong, but not uncomfortable.

'So where's Tilo?' I asked in the end.

'Tilo? Oh...' She put her hand up to shield her eyes. Then she pointed. 'There. You see? Over there. That is Tilo.'

Some way in the distance, I could see a figure, in what might have been a green T-shirt and a white sun cap, moving along the rising path towards Worcestershire Beacon[65].

'Tilo wished to go for a walk,' she said.

'You didn't want to go with him?'

'No. I decided to stay here.'

While she wasn't by any means the irate[66] customer from the cafe, neither was she quite the same person who'd been so warm and encouraging to me the day before. There was definitely something up, and I started preparing my defence about Hag Fraser's.

'By the way,' I said, 'I've been working a bit more on that song. You can hear it if you like.'

She gave this consideration, then said: 'If you do not mind, perhaps not just at this minute. You see, Tilo and I have just had a talk. You might call it a disagreement.'

'Oh okay. Sorry to hear that.'

'And now he has gone off for his walk.'

Again, we sat there not talking. Then I sighed and said: 'I think maybe this is all my fault.'

She turned to look at me. 'Your fault? Why do you say that?'

'The reason you've quarrelled, the reason your holiday's all messed up now. It's my fault. It's that hotel, isn't it? It wasn't very good, right?'

'The hotel?' She seemed puzzled. 'That hotel. Well, it has some weak points. But it is a hotel, like many others.'

'But you noticed, right? You noticed all the weak points. You must have done.'

She seemed to think this over, then nodded. 'It is true, I noticed the weak points. Tilo, however, did not. Tilo, of course, thought the hotel was splendid. We are so lucky, he kept saying. So lucky to find such a hotel. Then this morning we have our breakfast. For Tilo, this is a fine breakfast, the best breakfast ever. I say, Tilo, don't be stupid. This is not a good breakfast. This is not a good hotel. He says, no, no, we are so very lucky. So I become angry. I tell the proprietress[67] everything that is wrong. Tilo leads me away. Let's go for a walk, he says. You will feel better then. So we come out here. And he says, Sonja, look at these hills, aren't they so beautiful? Aren't we fortunate to come to such a place as this for our vacation? These hills, he says, are even more wonderful than he imagined them when we listen to Elgar. He asks me, isn't this so? Perhaps I become angry again. I tell him, these hills are not so wonderful. It is not how I imagine them when I hear Elgar's music. Elgar's hills are majestic and mysterious. Here, this is just like a park. This is what I say to him, and then it is his turn to be cross. He says in that case, he will walk by himself. He says we are finished, we never agree on anything now. Yes, he says, Sonja, you and me, we are finished. And off he goes! So there you are. That is why he is up there and I am down here.' She shielded her eyes again and watched Tilo's progress.

'I'm really sorry,' I said. 'If only I hadn't sent you to that hotel in the first place...'

'Please. The hotel is not important.' She leaned forward to get a better view of Tilo. Then she turned to me and smiled, and I thought maybe there were little tears in her eyes. 'Tell me,' she said. 'Today, you mean to write more songs?'

'That's the plan. Or at least, I want to finish the one I've been working on. The one you heard yesterday.'

'That was beautiful. And what will you do then, once you have finished writing your songs here? You have a plan?'

'I'll go back to London and form a band. These songs need just the right band or they won't work.'

'How exciting. I do wish you luck.'

After a moment, I said, quite quietly: 'Then again, I may not bother. It's not so easy, you know.'

She didn't reply, and it occurred to me she hadn't heard, because she'd turned away again, to look towards Tilo.

'You know,' she said eventually, 'when I was younger, nothing could make me angry. But now I get angry at many things. I don't know how I have become this way. It is not good. Well, I do not think Tilo is coming back here. I will return to the hotel and wait for him.' She got to her feet, her gaze still fixed on his distant figure.

'It's a shame,' I said, also getting up, 'you having a row on your holiday. And yesterday, when I was playing to you, you seemed so happy together.'

'Yes, that was a good moment. Thank you for that.' Suddenly, she held out her hand to me, smiling warmly. 'It has been so nice to meet you.'

We shook hands, in the slightly limp way you do with women. She started to walk away, then stopped and looked at me.

'If Tilo were here,' she said, 'he would say to you, never be discouraged. He would say, of course, you must go to London and try and form your band. Of course you will be successful. That is what Tilo would say to you. Because that is his way.'

'And what would you say?'

'I would like to say the same. Because you are young and talented. But I am not so certain. As it is, life will bring enough disappointments. If on top, you have such dreams as this ...' She smiled again and shrugged. 'But I should not say these things. I am not a good example to you. Besides, I can see you are much more like Tilo. If disappointments do come, you will carry on still. You will say, just as he does, I am so lucky.' For a few seconds, she went on gazing at me, like she was memorising the way I looked. The breeze was blowing her hair about, making her seem older than she usually did. 'I wish you much luck,' she said finally.

'Good luck yourself,' I said. 'And I hope you two make it up okay.'

She waved a last time, then went off down the path out of my view.

I took the guitar from its case and sat back on the bench. I didn't play anything for a while though, because I was looking into the distance, towards Worcestershire Beacon, and Tilo's tiny figure up on the incline. Maybe it was to do with the way the sun was hitting that part of the hill, but I could see him much more clearly now than before, even though he'd got further away. He'd paused for a moment on the path, and seemed to be looking about him at the surrounding hills, almost like he was trying to reappraise them. Then his figure started to move again.

I worked on my song for a few minutes, but kept losing concentration, mainly because I was thinking about the way Hag Fraser's face must have looked as Sonja laid into her that morning. Then I gazed at the clouds, and at the sweep of land below me, and I made myself think, again about my song, and the bridge passage I still hadn't got right.

Notes

1. Malvern Hills: a range of hills in the western England, mainly within English counties of Worcestershire, Herefordshire. The highest point is Worcestershire Beacon, a hill rising to 425 meters.
2. interlude: a period of time between two events or activities during which something different happens
3. paranoid: unreasonably suspicious or anxious
4. Camden Town: an important district in London, where businesses like retail, tourism and entertainment flourish with numerous well-known markets and music venues
5. West End: the shopping and entertainment area in the western part of central London
6. audition: a short performance given by a singer, actor, etc., as a test of their ability or suitability
7. shambolic: completely disordered; chaotic
8. acoustic: (of a musical instrument) making natural sound, without being amplified by electrical instruments
9. vocal: the part of a song which is sung
10. harmony: the way in which different musical notes are played or sung at the same time for a pleasing effect
11. amp: an amplifier, an electrical device to make sound louder
12. number: a song or dance, as part of a longer performance

13. umpteenth: a lot of
14. wanker: an expression used to insult somebody, especially a man
15. Great Malvern: the chief town and administrative centre of Malvern Hills district in Worcestershire, England. It is a market and resort town and a local cultural center.
16. A road: a road, in Britain, which is less important than a motorway, but wider and straighter than a B road
17. Herefordshire: a historic county in the western England
18. Geoff: the brother-in-law of the narrator in the story
19. brigade: a group of people similar in some way
20. make a point of: to make a special effort to do something necessary or important
21. strum: play (a musical instrument) by moving one's fingers up or down the strings
22. Pershore: a market town of the county of Worcestershire in England
23. claustrophobia: irrational fear of being in a small enclosed space
24. grill: ask someone many questions, often in an unpleasant way
25. bollocking: shouting at me and telling me that she is angry with me
26. gospel: the absolute truth
27. swat: hit with a hand or a flat object
28. cash-and-carry: a system of buying and selling goods, by which goods in large quantities are paid at low prices at once and taken away by the buyer
29. Elgar Route: a circular route containing many landmarks associated with Edward Elgar (1857—1934), who is an English composer.
30. hold the fort: look after everything when someone else is temporarily away
31. Kraut: an insulting expression for a person from Germany
32. ploughman's: or ploughman's lunch, a simple meal of bread and cheese, pickle and salad, often served in a pub
33. mayo: or mayonnaise, which is a thick cold yellowish sauce used to add flavor to salads or other cold food
34. baguette: or French loaf, which is a long, narrow loaf of white bread
35. parasol: a light umbrella to protect people from the sun
36. trainer: a shoe for sports or casual wear
37. tune out: stop paying attention
38. Abba: a Swedish pop group which was formed in 1972 and broke up in 1982. Abba is an acronym of the first letters of the group members' first names.
39. perturbed: disturbed
40. reflex: an action performed without thinking
41. livid: very angry
42. notch: a degree or level on a scale
43. stumped: asked someone a question too difficult to answer
44. incline: a slope
45. quip: a quick and amusing remark
46. pull a fast one on them: deceive them

47. get even with me: cause me the same amount of trouble as I had caused them
48. doodle: a picture, or anything, produced aimlessly
49. lovey-dovey: excessively romantic
50. snuggled: settled into a comfortable position
51. clarinet: a musical instrument of the woodwind group (单簧管)
52. Janáček: a Czech composer
53. Vaughan Williams: an English composer
54. Interlaken: a well-known tourist destination in Switzerland
55. Höheweg: a street in Interlaken
56. the Eiger: a mountain in the western part of the Alps in Switzerland
57. the Mönch: a mountain in the western part of the Alps in Switzerland
58. the Jungfrau: a mountain in the western part of the Alps in Switzerland. The word "Jungfrau" means "maiden".
59. Düsseldorf: a city in Germany, an international business and financial center. In the story this is where Peter, the son of Toli and Sonja, lives.
60. pull one's finger out: start to work hard
61. Sugarloaf: a hill in the area
62. course: flow quickly
63. moron: a stupid person
64. face the music: to confront the unpleasant consequences of one's actions
65. Worcestershire Beacon: also known as the Beacon, which is the highest point of the range of Malvern Hills
66. irate: very angry
67. proprietress: the owner of a business

Questions

1. In the light of Ishiguro's intention of writing "international novels", does this story contain "a vision of life that is of importance to people of varied backgrounds around the world"?
2. The subtitle of the collection *Nocturnes: Five Stories of Music and Nightfall* highlights two words "music" and "nightfall". What role do they play for the story taking place in "Malvern Hills"?
3. The first-person narration is one of distinctive techniques preferred by Ishiguro. How is this point of view conducive to the plot of the story? What difference will it make if another perspective is employed?

Chapter Ten   Utopia and Dystopia

The term "utopia" designates an idealized and nonexistent society or community. The term, which literally means "no place", was first coined by Sir Thomas More in his Latin masterpiece *Utopia*, in which More creates his ideal island state. An idea of human life, utopia is a subject of interest for various disciplines, such as history, philosophy, politics, sociology, and literature. In literature, utopian longing for a better world can be traced back to ancient classics, but the first greatest example of the literary utopias is the city in Plato's *Republic*, in which a perfect commonwealth is set forth. Demonstrating social, political, and religious perfection, most literary utopias set their stable and orderly society or community in a remote land reached by an adventurous traveler and aim ultimately at social and technological progress in the actual world. Notable examples of utopian visions include Tommaso Campanella's *City of the Sun* (1623), Francis Bacon's *New Atlantis* (1627), Edward Bellamy's *Looking Backward* (1888), William Morris' *News from Nowhere* (1891), and James Hilton's *Lost Horizon* (1934).

The term "dystopia", opposite of "utopia", represents an undesirable and frightening imaginary world. Literary dystopias, initially emerging by the end of the nineteenth century, dramatize the menacing tendencies of social, political, and technological order in the present society into disastrous scenarios and aim at a warning to the readers. Denying the possibility of a better future, they often feature dehumanization, totalitarian governments, environmental disasters, or other forms of decline in society. Representative works of this category include Samuel Butler's *Erewhon* (1872), Aldous Huxley's *Brave New World* (1932), George Orwell's *1984* (1949), and Yevgeny Zamyatin's *We* (1921), Anthony Burgess' *A Clockwork Orange* (1962), and Margaret Atwood's *The Handmaid's Tale* (1985).

As an essential part of world literature, English literature has nurtured its own utopian and dystopian creations, addressing a wide range of topics, among which are the issues concerning political and social systems, economic institutions, legal systems, religion, communal living, science, and technology, environment problems, and women's role in society, the attitude towards education and that towards the family. To bring their social force into full play, English utopias and dystopias have been woven with the aid of varied literary devices. Either positive or negative fictional systems, they assume the role of a satiric force zeroing in on the present society and human life. By contrasting the present world with the fictional one, they criticize the values and conditions of the actual society. Of the four selected works in this chapter, More's *Utopia* satirizes the conditions in the England in his day; Swift's *Gulliver's Travels* examines the strengths and weaknesses of mankind and reflects on the political, economic, and social conditions as well as the prevailing philosophical and scientific thoughts of his time; Wells, in *The Time Machine*, reflects critically on the social and technological concerns of his day; Orwell attacks the corruption and lies in his *Animal Farm*. In addition, other devices for characterization and plot development, such as shipwrecks, accidents in space, the narrative techniques of the fable, the fantasy, and the science fiction, are carefully applied by their creators in these utopian and dystopian works so as to present distinctive models for possible consideration and imitation on the part of readers.

Thomas More
1478—1535

Thomas More

Thomas More, an English essayist, poet, dialogue writer, a statesman, saint, and humanist, was born in London in 1478. His father, Sir John More, was a barrister. More first went to St. Anthony's School in Threadneedle Street and then was sent to the household of John Morton, archbishop of Canterbury and Lord Chancellor, who sent this exceedingly promising page to Oxford University in about 1492. At the university, More devoted himself to study and soon became well versed in the classics, French, history, mathematics, and music. Nevertheless, possibly pressured by his father, More left Oxford two years later and studied law in London, and eventually became a lawyer. He excelled inside and outside the legal community, meanwhile trying his hand at literary creation. He broadened and deepened his acquaintanceship with distinguished scholars, like Dutch humanist Desiderius Erasmus. From 1499 to 1503, driven by his intention of becoming a priest, More shifted to four years of ascetic life, living in the Carthusian monastery, at the end of which he decided to serve God and his fellowmen as a lay Christian. In 1504 he was elected to parliament.

In 1510 More was made Under-Sheriff of London and was highly esteemed as an impartial judge and the patron of the poor. His unusual abilities made him a member of royal service and the publication of *Utopia* in 1516 enhanced his reputation in Europe. Knighted in 1521, he was offered important positions one after another, sub-treasurer, Speaker of the House of Commons, Chancellor of the Duchy of Lancaster. In October, 1529, he succeeded Wolsey as Chancellor of England. Confronted with Henry VIII's plan to divorce Queen Catherine, and to make himself the supreme head of the English Church, More remained silent and consequently enraged the king. He was imprisoned in the Tower of London in 1534. With false evidence presented, he was tried and convicted of high treason and was beheaded on July 6, 1535. He was beatified by Pople Leo XIII in 1886 and canonized by Pope Pius XI in 1935.

One of the greatest minds of the sixteenth century, More established his literary reputation chiefly on his masterpiece *Utopia*. He also produced influential anti-heretical polemics and devotional works. England in More's day saw the decline of feudalism and the rise of the bourgeoisie, the invigorating influence of the Renaissance and the pervading impact of the Reformation. More's writings, on the whole, reflect the political, economic, religious and cultural transition and contradiction that marked his age and bear testimony to his consistent stance, at different stages of life, of being a man of "exemplary faith, piety and learning". His early works, including poems and biographies, are imbued with humanism, the essence of the Renaissance, which revived the close study of ancient Greek and Roman classics and celebrated the rational capacity of human beings of cultivating themselves and molding the earthly world in the direction of perfection. An eyewitness to the radical societal changes in his day, More accomplished *Utopia*, both an ancestor of utopian literature and a representative work of English humanism, in which More conveyed his hatred of oppression and corruption in actual society, his aspiration for a happy and classless society without poverty and exploitation and his belief in man's potential for goodness and rationality. It has given impetus to many imaginary societies in the upcoming centuries and influenced endeavors at social reforms up to the present century. In addition, More is no less known for his anti-heretical polemics and devotional works, which have evidenced his unwavering exertion of defending the authority of the Catholic Church for all the political and religious turbulence. *Responsio ad Lutherum* (1523), an attack on Martin Luther's response to Henry VIII's defense of the Catholic Church, and *A Dialogue* (1529), a condemnation of the English reformer William Tyndale, are notable examples of his controversial works; *A Treatice upon the Passion of Chryste* and *A Dialogue of Comfort against Tribulation* are best-known among his devotional works.

Utopia

A monument to Renaissance humanism, *Utopia* has presented an ideal state governed by reason, where everything is shared equally and everybody lives in plenty. The word "Utopia" is coined by More, based on two Greek words "outopos" (no place) and "eutopos" (good place). To secure the satirical effect in the work, More has adopted the traditional device of dialogue and integrated fact and fiction so as to expound on his humanist ideals. His visionary literary exploration has inspired more significant creations in literature and social reforms in reality.

The great work comprises Book I and Book II, both through the narration of an experienced traveler Raphael Hythloday. The majority part of the work involves a long conversation between More and Hythloday in a garden in Antwerp. More presents himself in Book I, where he is introduced, by a friend Peter Giles, to Raphael Hythloday, who has traveled to many foreign lands. With his varied exotic experiences and extraordinarily keen insight, Raphael puts forward his observations of foreign lands, especially European nations like England. He criticizes vehemently the different respects of the English society in More's day, such as legal system, war policy, foreign affairs, the enclosing of the land of common people, poverty rampant among common people. Raphael considers these existing systems neither just nor practical. By contrast, he then touches on the justly and happily governed state Utopia, arousing the interest of More. Upon the request of More and Peter, Raphael describes at length the fundamental aspects of the desirable life in Utopia—geography, cities, agriculture, officials, occupations, social and business relations, travel and trade, attitudes towards gold and silver, moral philosophy, people's delight in learning, marriage customs, legal procedures, foreign relations, principles concerning wars, religions—which in all constitute Book II. Although More does not agree with all that is described by Raphael, More does wish some of the Utopian practices would be implemented in his own country.

Originally written in Latin, *Utopia* is characterized with simple, conversational and everyday prose. It has a variety of English translations across time. Among them, Ralph Robynson's 1551 translation stands the test of time and is considered close to the original. The following selections are from the English version translated by Robert M. Adams, who is Professor of English at the University of California at Los Angeles and has also taught at Columbia, and at Wisconsin, Rutgers, and Cornell.

The Geography of Utopia

The island of Utopians is two hundred miles across in the middle part where it is widest, and is nowhere much narrower than this except toward the two ends. These ends, drawn toward one another in a five-hundred-mile circle, make the island crescent-shaped like a new moon. Between the horns of the crescent, which are about eleven miles apart, the sea enters and spreads into a broad bay. Being sheltered from the wind by the surrounding land, the bay is never rough, but quiet and smooth instead, like a big lake. Thus, nearly the whole inner coast is one great harbor, across which ships pass in every direction, to the great advantage of the people. What with[1] shallows[2] on one side, and rocks on the other, the entrance into the bay is very dangerous. Near the middle of the channel, there is one rock that rises above the water, and so presents no dangers in itself; on top of it a tower has been built, and there a garrison[3] is kept. Since the other rocks lie under water, they are very dangerous to navigation. The channels are known only to the Utopians, so hardly any strangers enter the bay without one of their pilots; and even they themselves could not enter safely if they did not direct themselves by some landmarks on the coast. If they should shift these landmarks about, they could lure[4] to destruction an enemy fleet coming against them, however big it was.

On the outer side of the island there are likewise occasional harbors; but the coast is rugged by nature, and so well fortified that a few defenders could beat off the attack of a strong force. They say (and the appearance of the place confirms this) that their land was not always an island. But Utopus, who conquered the country and gave it his name (it had previously been called Abraxa[5]), brought its rude and uncouth[6] inhabitants to such a high level of culture and humanity that they now excel in that regard almost every other people. After subduing them at his first landing, he cut a channel fifteen miles wide where their land joined the continent, and caused the sea to flow around the country. He put not only the natives to work at this task, but all his own soldiers too, so that the vanquished[7] would not think the labor a disgrace. With the work divided among so many hands, the project was finished quickly, and the neighboring peoples, who at first had laughed at his folly, were struck with wonder and terror at his success.

There are fifty-four cities on the island, all spacious and magnificent, identical in language, customs, institutions, and laws. So far as the location permits, all of them are built on the same plan, and have the same appearance. The nearest are at least twenty-four miles apart, and the farthest are not so remote that a man cannot go on foot from one to the other in a day.

Once a year each city sends three of its old and experienced citizens to Amaurot[8] to consider affairs of common interest to the island. Amaurot is the chief city, lies near the omphalos[9] of the land, so to speak[10], and convenient to every other district, so it acts as a capital. Every city has enough ground assigned to it so that at least ten miles of farm land are available in every direction, though where the cities are farther apart, they have much more land. No city wants to enlarge its boundaries, for the inhabitants consider themselves good tenants rather than landlords. At proper intervals all over the countryside they have built houses and furnished them with farm equipment. These houses are inhabited by citizens who come to the country by turns to occupy them. No rural house has fewer than forty men and women in it, besides two slaves. A master and mistress, serious and mature persons, are in charge of each household. Over every thirty households is placed a single phylarch[11]. Each year twenty persons from each rural household move back to the city, after completing a two-year stint[12] in the country. In their place, twenty others are sent out from town, to learn farm work from those who have already been in the country for a year, and who are better skilled in farming. They, in turn, will teach those who come the following year. If all were equally ignorant of farm work, and new to it, they might harm the crops out of ignorance. This custom of alternating farm workers is solemnly established so that no one will have to do such hard work against his will for more than two years; but many of them who take a natural pleasure in farm life ask to stay longer.

The farm workers till the soil, raise cattle, hew[13] wood, and take it to the city by land or water, as is most convenient. They breed an enormous number of chickens by a marvelous method. Men, not hens, hatch the eggs by keeping them in a warm place at an even temperature. As soon as they come out of the shell, the chicks recognize the men, follow them around, and are devoted to them instead of to their real mothers.

They raise very few horses, and these full of mettle[14], which they keep only to exercise the young men in the art of horsemanship. For the heavy work of plowing and hauling they use oxen, which they agree are inferior to horses over the short haul, but which can hold out longer under heavy burdens, are less subject to disease (as they suppose), and so can be kept with less cost and trouble. Moreover, when oxen are too old for work, they can be used for meat.

Grain they use only to make bread. They drink wine, apple or pear cider, or simple water, which they sometimes mix with honey or licorice, of which they have an abundance. Although they know very well, down to the last detail, how much grain each city and its surrounding district will consume, they produce much more grain and cattle than they need for themselves, and share the surplus with their neighbors. Whatever goods the folk in the country need which cannot be produced there, they request of the town magistrates, and since there is nothing to be paid or exchanged, they get what they want at once, without any haggling[15]. They generally go to town once a month in any case, to observe the holy days. When harvest time approaches, the phylarchs in the country notify the town-magistrates how many hands will be needed. Crews of harvesters come just when they're wanted, and in one day of good weather they can usually get in the whole crop.

Their Occupations

Agriculture is the one occupation at which everyone works, men and women alike, with no exceptions. They are trained in it from childhood, partly in the schools where they learn theory, and partly through field trips to nearby farms, which make something like a game of practical instruction. On these trips they not only watch the work being done, but frequently pitch in and get a workout by doing the jobs themselves.

Besides farm work (which, as I said, everybody performs), each person is taught a particular trade of his own, such as wool-working, linen-making, masonry[16], metal-work, or carpentry. There is no other craft that is practiced by any considerable number of them. Throughout the island people wear, and down through the centuries they have always worn, the same style of clothing, except for the distinction between the sexes, and between married and unmarried persons. Their clothing is attractive, does not hamper bodily movement, and serves for warm as well as cold weather; what is more, each household can make its own.

Every person (and this includes women as well as men) learns a second trade, besides agriculture. As the weaker sex, women practice the lighter crafts, such as working in wool or linen; the heavier crafts are assigned to the men. As a rule, the son is trained to his father's craft, for which most feel a natural inclination. But if anyone is attracted to another occupation, he is transferred by adoption into a family practicing the trade he prefers. When anyone makes such a change, both his father and the authorities make sure that he is assigned to a grave and responsible householder. After a man has learned one trade, if he wants to learn another, he gets the same permission. When he has learned both, he pursues whichever he likes better, unless the city needs one more than the other.

The chief and almost the only business of the syphogrants[17] is to manage matters so that no one sits around in idleness, and assure that everyone works hard at his trade. But no one has to exhaust himself with endless toil from early morning to late at night, as if he were a beast of burden. Such wretchedness, really worse than slavery, is the common lot of workmen in all countries, except Utopia. Of the day's twenty-four hours, the Utopians devote only six to work. They work three hours before noon, when they go to dinner. After dinner they rest for a couple of hours, then go to work for another three hours. Then they have supper, and at eight o'clock (counting the first hour after noon as one), they go to bed and sleep eight hours.

The other hours of the day, when they are not working, eating, or sleeping, are left to each man's individual discretion[18], provided he does not waste them in roistering[19] or sloth[20], but uses them busily in some occupation that pleases him. Generally these periods are devoted to intellectual activity. For they have an established custom of giving public lectures before daybreak; attendance at these lectures is required only of those who have been specially chosen to devote themselves to learning, but a great many other people, both men and women, choose voluntarily to attend. Depending on their interests, some go to one lecture, some to another. But if anyone would rather devote his spare time to his trade, as many do who don't care for the intellectual life, this is not discouraged; in fact, such persons are commended as especially useful to the commonwealth.

After supper, they devote an hour to recreation, in their gardens when the weather is fine, or during winter weather in the common halls where they have their meals. There they either play music or amuse themselves with conversation. They know nothing about gambling with dice, or other such foolish and ruinous games. They do play two games not unlike our own chess. One is a battle of numbers, in which one number captures another. The other is a game in which the vices fight a battle against the virtues. The game is set up to show how the vices oppose one another, yet readily combine against the virtues; then what vices oppose what virtues, how they try to assault them openly or undermine them in secret; how the virtues can break the strength of the vices or turn their purposes to good; and finally, by what means one side or the other gains the victory.

But in all this, you may get a wrong impression, if we don't go back and consider one point more carefully. Because they allot only six hours to work, you might think the necessities of life would be in scant[21] supply. This is far from the case. Their working hours are ample to provide not only enough but more than enough of the necessities and even the conveniences of life. You will easily appreciate this if you consider how large a part of the population in other countries exists without doing any work at all. In the first place, hardly any of the women, who are a full half of the population, work; or, if they do, then as a rule their husbands lie snoring[22] in the bed. Then there is a great lazy gang of priests and so-called religious men. Add to them all the rich, especially the landlords, who are commonly called gentlemen and nobility. Include with them their retainers[23], that mob of swaggering[24] bullies. Finally, reckon in[25] with these the sturdy[26] and lusty[27] beggars, who go about feigning[28] some disease as an excuse for their idleness. You will certainly find that the things which satisfy our needs are produced by far fewer hands than you had supposed.

And now consider how few of those who do work are doing really essential things. For where money is the standard of everything, many superfluous[29] traders are bound to be carried on simply to satisfy luxury and licentiousness[30]. Suppose the multitude of those who now work were limited to a few trades, and set to producing more and more of those conveniences and commodities that nature really requires. They would be bound to produce so much that the prices would drop, and the workmen would be unable to gain a living. But suppose again that all the workers in useless trades were put to useful ones, and that all the idlers (who now guzzle[31] twice as much as the workingmen who make what they consume) were assigned to productive tasks — well, you can easily see how little time each man would have to spend working, in order to produce all the goods that human needs and conveniences require — yes, and human pleasure too, as long as it's true and natural pleasure.

The experience of Utopia makes this perfectly apparent. In each city and its surrounding countryside barely five hundred of those men and women whose age and strength make them fit for work are exempted from it. Among these are the syphogrants, who by law are free not to work; yet they don't take advantage of the privilege, preferring to set a good example to their fellow citizens. Some others are permanently exempted from work so that they may devote themselves to study, but only on the recommendation of the priests and through a secret vote of the syphogrants. If any of these scholars disappoints their hopes, he becomes a workman again. On the other hand, it happens from time to time that a craftsman devotes his leisure so earnestly to study, and makes such progress as a result, that he is relieved of manual labor, and promoted to the class of learned men. From this class of scholars are chosen ambassadors, priests, tranibors[32], and the prince himself, who used to be called Barzanes[33], but in their modern tongue is known as Ademus[34]. Since all the rest of the population is neither idle nor occupied in useless trades, it is easy to see why they produce so much in so short a working day.

Apart from all this, in several of the necessary crafts their way of life requires less total labor than does that of people elsewhere. In other countries, building and repairing houses requires the constant work of many men, because what a father has built, his thriftless heir lets fall into ruin; and then his successor has to repair, at great expense, what could easily have been maintained at a very small charge. Further, even when a man has built a splendid house at large cost, someone else may think he has finer taste, let the first house fall to ruin, and then build another one somewhere else for just as much money. But among the Utopians, where everything has been established, and the commonwealth is carefully regulated, building a brand-new home on a new site is a rare event. They are not only quick to repair damage, but foresighted in preventing it. The result is that their buildings last for a very long time with minimum repairs; and the carpenters and masons sometimes have so little to do, that they are set to hewing timber and cutting stone in case some future need for it should arise.

Consider, too, how little labor their clothing requires. Their work clothes are loose garments made of leather which last as long as seven years. When they go out in public, they cover these rough working-clothes with a cloak. Throughout the entire island, everyone wears the same colored cloak, which is the color of natural wool. As a result, they not only need less wool than people in other countries, but what they do need is less expensive. They use linen cloth most, because it requires least labor. They like linen cloth to be white and wool cloth to be clean; but they put no price on fineness of texture. Elsewhere a man is not satisfied with four or five woolen cloaks of different colors and as many silk shirts, or if he's a show-off, even then of each are not enough. But a Utopian is content with a single cloak, and generally wears it for two seasons. There is no reason at all why he should want any others, for it he had them, he would not be better protected against the cold, nor would he appear in any way better dressed.

When there is an abundance of everything, as a result of everyone working at useful trades, and nobody consuming to excess, then great numbers of the people often go out to work on the roads, if any of them need repairing. And when there is no need even for this sort of public work, then the officials very often proclaim a shorter work day, since they never force their citizens to perform useless labor. The chief aim of their constitution and government is that, whenever public needs permit, all citizens should be free, so far as possible, to withdraw their time and energy from the service of the body, and devote themselves to the freedom and culture of the mind. For that, they think, is the real happiness of life.

Notes

1. What with: Because of
2. shallows: a shallow area in a river, a lake or the sea
3. garrison: a group of soldiers who guard a place or fort
4. lure: tempt
5. Abraxa: the Greek letters comprising this word have numerical equivalents which amount to 356.
6. uncouth: not having good manners
7. vanquished: defeated completely

8. Amaurot: the city of the most significance in Utopia. The narrator Raphael in the book lived there for five full years.
9. omphalos: the center of something
10. so to speak: as one might say
11. phylarch: head of a tribe. The word is from the Greek.
12. stint: a fixed period of time for a particular activity
13. hew: cut with an axe
14. mettle: the determination to do something successfully despite difficulties
15. haggling: arguing in order to fix a price
16. masonry: the craft of cutting and preparing stone for building
17. syphogrant: an equivalent for the word "phylarch" [see note 11]. Both of the words refer to officials in Utopia, as Raphael Hythloday narrates in another section of Book II of *Utopia*: "Once a year, every group of thirty households elects an official, formerly called the syphogrant, but now called the phylarch."
18. discretion: the right or ability to decide what should be done on a particular occasion
19. roister: have fun noisily
20. sloth: laziness
21. scant: hardly sufficient
22. snore: breathe noisily through one's nose and mouth when one is sleeping
23. retainer: a servant, especially one who has worked for a person or family for a long time
24. swaggering: walking or behaving in an extremely arrogant way
25. reckon in: include
26. sturdy: strong and healthy
27. lusty: strong, healthy and energetic
28. feign: pretend to have
29. superfluous: more than is necessary
30. licentiousness: the state of being sexually unrestrained
31. guzzle: eat or drink eagerly, quickly
32. tranibor: the title for an official senior to a syphorant, as is described in one section of Book II of Utopia: "Over every group of ten syphogrants with their households there is another official, once called the tranibor but now known as the head phylarch."
33. Barzanes: Son of Zeus
34. Ademus: without people

Questions

1. Have you ever thought about engaging in farming? Is the practice of agriculture in Utopia inviting to you? Concerning the issue of whether to live to work or to work to live, what is the choice by Utopians? For Utopians, what does the real happiness of life consist in?
2. The representation of the land of Utopia, an ideal and nonexistent political and social way of life, is a vehicle for satire on the society in More's day. Are those descriptions enlightening for us today?

3. In the notes to his English translation of *Utopia*, Robert M. Adams compares translations to mistresses: "the faithful ones are apt to be ugly, and the beautiful ones false". Compare one part of Adams' translation, for instance, the beginning part of Book II, *Utopia*, with that accomplished by Ralph Robynson and think about the role translators play in the transmission and promotion of influential thoughts and literature legacy.

Jonathan Swift
1667—1745

Jonathan Swift

Jonathan Swift, an Anglo-Irish satirist, essayist, poet, a prominent political and religious figure in his day, was born in Ireland on November 30, 1667, shortly after the unexpected death of his father. Later on his mother had been absent from his life for some time. He was thus left in the care of relatives. However, he was well-educated, first at Kilkenny School, the best in Ireland, and then at Trinity College of Dublin. He received the Bachelor of Arts degree in 1686. Under the uncertain political situation after the Glorious Revolution, he went to England where he served as secretary to Sir William Temple, a scholar and former member of Parliament, living at Temple's home Moor Park.

At Moor Park Swift read widely in Temple's rich library, and tried his hand at literary creation. From 1694 to 1696, he made two trips to Ireland. When Temple died in 1699, Swift returned to Ireland as a chaplain and secretary to the Earl of Berkeley. From 1699 to 1710, he shuttled between Dublin and London and produced a lot of writings in support of his Whig political beliefs in this course and his consistent religious ones in Anglican Church. His works were popular, especially those published under the pseudonym of Isaac Bickerstaff. When the Whig fell and was substituted by the Tory ministry, with those political beliefs already being questioned, he was won over by the Tories and became the Tory ministry's chief political writer. He edited the journal *The Examiner* from 1710 to 1711. After the Whigs came into power again, Swift returned to Ireland in 1714, and assumed his role as a dean at St. Patrick's Cathedral in Dublin. Apart from short visits to London, he spent the rest of his life in Ireland. He died in 1745 and was buried in St. Patrick's Cathedral.

As for his literary career, Swift is chiefly remembered as one of greatest satirists in world literature. He defined "satire" as "a sort of glass wherein beholders do generally discover everybody's face but their own, which is the chief reason for that kind of reception it meets in the world, and that so very few are offended with it." He employed it to scrutinize both the strengths and weaknesses of individuals and society. Among his satirical works, the most prestigious are the following: his earlier writings *A Tale of a Tub* (1704) and *The Battle of the Books* (1704), the former a satire on chief sects of Christianity as well as literary and scholarly pedants of his day and the latter a debate between the ancient Greek and Roman learning and the modern learning; his pamphlets on Ireland *The Drapier's Letters* (1724) which calls on Irish people to boycott the new copper coins with reduced value imposed by the English government and *A Modest Proposal* (1729) which ironically suggests the impoverished Irish people relieving themselves from the increasingly severe conditions by eating their own children; and his masterpiece *Gulliver's Travels* (1726). When it comes to the utopian literary tradition, *Gulliver's Travels* unquestionably stands out as a representative of the eighteenth century utopian works. In the period of burgeoning English Enlightenment, a progressive intellectual movement with more emphasis on "reason" rather than "emotion", Swift, like other enlighteners, considered the "enlightenment" of the people his bounden duty. He dramatized the contrasts between what he thought constituted proper moral standards and social justice and the actual practices of the bourgeoisie-aristocratic society of his day by weaving both utopian and dystopian elements into the depictions of Gulliver's unexpected travels in those imaginary lands in order to propose a hint of the direction of progress beyond his physical English society.

An eminent prose satirist in the English language, Swift distinguishes his works with his signature satiric techniques such as a literary voice in disguise, exaggeration, dramatized examples, vivid comparisons, abundant concrete details, irony, understatement, all of these serving as a vehicle for his faith, intelligence and his hope for humankind.

Gulliver's Travels

In his greatest work *Gulliver's Travels*, Swift demonstrates his brilliant satirical power by touching on a wide range of subjects, involving the accomplishments and shortcomings of humankind and the political, economic, and social conditions of his time as well as the philosophical and scientific thoughts that then prevailed, through which his insightful views on the power of reason and human society are communicated. With both utopian and dystopian aspects, the work itself comprises four parts revolving around the narrator Lemuel Gulliver, a surgeon in the beginning and a captain in the end, who voyaged to "several remote nations of the world" over about sixteen years and seven months. Swift considers all Gulliver's travels admirable things and likely to mend the physical world.

In part I "A Voyage to Lilliput", Gulliver, after surviving a shipwreck, finds himself in a kingdom where inhabitants stand not more than six inch high. Gulliver has been confined for some time before finally granted conditional liberty. He doesn't intend to involve himself in the violent faction between the two parties which distinguish each other by the height of their shoe heels. In the war against another empire Blefuscu, which takes advantage of the debate in the Lilliput over whether to break eggs on large ends or small ones, Gulliver serves the Lilliput emperor and prevents an invasion intended by Blefuscu, but doesn't help with the emperor's plan to make that country a province of his own kingdom. When a scheme is forming against him, Gulliver flees Lilliput.

In part II "A Voyage to Brobdingnag", Gulliver is left behind by other sailors on an unknown island of giants. A farmer takes tiny Gulliver home and later shows him through half of the kingdom for money before finally selling him to the queen, who is passionately fond of Gulliver. Glumdalclitch, his nine-year-old daughter, on the other hand, takes great care of Gulliver all through the way and afterwards. In favor with both the king and the queen, Gulliver lives a happy life despite some troublesome accidents. He stands up for the honor of England when the king asks him of England and then makes negative remarks. Gulliver leaves the kingdom Brobdingnag accidentally when an eagle takes away the travelling-box Gulliver is in and drops it to the sea.

In part III "A Voyage to Laputa, Balnibarbi, Luggnagg, Glubbdubdrib, and Japan", Gulliver visits more nations. At the flying island of Laputa, people, with shapes, habits and appearances distinctive as a race, are obsessed with mathematics and music. Gulliver learns about the theories of the floating of the island and the methods the king would resort to to suppress the towns below. At Balnibarbi, a continent below the flying island, Gulliver is baffled by the poorly-cultivated land, strangely-built houses and miserable-looking people until he is allowed to visit the Grand Academy of Lagado, where researchers indulge themselves in whimsical projects such as extracting sun beam out of cucumbers, reducing human excrement to its original food, changing ice into gunpowder. During a short voyage to Glubbdubdrib, a small island, Gulliver encounters a tribe of magicians. Assisted by the magic practiced by the governor, he interviews the spirits of many historical celebrities such as Alexander the Great, Caesar, Homer, Aristotle, Descartes. At the kingdom of Luggnagg, Gulliver hears about the horrifying lives of struldbruggs, immortal beings of the kingdom, before seeing them in person. He is consequently disillusioned with the long-held dream of enjoying a perpetual life.

In part IV "A Voyage to the Country of the Houyhnhnms", Gulliver sets out as Captain of a ship. His men conspire against him so he is left alone in an unknown land where the Houyhnhnms, a species of rational, virtuous, intelligent horses, preside over the nation. He finds another distinct breed inhabiting the same land, Yahoos, the savage, ugly, ignorant ape-like humans. He is so amazed at all virtues, such as friendship, benevolence, order and harmony, displayed by the Houyhnhnms that he is eager to live there for the rest of the life. However, he has to leave on the request of his horse master for the purity of the horse country. He leaves with infinite regret.

The selections below are all from part IV "A Voyage to the Country of the Houyhnhnms", an utopian land of reason in the eyes of Gulliver. Chapter II describes Gulliver's first meeting with a horse family after he finds himself in the country of the Houyhnhnms, chapter IV narrates Gulliver's talks with his horse master about some concepts, the horses and his fellowmen in England, and the excerpt from chapter VIII includes Gulliver's accounts of the virtues of the Houyhnhnms, and some customs of the Houyhnhnms' country.

Chapter II

[The author conducted by a Houyhnhnm to his house. The house described. The author's

reception. The food of the Houyhnhnms. The author in distress for want of meat, is at last relieved. His manner of feeding in that country.]

Having travelled about three miles, we came to a long kind of building, made of timber stuck in the ground, and wattled¹ across; the roof was low, and covered with straw. I now began to be a little comforted, and took out some toys, which travellers usually carry for presents to the savage Indians of America and other parts, in hopes the people of the house would be thereby encouraged to receive me kindly. The horse made me a sign to go in first; it was a large room with a smooth clay floor, and a rack and manger extending the whole length on one side. There were three nags², and two mares³, not eating, but some of them sitting down upon their hams⁴, which I very much wondered at; but wondered more to see the rest employed in domestic business. They seemed but ordinary cattle; however, this confirmed my first opinion, that a people who could so far civilize brute animals must needs⁵ excel in wisdom all the nations of the world. The grey came in just after, and thereby prevented any ill treatment which the others might have given me. He neighed⁶ to them several times in a style of authority, and received answers.

Beyond this room, there were three others, reaching the length of the house, to which you passed through three doors, opposite to each other, in the manner of a vista; we went through the second room towards the third; here the grey walked in first, beckoning me to attend: I waited in the second room, and got ready my presents for the master and mistress of the house: they were two knives, three bracelets of false pearl, a small looking-glass and a bead necklace. The horse neighed three or four times, and I waited to hear some answers in a human voice, but I heard no other returns than in the same dialect, only one or two a little shriller than his. I began to think that this house must belong to some person of great note⁷ among them, because there appeared so much ceremony before I could gain admittance. But that a man of quality should be served all by horses was beyond my comprehension. I feared my brain was disturbed by my sufferings and misfortunes: I roused myself, and looked about me in the room where I was left alone; this was furnished as the first, only after a more elegant manner. I rubbed my eyes often, but the same objects still occurred. I pinched my arms and sides, to awake myself, hoping I might be in a dream. I then absolutely concluded, that all these appearances could be nothing else but necromancy⁸ and magic. But I had no time to pursue these reflections; for the grey horse came to the door, and made me a sign to follow him into the third room, where I saw a very comely⁹ mare, together with a colt and foal¹⁰, sitting on their haunches¹¹, upon mats of straw, not unartfully made, and perfectly neat and clean.

The mare, soon after my entrance, rose from her mat, and coming up close, after having nicely observed my hands and face, gave me a most contemptuous look; and turning to the horse, I heard the word *Yahoo* often repeated betwixt¹² them; the meaning of which word I could not then comprehend, although it were the first I had learned to pronounce; but I was soon better informed, to my everlasting mortification¹³: for the horse beckoning to me with his head, and repeating the word *hhuun, hhuun,* as he did upon the road, which I understood was to attend him, led me out into a kind of court, where was another building at some distance from the house. Here we entered, and I saw three of those detestable creatures, which I first met after my landing, feeding upon roots, and the flesh of some animals, which I afterwards found to be that of asses and dogs, and now and then a cow dead by accident or disease. They were all tied by the neck with strong withes[14], fastened to a beam; they held their food between the claws of their forefeet, and tore it with their teeth.

The master horse ordered a sorrel[15] nag, one of his servants, to untie the largest of these animals, and take him into the yard. The beast and I were brought close together, and our countenances diligently compared, both by master and servant, who thereupon repeated several times the word *Yahoo*. My horror and astonishment are not to be described, when I observed, in this abominable animal, a perfect human figure; the face of it indeed was flat and broad, the nose depressed, the lips large, and the mouth wide. But these differences are common to all savage nations, where the lineaments[16] of the countenance are distorted by the natives suffering their infants to lie grovelling[17] on the earth, or by carrying them on their backs, nuzzling with their face against the mothers' shoulders. The forefeet of the *Yahoo* differed from my hands in nothing else but the length of the nails, the coarseness and brownness of the palms, and the hairiness on the backs. There was the same resemblance between our feet, with the same differences, which I knew very well, although the horses did not, because of my shoes and stockings; the same in every part of our bodies, except as to hairiness and colour, which I have already described.

The great difficulty that seemed to stick with the two horses, was, to see the rest of my body so very different from that of a Yahoo, for which I was obliged[18] to my clothes, whereof they had no conception: the sorrel nag offered me a root, which he held (after their manner, as we shall describe in its proper place) between his hoof[19] and pastern[20]; I took it in my hand, and having smelt it, returned it to him again as civilly as I could. He brought out of the Yahoos' kennel a piece of ass's flesh, but it smelt so offensively that I turned from it with loathing: he then threw it to the Yahoo, by whom it was greedily devoured. He afterwards showed me a wisp of hay, and a fetlock[21] full of oats; but I shook my head, to signify, that neither of these were food for me. And indeed, I now apprehended, that I must absolutely starve, if I did not get to some of my own species: for as to those filthy Yahoos, although there were few greater lovers of mankind, at that time, than myself; yet I confess I never saw any sensitive being so detestable on all accounts; and the more I came near them, the more hateful they grew, while I stayed in that country. This the master horse observed by my behaviour, and therefore sent the Yahoo back to his kennel. He then put his fore-hoof to his mouth, at which I was much surprised, although he did it with ease, and with a motion that appeared perfectly natural, and made other signs to know what I would eat; but I could not return him such an answer as he was able to apprehend; and if he had understood me, I did not see how it was possible to contrive any way for finding myself nourishment. While we were thus engaged, I observed a cow passing by, whereupon I pointed to her, and expressed a desire to let me go and milk her. This had its effect; for he led me back into the house, and ordered a mare-servant to open a room, where a good store of milk lay in earthen and wooden vessels, after a very orderly and cleanly manner. She gave me a large bowl full, of which I drank very heartily, and found myself well refreshed.

About noon I saw coming towards the house a kind of vehicle drawn like a sledge by four Yahoos. There was in it an old steed[22], who seemed to be of quality; he alighted[23] with his hind feet forward, having by accident got a hurt in his left forefoot. He came to dine with our horse, who received him with great civility. They dined in the best room, and had oats boiled in milk for the second course, which the old horse ate warm, but the rest cold. Their mangers were placed circular in the middle of the room, and divided into several partitions, round which they sat on their haunches upon bosses of straw. In the middle was a large rack with angles answering to every partition of the manger. So that each horse and mare ate their own hay, and their own mash of oats and milk, with much decency and regularity. The behaviour of the young colt and foal appeared very modest, and that of the master and mistress extremely cheerful and complaisant[24] to their guest. The grey ordered me to stand by him and much discourse passed between him and his friend concerning me, as I found by the stranger's often looking on me, and the frequent repetition of the word Yahoo.

I happened to wear my gloves, which the master grey observing, seemed perplexed, discovering signs of wonder what I had done to my forefeet; he put his hoof three or four times to them, as if he would signify, that I should reduce them to their former shape, which I presently did, pulling off both my gloves, and putting them into my pocket. This occasioned[25] farther talk, and I saw the company was pleased with my behaviour, whereof[26] I soon found the good effects. I was ordered to speak the few words I understood, and while they were at dinner, the master taught me the names for oats, milk, fire, water, and some others: which I could readily pronounce after him, having from my youth a great facility in learning languages.

When dinner was done, the master horse took me aside, and by signs and words made me understand the concern he was in, that I had nothing to eat. Oats in their tongue are called *hlunnh*. This word I pronounced two or three times; for although I had refused them at first, yet upon second thoughts, I considered that I could contrive to make of them a kind of bread, which might be sufficient with milk to keep me alive, till I could make my escape to some other country, and to creatures of my own species. The horse immediately ordered a white mare-servant of his family to bring me a good quantity of oats in a sort of wooden tray. These I heated before the fire as well as I could, and rubbed them till the husks came off, which I made a shift to winnow[27] from the grain; I ground and beat them between two stones, then took water, and made them into a paste or cake, which I toasted at the fire, and ate warm with milk. It was at first a very insipid[28] diet, although common enough in many parts of Europe, but grew tolerable by time; and having been often reduced to hard fare[29] in my life, this was not the first experiment I had made how easily nature is satisfied. And I cannot but[30] observe, that I never had one hour's sickness, while I stayed in this island. It is true, I sometimes made a shift to catch a rabbit, or bird, by springes made of Yahoos' hairs, and I often gathered wholesome herbs, which I boiled, and ate as salads with my bread, and now and then, for a rarity, I made a little butter, and drank the whey[31]. I was at first at a great loss for salt; but custom soon reconciled the want of it; and I am confident that the frequent use of salt among us is an effect of luxury, and was first introduced only as a provocative to drink; except where it is necessary for preserving of flesh in long voyages, or in places remote from great markets. For we observe no animal to be fond of it but man: and as to myself, when I left this country, it was a great while before I could endure the taste of it in anything that I ate.

This is enough to say upon the subject of my diet, wherewith other travellers fill their books, as if the readers were personally concerned whether we fared well[32] or ill. However, it was necessary to mention this matter, lest the world should think it impossible that I could find sustenance for three years in such a country, and among such inhabitants.

When it grew towards evening, the master horse ordered a place for me to lodge in; it was but six yards from the house, and separated from the stable of the Yahoos. Here I got some straw, and covering myself with my own clothes, slept very sound. But I was in a short time better accommodated, as the reader shall know hereafter, when I come to treat more particularly about my way of living.

Chapter IV

[*The Houyhnhnms' notion of truth and falsehood. The author's discourse disapproved by his master. The author gives a more particular account of himself, and the accidents of his voyage.*]

My master heard me with great appearances of uneasiness in his countenance, because *doubting or not believing,* are so little known in this country, that the inhabitants cannot tell how to behave themselves under such circumstances. And I remember in frequent discourses with my master concerning the nature of manhood, in other parts of the world, having occasion to talk of *lying and false representation*, it was with much difficulty that he comprehended what I meant, although he had otherwise a most acute judgment. For he argued thus; that the use of speech was to make us understand one another, and to receive information of facts; now if any one *said the thing which was not,* these ends were defeated; because I cannot properly be said to understand him, and I am so far from receiving information, that he leaves me worse than in ignorance, for I am led to believe a thing *black* when it is *white*, and *short* when it is *long*. And these were all the notions he had concerning that faculty of *lying*, so perfectly well understood, and so universally practised among human creatures.

To return from this digression; when I asserted that the Yahoos were the only governing animals in my country, which my master said was altogether past his conception, he desired to know, whether we had Houyhnhnms among us, and what was their employment: I told him, we had great numbers, that in summer they grazed in the fields, and in winter were kept in houses, with hay and oats, where Yahoo servants were employed to rub their skins smooth, comb their manes[33], pick their feet, serve them with food, and make their beds. I understand you well, said my master, it is now very plain, from all you have spoken, that whatever share of reason the Yahoos pretend to, the Houyhnhnms are your masters; I heartily wish our Yahoos would be so tractable[34]. I begged his Honour would please to excuse me from proceeding any farther, because I was very certain that the account he expected from me would be highly displeasing. But he insisted in commanding me to let him know the best and the worst: I told him, he should be obeyed. I owned[35], that the Houyhnhnms among us, whom we called horses, were the most generous and comely animals we had, that they excelled in strength and swiftness; and when they belonged to persons of quality, employed in travelling, racing, or drawing chariots, they were treated with much kindness and care, till they fell into diseases, or became foundered[36] in the feet; but then they were sold, and used to all kind of drudgery[37] till they died; after which their skins were stripped and sold for what they were worth, and their bodies left to be devoured by dogs and birds of prey. But the common race of horses had not so good fortune, being kept by farmers and carriers and other mean people, who put them to greater labour, and feed them worse. I described, as well as I could, our way of riding, the shape and use of a bridle, a saddle, a spur, and a whip; of harness and wheels. I added, that we fastened plates of a certain hard substance called "iron", at the bottom of their feet, to preserve their hoofs from being broken by the stony ways on which we often travelled.

My master, after some expressions of great indignation, wondered how we dared to venture upon a Houyhnhnm's back, for he was sure, that the weakest servant in his house would be able to shake off the strongest Yahoo, or by lying down, and rolling upon his back, squeeze the brute to death. I answered, that our horses were trained up from three or four years old to the several uses we intended them for; that if any of them proved intolerably vicious, they were employed for carriages, that they were severely beaten while they were young, for any mischievous tricks; that the males, designed for the common use of riding or draught, were generally castrated about two years after their birth, to take down their spirits, and make them more tame and gentle; that they were indeed sensible of rewards and punishments; but his Honour would please to consider, that they had not the least tincture[38] of reason any more than the Yahoos in this country.

It put me to the pains of many circumlocutions[39] to give my master a right idea of what I spoke; for their language doth not abound in variety of words, because their wants and passions are fewer than among us. But it is impossible to express his noble resentment at our savage treatment of the Houyhnhnm race, particularly after I had explained the manner and use of castrating horses among us, to hinder them from propagating[40] their kind, and to render them more servile[41]. He said, if it were possible there could be any country where Yahoos alone were endued[42] with reason, they certainly must be the governing animal, because reason will in time always prevail against brutal strength. But, considering the frame of our bodies, and especially of mine, he thought no creature of equal bulk was so ill contrived for employing that reason in the common offices of life; whereupon he desired to know whether those among whom I lived, resembled me or the Yahoos of his country. I assured him, that I was as well shaped as most of my age; but the younger and the females were much more soft and tender, and the skins of the latter generally as white as milk. He said, I differed indeed from other Yahoos, being much more cleanly, and not altogether so deformed, but in point of real advantage he thought I differed for the worse. That my nails were of no use either to my fore or hinder feet; as to my forefeet, he could not properly call them by that name, for he never observed me to walk upon them; that they were too soft to bear the ground; that I generally went with them uncovered, neither was the covering I sometimes wore on them of the same shape or so strong as that on my feet behind. That I could not walk with any security, for if either of my hinder feet slipped, I must inevitably fall. He then began to find fault with other parts of my body, the flatness of my face, the prominence of my nose, my eyes placed directly in front, so that I could not look on either side without turning my head: that I was not able to feed myself without lifting one of my forefeet to my mouth: and therefore nature had placed those joints to answer that necessity. He knew not what could be the use of those several clefts and divisions in my feet behind; that these were too soft to bear the hardness and sharpness of stones without a covering made from the skin of some other brute; that my whole body wanted a fence against heat and cold, which I was forced to put on and off every day with tediousness and trouble. And lastly, that he observed every animal in this country naturally to abhor the Yahoos, whom the weaker avoided, and the stronger drove from them. So that supposing us to have the gift of reason, he could not see how it were possible to cure that natural antipathy which every creature discovered against us; nor consequently, how we could tame and render them serviceable. However, he would (as he said) debate the matter no farther, because he was more desirous to know my own story, the country, where I was born, and the several actions and events of my life before I came hither[43].

I assured him how extremely desirous I was that he should be satisfied in every point; but I doubted much, whether it would be possible for me to explain myself on several subjects whereof his Honour could have no conception, because I saw nothing in his country to which I could resemble them. That however, I would do my best, and strive to express myself by similitudes[44], humbly desiring his assistance when I wanted proper words, which he was pleased to promise me.

I said, my birth was of honest parents, in an island called England, which was remote from this country as many days' journey as the strongest of his Honour's servants could travel in the annual course of the sun. That I was bred a surgeon, whose trade it is to cure wounds and hurts in the body, got by accident or violence. That my country was governed by a female man, whom we called *queen*. That I left it to get riches, whereby I might maintain myself and family when I should return. That in my last voyage I was commander of the ship, and had about fifty Yahoos under me, many of which died at sea, and I was forced to supply them by others picked out from several nations. That our ship was twice in danger of being sunk; the first time by a great storm, and the second, by striking against a rock. Here my master interposed[45], by asking me, how I could persuade strangers out of different countries to venture with me, after the losses I had sustained, and the hazards I had run. I said, they were fellows of desperate fortunes, forced to fly from the places of their birth, on account of their poverty or their crimes. Some were undone[46] by lawsuits; others spent all they had in drinking, whoring and gaming; others fled for treason; many for murder, theft, poisoning, robbery, perjury[47], forgery, coining false money; for committing rapes or sodomy; for flying from their colours, or deserting to the enemy; and most of them had broken prison; none of these durst[48] return to their native countries for fear of being hanged, or of starving in a jail; and therefore they were under a necessity of seeking a livelihood in other places.

During this discourse, my master was pleased often to interrupt me; I had made use of many circumlocutions in describing to him the nature of the several crimes, for which most of our crew had been forced to fly their country. This labour took up several days' conversation before he was able to comprehend me. He was wholly at a loss to know what could be the use or necessity of practising those vices. To clear up which I endeavoured to give him some ideas of the desire of power and riches; of the terrible effects of lust, intemperance[49], malice, and envy. All this I was forced to define and describe by putting of cases, and making suppositions. After which, like one whose imagination was struck with something never seen or heard of before, he would lift up his eyes with amazement and indignation. Power, government, war, law, punishment, and a thousand other things had no terms wherein that language could express them, which made the difficulty almost insuperable to give my master any conception of what I meant. But being of an excellent understanding, much improved by contemplation and converse, he at last arrived at a competent knowledge of what human nature in our parts of the world is capable to perform, and desired I would give him some particular account of that land which we call Europe, especially of my own country.

Chapter VIII

[The author relates several particulars of the Yahoos. The great virtues of the Houyhnhnms. The education and exercise of their youth. Their general assembly.]

[...]

Having already lived three years in this country, the reader I suppose will expect that I should, like other travellers, give him some account of the manners and customs of its inhabitants, which it was indeed my principal study to learn.

As these noble Houyhnhnms are endowed by nature with a general disposition to all virtues, and have no conceptions or ideas of what is evil in a rational creature, so their grand maxim[50] is to cultivate *reason*, and to be wholly governed by it. Neither is *reason* among them a point problematical as with us, where men can argue with plausibility[51] on both sides of a question; but strikes you with immediate conviction; as it must needs do where it is not mingled, obscured, or discoloured by passion and interest. I remember it was with extreme difficulty that I could bring my master to understand the meaning of the word *opinion*, or how a point could be disputable; because *reason* taught us to affirm or deny only where we are certain; and beyond our knowledge we cannot do either. So that controversies, wranglings[52], disputes, and positiveness in false or dubious propositions are evils unknown among the Houyhnhnms. In the like manner, when I used to explain to him our several systems of *natural philosophy*, he would laugh that a creature pretending to *reason* should value itself upon the knowledge of other people's conjectures, and in things where that knowledge, if it were certain, could be of no use. Wherein[53] he agreed entirely with the sentiments of Socrates, as Plato delivers them; which I mention as the highest honour I can do that prince of philosophers. I have often since reflected what destruction such a doctrine would make in the libraries of Europe, and how many paths to fame would be then shut up in the learned world.

Friendship and *benevolence* are the two principal virtues among the Houyhnhnms, and these not confined to particular objects, but universal to the whole race. For a stranger from the remotest part is equally treated with the nearest neighbour, and wherever he goes, looks upon himself as at home. They preserve *decency* and *civility* in the highest degrees, but are altogether ignorant of *ceremony*. They have no fondness for their colts or foals, but the care they take in educating them proceeds entirely from the dictates[54] of *reason*. And I observed my master to show the same affection to his neighbour's issue that he had for his own. They will have it that *Nature* teaches them to love the whole species, and it is *reason* only that maketh a distinction of persons, where there is a superior degree of virtue.

When the matron Houyhnhnms have produced one of each sex, they no longer accompany with their consorts[55], except they lose one of their issue[56] by some casualty, which very seldom happens: but in such a case they meet again; or when the like accident befalls a person whose wife is past bearing, some other couple bestows on him one of their own colts, and then go together a second time till the mother is pregnant. This caution is necessary to prevent the country from being overburdened with numbers. But the race of inferior Houyhnhnms bred up to be servants is not so strictly limited upon this article; these are allowed to produce three of each sex, to be domestics[57] in the noble families.

In their marriages they are exactly careful to choose such colours as will not make any disagreeable mixture in the breed. *Strength* is chiefly valued in the male, and *comeliness* in the female, not upon the account of *love*, but to preserve the race from degenerating: for where a female happens to excel in *strength*, a consort is chosen with regard to *comeliness*. Courtship, love, presents, jointures[58], settlements[59], have no place in their thoughts, or terms whereby[60] to express them in their language. The young couple meet and are joined, merely because it is the determination of their parents and friends: it is what they see done every day, and they look upon it as one of the necessary actions in a reasonable being. But the violation of marriage, or any other unchastity, was never heard of: and the married pair pass their lives with the same friendship and mutual benevolence that they bear to all others of the same species who come in their way; without jealousy, fondness, quarrelling, or discontent.

In educating the youth of both sexes, their method is admirable, and highly deserves our imitation. These are not suffered to taste a grain of oats, except upon certain days, till eighteen years old; nor milk, but very rarely; and in summer they graze two hours in the morning, and as many in the evening, which their parents likewise observe; but the servants are not allowed above half that time; and a great part of their grass is brought home, which they eat at the most convenient hours, when they can be best spared from work.

Temperance, industry, exercise, and *cleanliness*, are the lessons equally enjoined[61] to the young ones of both sexes: and my master thought it monstrous in us to give the females a different kind of education from the males, except in some articles of domestic management; whereby, as he truly observed, one half of our natives were good for nothing but bringing children into the world: and to trust the care of their children to such useless animals, he said, was yet a greater instance of brutality.

But the Houyhnhnms train up their youth to strength, speed, and hardiness, by exercising them in running races up and down steep hills, and over hard stony grounds, and when they are all in a sweat, they are ordered to leap over head and ears into a pond or a river. Four times a year the youth of certain districts meet to show their proficiency in running and leaping, and other feats of strength or agility; where the victor is rewarded with a song made in his or her praise. On this festival the servants drive a herd of Yahoos into the field, laden with hay, and oats, and milk for a repast[62] to the Houyhnhnms; after which these brutes are immediately driven back again, for fear of being noisome[63] to the assembly.

Every fourth year, at the vernal equinox, there is a representative council of the whole nation, which meets in a plain about twenty miles from our house, and continues about five or six days. Here they inquire into the state and condition of the several districts; whether they abound or be deficient in hay or oats, or cows or Yahoos. And wherever there is any want (which is but seldom) it is immediately supplied by unanimous consent and contribution. Here likewise the regulation of children is settled: as for instance, if a Houyhnhnm has two males, he changeth one of them with another who hath two females: and when a child hath been lost by any casualty, where the mother is past breeding, it is determined what family in the district shall breed another to supply the loss.

Notes

Chapter II

1. wattle: make fences or walls with branches and poles
2. nag: an old horse
3. mare: a female horse
4. ham: the upper part of the legs and buttocks
5. must needs: (*old use*) unavoidably; inevitably
6. neigh: make the loud long sound that a horse makes
7. of great note: of great importance
8. necromancy: the practice of communicating with the dead in order to learn about the future
9. comely: attractive; good-looking
10. foal: a young horse
11. haunch: the part of the body between the waist and legs
12. betwixt: (*old use*) between
13. mortification: the feeling of shame, embarrassment or humiliation
14. withe: a flexible branch of
15. sorrel: a light reddish-brown color
16. lineament: a distinctive feature of a face
17. grovelling: lying or moving flat on the ground with one's face downwards
18. I was obliged: I was grateful
19. hoof: the hard part of the foot of a horse
20. pastern: the part of a horse's foot between the fetlock and the hoof
21. fetlock: the back part of a horse's leg, above the hoof, where long hair grows
22. steed: a horse for riding
23. alight: get off a vehicle
24. complaisant: ready to please others
25. occasion: cause
26. whereof: (*old use*) of which
27. winnow: blow a current of air to remove the outer covering, or husks
28. insipid: lacking flavor
29. fare: food of a particular kind
30. cannot but: have to
31. whey: the watery part of sour milk after the curd has been removed
32. fared well: be successful in a specified situation

Chapter IV

33. mane: the long hair on the neck of a horse
34. tractable: easy to control
35. own: admit
36. foundered: unable to walk well because the foot has some kind of weakness

37. drudgery: hard dull work
38. tincture: a very small amount of
39. circumlocution: using more words than are necessary so as to answer a difficult question in an indirect way
40. propagae: produce the young of one's own kind
41. servile: too eager to obey others
42. endued: provided with (a good quality)
43. hither: (*old use*) to this place
44. similitude: the state of being similar to something
45. interpose: interrupt
46. undone: ruined
47. perjury: telling a lie deliberately in court
48. durst: old past tense of the verb "dare"
49. intemperance: the quality of lacking self-control

Chapter VIII
50. maxim: a short saying which expresses a general truth or a rule for good conduct
51. plausibility: the quality of being seemingly reasonable
52. wrangling: arguing angrily and noisily for a long time
53. Wherein: In which
54. dictate: an order or a principle which one must obey
55. consort: a husband or companion
56. issue: children of one's own
57. domestic: a servant working in a house
58. jointure: the property set aside to support the wife of a man after his death
59. settlement: a formal gift of money or property
60. whereby: by which
61. enjoined: ordered (something to be done)
62. repast: a meal
63. noisome: very unpleasant

Questions

1. One critic once argued that *Gulliver's Travels* challenged readers' "assurance that as rational animals they occupied a privileged position in the Chain of Being". How do chapter II and chapter IV bear evidence of Swift's satiric techniques?
2. In chapter VIII, the word "reason" has been used several times. What's its significant for this prestigious satirical work?
3. Gulliver is fascinated with the virtuous and harmonious life in the country of horses. Do you think the country of the Houyhnhnms a utopia? From your perspective, are there any limitations of this country, which is highly esteemed by Gulliver?

Herbert George Wells
1866—1946

Herbert George Wells, an English novelist, short story writer, journalist, and historian, was born into a poor family in Bromley, Kent on September 21, 1866. His father was an unsuccessful shopkeeper and his mother a housekeeper. Wells developed an interest in literature at an early age. He won a scholarship to the Normal School of Science in South Kensington. There he studied biology, geology, and astronomical physics and was particularly influenced by Thomas H. Huxley, who instilled into Wells beliefs in both biological and social evolution. Besides, he read widely, committed himself to socialism, engaged in debating society and contributed to the college magazine. After graduation, Wells worked as a teacher for a time and sent contributions to newspapers and magazines. In 1893 he completed a textbook of biology before he finally settled as a professional writer.

Herbert George Wells

Best-known as the father of modern science fiction, an honor he shares with Jules Verne, Wells is prolific in both fiction and non-fiction writing. He began with science fiction, an interest stemming from his scientific training. His science-fiction novels such as *The Time Machine* (1895), *The Island of Doctor Moreau* (1896), *The Invisible Man* (1897), *The War of the Worlds* (1898), and several short stories like "The Stolen Bacillus", "The Country of the Blind", and "The Man Who Could Work Miracles" have been regarded as classics and have profoundly influenced the course of modern science fiction and fantasy, winning him the reputation as a prophet of scientific developments and human destiny. The years that followed saw Wells concentrate more on realistic novels on the basis of his youthful experiences. Classics such as *Kipps* (1905), *Tono-Bungay* (1908), *The History of Mr. Polly* (1910), demonstrate Wells's humour and his sympathy for ordinary people. Among his nonfiction works, another kind of vehicles for his political ideals and philosophical concepts, *The Outline of History* (1920) stands out, specifying his ideal of cosmopolitanism.

As a writer of outstanding originality and with a world of ideas, Wells has infused his passionate concerns for human society into his works. His lower social class origin and his scientific education background account for much of his perspectives in his long-standing works. Contrasted with Jules Verne, Wells has foreseen the impact science would make on social organization and the lives of humanity and has thereby distinguished himself in his literary creation by exploring the impact of technology on human affairs and the moral responsibility of scientists for the potentially harmful applications of their research, and consequently satirizing his own culture and times. On the other hand, the miserable life in his early years made it easier for him to see the terrible social injustice and to accept the progressive ideas of socialism. He openly embraced socialism while at university and joined the Fabian society in 1903. His realistic novels are based on his keen observation of the poverty and injustice in British society. As for Wells's attitude towards the future of humankind, early readings like Plato's *Republic* laid a foundation of his idea of building up a utopia through the growth of science and socialism. A just and efficient world state is his ideal of human society. Yet his prospect of humankind, throughout his lifetime, has shifted over decades, which is reflected in the wavering between dystopian and utopian scenarios in his works.

The Time Machine

The best-known of Wells's science fiction, *The Time Machine* revolves around a time traveler who travels into the distant future. There his long-held utopian anticipation of future ages has collapsed as he witnesses two futuristic human races being on the wane. Presenting a possibility that could occur, the story conveys Wells's somewhat dystopian attitude toward the social, political and technological concerns in his day and hence compels further reflection upon the contemporary human society as a whole.

The story unfolds as the nameless time traveler expounds passionately to some guests his idea of time being the fourth dimension indispensible to the real existence of a solid body. Having failed to convince his guests, he shows them a time machine by which he plans to explore time. Several days later, as his guests are being confused about his mysterious disappearance, the time traveler presents himself in an unexpected plight. He later relates his thrilling yet unpleasant experience of time travelling, during which he is flung into a future place, by his elaborate ivory, crystal and brass contraption, in the year eight hundred and two thousand odd. There and then he comes across a race of human beings in the future, the Eloi. Nevertheless, his passion for the future age gradually ebbs away as more respects of this futuristic world are revealed, such as the Eloi looking beautiful, graceful yet lacking knowledge and intellectual curiosity, big buildings assuming dilapidated looks, the indifference demonstrated by the Eloi to their peers in danger, differences between men and women on the wane. Confronting the decadent humanity in this future age, the time traveler comes up with some plausible explanations, indicative of the situation in his own day. Later he is abruptly panicked when he finds no trace of the time machine. Searching around for it, he finds another race of human descendants, the under-world Morlocks, the odious creatures preying on the graceful upper-world race the Eloi. The striking contrast between the two races reminds the traveler of the widening difference between the Capitalist and the Laborer in his day. He is sure that Morlocks have taken his machine and thus risks his life to descend, through one waterless well, to the frightful under-world, where Morlocks inhabits. He hardly fails to escape. After some desperate struggles against Morlocks, the traveler regains his time machine. His encounter with the Eloi girl Weena and their joint adventures all the way through add warmth and hope to the otherwise depressing age. Afterwards he travels to the future age of more than thirty million years, where desolate scene frightens him. When the time traveler finishes the adventurous story, the guests of his own age do not believe his accounts. Though pessimistic about the advancement of mankind, the traveler prepares for another time travel, leaves the next day and doesn't return until the story concludes.

Quite imaginative and innovative, the selected part in the following delineates how the time traveler embarks on the enthralling adventure through time and how he goes through the first future age he is hurtled into when he just arrives there.

Chapter III

'I told some of you last Thursday of the principles of the Time Machine, and showed you the actual thing itself, incomplete in the workshop. There it is now, a little travel-worn, truly; and one of the ivory bars is cracked, and a brass rail bent; but the rest of it's sound enough. I expected to finish it on Friday, but on Friday, when the putting together was nearly done, I found that one of the nickel bars was exactly one inch too short, and this I had to get remade; so that the thing was not complete until this morning. It was at ten o'clock today that the first of all Time Machines began its career. I gave it a last tap, tried all the screws again, put one more drop of oil on the quartz rod, and sat myself in the saddle. I suppose a suicide who holds a pistol to his skull feels much the same wonder at what will come next as I felt then. I took the starting lever in one hand and the stopping one in the other, pressed the first, and almost immediately the second. I seemed to reel; I felt a nightmare sensation of falling; and, looking round, I saw the laboratory exactly as before. Had anything happened? For a moment I suspected that my intellect had tricked me. Then I noted the clock. A moment before, as it seemed, it had stood at a minute or so past ten; now it was nearly half-past three!

'I drew a breath, set my teeth, gripped the starting lever with both hands, and went off with a thud[1]. The laboratory got hazy and went dark. Mrs. Watchett came in and walked, apparently without seeing me, towards the garden door. I suppose it took her a minute or so to traverse the place, but to me she seemed to shoot across the room like a rocket. I pressed the lever over to its extreme position. The night came like the turning out of a lamp, and in another moment came tomorrow. The laboratory grew faint and hazy, then fainter and ever fainter. Tomorrow night came black, then day again, night again, day again, faster and faster still. An eddying[2] murmur filled my ears, and a strange, dumb confusedness descended on my mind.

'I am afraid I cannot convey the peculiar sensations of time travelling. They are excessively unpleasant. There is a feeling exactly like that one has upon a switchback[3] — of a helpless headlong[4] motion! I felt the same horrible anticipation, too, of an imminent[5] smash. As I put on pace, night followed day like the flapping of a black wing. The dim suggestion of the laboratory seemed presently to fall away from me, and I saw the sun hopping swiftly across the sky, leaping it every minute, and every minute marking a day. I supposed the laboratory had been destroyed and I had come into the open air. I had a dim impression of scaffolding[6], but I was already going too fast to be conscious of any moving things. The slowest snail that ever crawled dashed by too fast for me. The twinkling succession of darkness and light was excessively painful to the eye. Then, in the intermittent[7] darknesses, I saw the moon spinning swiftly through her quarters[8] from new to full, and had a faint glimpse of the circling stars. Presently, as I went on, still gaining velocity, the palpitation of night and day merged into one continuous greyness; the sky took on a wonderful deepness of blue, a splendid luminous color like that of early twilight; the jerking sun became a streak of fire, a brilliant arch, in space; the moon a fainter fluctuating band; and I could see nothing of the stars, save now and then a brighter circle flickering in the blue.

'The landscape was misty and vague. I was still on the hill-side upon which this house now stands, and the shoulder rose above me grey and dim. I saw trees growing and changing like puffs of vapour, now brown, now green; they grew, spread, shivered, and passed away. I saw huge buildings rise up faint and fair, and pass like dreams. The whole surface of the earth seemed changed — melting and flowing under my eyes. The little hands upon the dials that registered my speed raced round faster and faster. Presently I noted that the sun belt swayed up and down, from solstice to solstice, in a minute or less, and that consequently my pace was over a year a minute; and minute by minute the white snow flashed across the world, and vanished, and was followed by the bright, brief green of spring.

'The unpleasant sensations of the start were less poignant[9] now. They merged at last into a kind of hysterical exhilaration. I remarked indeed a clumsy swaying of the machine, for which I was unable to account. But my mind was too confused to attend to it, so with a kind of madness growing upon me, I flung myself into futurity. At first I scarce thought of stopping, scarce thought of anything but these new sensations. But presently a fresh series of impressions grew up in my mind — a certain curiosity and therewith[10] a certain dread — until at last they took complete possession of me. What strange developments of humanity, what wonderful advances upon our rudimentary civilization, I thought, might not appear when I came to look nearly into the dim elusive world that raced and fluctuated before my eyes! I saw great and splendid architecture rising about me, more massive than any buildings of our own time, and yet, as it seemed, built of glimmer and mist. I saw a richer green flow up the hill-side, and remain there, without any wintry intermission. Even through the veil of my confusion the earth seemed very fair. And so my mind came round to the business of stopping.

'The peculiar risk lay in the possibility of my finding some substance in the space which I, or the machine, occupied. So long as I travelled at a high velocity through time, this scarcely mattered; I was, so to speak, attenuated[11] — was slipping like a vapour through the interstices[12] of intervening substances! But to come to a stop involved the jamming of myself, molecule by molecule, into whatever lay in my way; meant bringing my atoms into such intimate contact with those of the obstacle that a profound chemical reaction — possibly a far-reaching explosion — would result, and blow myself and my apparatus out of all possible dimensions — into the Unknown. This possibility had occurred to me again and again while I was making the machine; but then I had cheerfully accepted it as an unavoidable risk — one of the risks a man has got to take! Now the risk was inevitable, I no longer saw it in the same cheerful light. The fact is that, insensibly, the absolute strangeness of everything, the sickly jarring[13] and swaying of the machine, above all, the feeling of prolonged falling, had absolutely upset my nerve. I told myself that I could never stop, and with a gust of petulance[14] I resolved to stop forthwith. Like an impatient fool, I lugged[15] over the lever, and incontinently[16] the thing went reeling over, and I was flung headlong through the air.

'There was the sound of a clap of thunder in my ears. I may have been stunned for a moment. A pitiless hail was hissing round me, and I was sitting on soft turf in front of the overset machine. Everything still seemed grey, but presently I remarked[17] that the confusion in my ears was gone. I looked round me. I was on what seemed to be a little lawn in a garden, surrounded by rhododendron[18] bushes, and I noticed that their mauve and purple blossoms were dropping in a shower under the beating of the hail-stones. The rebounding, dancing hail hung in a cloud over the machine, and drove along the ground like smoke. In a moment I was wet to the skin. "Fine hospitality," said I, "to a man who has travelled innumerable years to see you."

'Presently I thought what a fool I was to get wet. I stood up and looked round me. A colossal figure, carved apparently in some white stone, loomed indistinctly beyond the rhododendrons through the hazy downpour. But all else of the world was invisible.

'My sensations would be hard to describe. As the columns of hail grew thinner, I saw the white figure more distinctly. It was very large, for a silver birch-tree touched its shoulder. It was of white marble, in shape something like a winged sphinx, but the wings, instead of being carried vertically at the sides, were spread so that it seemed to hover. The pedestal[19], it appeared to me, was of bronze, and was thick with verdigris[20]. It chanced that the face was towards me; the sightless eyes seemed to watch me; there was the faint shadow of a smile on the lips. It was greatly weather-worn, and that imparted an unpleasant suggestion of disease. I stood looking at it for a little space — half a minute, perhaps, or half an hour. It seemed to advance and to recede as the hail drove before it denser or thinner. At last I tore my eyes from it for a moment and saw that the hail curtain had worn threadbare, and that the sky was lightening with the promise of the sun.

'I looked up again at the crouching white shape, and the full temerity[21] of my voyage came suddenly upon me. What might appear when that hazy curtain was altogether withdrawn? What might not have happened to men? What if cruelty had grown into a common passion? What if in this interval the race had lost its manliness and had developed into something inhuman, unsympathetic, and overwhelmingly powerful? I might seem some old-world savage animal, only the more dreadful and disgusting for our common likeness — a foul creature to be incontinently slain.

'Already I saw other vast shapes — huge buildings with intricate parapets and tall columns, with a wooded hill-side dimly creeping in upon me through the lessening storm. I was seized with a panic fear. I turned frantically to the Time Machine, and strove hard to readjust it. As I did so the shafts[22] of the sun smote through the thunderstorm. The grey downpour was swept aside and vanished like the trailing garments of a ghost. Above me, in the intense blue of the summer sky, some faint brown shreds of cloud whirled into nothingness. The great buildings about me stood out clear and distinct, shining with the wet of the thunderstorm, and picked out in white by the unmelted hailstones piled along their courses. I felt naked in a strange world. I felt as perhaps a bird may feel in the clear air, knowing the hawk wings above and will swoop[23]. My fear grew to frenzy. I took a breathing space, set my teeth, and again grappled[24] fiercely, wrist and knee, with the machine. It struck my chin violently. One hand on the saddle, the other on the lever, I stood panting heavily in attitude to mount again.

'But with this recovery of a prompt retreat my courage recovered. I looked more curiously and less fearfully at this world of the remote future. In a circular opening, high up in the wall of the nearer house, I saw a group of figures clad in rich soft robes. They had seen me, and their faces were directed towards me.

'Then I heard voices approaching me. Coming through the bushes by the White Sphinx were the heads and shoulders of men running. One of these emerged in a pathway leading straight to the little lawn upon which I stood with my machine. He was a slight creature — perhaps four feet high — clad in a purple tunic, girdled at the waist with a leather belt. Sandals or buskins — I could not clearly distinguish which — were on his feet; his legs were bare to the knees, and his head was bare. Noticing that, I noticed for the first time how warm the air was.

'He struck me as being a very beautiful and graceful creature, but indescribably frail. His flushed face reminded me of the more beautiful kind of consumptive — that hectic beauty of which we used to hear so much. At the sight of him I suddenly regained confidence. I took my hands from the machine.

Chapter IV

'In another moment we were standing face to face, I and this fragile thing out of futurity. He came straight up to me and laughed into my eyes. The absence from his bearing[25] of any sign of fear struck me at once. Then he turned to the two others who were following him and spoke to them in a strange and very sweet and liquid tongue.

'There were others coming, and presently a little group of perhaps eight or ten of these exquisite creatures were about me. One of them addressed me. It came into my head, oddly enough, that my voice was too harsh and deep for them. So I shook my head, and, pointing to my ears, shook it again. He came a step forward, hesitated, and then touched my hand. Then I felt other soft little tentacles upon my back and shoulders. They wanted to make sure I was real. There was nothing in this at all alarming. Indeed, there was something in these pretty little people that inspired confidence — a graceful gentleness, a certain childlike ease. And besides, they looked so frail that I could fancy myself flinging the whole dozen of them about like nine-pins. But I made a sudden motion to warn them when I saw their little pink hands feeling at the Time Machine. Happily then, when it was not too late, I thought of a danger I had hitherto[26] forgotten, and reaching over the bars of the machine I unscrewed the little levers that would set it in motion, and put these in my pocket. Then I turned again to see what I could do in the way of communication.

'And then, looking more nearly into their features, I saw some further peculiarities in their Dresden[27]-china type of prettiness. Their hair, which was uniformly curly, came to a sharp end at the neck and cheek; there was not the faintest suggestion of it on the face, and their ears were singularly minute. The mouths were small, with bright red, rather thin lips, and the little chins ran to a point. The eyes were large and mild; and — this may seem egotism on my part — I fancied even that there was a certain lack of the interest I might have expected in them.

'As they made no effort to communicate with me, but simply stood round me smiling and speaking in soft cooing[28] notes to each other, I began the conversation. I pointed to the Time Machine and to myself. Then hesitating for a moment how to express time, I pointed to the sun. At once a quaintly[29] pretty little figure in chequered purple and white followed my gesture, and then astonished me by imitating the sound of thunder.

'For a moment I was staggered, though the import of his gesture was plain enough. The question had come into my mind abruptly: were these creatures fools? You may hardly understand how it took me. You see I had always anticipated that the people of the year Eight Hundred and Two Thousand odd would be incredibly in front of us in knowledge, art, everything. Then one of them suddenly asked me a question that showed him to be on the intellectual level of one of our five-year-old children — asked me, in fact, if I had come from the sun in a thunderstorm! It let loose the judgment I had suspended upon their clothes, their frail light limbs, and fragile features. A flow of disappointment rushed across my mind. For a moment I felt that I had built the Time Machine in vain.

'I nodded, pointed to the sun, and gave them such a vivid rendering[30] of a thunderclap as startled them. They all withdrew a pace or so and bowed. Then came one laughing towards me, carrying a chain of beautiful flowers altogether new to me, and put it about my neck. The idea was received with melodious applause; and presently they were all running to and fro for flowers, and laughingly flinging them upon me until I was almost smothered with blossom. You who have never seen the like can scarcely imagine what delicate and wonderful flowers countless years of culture had created. Then someone suggested that their plaything should be exhibited in the nearest building, and so I was led past the sphinx of white marble, which had seemed to watch me all the while with a smile at my astonishment, towards a vast grey edifice[31] of fretted stone. As I went with them the memory of my confident anticipations of a profoundly grave and intellectual posterity came, with irresistible merriment, to my mind.

'The building had a huge entry, and was altogether of colossal dimensions. I was naturally most occupied with the growing crowd of little people, and with the big open portals that yawned before me shadowy and mysterious. My general impression of the world I saw over their heads was a tangled waste of beautiful bushes and flowers, a long neglected and yet weedless garden. I saw a number of tall spikes of strange white flowers, measuring a foot perhaps across the spread of the waxen petals. They grew scattered, as if wild, among the variegated[32] shrubs, but, as I say, I did not examine them closely at this time. The Time Machine was left deserted on the turf among the rhododendrons.

'The arch of the doorway was richly carved, but naturally I did not observe the carving very narrowly, though I fancied I saw suggestions of old Phoenician[33] decorations as I passed through, and it struck me that they were very badly broken and weather-worn. Several more brightly clad people met me in the doorway, and so we entered, I, dressed in dingy[34] nineteenth-century garments, looking grotesque enough, garlanded with flowers, and surrounded by an eddying mass of bright, soft-colored robes and shining white limbs, in a melodious whirl of laughter and laughing speech.

'The big doorway opened into a proportionately great hall hung with brown. The roof was in shadow, and the windows, partially glazed[35] with coloured glass and partially unglazed, admitted a tempered light. The floor was made up of huge blocks of some very hard white metal, not plates nor slabs — blocks, and it was so much worn, as I judged by the going to and fro of past generations, as to be deeply channelled along the more frequented ways. Transverse to the length were innumerable tables made of slabs of polished stone, raised perhaps a foot from the floor, and upon these were heaps of fruits. Some I recognized as a kind of hypertrophied raspberry and orange, but for the most part they were strange.

'Between the tables was scattered a great number of cushions. Upon these my conductors seated themselves, signing for me to do likewise. With a pretty absence of ceremony they began to eat the fruit with their hands, flinging peel and stalks, and so forth, into the round openings in the sides of the tables. I was not loath to follow their example, for I felt thirsty and hungry. As I did so I surveyed the hall at my leisure[36].

'And perhaps the thing that struck me most was its dilapidated look. The stained-glass windows, which displayed only a geometrical pattern, were broken in many places, and the curtains that hung across the lower end were thick with dust. And it caught my eye that the corner of the marble table near me was fractured. Nevertheless, the general effect was extremely rich and picturesque. There were, perhaps, a couple of hundred people dining in the hall, and most of them, seated as near to me as they could come, were watching me with interest, their little eyes shining over the fruit they were eating. All were clad in the same soft and yet strong, silky material.

'Fruit, by the by[37], was all their diet. These people of the remote future were strict vegetarians, and while I was with them, in spite of some carnal cravings, I had to be frugivorous[38] also. Indeed, I found afterwards that horses, cattle, sheep, dogs, had followed the Ichthyosaurus[39] into extinction. But the fruits were very delightful; one, in particular, that seemed to be in season all the time I was there — a floury thing in a three-sided husk — was especially good, and I made it my staple. At first I was puzzled by all these strange fruits, and by the strange flowers I saw, but later I began to perceive their import.

'However, I am telling you of my fruit dinner in the distant future now. So soon as my appetite was a little checked, I determined to make a resolute attempt to learn the speech of these new men of mine. Clearly that was the next thing to do. The fruits seemed a convenient thing to begin upon, and holding one of these up I began a series of interrogative sounds and gestures. I had some considerable difficulty in conveying my meaning. At first my efforts met with a stare of surprise or inextinguishable laughter, but presently a fair-haired little creature seemed to grasp my intention and repeated a name. They had to chatter and explain the business at great length to each other, and my first attempts to make the exquisite little sounds of their language caused an immense amount of amusement. However, I felt like a schoolmaster amidst children, and persisted, and presently I had a score of noun substantives[40] at least at my command; and then I got to demonstrative pronouns, and even the verb "to eat." But it was slow work, and the little people soon tired and wanted to get away from my interrogations, so I determined, rather of necessity, to let them give their lessons in little doses when they felt inclined. And very little doses I found they were before long, for I never met people more indolent[41] or more easily fatigued.

'A queer thing I soon discovered about my little hosts, and that was their lack of interest. They would come to me with eager cries of astonishment, like children, but like children they would soon stop examining me and wander away after some other toy. The dinner and my conversational beginnings ended, I noted for the first time that almost all those who had surrounded me at first were gone. It is odd, too, how speedily I came to disregard these little people. I went out through the portal[42] into the sunlit world again as soon as my hunger was satisfied. I was continually meeting more of these men of the future, who would follow me a little distance, chatter and laugh about me, and, having smiled and gesticulated[43] in a friendly way, leave me again to my own devices.

'The calm of evening was upon the world as I emerged from the great hall, and the scene was lit by the warm glow of the setting sun. At first things were very confusing. Everything was so entirely different from the world I had known — even the flowers. The big building I had left was situated on the slope of a broad river valley, but the Thames had shifted perhaps a mile from its present position. I resolved to mount to the summit of a crest, perhaps a mile and a half away, from which I could get a wider view of this our planet in the year Eight Hundred and Two Thousand Seven Hundred and One A.D. For that, I should explain, was the date the little dials of my machine recorded.

'As I walked I was watching for every impression that could possibly help to explain the condition of ruinous splendour in which I found the world — for ruinous it was. A little way up the hill, for instance, was a great heap of granite, bound together by masses of aluminum, a vast labyrinth of precipitous walls and crumpled heaps, amidst which were thick heaps of very beautiful pagoda-like plants — nettles possibly — but wonderfully tinted with brown about the leaves, and incapable of stinging. It was evidently the derelict[44] remains of some vast structure, to what end built I could not determine. It was here that I was destined, at a later date, to have a very strange experience — the first intimation of a still stranger discovery — but of that I will speak in its proper place.

'Looking round with a sudden thought, from a terrace on which I rested for a while, I realized that there were no small houses to be seen. Apparently the single house, and possibly even the household, had vanished. Here and there among the greenery were palace-like buildings, but the house and the cottage, which form such characteristic features of our own English landscape, had disappeared.

'"Communism," said I to myself.

'And on the heels of that came another thought. I looked at the half-dozen little figures that were following me. Then, in a flash, I perceived that all had the same form of costume, the same soft hairless visage, and the same girlish rotundity[45] of limb. It may seem strange, perhaps, that I had not noticed this before. But everything was so strange. Now, I saw the fact plainly enough. In costume, and in all the differences of texture and bearing that now mark off the sexes from each other, these people of the future were alike. And the children seemed to my eyes to be but the miniatures of their parents. I judged, then, that the children of that time were extremely precocious[46], physically at least, and I found afterwards abundant verification of my opinion.

'Seeing the ease and security in which these people were living, I felt that this close resemblance of the sexes was after all what one would expect; for the strength of a man and the softness of a woman, the institution of the family, and the differentiation of occupations are mere militant necessities of an age of physical force; where population is balanced and abundant, much child-bearing becomes an evil rather than a blessing to the State; where violence comes but rarely and off-spring are secure, there is less necessity — indeed there is no necessity — for an efficient family, and the specialization of the sexes with reference to their children's needs disappears. We see some beginnings of this even in our own time, and in this future age it was complete. This, I must remind you, was my speculation at the time. Later, I was to appreciate how far it fell short of the reality.

'While I was musing upon these things, my attention was attracted by a pretty little structure, like a well under a cupola[47]. I thought in a transitory way of the oddness of wells still existing, and then resumed the thread of my speculations. There were no large buildings towards the top of the hill, and as my walking powers were evidently miraculous, I was presently left alone for the first time. With a strange sense of freedom and adventure I pushed on up to the crest.

'There I found a seat of some yellow metal that I did not recognize, corroded[48] in places with a kind of pinkish rust and half smothered in soft moss, the arm-rests cast and filed into the resemblance of griffins' heads. I sat down on it, and I surveyed the broad view of our old world under the sunset of that long day. It was as sweet and fair a view as I have ever seen. The sun had already gone below the horizon and the west was flaming gold, touched with some horizontal bars of purple and crimson. Below was the valley of the Thames, in which the river lay like a band of burnished steel. I have already spoken of the great palaces dotted about among the variegated greenery, some in ruins and some still occupied. Here and there rose a white or silvery figure in the waste garden of the earth, here and there came the sharp vertical line of some cupola or obelisk[49]. There were no hedges, no signs of proprietary rights, no evidences of agriculture; the whole earth had become a garden.

'So watching, I began to put my interpretation upon the things I had seen, and as it shaped itself to me that evening, my interpretation was something in this way. (Afterwards I found I had got only a half-truth — or only a glimpse of one facet of the truth.)

'It seemed to me that I had happened upon humanity upon the wane. The ruddy sunset set me thinking of the sunset of mankind. For the first time I began to realize an odd consequence of the social effort in which we are at present engaged. And yet, come to think, it is a logical consequence enough. Strength is the outcome of need; security sets a premium[50] on feebleness. The work of ameliorating[51] the conditions of life — the true civilizing process that makes life more and more secure — had gone steadily on to a climax. One triumph of a united humanity over Nature had followed another. Things that are now mere dreams had become projects deliberately put in hand and carried forward. And the harvest was what I saw!

'After all, the sanitation and the agriculture of today are still in the rudimentary stage. The science of our time has attacked but a little department of the field of human disease, but, even so, it spreads its operations very steadily and persistently. Our agriculture and horticulture destroy a weed just here and there and cultivate perhaps a score or so of wholesome plants, leaving the greater number to fight out a balance as they can. We improve our favourite plants and animals — and how few they are — gradually by selective breeding; now a new and better peach, now a seedless grape, now a sweeter and larger flower, now a more convenient breed of cattle. We improve them gradually, because our ideals are vague and tentative, and our knowledge is very limited; because Nature, too, is shy and slow in our clumsy hands. Some day all this will be better organized, and still better. That is the drift of the current in spite of the eddies[52]. The whole world will be intelligent, educated, and co-operating; things will move faster and faster towards the subjugation of Nature. In the end, wisely and carefully we shall readjust the balance of animal and vegetable life to suit our human needs.

'This adjustment, I say, must have been done, and done well; done indeed for all Time, in the space of Time across which my machine had leaped. The air was free from gnats, the earth from weeds or fungi; everywhere were fruits and sweet and delightful flowers; brilliant butterflies flew hither and thither. The ideal of preventive medicine was attained. Diseases had been stamped out. I saw no evidence of any contagious diseases during all my stay. And I shall have to tell you later that even the processes of putrefaction[53] and decay had been profoundly affected by these changes.

'Social triumphs, too, had been effected. I saw mankind housed in splendid shelters, gloriously clothed, and as yet I had found them engaged in no toil. There were no signs of struggle, neither social nor economical struggle. The shop, the advertisement, traffic, all that commerce which constitutes the body of our world, was gone. It was natural on that golden evening that I should jump at the idea of a social paradise. The difficulty of increasing population had been met, I guessed, and population had ceased to increase.

'But with this change in condition comes inevitably adaptations to the change. What, unless biological science is a mass of errors, is the cause of human intelligence and vigour? Hardship and freedom: conditions under which the active, strong, and subtle survive and the weaker go to the wall; conditions that put a premium upon the loyal alliance of capable men, upon self-restraint, patience, and decision. And the institution of the family, and the emotions that arise therein, the fierce jealousy, the tenderness for offspring, parental self-devotion, all found their justification and support in the imminent dangers of the young. Now, where are these imminent dangers? There is a sentiment arising, and it will grow, against connubial[54] jealousy, against fierce maternity, against passion of all sorts; unnecessary things now, and things that make us uncomfortable, savage survivals, discords in a refined and pleasant life.

'I thought of the physical slightness of the people, their lack of intelligence, and those big abundant ruins, and it strengthened my belief in a perfect conquest of Nature. For after the battle comes Quiet. Humanity had been strong, energetic, and intelligent, and had used all its abundant vitality to alter the conditions under which it lived. And now came the reaction of the altered conditions.

'Under the new conditions of perfect comfort and security, that restless energy, that with us is strength, would become weakness. Even in our own time certain tendencies and desires, once necessary to survival, are a constant source of failure. Physical courage and the love of battle, for instance, are no great help — may even be hindrances — to a civilized man. And in a state of physical balance and security, power, intellectual as well as physical, would be out of place. For countless years I judged there had been no danger of war or solitary violence, no danger from wild beasts, no wasting disease to require strength of constitution, no need of toil. For such a life, what we should call the weak are as well equipped as the strong, are indeed no longer weak. Better equipped indeed they are, for the strong would be fretted by an energy for which there was no outlet. No doubt the exquisite beauty of the buildings I saw was the outcome of the last surgings of the now purposeless energy of mankind before it settled down into perfect harmony with the conditions under which it lived — the flourish of that triumph which began the last great peace. This has ever been the fate of energy in security; it takes to art and to eroticism, and then come languor[55] and decay.

'Even this artistic impetus[56] would at last die away — had almost died in the Time I saw. To adorn themselves with flowers, to dance, to sing in the sunlight: so much was left of the artistic spirit, and no more. Even that would fade in the end into a contented inactivity. We are kept keen on the grindstone of pain and necessity, and, it seemed to me, that here was that hateful grindstone broken at last!

'As I stood there in the gathering dark I thought that in this simple explanation I had mastered the problem of the world — mastered the whole secret of these delicious people. Possibly the checks they had devised for the increase of population had succeeded too well, and their numbers had rather diminished than kept stationary. That would account for the abandoned ruins. Very simple was my explanation, and plausible enough — as most wrong theories are!

Notes

Chapter III

1. thud: a dull heavy sound which is made when a heavy object hits something else
2. eddying: moving gently in the air or in water around and around
3. switchback: a road with sharp bends
4. headlong: with the head going first and the rest of the body following
5. imminent: almost certain to happen very soon
6. scaffolding: poles and boards made into a structure to support workers and materials during the construction or repair of a building
7. intermittent: happening occasionally
8. quarter: the period of time twice a month when a quarter of the moon is visible
9. poignant: having a strong effect on one's feelings and making one feel sad or regretful
10. therewith: with or in the thing mentioned
11. attenuated: very thin
12. interstice: a small crack between things
13. jarring: moving with a rather hard shaking manner
14. petulance: the state of being unreasonably irritable
15. lug: carry or drag with a lot of effort
16. incontinently: unable to control oneself
17. remark: notice
18. rhododendron: a bush with red, pink or purple flowers (杜鹃花)
19. pedestal: a base on which something stands, such as a statue
20. verdigris: the greenish substance that forms on the metals copper, brass, and bronze when they are exposed to wet conditions
21. temerity: reckless boldness
22. shaft: a ray of light
23. swoop: move suddenly and quickly downward in order to attack
24. grapple: take a firm hold of something and struggle with it

Chapter IV

25. bearing: the way one behaves
26. hitherto: until the particular time one is talking about
27. Dresden: an industrial city in southeastern Germany, famous for its china manufacturing
28. cooing: making a gentle low sound
29. quaintly: in an attractively usual way

30. rendering: the particular way something is performed
31. edifice: a large and impressive building
32. variegated: having spots, streaks or patches of different colors
33. Phoenician: of Phoenicia, an ancient east Mediterranean country
34. dingy: dirty and discolored
35. glazed: fitted with glass
36. at my leisure: when I had free time
37. by the by: by the way
38. frugivorous: fruit-eating
39. Ichthyosaurus: an extinct marine Mesozoic reptile
40. substantive: a noun or pronoun in place of a noun
41. indolent: lazy
42. portal: a large and impressive entrance
43. gesticulate: move expressive gestures with hands and arms while talking
44. derelict: deserted and falling into ruins
45. rotundity: the state of being plump
46. precocious: having matured at a much younger age than usual
47. cupola: a roof or ceiling in the form of dome
48. corroded: destroyed something slowly by chemical action or rusting
49. obelisk: a four-sided stone column that tapers to a pyramid top
50. premium: the extra amount of money added to a standard rate
51. ameliorate: improve
52. eddy: the circular movement of water or air
53. putrefaction: the process of decay, producing an offensive smell
54. connubial: related to marriage
55. languor: physical or mental laziness or weariness
56. impetus: a driving force

Questions

1. In an introduction to a 1964 edition of *The Time Machine* by Airmont Publishing Company, Donald A. Wollheim remarked, "(the novel) embodies the theme Wells was to stress throughout his life as a social critic and prophet". How does the selected part justify this remark?
2. In the light of the definitions of utopia and dystopia and the selected part here, which word—utopian or dystopian—will you apply to define Wells's attitude to the future of humankind?
3. Compare this science-fiction story with the one you are most familiar with. Are they different from each other?

George Orwell
1903—1950

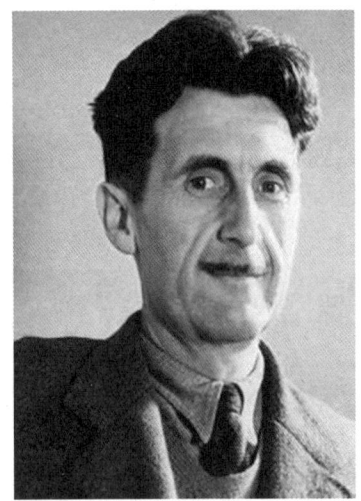
George Orwell

George Orwell (pseudonym of Eric Arthur Blair), a British novelist, essayist, critic and journalist, was born on June 25, 1903 in Bengal, India, where his father worked as a minor official for the Opium Department of the Government of India. In 1905 he was brought back to England and received a conventional upbringing there. Later, he enrolled in Eton, the civilized atmosphere of which nourished the values of patriotism, tradition and tolerance within him. It was at Eton that he published the first writing. Leaving Eton, he joined the Indian Imperial Police in Burma, but left five years later out of his disgust at the brutality of the colonial rule. Having returned to England, Orwell decided to pursue the career as a writer.

Orwell's magnitude in the twentieth century literature derives from his uncompromising commitment to human freedom and social justice. He was, by some critics, compared to a barometer to an understanding of the conflicts and mood of the 1930s and 1940s, a time of cultural and political crisis. A penetrating observer and perceptive social analyst, he reflects relentlessly on the subjects such as Burma, unemployment, popular culture, political power, poverty and social oppression, drawing heavily on his own experiences to create his distinctive works. *Burmese Days* (1934), reflecting the effects of living under colonialism, is based on his experiences as a policeman in Burma. *Down and Out in Paris and London* (1933), examining the life of the poor, is based on the year he spent in self-imposed poverty in London and Paris after he returned from Burma. *The Road to Wigan Pier* (1937) describes the life of English coal miners, emphasizing the importance of traditional values to English common culture. *Homage to Catalonia* (1938) is anchored in his experiences as a common soldier in the Spanish Civil War, delineating the absurdities of war and the decency of ordinary people entangled in the events beyond their control. Among all his books, two masterpieces are most widely read: *Animal Farm* (1945) and *1984* (1949), the former a political allegory and the latter a dystopian satire of his own society. Besides the above accomplishments, Orwell is a renowned essayist in English Language as well. With his highly independent view of modern society, politics, and literature, Orwell presents the complex ideas and observations in an outstanding collection of essays. The most esteemed among them are "Shooting an Elephant" and "A Hanging", two pieces from his Burmese days, creating anew the brutal realities he experienced in Burma; "How the Poor Die", generated from his subsistence living in Paris and London; "The Whale", emphasizing writers' obligation. Other most acclaimed essays also include "Raffles and Miss Blandish," "The Art of Donald McGill", "Boy's Weeklies", "England Your England" and "The English People", and "Politics and the English Language", the last piece exploring how language might be politically manipulated.

Highly lauded as "the conscience of his generation", Orwell has persistently committed himself to the role of the writer in influencing the awareness of his people and affecting the direction and order of his society. To make people conscious of what is happening around them and thus enlarge their sympathies, he has explored and eventually established his own language style and literary style. As an essayist, he is best-known for his lucid and forceful presentation of both ideas and observations, which is a model for students dedicating themselves to writing. As for his works of other categories, he has made varied attempts all the way through.

Animal Farm

First published in 1945, *Animal Farm* has been highly acclaimed as a masterpiece fusing both artistic and political purpose. Containing both utopian and dystopian scenarios, the novel evolves around a rebellion raised by the animals on a farm in England.

One night on Manor Farm, Major, a highly regarded boar, is communicating to all other animals his understanding of nature of life, that is, man is the only real enemy animals have and removing man can not only eradicate the root cause of hunger and overwork imposed on animals but also ensure happiness and prosperity of all animals. He then sings a song, called "Beasts of England", which describes an idealistic animal utopia where man has vanished.

Major's speech gives the other animals a brand-new outlook on life and inspires them to prepare for a rebellion. Among them, three clever pigs Snowball, Napoleon and Squealer, elaborate Major's teachings into Animalism, aiming at equality among all animals, and expound these principles to other animals. Whether for or against their preaching, all animals soon find themselves engaged in a rebellion, driving away their human master Mr. Jones and his family and taking over the farm. "Manor Farm" is replaced by "Animal Farm", where animals work and live happily. Jointly and successfully, they soon frustrate Mr. Jones's attempt to recapture the farm. However, the seemingly thriving utopian scenes are gradually obscured. Shortly after the triumph over man, while working on the farm, pigs are so clever that they do not work but direct and supervise the others. As for food, Squealer soon manages to hoax other animals into accepting the fact that pigs are entitled to take apples and milk. When it comes to the farm policies, Snowball and Napoleon always set themselves against each other. The conflict culminates at a Sunday morning Meeting where Snowball vehemently expounds his reasons for advocating the building of the windmill so as to call for support from other animals. Unexpectedly, he is expelled by Napoleon, who, with the help of nine enormous fierce dogs, thus becomes the only leader on the farm. Despite their misgivings and dismay, other animals are coerced into subjecting themselves to Napoleon. Surprisingly, the plan of windmill is soon resumed and yet proceeds with much difficulty. Squealer, on behalf of Napoleon, is, from time to time, sent to explain the new arrangements to the other animals and at the same time speak ill of Snowball, who is constantly exploited by Napoleon and Squealer to their own advantage in the years to come. On the other hand, animals find themselves live no better than before. What's worse, the fundamental principles on which the animal farm is initially founded, are gradually breached over years. With the threatening pressure by Napoleon, animals have no alternative. Those who dare to protest against his orders are punished harshly. Meanwhile Squealer goes all out to justify all the betrayals of those earliest resolutions passed at the first triumphant meeting after Jones is expelled. Animals are dismayed that their utopian vision of life is far from being fulfilled. What they are going through is not that all animals are equal but that pigs are superior to all other species on the farm. Eventually all the pigs are seen walking on their hind legs and holding parties with local farmers. Napoleon abolishes the name "Animal Farm" and restores the name "Manor Farm", the one in Jones's day.

Part of a masterly graphic account of how utopian ideal is breached by corruption and lies, the selected sections are respectively about the early vibrant days after the triumphant rebellion on the farm and the gloomy days after the principles of Animalism are outright abolished.

Chapter II (Excerpt)

But they woke at dawn as usual, and suddenly remembering the glorious thing that had happened, they all raced out into the pasture together. A little way down the pasture there was a knoll[1] that commanded a view of most of the farm. The animals rushed to the top of it and gazed round them in the clear morning light. Yes, it was theirs — everything that they could see was theirs! In the ecstasy of that thought they gambolled[2] round and round, they hurled themselves into the air in great leaps of excitement. They rolled in the dew, they cropped[3] mouthfuls of the sweet summer grass, they kicked up clods[4] of the black earth and snuffed[5] its rich scent. Then they made a tour of inspection of the whole farm and surveyed with speechless admiration the ploughland, the hayfield, the orchard, the pool, the spinney[6]. It was as though they had never seen these things before, and even now they could hardly believe that it was all their own.

Then they filed[7] back to the farm buildings and halted in silence outside the door of the farmhouse. That was theirs too, but they were frightened to go inside. After a moment, however, Snowball and Napoleon butted[8] the door open with their shoulders and the animals entered in single file, walking with the utmost care for fear of disturbing anything. They tiptoed from room to room, afraid to speak above a whisper and gazing with a kind of awe at the unbelievable luxury, at the beds with their feather mattresses, the looking-glasses, the horsehair sofa, the Brussels carpet, the lithograph[9] of Queen Victoria over the drawing-room mantelpiece. They were just coming down the stairs when Mollie was discovered to be missing. Going back, the others found that she had remained behind in the best bedroom. She had taken a piece of blue ribbon from Mrs. Jones's dressing-table, and was holding it against her shoulder and admiring herself in the glass in a very foolish manner. The others reproached her sharply, and they went outside. Some hams hanging in the kitchen were taken out for burial, and the barrel of beer in the scullery[10] was stove in with a kick from Boxer's hoof, otherwise nothing in the house was touched. A unanimous resolution was passed on the spot that the farmhouse should be preserved as a museum. All were agreed that no animal must ever live there.

The animals had their breakfast, and then Snowball and Napoleon called them together again.

'Comrades,' said Snowball, 'it is half past six and we have a long day before us. Today we begin the hay harvest. But there is another matter that must be attended to first.'

The pigs now revealed that during the past three months they had taught themselves to read and write from an old spelling book which had belonged to Mr. Jones's children and which had been thrown on the rubbish heap. Napoleon sent for pots of black and white paint and led the way down to the five-barred gate that gave on to the main road. Then Snowball (for it was Snowball who was best at writing) took a brush between the two knuckles of his trotter[11], painted out MANOR FARM from the top bar of the gate and in its place painted ANIMAL FARM. This was to be the name of the farm from now onwards. After this they went back to the farm buildings, where Snowball and Napoleon sent for a ladder which they caused to be set against the end wall of the big barn. They explained that by their studies of the past three months the pigs had succeeded in reducing the principles of Animalism to Seven Commandments. These Seven Commandments would now be inscribed on the wall; they would form an unalterable law by which all the animals on Animal Farm must live for ever after. With some difficulty (for it is not easy for a pig to balance himself on a ladder) Snowball climbed up and set to work, with Squealer a few rungs[12] below him holding the paint-pot. The Commandments were written on the tarred wall in great white letters that could be read thirty yards away. They ran thus:

THE SEVEN COMMANDMENTS

1. Whatever goes upon two legs is an enemy.

2. Whatever goes upon four legs, or has wings, is a friend.

3. No animal shall wear clothes.

4. No animal shall sleep in a bed.

5. No animal shall drink alcohol.

6. No animal shall kill any other animal.

7. All animals are equal.

It was very neatly written, and except that 'friend' was written 'freind' and one of the 'S's' was the wrong way round, the spelling was correct all the way through. Snowball read it aloud for the benefit of the others. All the animals nodded in complete agreement, and the cleverer ones at once began to learn the Commandments by heart.

'Now, comrades,' cried Snowball, throwing down the paint-brush, 'to the hayfield! Let us make it a point of honour to get in the harvest more quickly than Jones and his men could do.'

But at this moment the three cows, who had seemed uneasy for some time past, set up a loud lowing. They had not been milked for twenty-four hours, and their udders were almost bursting. After a little thought, the pigs sent for buckets and milked the cows fairly successfully, their trotters being well adapted to this task. Soon there were five buckets of frothing[13] creamy milk at which many of the animals looked with considerable interest.

'What is going to happen to all that milk?' said someone.

'Jones used sometimes to mix some of it in our mash[14],' said one of the hens.

'Never mind the milk, comrades!' cried Napoleon, placing himself in front of the buckets. 'That will be attended to. The harvest is more important. Comrade Snowball will lead the way. I shall follow in a few minutes. Forward, comrades! The hay is waiting.'

So the animals trooped down to the hayfield to begin the harvest, and when they came back in the evening it was noticed that the milk had disappeared.

Chapter III

How they toiled and sweated to get the hay in! But their efforts were rewarded, for the harvest was an even bigger success than they had hoped.

Sometimes the work was hard; the implements had been designed for human beings and not for animals, and it was a great drawback that no animal was able to use any tool that involved standing on his hind legs. But the pigs were so clever that they could think of a way round every difficulty. As for the horses, they knew every inch of the field, and in fact understood the business of mowing and raking far better than Jones and his men had ever done. The pigs did not actually work, but directed and supervised the others. With their superior knowledge it was natural that they should assume the leadership. Boxer and Clover would harness themselves to the cutter or the horse-rake (no bits or reins were needed in these days, of course) and tramp steadily round and round the field with a pig walking behind and calling out 'Gee up, comrade!' or 'Whoa back, comrade!' as the case might be. And every animal down to the humblest worked at turning the hay and gathering it. Even the ducks and hens toiled to and fro all day in the sun, carrying tiny wisps of hay in their beaks. In the end they finished the harvest in two days' less time than it had usually taken Jones and his men. Moreover, it was the biggest harvest that the farm had ever seen. There was no wastage[15] whatever; the hens and ducks with their sharp eyes had gathered up the very last stalk. And not an animal on the farm had stolen so much as a mouthful.

All through that summer the work of the farm went like clockwork. The animals were happy as they had never conceived it possible to be. Every mouthful of food was an acute positive pleasure, now that it was truly their own food, produced by themselves and for themselves, not doled out[16] to them by a grudging master. With the worthless parasitical human beings gone, there was more for everyone to eat. There was more leisure too, inexperienced though the animals were. They met with many difficulties — for instance, later in the year, when they harvested the corn, they had to tread it out in the ancient style and blow away the chaff[17] with their breath, since the farm possessed no threshing machine — but the pigs with their cleverness and Boxer with his tremendous muscles always pulled them through. Boxer was the admiration of everybody. He had been a hard worker even in Jones's time, but now he seemed more like three horses than one; there were days when the entire work of the farm seemed to rest upon his mighty shoulders. From morning to night he was pushing and pulling, always at the spot where the work was hardest. He had made an arrangement with one of the cockerels[18] to call him in the mornings half an hour earlier than anyone else, and would put in some volunteer labour at whatever seemed to be most needed, before the regular day's work began. His answer to every problem, every setback, was 'I will work harder!' — which he had adopted as his personal motto.

But everyone worked according to his capacity. The hens and ducks, for instance, saved five bushels of corn at the harvest by gathering up the stray grains. Nobody stole, nobody grumbled over his rations, the quarrelling and biting and jealousy which had been normal features of life in the old days had almost disappeared. Nobody shirked — or almost nobody. Mollie, it was true, was not good at getting up in the mornings, and had a way of leaving work early on the ground that there was a stone in her hoof. And the behaviour of the cat was somewhat peculiar. It was soon noticed that when there was work to be done the cat could never be found. She would vanish for hours on end, and then reappear at meal-times, or in the evening after work was over, as though nothing had happened. But she always made such excellent excuses, and purred so affectionately, that it was impossible not to believe in her good intentions. Old Benjamin, the donkey, seemed quite unchanged since the Rebellion. He did his work in the same slow obstinate way as he had done it in Jones's time, never shirking and never volunteering for extra work either. About the Rebellion and its results he would express no opinion. When asked whether he was not happier now that Jones was gone, he would say only 'Donkeys live a long time. None of you has ever seen a dead donkey,' and the others had to be content with this cryptic[19] answer.

On Sundays there was no work. Breakfast was an hour later than usual, and after breakfast there was a ceremony which was observed every week without fail. First came the hoisting of the flag. Snowball had found in the harness-room an old green tablecloth of Mrs. Jones's and had painted on it a hoof and a horn in white. This was run up the flagstaff in the farmhouse garden every Sunday morning. The flag was green, Snowball explained, to represent the green fields of England, while the hoof and horn signified the future Republic of the Animals which would arise when the human race had been finally overthrown. After the hoisting of the flag all the animals trooped into the big barn for a general assembly which was known as the Meeting. Here the work of the coming week was planned out and resolutions were put forward and debated. It was always the pigs who put forward the resolutions. The other animals understood how to vote, but could never think of any resolutions of their own. Snowball and Napoleon were by far the most active in the debates. But it was noticed that these two were never in agreement: whatever suggestion either of them made, the other could be counted on to oppose it. Even when it was resolved — a thing no one could object to in itself — to set aside the small paddock[20] behind the orchard as a home of rest for animals who were past work, there was a stormy debate over the correct retiring age for each class of animal. The Meeting always ended with the singing of 'Beasts of England', and the afternoon was given up to recreation.

Chapter X

YEARS passed. The seasons came and went, the short animal lives fled by. A time came when there was no one who remembered the old days before the Rebellion, except Clover, Benjamin, Moses the raven, and a number of the pigs.

Muriel was dead; Bluebell, Jessie, and Pincher were dead. Jones too was dead — he had died in an inebriate's[21] home in another part of the country. Snowball was forgotten. Boxer was forgotten, except by the few who had known him. Clover was an old stout mare now, stiff in the joints, and with a tendency to rheumy[22] eyes. She was two years past the retiring age, but in fact no animal had ever actually retired. The talk of setting aside a corner of the pasture for superannuated[23] animals had long since been dropped. Napoleon was now a mature boar of twenty-four stone[24]. Squealer was so fat that he could with difficulty see out of his eyes. Only old Benjamin was much the same as ever, except for being a little greyer about the muzzle, and, since Boxer's death, more morose[25] and taciturn[26] than ever.

There were many more creatures on the farm now, though the increase was not so great as had been expected in earlier years. Many animals had been born to whom the Rebellion was only a dim tradition, passed on by word of mouth, and others had been bought who had never heard mention of such a thing before their arrival. The farm possessed three horses now besides Clover. They were fine upstanding beasts, willing workers and good comrades, but very stupid. None of them proved able to learn the alphabet beyond the letter B. They accepted everything that they were told about the Rebellion and the principles of Animalism, especially from Clover, for whom they had an almost filial respect; but it was doubtful whether they understood very much of it.

The farm was more prosperous now, and better organized: it had even been enlarged by two fields which had been bought from Mr. Pilkington. The windmill had been successfully completed at last, and the farm possessed a threshing machine and a hay elevator of its own, and various new buildings had been added to it. Whymper had bought himself a dogcart[27]. The windmill, however, had not after all been used for generating electrical power. It was used for milling corn, and brought in a handsome money profit. The animals were hard at work building yet another windmill; when that one was finished, so it was said, the dynamos[28] would be installed. But the luxuries of which Snowball had once taught the animals to dream, the stalls with electric light and hot and cold water, and the three-day week, were no longer talked about. Napoleon had denounced such ideas as contrary to the spirit of Animalism. The truest happiness, he said, lay in working hard and living frugally.

Somehow it seemed as though the farm had grown richer without making the animals themselves any richer — except, of course, for the pigs and the dogs. Perhaps this was partly because there were so many pigs and so many dogs. It was not that these creatures did not work, after their fashion. There was, as Squealer was never tired of explaining, endless work in the supervision and organization of the farm. Much of this work was of a kind that the other animals were too ignorant to understand. For example, Squealer told them that the pigs had to expend enormous labours every day upon mysterious things called 'files', 'reports', 'minutes', and 'memoranda'. These were large sheets of paper which had to be closely covered with writing, and as soon as they were so covered, they were burnt in the furnace. This was of the highest importance for the welfare of the farm, Squealer said. But still, neither pigs nor dogs produced any food by their own labour; and there were very many of them, and their appetites were always good.

As for the others, their life, so far as they knew, was as it had always been. They were generally hungry, they slept on straw, they drank from the pool, they laboured in the fields; in winter they were troubled by the cold, and in summer by the flies. Sometimes the older ones among them racked[29] their dim memories and tried to determine whether in the early days of the Rebellion, when Jones's expulsion was still recent, things had been better or worse than now. They could not remember. There was nothing with which they could compare their present lives: they had nothing to go upon except Squealer's lists of figures, which invariably demonstrated that everything was getting better and better. The animals found the problem insoluble; in any case, they had little time for speculating on such things now. Only old Benjamin professed to remember every detail of his long life and to know that things never had been, nor ever could be much better or much worse — hunger, hardship, and disappointment being, so he said, the unalterable law of life.

And yet the animals never gave up hope. More, they never lost, even for an instant, their sense of honour and privilege in being members of Animal Farm. They were still the only farm in the whole county — in all England! — owned and operated by animals. Not one of them, not even the youngest, not even the newcomers who had been brought from farms ten or twenty miles away, ever ceased to marvel at that. And when they heard the gun booming and saw the green flag fluttering at the masthead, their hearts swelled with imperishable pride, and the talk always turned towards the old heroic days, the expulsion of Jones, the writing of the Seven Commandments, the great battles in which the human invaders had been defeated. None of the old dreams had been abandoned. The Republic of the Animals which Major had foretold, when the green fields of England should be untrodden by human feet, was still believed in. Some day it was coming: it might not be soon, it might not be within the lifetime of any animal now living, but still it was coming. Even the tune of 'Beasts of England' was perhaps hummed secretly here and there: at any rate, it was a fact that every animal on the farm knew it, though no one would have dared to sing it aloud. It might be that their lives were hard and that not all of their hopes had been fulfilled; but they were conscious that they were not as other animals. If they went hungry, it was not from feeding tyrannical human beings; if they worked hard, at least they worked for themselves. No creature among them went upon two legs. No creature called any other creature 'Master'. All animals were equal.

One day in early summer Squealer ordered the sheep to follow him, and led them out to a piece of waste ground at the other end of the farm, which had become overgrown with birch saplings[30]. The sheep spent the whole day there browsing at the leaves under Squealer's supervision. In the evening he returned to the farmhouse himself, but, as it was warm weather, told the sheep to stay where they were. It ended by their remaining there for a whole week, during which time the other animals saw nothing of them. Squealer was with them for the greater part of every day. He was, he said, teaching them to sing a new song, for which privacy was needed.

It was just after the sheep had returned, on a pleasant evening when the animals had finished work and were making their way back to the farm buildings, that the terrified neighing[31] of a horse sounded from the yard. Startled, the animals stopped in their tracks. It was Clover's voice. She neighed again, and all the animals broke into a gallop and rushed into the yard. Then they saw what Clover had seen.

It was a pig walking on his hind legs.

Yes, it was Squealer. A little awkwardly, as though not quite used to supporting his considerable bulk in that position, but with perfect balance, he was strolling across the yard. And a moment later, out from the door of the farmhouse came a long file of pigs, all walking on their hind legs. Some did it better than others, one or two were even a trifle[32] unsteady and looked as though they would have liked the support of a stick, but every one of them made his way right round the yard successfully. And finally there was a tremendous baying[33] of dogs and a shrill crowing from the black cockerel, and out came Napoleon himself, majestically upright, casting haughty glances from side to side, and with his dogs gambolling round him.

He carried a whip in his trotter.

There was a deadly silence. Amazed, terrified, huddling together, the animals watched the long line of pigs march slowly round the yard. It was as though the world had turned upside-down. Then there came a moment when the first shock had worn off and when, in spite of everything — in spite of their terror of the dogs, and of the habit, developed through long years, of never complaining, never criticizing, no matter what happened — they might have uttered some word of protest. But just at that moment, as though at a signal, all the sheep burst out into a tremendous bleating of —

'Four legs good, two legs *better!* Four legs good, two legs *better!* Four legs good, two legs *better!*'

It went on for five minutes without stopping. And by the time the sheep had quieted down, the chance to utter any protest had passed, for the pigs had marched back into the farmhouse.

Benjamin felt a nose nuzzling[34] at his shoulder. He looked round. It was Clover. Her old eyes looked dimmer than ever. Without saying anything, she tugged gently at his mane[35] and led him round to the end of the big barn, where the Seven Commandments were written. For a minute or two they stood gazing at the tatted wall with its white lettering.

'My sight is failing,' she said finally. 'Even when I was young I could not have read what was written there. But it appears to me that that wall looks different. Are the Seven Commandments the same as they used to be, Benjamin?'

For once Benjamin consented to break his rule, and he read out to her what was written on the wall. There was nothing there now except a single Commandment. It ran:

ALL ANIMALS ARE EQUAL

BUT SOME ANIMALS ARE MORE

EQUAL THAN OTHERS

After that it did not seem strange when next day the pigs who were supervising the work of the farm all carried whips in their trotters. It did not seem strange to learn that the pigs had bought themselves a wireless set, were arranging to install a telephone, and had taken out subscriptions to *John Bull, TitBits,* and the *Daily Mirror.* It did not seem strange when Napoleon was seen strolling in the farmhouse garden with a pipe in his mouth — no, not even when the pigs took Mr. Jones's clothes out of the wardrobes and put them on. Napoleon himself appearing in a black coat, ratcatcher breeches, and leather leggings, while his favourite sow appeared in the watered silk dress which Mrs Jones had been used to wear on Sundays.

A week later, in the afternoon, a number of dogcarts drove up to the farm. A deputation[36] of neighbouring farmers had been invited to make a tour of inspection. They were shown all over the farm, and expressed great admiration for everything they saw, especially the windmill. The animals were weeding the turnip field. They worked diligently, hardly raising their faces from the ground, and not knowing whether to be more frightened of the pigs or of the human visitors.

That evening loud laughter and bursts of singing came from the farmhouse. And suddenly, at the sound of the mingled voices, the animals were stricken with curiosity. What could be happening in there, now that for the first time animals and human beings were meeting on terms of equality? With one accord they began to creep as quietly as possible into the farmhouse garden.

At the gate they paused, half frightened to go on but Clover led the way in. They tiptoed up to the house, and such animals as were tall enough peered in at the dining-room window. There, round the long table, sat half a dozen farmers and half a dozen of the more eminent pigs, Napoleon himself occupying the seat of honour at the head of the table. The pigs appeared completely at ease in their chairs The company had been enjoying a game of cards but had broken off for a moment, evidently in order to drink a toast. A large jug was circulating, and the mugs were being refilled with beer. No one noticed the wondering faces of the animals that gazed in at the window.

Mr. Pilkington of Foxwood had stood up, his mug in his hand. In a moment, he said, he would ask the present company to drink a toast. But before doing so, there were a few words that he felt it incumbent[37] upon him to say.

It was a source of great satisfaction to him, he said — and, he was sure, to all others present — to feel that a long period of mistrust and misunderstanding had now come to an end. There had been a time — not that he, or any of the present company, had shared such sentiments — but there had been a time when the respected proprietors[38] of Animal Farm had been regarded, he would not say with hostility, but perhaps with a certain measure of misgiving, by their human neighbours. Unfortunate incidents had occurred, mistaken ideas had been current. It had been felt that the existence of a farm owned and operated by pigs was somehow abnormal and was liable[39] to have an unsettling effect in the neighbourhood. Too many farmers had assumed without due inquiry, that on such a farm a spirit of licence and indiscipline would prevail. They had been nervous about the effects upon their own animals, or even upon their human employees. But all such doubts were now dispelled. Today he and his friends had visited Animal Farm and inspected every inch of it with their own eyes, and what did they find? Not only the most up-to-date methods, but a discipline and an orderliness which should be an example to all farmers everywhere. He believed that he was right in saying that the lower animals on Animal Farm did more work and received less food than any animals in the county. Indeed, he and his fellow-visitors today had observed many features which they intended to introduce on their own farms immediately.

He would end his remarks, he said, by emphasizing once again the friendly feelings that subsisted, and ought to subsist, between Animal Farm and its neighbours. Between pigs and human beings there was not, and there need not be, any clash of interests whatever. Their struggles and their difficulties were one. Was not the labour problem the same everywhere? Here it became apparent that Mr. Pilkington was about to spring some carefully prepared witticism[40] on the company, but for a moment he was too overcome by amusement to be able to utter it. After much choking, during which his various chins turned purple, he managed to get it out: 'If you have your lower animals to contend with,' he said, 'we have our lower classes!' This *bon mot*[41] set the table in a roar; and Mr. Pilkington once again congratulated the pigs on the low rations, the long working hours, and the general absence of pampering[42] which he had observed on Animal Farm.

And now, he said finally, he would ask the company to rise to their feet and make certain that their glasses were full. 'Gentlemen,' concluded Mr. Pilkington, 'gentlemen, I give you a toast: to the prosperity of Animal Farm!'

There was enthusiastic cheering and stamping of feet. Napoleon was so gratified that he left his place and came round the table to clink his mug against Mr. Pilkington's before emptying it. When the cheering had died down, Napoleon, who had remained on his feet, intimated that he too had a few words to say.

Like all of Napoleon's speeches, it was short and to the point. He too, he said, was happy that the period of misunderstanding was at an end. For a long time there had been rumours — circulated, he had reason to think, by some malignant enemy — that there was something subversive and even revolutionary in the outlook of himself and his colleagues. They had been credited with attempting to stir up rebellion among the animals on neighbouring farms. Nothing could be further from the truth! Their sole wish, now and in the past, was to live at peace and in normal business relations with their neighbours. This farm which he had the honour to control, he added, was a cooperative enterprise. The title-deeds[43], which were in his own possession, were owned by the pigs jointly.

He did not believe, he said, that any of the old suspicions still lingered, but certain changes had been made recently in the routine of the farm which should have the effect of promoting confidence still further. Hitherto[44] the animals on the farm had had a rather foolish custom of addressing one another as 'Comrade'. This was to be suppressed. There had also been a very strange custom, whose origin was unknown, of marching every Sunday morning past a boar's skull which was nailed to a post in the garden. This, too, would be suppressed, and the skull had already been buried. His visitors might have observed, too, the green flag which flew from the masthead. If so, they would perhaps have noted that the white hoof and horn with which it had previously been marked had now been removed. It would be a plain green flag from now onwards.

He had only one criticism, he said, to make of Mr. Pilkington's excellent and neighbourly speech. Mr. Pilkington had referred throughout to 'Animal Farm'. He could not of course know — for he, Napoleon, was only now for the first time announcing it — that the name 'Animal Farm' had been abolished. Henceforward the farm was to be known as the 'Manor Farm' — which, he believed, was its correct and original name.

'Gentlemen,' concluded Napoleon, 'I will give you the same toast as before, but in a different form. Fill your glasses to the brim. Gentlemen, here is my toast: To the prosperity of the Manor Farm!'

There was the same hearty cheering as before, and the mugs were emptied to the dregs[45]. But as the animals outside gazed at the scene, it seemed to them that some strange thing was happening. What was it that had altered in the faces of the pigs? Clover's old dim eyes flitted[46] from one face to another. Some of them had five chins, some had four, some had three. But what was it that seemed to be melting and changing? Then, the applause having come to an end, the company took up their cards and continued the game that had been interrupted, and the animals crept silently away.

But they had not gone twenty yards when they stopped short. An uproar of voices was coming from the farmhouse. They rushed back and looked through the window again. Yes, a violent quarrel was in progress. There were shoutings, bangings on the table, sharp suspicious glances, furious denials. The source of the trouble appeared to be that Napoleon and Mr. Pilkington had each played an ace of spades simultaneously.

Twelve voices were shouting in anger, and they were all alike. No question, now, what had happened to the faces of the pigs. The creatures outside looked from pig to man, and from man to pig, and from pig to man again; but already it was impossible to say which was which.

Chapter Ten Utopia and Dystopia

Notes

Chapter II

1. knoll: a small round hill
2. gambol: jump about playfully
3. crop: (of an animal) bite off and eat the tops of (plants)
4. clod: a lump of earth or clay
5. snuff: inhale noisily through the nose
6. spinney: a small area of trees and bushes
7. file: march or walk in a line of people, one after another
8. butt: strike or hit (something or someone) with the head or horns
9. lithograph: a picture made by lithography, a method of printing in which a flat surface is specially treated so that ink sticks to some areas required for printing
10. scullery: a small room, next to the kitchen, used for washing dishes and other rough cleaning work
11. trotter: the foot of a pig
12. rung: a horizontal bar forming a step of a ladder
13. frothing: producing a mass of small bubbles on the surface of a liquid
14. mash: grain, bran mixed with water, used as food for animals

Chapter III

15. wastage: loss or destruction of something, especially due to lack of care
16. dole out: giave (money or food) in small quantities
17. chaff: the outer covering separated from the grain during threshing
18. cockerel: a young cock
19. cryptic: having a meaning that is difficult to understand
20. paddock: a small field for keeping or exercising horses

Chapter X

21. inebriate: a drunkard
22. rheumy: having a watery fluid that collects in eyes
23. superannuated: too old to be useful for work
24. stone: a measure of weight, which is equal to 6.35 kg
25. morose: unhappy and unwilling to talk very much
26. taciturn: tending to say little
27. dogcart: a two-wheeled vehicle drawn by a horse
28. dynamo: a device for changing mechanical energy into electricity
29. rack: try very hard to think of something
30. sapling: a young tree
31. neighing: (a horse) making a long loud sound
32. a trifle: slightly

33. baying: (a dog) making repeatedly the long deep cry
34. nuzzling: touching gently with the nose
35. mane: the long hair on the neck of an animal
36. deputation: a group of people appointed to represent others
37. incumbent: necessary as a duty or responsibility
38. proprietor: an owner
39. liable: likely
40. witticism: a witty remark
41. *bon mot*: a clever remark
42. pampering: treating (someone) with too much care
43. title-deed: a piece of paper giving legal proof that someone is the owner of a house, etc.
44. Hitherto: Until now
45. dregs: the remnants of a liquid left in a container
46. flit: move quickly

Questions

1. From the preceding chapters to the concluding chapter, what does Orwell aim at via the increasingly deteriorating scenes? In chapter II and III, are there any signs indicative of the resulting chapter? Look up some reference books if necessary.
2. Based on the selected chapters, what, do you think, account(s) for the transformation of the farm from "Manor Farm" to "Animal Farm", and eventually the one from "Animal Farm" back to "Manor Farm"? What do you think of those animals on the farm? Are they responsible for those changes? Can they be categorized? What are their allegorical meanings?
3. Orwell is renowned for his precise, clear and vivid prose style. His ideal of prose is "like a window pane". Does this animal fable exemplify his intention?